B
U
P

Oreste Pollicino · Marco Bassini · Giovanni De Gregorio

INTERNET LAW AND PROTECTION OF FUNDAMENTAL RIGHTS

Typesetting: Laura Panigara, Cesano Boscone (Milan)
Cover: Cristina Bernasconi, Milan

EGEA S.p.A.
Via Salasco, 5 - 20136 Milano
Tel. 02/5836.5751 – Fax 02/5836.5753
egea.edizioni@unibocconi.it – www.egeaeditore.it

First edition: September 2022

ISBN Domestic Edition 978-88-99902-93-3
ISBN International Edition 978-88-31322-70-6
ISBN Digital International Edition 978-88-31322-72-0
ISBN Digital Domestic Edition 978-88-238-8526-4

Print: Logo S.r.l, Borgoricco (Padua)

Table of Contents

Part II – Freedom of Expression

Introduction

The protection of fundamental rights in the digital age is increasingly at the core of Internet law. The massive spread of digital and algorithmic technologies is raising questions that are inherently constitutional. Rights and freedoms are exposed to the opportunities and challenges of digital technologies, thus leading to different constitutional responses.

We believe that developing skills and expertise in this area is critical for law students, and this idea has driven us to work on this book based on our experience in teaching courses on Internet law and constitutional law at Bocconi University, particularly the LL.M. in Law of Internet Technologies. This book is a collective enterprise that is in line not only with our research interest but also with our teaching focus.

The book is structured in three parts. It begins by providing a focus on the primary questions around the Internet, particularly the regulation and governance of the digital environment, the jurisdictional challenge and the access to the Internet. The second part of the book examines the law of online content, looking at the protection of freedom of expression in the real and the digital world, the law of online intermediaries, the challenges raised by disinformation and hate speech and specific sectors such as copyright and audiovisual media services. The third part analyzes the field of privacy and data protection by looking at their historical roots, the role of the General Data Protection Regulation and specific challenges, particularly the right to be forgotten, data retention and the transfer of data.

We believe that the first edition of this book can provide our students with a benchmark for understanding the constitutional challenges of the digital age. The book can be a valuable resource for undergraduate and graduate courses such as advanced constitutional law, Internet law, fundamental rights, privacy and data protection. We also believe that this book can provide a first overview for entering this area and address the constitutional questions that the development of digital technologies has raised in recent years.

This volume is also the result of the work of our research team. They have played an important role in this project, particularly at the editing stage. Therefore, we would like to express our gratitude to Flavia Bavetta, Pietro Dunn and Federica Paolucci for their support and commitment to this project.

Last but not least, we owe a world of gratitude to our students at Bocconi University who were the inspiration for this book over recent years in various undergraduate and postgraduate courses where we had the chance to teach these thrilling subjects in an intellectually vibrant and genuinely committed community.

Part I
The Internet Landscape

1 The Law of the Internet

1.1 Introduction

The advent of the Internet has triggered global transformations. Since the end of the 20th century, this new space has led to the consolidation of the information society, which can be considered a modern society whose progress is no longer strictly related to the production and distribution of material goods and services but is also of a digital nature. Data and information are the fuel of the economy of the new century, thus making digital services key to the development of society as a whole. Such a transformation would not have been possible without a global communication channel such as the Internet which has led to the paradigm shift from the analogue to the digital dimension or, in other words, from atoms to bits.

Developed from the military project ARPANet of the US Advanced Research Projects Agency (ARPA), the Internet spread during the 1990s thanks also to the creation of an architecture capable of simplifying the use of this means of communication: the World Wide Web. From a technical point of view, the Internet is a set of interconnected networks that form the so-called network of networks. The operation of the network is made possible thanks to the use of protocols that allow the various connected devices to be identified uniquely using an Internet Protocol number. The exchange of information takes place through data packets that constitute separate units capable of traveling independently and being exchanged conventionally through the TCP/IP protocol, while the resources found on the network are instead identified by a string of characters called the domain name.

TCP/IP stands for Transmission Control Protocol/Internet Protocol and is a suite of communication protocols used to interconnect network devices on the Internet. TCP/IP specifies how data is exchanged over the Internet by providing end-to-end communications that identify how it should be broken into packets, addressed, transmitted, routed and received at the destination. The two main protocols are the TCP, which defines how applications can create channels of communication across a network, and the IP, which defines how to address and route each packet to make sure it reaches the right destination. The IP address helps determine where to forward the message. TCP/IP thus uses a client–server model of communication in which a user or machine (a client) is provided a service, such as sending a webpage, by another computer (a server) in the network. The TCP/IP model is structured into four layers of communication for the transmission of the data packages: the physical layer; the network layer; the transport layer; and the application layer.

The development of this new digital dimension has led to the questioning of the role played by public and private actors in Internet governance. If, on the one hand, states have tried, and not always succeeded, to maintain their sovereign power within their own territory in relation to this new digital space, private actors, on the other hand, in particular supranational and multinational organizations, have extended their area of influence far beyond the confines of their headquarters. The law of the Internet then results from a mix of public and private influences that shape rights and freedoms in the digital age.

This framework has raised questions about the governance of the Internet. This chapter underlines the evolution of the debate around the law of the Internet. The first part addresses the libertarian approach that characterized the debate at the end of the 20th century (1.2–1.3). The second part examines the arguments against this libertarian approach and underlines the power of states and private actors to regulate the digital environment (1.4). The third part underlines the role of architecture as a possible means to regulate the digital environment (1.5). The fourth part focuses on the rise of the constitutional dimension of the Internet, particularly looking at the rise of Internet bills of rights (1.6) and new regulatory approaches to address the exercise of online platform powers (1.7).

1.2 The regulatory conundrum

One of the most debated questions posed by the rise of the Internet was whether, in view of the unprecedented decentralized and cross-border nature of cyberspace, states were still entitled to set and enforce rules governing conducts that take place online. 1995 is perhaps the year that marked the point of no return: the advent of browsers. Browsers retrieve, present and transfer information from the Word Wide Web in a visible and user-friendly way. As the Internet became popular, it was mainly understood as a "land of freedom" where individuals could employ new avenues for the exercise of a variety of human activities, most notably freedom of speech. In light of this view, any attempt to claim the applicability of state law was perceived as a threat to such freedom by a large group of activists who challenged states' ability to extend their sovereign power over cyberspace. Among others, John Perry Barlow, one of the founders of the Electronic Frontiers Foundation, is among the most influential digital rights activists. In his famous "A Declaration of the Independence of Cyberspace" he wrote:

> Governments of the Industrial World, you weary giants of flesh and steel, I come from Cyberspace, the new home of Mind. On behalf of the future, I ask you of the past to leave us alone. You are not welcome among us. You have no sovereignty where we gather.

It is not by coincidence that Barlow wrote the Declaration in 1996 as a reaction to the coming into force of the Communications Decency Act (CDA). The CDA is the first Act passed by the United States Congress with the specific purpose to regulate cyberspace, and most notably with a view to preventing minors from accessing indecent and patently offensive materials on the Internet. This statute was definitely seen as a threat to the unprecedented degree of freedom that cyberspace was meant to provide. The Supreme Court judgment in *Reno v. ACLU* (521 US 844, 1997), which one year later invalidated significant parts of the CDA, contributed to strengthening cyberlibertarians' convictions about the need to preserve Internet freedom. They saw the judgment as an act of enforcement of the First Amendment (which protects freedom of speech in the US Constitution) to its utmost degree, as the repeal of the first attempt to regulate cyberspace. Still today, the Declaration is regarded as the most powerful manifesto of the attitude vis-à-vis state regulation of the so-called cyberlibertarians. Barlow had no legal background, and the Declaration was not shaped in legal terms; however, this manifesto also proved influential among the first scholars who approached the rise of cyberspace and the regulatory dilemma.

Today, states are usually considered as able to enforce their legal norms "in the real world" and likewise on the Internet. Otherwise, cyberspace would amount to a "free zone" where conduct prohibited in the analogue world is tolerated "just because" it occurs on the Internet, where no state has authority. However, in 1996, it was hard to predict the actual development of cyberspace, including of its governance. The degree of novelty and the magnitude of the transformations generated by the Internet were seen as unprecedented. Perhaps other technological developments have caused similar challenges in the past. Indeed, like the Internet, the use of traditional media could definitely give rise to conduct having extraterritorial effects, thus triggering the problem of determining which state could properly assert jurisdiction.

Yet jurisdiction constitutes only one side of the coin. The next chapter will explore how courts dealt with the jurisdictional puzzle, particularly by resorting to traditional criteria or by adapting them to the digital reality. The other side of the coin concerns the unprecedented degree of freedom inherent to the availability of the Internet. Regardless of the jurisdiction conundrum, the Internet was fashioned as a metaphor of freedom, and the fear that regulation could undermine such freedom definitely influenced some scholars.

1.3 Cyberanarchy

David Johnson and David Post are by far the most important theorists of cyberanarchy among legal scholars. In a seminal article published in 1996 they argued that the rise of cyberspace, and therefore of cross-border communication networks, undermined both the feasibility and the legitimacy of applying laws based on geographic boundaries. By implicitly establishing cyberspace as a *separate place*, other than the real world of atoms, they maintained that new rules and institutions needed to be set. In rejecting the application of existing territorially-based laws and institutions, they also found self-regulation to be the most fitting option for the characteristics of cyberspace. They actually proposed that

> established territorial authorities … defer to the self-regulatory efforts of Cyberspace participants who care most deeply about this new digital trade in ideas, information, and services.

The assumption behind this proposal was that cyberspace could build its own institutions and rules on a purely *self-regulatory* basis, separated from territorial jurisdictions. Geographical boundaries in law-making, in Johnson and Post's view, do not make sense when it comes to cyberspace:

> Cyberspace radically undermines the relationship between legally significant (online) phenomena and physical location. The rise of the global computer network is destroying the link between geographical location and: (1) the power of local governments to assert control over online behavior; (2) the effects of online behavior on individuals or things; (3) the legitimacy of the efforts of a local sovereign to enforce rules applicable to global phenomena; and (4) the ability of physical location to give notice of which sets of rules apply.

In other words, cyberspace is simply a place where distinct laws apply. These rules, however, should be established by the cyberspace participants themselves. The community of online users and Internet service providers (ISPs) should take on the task of developing a self-governance system. Against this background,

> governments cannot stop electronic communications coming across their borders, even if they want to do so. Nor can they credibly claim a right to regulate the Net based on supposed local harms caused by activities that originate outside their borders and that travel electronically to many different nations; one nation's legal institutions should not, therefore, monopolize rule-making for the entire Net.

Additionally, they noted:

> Even so, established authorities likely will continue to claim that they must analyze and regulate the new online phenomena in terms of some physical locations. After all, the people engaged in online communications still inhabit the material world. And, so the argument goes, local legal authorities must have authority to remedy the problems created in the physical world by those acting on the Net. The rise of responsible law-making institutions within Cyberspace, however, will weigh heavily against arguments that would claim that the Net is "lawless" and thus tie regulation of online trade to physical jurisdictions.

But rules should not be identical everywhere in cyberspace. In the view of Johnson and Post, cyberspace also has internal borders; dividing lines can thus be created even between different spheres within the same digital realm. Therefore, there are more "territories" of "spheres of activity" within the cyberspace. The existence of "barriers" of such a nature allows for the development of distinct rule sets that may not only differ but also change and evolve over time. Since different communities exist in cyberspace, each one with its own set of rules, individuals can easily cross internal borders and relocate, moving among differing online spaces.

Finally, Johnson and Post believed that the new law created in cyberspace can be reconciled with current territorially based legal systems

> by treating it as a distinct doctrine, applicable to a clearly demarcated sphere, created primarily by legitimate, self-regulatory processes, and entitled to appropriate deference – but also subject to limitations when it oversteps its appropriate sphere.

1.4 Against cyberanarchy

Along with Tim Wu, Jack Goldsmith ranks among the commentators most thoroughly opposed to the cyberlibertarian (or cyberanarchic) view supported by Johnson and Post. A landmark piece by Goldsmith, published in 1999 and entitled "Against Cyberanarchy," directly challenges the conclusions reached by the Johnson and Post in their 1996 article. It is worth noting that Goldsmith wrote his piece in the aftermath of the *Reno v. ACLU* judgment delivered by the Supreme Court, when commentators were debating the true significance of the decision. As noted above, this judgment declared some provisions of the Communications Decency Act passed by Congress in 1996 – the first specific piece of content regulation applicable to the Internet – unconstitutional based on First Amendment rights. Some cyberlibertarians even claimed that this decision supported their arguments.

Goldsmith outlined the assumptions and the conclusions of the so-called regulation skeptics as follows:

> The regulation skeptics make both descriptive and normative claims. On the descriptive side, they claim that the application of geographically based conceptions of legal regulation and choice of law to a-geographical cyberspace activity either makes no sense or leads to hopeless confusion. On the normative side, they argue that because cyberspace transactions occur "simultaneously and equally" in all national jurisdictions, regulation of the flow of this information by any particular national jurisdiction illegitimately produces significant negative spillover effects in other jurisdictions. They also claim that the architecture of cyberspace precludes notice of governing law that is crucial to the law's legitimacy. In contrast, they argue, cyberspace participants are much better positioned than national regulators to design comprehensive legal rules that would both internalize the costs of cyberspace activity and give proper notice to cyberspace participants. The regulation skeptics conclude from these arguments that national regulators should "defer to the self-regulatory efforts of Cyberspace participants."

According to Goldsmith, the regulation skeptics make three errors. The first error is that they overstate the differences between cyberspace transactions and other transnational transactions:

> both involve people in real space in one territorial jurisdiction transacting with people in real space in another territorial jurisdiction in a way that sometimes causes real-world harms. In both contexts, the state in which the harms are suffered has a legitimate interest in regulating the activity that produces the harms.

The second error made by regulation skeptics, in Goldsmith's view, relates to the specific option of self-regulation that Johnson and Post pointed out as the most appropriate solution to govern cyberspace. In this respect,

> the skeptics do not attend to the distinction between default laws and mandatory laws. Their ultimate normative claim that cyberspace should be self-regulated makes sense with respect to default laws that, by definition, private parties can modify to fit their needs. It makes much less sense with respect to mandatory or regulatory laws that, for paternalistic reasons or in order to protect third parties, place limits on private legal ordering.

Finally, Goldsmith observed that the skeptics underestimate the value of traditional legal tools and technology in respect of cross-border regulatory issues implicated by cyberspace:

> Cyberspace transactions do not inherently warrant any more deference by national regulators, and are not significantly less resistant to the tools of conflict of laws, than other transnational transactions.

He argued, therefore, that regulation of cyberspace is both feasible and legitimate, as opposed to Johnson and Post's views. It is worth noting that Goldsmith does not delve into whether regulation per se is desirable, nor does he consider which type of regulation may be more appropriate to secure goals such as protection of freedom of speech and democracy. In a nutshell, his view is that in cyberspace there is no exceptionalism justifying a rejection of traditional regulatory schemes. It is not by coincidence that in his 2002 response to Goldsmith's article, David Post (in an article titled "Against 'Against Cyberanarchy'") specifically defined this approach as "unexceptionalism."

Post, claiming to be an "unrepentant exceptionalist," specifically addressed two points in Goldsmith's article. On the one hand, he challenged the idea that cyberspace is functionally identical to transnational activity mediated by other means such as mail or telephone. On the other hand, he disputed the capability of traditional principles and legal tools to capture problems arising in cyberspace. According to Post, no matter whether something happens in cyberspace, the questions posed by cyberspace are different and more difficult than those in the analogue world and cannot be solved using solutions applicable to the latter.

Besides Johnson, Post and Goldsmith, other scholars participated in this seminal debate that flourished in the second half of the 1990s in the United States. Trotter Hardy, for instance, called for the decentralization of the mechanisms by which behavior is regulated in cyberspace. In his view, some of the problems of cyberspace are genuinely new because they are unprecedented in the physical world, while other problems are new because they occur more frequently (e.g., anonymous messages) and require proper solutions. To determine such solutions, he endorsed decentralization as the most flexible and least intrusive rule-making process, particularly fitting in light of the evolving nature of cyberspace. A decentralized private regime is supposed to be more efficient and to properly complement top-down rules.

Other commentators such as Joel Reidenberg have pointed out that, in relation to cyberspace, other sources of rule-making come into play in addition to law and government regulation. He argued that user preferences and technical choices actually create default rules. These rules, imposed by technology and communication networks, constitute the so-called *Lex Informatica.* Such *Lex Informatica* may help resolve some of the issues emerging in cyberspace that traditional legal solutions fail to properly tackle, in light of its flexible and adaptable nature. Architecture itself can embody rules that allow the preservation of public order values. For this reason, policymakers should consider and recognize the *Lex Informatica* as a viable tool for the definition of information policy rules.

1.5 From the "law of the horse" to "code is law"

In addition to the debate between exceptionalists and unexceptionalists on the feasibility and legitimacy of state-centered regulation of cyberspace, another remarkable and intertwined debate concerned the need for a separate branch of law for cyberspace.

This key question was first raised by Judge Frank Easterbrook in a famous speech given in 1996, when he argued that there was no more need for a distinct law for cyberspace than there was a need for a separate "law of the horse." Easterbrook framed this metaphor to substantiate his view that "the best way to learn the law applicable to specialized endeavours it to study general rules." In his opinion,

> lots of cases deal with sales of horses; others deal with people kicked by horses; still more deal with the licensing and racing of horses, or with the care veterinarians give to horses, or with prizes at horse shows. Any effort to collect these strands into a course on "The Law of the Horse" is doomed to be shallow and to miss unifying principles.

According to Easterbrook, there is a risk of "multidisciplinary dilettantism" and no added value derives from thinking in particular about how law and cyberspace connect. Moreover, he noted that creating specific rules for cyberspace might be useless in light of the swift developments occurring in this specific field: this would likely make the rules established by lawmakers at a given time outdated and no longer fit for an environment subject to significant evolution that lawyers poorly understand. Thus, Easterbrook's argument was to

> do what is essential to permit the participants in this evolving world to make their own decisions. That means three things: make rules clear; create property rights where now there are none; and facilitate the formation of bargaining institutions. Then let the world of cyberspace evolve as it will, and enjoy the benefits.

In direct response to Easterbrook, in 1999, Lawrence Lessig wrote a detailed explanation of what cyberlaw might teach and why there are good reasons to think about law in cyberspace. First of all, Lessig rejects the view that cyberspace is unregulable. In his view, both the assumption that the nature of cyberspace is fixed and the assumption that governments can do nothing to change its architecture are wrong. This is why Lessig focuses specifically on how regulation can be conducted in cyberspace, starting from the observation of inherent differences between the analogue and the digital worlds that may frustrate the effectiveness of legal norms (for example, he points out that anonymity may to a certain degree be preserved online, thus allowing minors to engage in conduct or activities otherwise prohibited).

According to Lessig, behavior is regulated by four types of constraints in the physical world: *legal norms*; *social norms*; *the market*; and *architecture*. The latter factor consists of the physical world. The same paradigm is reproduced in cyberspace, where the architecture corresponds to the code, that is, the software and hardware that make cyberspace what it is:

> The substance of these constraints may vary, but they are all experienced as conditions on one's access to cyberspace. In some places, one must enter a password before one gains access; in other places, one can enter whether identified or not. In some places, the transactions that one engages in produce traces that link the transactions (the mouse droppings) back to the individual; in other places, this link is achieved only if the individual wants. In some places, one can select to speak a language that only the recipient can hear (through encryption); in other places, encryption is not an option. The code or software or architecture or protocols set these features; they are features selected by code writers; they constrain some behavior by making other behavior possible, or impossible. They imbed certain values, or they make certain values impossible. In this sense, they too are regulations, just as the architectures of real space code are regulations.

The four modalities operate and interact together. Each modality, according to Lessig, has both direct and indirect effects. It has indirect effects in the sense that it impacts on other modalities of regulation. Therefore, law and code (the most important constraints) can indirectly change each other and, in this way, ultimately change how behavior is regulated. Lessig believes that when it comes to cyberspace, the optimal mode of regulation is different from that applicable to the physical world. Cyberspace can be regulated *through its architecture*. The regulation of code is thus the most effective tool that law might use to regulate behavior online.

Murray went even further, underlining how the effectiveness of such regulation depends not only on the modality of regulation (e.g., network architecture) but also on the power that each point of the network can exercise over other points. It was already clear that the Internet would not entirely overcome state regulation. Nonetheless, public actors are no longer the only powerful regulators; they are just one piece of the fragmented framework of online governance. Even if states have not lost their power over the digital environment, there are new actors who are also expressing their influence on the digital environment. Online platforms in particular have become more influential, operating in the shadow of governments. They have developed their functions as proxies or delegated entities of public authorities to enforce public policies online or exercise autonomous functions that rely on the mix between market power and technological asymmetry.

Therefore, there are definitely good reasons to think about law and cyberspace (and therefore about Internet law): twenty-five years after the advent of cyberspace, we have witnessed countless developments that have brought to light the peculiarities of the digital environment.

1.6 From the regulatory dilemma to the rise of Internet bills of rights

The starting point for thinking about the relationship between the Internet and law has to be set at the origins of the debate on Internet regulation. The relevant literature shows a common, seminal research question, that is, whether states were entitled to claim their sovereignty over the Internet and to regulate it. Some early judgments (including the very well-known *Yahoo! v. LICRA* saga) dealt with the task of allocating among national courts the power to assert jurisdiction over cases involving the use of the Internet.

> *Yahoo! v. LICRA*, as will be discussed in the next chapter, concerned the case of the sale of Nazi memorabilia through the Internet. Whereas the sale of such items is not illegal within the United States, due to the strength of First Amendment guarantees of free speech, it represented a crime in France: therefore, the Paris *Tribunal de Grande Instance* ordered Yahoo! to cease the provision of those goods to French citizens. Yahoo! argued that French law should not apply to it, since the servers it used were based in the United States, and that the French Tribunal's order infringed its First Amendment rights. The US Appeals Court for the Ninth Circuit eventually held that Yahoo! had to comply with such an order.

These issues were of utmost importance at the time, since – as noted above – some commentators argued that the characteristics of the Internet were of such a nature as to make it incompatible with state regulation, and the Internet could therefore dismantle or undermine states' powers, weakening or even setting aside sovereign claims to regulate cyberspace and the power of domestic courts to adjudicate cases.

States proved to be capable of enforcing their own laws with respect to the Internet and the activities carried out thereon. There have been some examples of governmental interference with the functioning of the Internet, thus revealing that states have managed not only to lay down certain rules and policies for the Internet, but also to require service providers to enforce the same (ISPs' actions to arrange filtering measures in China is very telling in this respect). Digital players and most notably ISPs, whether as a "long arm" of public authorities or autonomously because of their growing market power, have thus become more and more influential.

In fact, once it had been ascertained that its flourishing was not going to result in a crisis for constitutional states, the Internet was no longer considered a subject deserving strong public regulation. On the contrary, private law significantly influenced the Internet and its functioning, particularly by means of the principles and rules governing the liability of online platforms. The debate thus shifted from the regulation–governance dilemma to a different one, relating to the protection of fundamental rights on the Internet.

Among others, Teubner has described the emergence of a number of civil constitutions as a real trend on a worldwide scale, where several autonomous subsystems of world society would undertake a process of constitutionalization. Teubner pointed out that an Internet constitution (different from the traditional political constitutions) would be the proper *sedes materiae* of digital constitutional principles and norms. In his view, these principles would have to be set forth in the process of "constitutionalizing" the Internet – a process which would determine, most crucially, whether

> business operators, even stimulated by economic stimulation in private–public co-regulation, should be entrusted with deciding on the limits of human rights.

Teubner also predicted a debate on the horizontal effect of fundamental rights, which according to him would allow individuals to assert their claims vis-à-vis political bodies and "social institutions, in particular centers of economic power."

In the wake of Teubner's view, Internet activists, members of international fora and supporters of Internet freedom have called for the adoption of an Internet bill of rights: notably, an international covenant binding both public and private actors to secure the protection of individual rights. Many propositions have been made in this respect, even among public authorities, such as in Brazil and Italy. Behind this stance is the idea that human rights have to be effectively protected (and thus enforced) vis-à-vis public authorities but also private actors. As the following chapters will show, this is one of the most important issues in the current debate, which is increasingly discussed in light of the alleged "public nature" of the services provided by operators such as social networks and search engines.

Thus, if the original concerns were related to possible governmental interference in the "sphere of freedom" that the cyberspace has created, there is a now a broader focus on the role of private actors, such as ISPs, which de facto act as "private powers." The recent calls for more in-depth regulation, most notably in the European Union, witnessed by the proposal for a regulation known as the "Digital Services Act," reflect this renewed attitude vis-à-vis the role of traditional institutions and rule-making processes. It goes without saying that governmental regulation should be consistent with the protection of human rights such as freedom of speech, which has found new avenues for its exercise on the Internet. However, it seems that national constitutions and international human rights charters and covenants (such as the Charter of Fundamental Rights of the European Union and the European Convention on Human Rights) have proven to incorporate proper safeguards, even if they were drafted before the rise of the Internet and despite the largely unsuccessful attempts to revise the relevant wording in order to encompass the digital world.

It should not come as a surprise that Internet law is mainly made up of case law, where courts have had to tackle the difficulties of enforcing in the digital age rules and principles established in the atomic world. The remarkable degree of legislative inertia in this field has definitely contributed to making courts the true "playmakers" of the shift to the digital world. Not by chance, important legislative reforms have been preceded by landmark cases where courts have had the chance to interpret old-fashioned legal provisions in light of technical developments and with a view to safeguarding the protection of human rights.

1.7 The constitutional dimension of the Internet

The Internet has increasingly challenged the protection of rights and freedoms, thus raising questions for constitutionalism in the digital age. In terms of speech, the digital environment has become a primary channel for individuals to exercise their rights and freedoms, especially freedom of expression. The Internet and related services have fostered the dissemination of information, increasing the opportunities of each individual to share ideas and opinions on a global scale without the infrastructural costs and content filters of traditional media outlets.

A technological optimism characterized the early days of the digital environment. At that time, the Internet promised an emancipation of the public sphere and democracy from public controls through decentralization and anonymity. This positive trend was confirmed in countless numbers of cases. It would be enough to mention how social media and search engines have provided irreplaceable tools for exercising the two sides of freedom of expression, precisely the right to inform and that to be informed. Online speech has shown its ability to influence elections, to expand the exchange of new ideas to a global scale, and to support minorities and political movements as an instrument of emancipation, such as during the Arab Spring. While at first glance this picture would suggest that the digital environment has enhanced freedom of expression while emancipating individual freedom from the interference of public authorities, a closer look reveals that the flow of information online is not without control. In recent years, states have taken steps to regulate online speech to tackle extreme content or the spread of unauthorized copyright content. In some cases, public actors have also relied on shutting down the Internet extensively despite the economic consequences.

Nonetheless, the control of online speech is not merely related to online censorship by public authorities that are already subject to constitutional obligations. The exercise of power over information also concerns private actors. Although the Internet has enhanced access to different types of information, this positive effect is lessened by a substantial restriction in the autonomy of users that are subject to governance of online platforms. Unlike public actors, online platforms are not required to ensure the same constitutional safeguards when they take decisions over the organization or removal of speech online. These actors can enforce and balance the vast amount of online information outside any public safeguard, primarily the rule of law, as also shown by the blocking of Donald Trump's accounts by Facebook and Twitter.

In this respect, scholars have repeatedly highlighted the significant shift from a dyadic to a triadic paradigm. Whereas 20th-century speech regulation saw an interaction between two actors (i.e., the state governing and regulating speech and individuals seeking to enjoy their freedom as fully as possible), 21st-century speech regulation has seen the rise of a third, increasingly relevant class of actors, represented by the private owners of digital infrastructures. Thus, in Balkin's own words, today "free speech is a triangle."

These considerations can also be extended to the field of data. At the end of the 20th century, the digital environment was considered a space to ensure the protection of privacy through anonymity and decentralization, which was seen as a way to protect freedoms from public interference. However, this framework of anonymity and decentralization has not been an obstacle for public actors, which have increasingly relied on the digital environment as an instrument of surveillance. The case of Snowden is just one example not only of the consolidation of a surveillance society, but also of the cooperation between the public and private sector in the field of data surveillance.

The paradigmatic idea of a public panopticon can be considered one of the primary concerns in the digital age. However, as in the case of freedom of expression, public actors have not been the only source of concerns about privacy and personal data. At the end of the 20th century, the development of new processing technologies driven by neoliberal narratives has allowed the rise of new business models based on the processing of multiple kinds of information, including personal data, which are increasingly collected, organized and processed not only by public actors for the pursuit of public tasks but also by businesses for purposes of profit. The processing of personal data has already highlighted serious constitutional challenges at the beginning of this century, especially with the evolution of profiling technologies. In this framework, online platforms play a critical role due to the vast amount of data they process and organize. Even if not exclusively, their business model is based or highly relies on the processing of data for profiling purposes to make profits from advertising revenues, targeted services or analysis of data. Like in the field of content, the value of data in the algorithmic society can be understood by focusing on artificial intelligence systems providing opportunities for extracting value from the processing of vast amounts of (personal) data.

The development and implementation of algorithmic technologies have increased concerns about the protection of fundamental rights. Furthermore, such challenges concern not only individual rights but also democratic values. For instance, the Cambridge Analytica scandal showed how these constitutional challenges also involve the collective interest and, more generally, democracy.

1.8 Conclusions

The advent of the Internet has increasingly shaped daily lives. This space has not only provided new opportunities but also raised critical challenges for the protection of rights and democratic values. This is why questions about the governance of this space have been at the center of the debate. At the end of the 20th century, the positions were primarily oriented towards allowing the Internet to follow its own path, primarily driven by self-regulation. This framework has been challenged by different public and private actors that have demonstrated how it is possible to exercise power on the Internet.

From a libertarian approach to the Internet, the debate has moved towards a different perspective on the law of the Internet by focusing on regulation of the architecture and the actors governing this space. In this case, the question is not only about whether the law applies to the Internet but also how different actors express their powers over this space. In this case, the primary concerns are related not only to the exercise of traditional public powers but also to new private interference with fundamental rights and democratic values.

Therefore, the focus has shifted towards the process of constitutionalization of the Internet, particularly looking at bills of rights. This has been just a first step that underlines the constitutional dimension of the Internet. The Internet has led to the amplification of rights and democratic values, thus raising questions about the role of constitutionalism in the digital age.

2 Internet and Jurisdiction

2.1 Introduction

The first chapter of this book illustrates how scholars faced the rise of cyberspace and its impact on legal categories and, most notably, state sovereignty. In spite of some calls for cyberanarchy, the advent of the Internet did not deprive governments of the power to regulate activities and conducts taking place in the digital realm. As one can easily notice in everyday life, territorial borders still matter and make a difference. However, a key problem that arose in the late 1990s concerned the definition of criteria for states to assert jurisdiction in cyberspace. At least at the very beginning, this problem did not concern prescriptive jurisdiction (i.e., the ability of states to exercise their rule-making authority over a particular conduct or individual) but rather adjudicative jurisdiction (i.e., the power of courts to hear and adjudicate a specific matter) and enforcement jurisdiction (i.e., the ability of governments to ensure compliance with certain measures adopted by state authorities).

The ability of courts to assert their jurisdiction (and then, implicitly, the relevant national law) contributed to weakening the claim that cyberspace was a land of anarchy where states had no ability to impose their own laws and regulations. This chapter will show how the key problem, in the eyes of courts, has never been whether state law was applicable as such, but rather which state law was the applicable one and which court could, therefore, hear a case. In a way, the approach of courts was a reaction to the claim of cyberanarchy endorsed by some scholars in earlier years.

The issue of jurisdiction thus became critical first of all in the United States. US courts approached the problems raised by the apparently borderless nature of the Internet by revisiting the traditional criteria for a court to assert jurisdiction over a case. This is an even more sensitive issue to the extent that transnational disputes may involve different standards of protection of the same right, such as freedom of expression or the right to privacy, and therefore may become a matter of "digital sovereignty."

2.2 Cyberspace and jurisdiction

A well-known test in US common law to determine if a state has jurisdiction over a case is based on so-called minimum contact. US courts attached relevance to various circumstances to establish that such minimum contact was actually met. Most frequently, they relied on the existence of a "purposeful availment": without requiring physical presence or contact, they established personal jurisdiction over defendants on the assumption that they had taken deliberate action toward the forum state. Such a test was taken into account also in the context of the first cases dealing with the novelty of cyberspace. Courts focused on whether certain activities carried out on the Internet constituted a purposeful availment of such a nature to meet the minimum contact test. For instance, in *CompuServe Inc v Patterson*, a 1996 case, the US Court of Appeals for the Sixth Circuit held that the defendant, a Texas resident, purposefully availed himself of the privilege of doing business in Ohio by electronically transmitting shareware software files to CompuServe, which, in turn, advertised and distributed them to its subscribers over the Internet. In contrast, in *Bensusan Restaurant v King,* a 1997 judgment, the US Court of Appeals for the Second Circuit ruled that the simple creation of a passive website did not constitute a purposeful availment, since it only permitted users located everywhere in the world to access it.

In 1997, a landmark case was delivered in *Zippo Manufacturing v Zippo Dot Com.* The US District Court for the Western District of Pennsylvania developed the well-known "sliding-scale test," differentiating and categorizing websites according to three levels of interactivity: "the likelihood that personal jurisdiction can be constitutionally exercised is directly proportional to the nature and quality of the commercial activity that an entity conducts over the Internet" (952 F.Supp. 1124). The court focused first on subjects that operate websites for the purpose of doing business: in such cases, "if the defendant enters into contracts with residents of a foreign jurisdiction that involve the knowing and repeated transmission of computer files over the Internet, personal jurisdiction is proper" (952 F.Supp. 1124). Second, the court pointed out that, unlike active websites, passive websites are used only to post information and make it available in other countries; therefore, such activities do not amount to a sound basis for personal jurisdiction. Finally, the court held that "the middle ground is occupied by interactive Web sites where a user can exchange information with the host computer. In these cases, the exercise of jurisdiction is determined by examining the level of interactivity and commercial nature of the exchange of information that occurs on the web site" (952 F.Supp. 1124).

Having that said, the District Court concluded that Zippo Dot Com, a California corporation, had entered into contact via its website with Pennsylvania residents for business purposes. Such "purposeful availment" was deemed sufficient to meet the minimum contact test; thus, the court had jurisdiction and rejected Zippo Dot Com's motion to dismiss the case.

Commentators have criticized the sliding-scale test developed in *Zippo* and discouraged overreliance on the value of such a test (in particular, on its ability to replace the minimum contact test). The test was based on a very basic functioning of websites, the structure of which were much simpler than they are today. Moreover, the understanding of the potential of the Internet was still very limited at that time. Problems with which everyone is familiar nowadays, such as international data transfers and the relevant data protection issues, were not yet apparent, and the still-limited complexity of websites led to designing this test.

Courts have in fact relied on *Zippo*'s sliding-scale test in a few cases. In *ALS Scan v Digital Service Consultants*, the US Court of Appeals for the Fourth Circuit applied *Zippo* in a suit for copyright infringement caused by the defendant's posting of copyrighted materials on the Internet. The court also relied on the "effects test" developed by the US Supreme Court in *Calder v Jones*, 465 US 783 (1984), in which the court ruled that the infringer could not be subject to the jurisdiction of Maryland (where the plaintiff had filed suit) since its website was at most passive and had not established any contact with the forum state. Likewise, in *Cybersell v Cybersell*, the US Court of Appeals for the Ninth Circuit found that the posting on the website of Cybersell (which was incorporated in California) of an allegedly infringing service mark for which an eponymous Arizona company had filed an application did not establish personal jurisdiction in Arizona, as the passive nature of the website (which only advertised the owner's services) did not qualify as purposeful availment of the benefits and protections of Arizona.

In contrast, the US District Court for the Western District of Wisconsin declined to adopt the sliding-scale test in *Hy Cite Corporation v BadBusinessBureau.com*. The court significantly revisited the test, noting that the degree of interactivity of a website is just "one component of a determination whether a defendant has availed itself purposefully of the benefits or privileges of the forum state" 297 F. Supp. 2d 1161 (W.D. Wis. 2004).

Furthermore, in *Amway Corp. v The Procter & Gamble Company*, a plaintiff incorporated in Michigan brought a tort liability claim against the owner of a website that had posted defamatory information concerning the former. The US District Court for the Western District of Michigan applied the *Calder* effects test in order to determine whether it had jurisdiction over the defendant, who resided in Oregon. First, it established that the defendant had committed an intentional tort, thus fulfilling the first prong of the *Calder* test. Second, the court acknowledged that the brunt of the harm had been felt by the plaintiff in the forum state, so that it could be said to be "the focal point of the harm" suffered by him. Third, the plaintiff had proved that the defendant inflicted the tortious action knowing that the brunt of the harm would be suffered there. Therefore, the court held that it had jurisdiction over the defendant.

2.3 Beyond US courts

US courts have not been the only ones to face problems of jurisdiction over the Internet. In 2002, for example, the High Court of Australia released a landmark judgment in *Dow Jones & Company v Gutnick*, concerning a case of online defamation. The plaintiff filed a complaint against the defendant, a financial information firm, as a result of an article that appeared on its online newspaper. Only a few of the subscribers were located in Australia; however, the High Court of Australia decided to hear the case. According to the court, "if people wish to do business in, or indeed travel to, or live in, or utilize the infrastructure of different countries, they can hardly expect to be absolved from compliance with the laws of those countries. The fact that publication might occur everywhere does not mean that it occurs nowhere" ([2002] HCA 56, 186). The court also noted that "harm to reputation is done when a defamatory publication is comprehended by the reader, the listener, or the observer. Until then, no harm is done by it" ([2002] HCA 56, 26). Accordingly,

> defamation is to be located at the place where the damage to reputation occurs … It is only when the material is in comprehensible form that the damage to reputation is done ... In the case of material on the World Wide Web, it is not available in comprehensible form until downloaded on to the computer of a person who has used a web browser to pull the material from the web server. It is where that person downloads the material that the damage to reputation may be done. ([2002] HCA 56, 44)

Similarly, in 2004 a UK court heard a complaint brought by an American citizen against the authors of defamatory texts posted on a website based in California. Both the plaintiff and the defendant were US residents, and the website on which the defamation appeared was operated in California. However, the plaintiff went before a British court, assuming that the defamatory content could also be accessed in the United Kingdom, creating a harm to his reputation there. In *Lewis v King*, the England and Wales Court of Appeal found that it had jurisdiction because defamation occurs whenever a libelous statement is posted on the web and becomes accessible in the United Kingdom (or specifically England and Wales). Accordingly, since the plaintiff had a reputation in that country, the harmful event was suffered (also) in the United Kingdom and the domestic court did not lack jurisdiction.

2.4 Jurisdiction and cyberspace in Europe

In the legal system of the European Union, it was up to the Court of Justice of the European Union (ECJ) to apply the EU rules on jurisdiction laid down by the Brussels I Regulation to cyberspace transactions. Article 7(2) of Regulation No. 1215/2012, which repealed Regulation 44/2001, on jurisdiction and the recognition and enforcement of judgments in civil and commercial matters establishes that a person domiciled in a Member State may, in another Member State, be sued in matters relating to tort, delict or quasi-delict, in the courts for the place where the harmful event occurred. In its case law, even before the rise of the Internet, the ECJ has consistently understood this provision as implying that the "place where the harmful event occurred" covers both the place where the damage occurred and the location of the event giving rise to the damage. In particular, in *Shevill* (C-68/93) the ECJ said that

> the victim of a libel by a newspaper article distributed in several Contracting States may bring an action for damages against the publisher either before the courts of the Contracting State of the place where the publisher of the defamatory publication is established, which have jurisdiction to award damages for all the harm caused by the defamation, or

> before the courts of each Contracting State in which the publication was distributed and where the victim claims to have suffered injury to his reputation, which have jurisdiction to rule solely in respect of the harm caused in the State of the court seised. (ECJ, C-68/93, 33)

In the view of the ECJ, the plaintiffs had two options: suing the offender and seeking the full compensation of damages before the courts of the place of publication, or alternatively at the place where the harm was suffered (including the place of residence). However, in the latter scenario the claimant is entitled to seek a limited amount of damages, corresponding to the harm suffered in that specific jurisdiction.

The advent of the Internet required the ECJ to test the persistent validity of these holdings. In *eDate Advertising* (C-509/09), the ECJ had the chance to return to this issue with respect to online content infringing personality rights. The ECJ ruled that

> in the event of an alleged infringement of personality rights by means of content placed online on an internet website, the person who considers that his rights have been infringed has the option of bringing an action for liability, in respect of all the damage caused, either before the courts of the Member State in which the publisher of that content is established or before the courts of the Member State in which the centre of his interests is based. That person may also, instead of an action for liability in respect of all the damage caused, bring his action before the courts of each Member State in the territory of which content placed online is or has been accessible. Those courts have jurisdiction only in respect of the damage caused in the territory of the Member State of the court seised. (ECJ, C-509/09, 52)

In *Bolagsupplysningen OÜ* (C-194/16) once again the ECJ was asked to rule on the application of the Brussels I Regulation, as amended in 2012, to the Internet. The proceedings concerned a request to rectify information and to delete comments available online. The ECJ pointed out that, given the ubiquitous nature of information on the Internet and the fact that the pieces of content available online are subject to universal distribution, a request for rectification and removal of comments amounts to a single claim. As result, it can be filed only before a court having jurisdiction over the entirety of a claim seeking compensation for losses under the *Shevill* and *eDate* case law, and not before a court that lacks jurisdiction to do so.

The ECJ also had the chance to rule in cases concerning intellectual property law. In *Wintersteiger* (C-523/10), the ECJ rejected the argument that jurisdiction should be based on the location of the damage, specifically the place where a website can be accessed. Instead, it pointed out that the place of the damage where all losses can be claimed is the place where a national trademark is registered.

Despite this precedent, the ECJ adopted a different interpretation of Article 5(3) in the area of copyright law. In *Pinckney* (C-170/12) the ECJ had to rule on the unauthorized reproduction and distribution of a French author's songs in the United Kingdom. The preliminary question raised to the ECJ concerned the interpretation of (the former) Article 5(3) of Regulation 44/2001. The ECJ drew a clear distinction between cases of copyright infringement and cases involving personality rights, noting that

> in applying those principles, for the purpose of identifying the place where damage allegedly caused over the Internet has occurred, the Court has distinguished between infringements of personality rights and infringement of intellectual and industrial property rights. Thus, the alleged victim of an infringement of personality rights by means of content placed online, which is protected in all the Member States may, on the basis that the harmful even occurred there, bring his action before the courts of each Member State in the territory of which content placed online is or has been accessible … Furthermore, given that the impact which material placed online is liable to have on an individual's personality rights might best be assessed by the court of the place where the alleged victim has his centre of interests, the alleged victim may choose to bring an action in one forum in respect of all of the damage caused. However, the allegation of an infringement of an intellectual and industrial property right, in respect of which the protection granted by registration is limited to the territory of the Member State of registration, must be brought before the courts of that State. It is the courts of the Member State of registration which are the best placed to ascertain whether the right at issue has been infringed. (ECJ, C-170/12, 35–36)

That said, since copyright enjoys harmonized protection throughout the European Union and does not depend on national registration, the ECJ recognized that the fact that a website is accessible is sufficient to establish jurisdiction for the purposes of Article 5(3) of Regulation 44/2001. In *Hejduk* (C-441/13), the ECJ heard a case regarding a violation of copyright due to the publication of photographs on a website. The defendant argued that, since the company was established in Germany and there was no redirection from the German domain name, the German court was the one having jurisdiction. The ECJ confirmed its approach in *Pinckney*, saying that the court of the place where the infringing content is accessible has jurisdiction only with respect to the damages occurred in that territory. In this way, the ECJ rejected the view of the Advocate General, who had noted that the divulgation of content "can hardly be considered as occurring in a specific place that can be defined according to a territoriality criterion," highlighting the "dematerialization" occurring to damages and the consequent delocalization.

2.5 Conclusions

As case law demonstrates, courts have rejected the views sympathetic to cyberanarchy. The very idea of the Internet as an anarchic dream completely free from national laws has collapsed. Within this perspective, some important remarks concerning jurisdiction over the Internet may be made with reference to the case law discussed above. As Reidenberg highlighted:

> The maturation of the analysis reflects an evolution from a somewhat naïve view of the Internet to a rejection of the Internet activists' simple denial of law. The Internet became popular precisely because of the promise of a global audience. But, this promise could not absolve online activities of legal responsibility. While online technologies were initially designed for geographically indifferent access, nothing fixed the technology in

stone. Commercial pressures and the dynamic nature of the Internet have resulted in geolocation and the re-creation of geographic origin and destination.

On that premise, some important observations can be made.

It is worth noting, first of all, that the concept of sovereignty that was frequently called into question in the 1990s in the context of the rise of the Internet was already quite old-fashioned. This idea of sovereignty relied on the ability of a nation to exercise full enforcement jurisdiction over persons and properties within its borders. This view may have been valid a century ago, when, in 1895, in the case of *Carrick v Hancock*, Lord Russell of Killowen CJ famously declared that "the jurisdiction of a court was based upon the principle of territorial dominion, and that all the persons within territorial dominion owe their allegiance to its sovereign power and obedience to all its laws and to the lawful jurisdiction of its courts." But such an absolutist concept of sovereignty, based on the exclusivity of the power of control that states retain within their territory, does not fit well with a globalized society. And this is not because of the Internet, although the rise of cyberspace has made even clearer the inadequacy of this understanding of sovereignty.

A second aspect that is worth noting is that, in light of the case law discussed above, despite cyberanarchist predictions, digital technology seems to have empowered sovereign states to assert their jurisdiction over online activities and conduct rather than dismantling it. Concerns about multi-jurisdictional regulatory exposure (i.e., the fact that individuals and entities are supposed to comply with laws and regulations applicable in a variety of states) have been centered on the idea that a content provider or Internet service provider with a multi-jurisdictional presence cannot monitor or control the geographical flow of information over the Internet. However, many techniques, such as geo-localization, have been developed to allow geographical content discrimination. The latter may be more or less desirable depending, for instance, on the costs or the consequences they may incur; however, it cannot be disputed that it is feasible, so this can no longer be an argument in support of cyberanarchy. Moreover, it must be stressed that many regulatory regimes have become transnational in recent decades, at least in the EU legal system. This does not resolve all possible issues; however, it is a step forward that ultimately reduces the likelihood of clashes between different legal systems and the risks associated with multi-jurisdictional exposure.

When it comes to jurisdiction, enforcement plays a key value in the context of the digital sphere. If the case law overview above sheds some light on the ability of states to exercise their prescriptive and adjudicative jurisdiction even in cyberspace, the new structure of the digital sphere (where "free speech is a triangle," in Jack Balkin's words) poses some challenges with respect to the enforcement jurisdiction. Increasingly the actual enforcement of courts' orders or decisions depends on the operators having the technical ability to ensure compliance, that is, online intermediaries. As the next chapters will bring to light, intermediaries were created mostly in the United States, where they were subject to a relatively favorable regulatory regime that is sympathetic to the extensive protection of freedom of speech under the First

Amendment. However, they now operate on a global scale, including in jurisdictions where a different standard of protection may apply.

This scenario is not merely theoretical. A very telling case that illustrates the challenges deriving from the difference in the degree of protection of rights and interests in the context of the Internet is the well-known *Yahoo! Licra* saga. This is one of the oldest and most important cases in this field, which arose out of the creation of a website that held auctions for Nazi relics, which was hosted by Yahoo! and managed by third parties in the United States. Certain anti-discrimination organizations, including Ligue Internationale Contre le Racisme et l'Antisémitisme (LICRA), sued to block the website in France, on the grounds that the activities were expressly prohibited under the French Criminal Code. In May 2000, the High Court of Paris ordered Yahoo! to take the technological steps necessary to prevent the site from being accessed within France. Yahoo! had strongly objected to the requests made by the plaintiffs in this case, and it had expressed its intention not to comply with the order issued by the French court, claiming it was immune from that court's jurisdiction. In its defense, Yahoo! argued, inter alia, that the servers hosting the site were located in the United States, and that the site's principal, although not exclusive, target was citizens of the United States, a country in which the sale of Nazi relics is not prohibited but is protected under the broad umbrella of the First Amendment.

Another point raised by Yahoo! focused on the alleged impossibility of limiting access to a website to residents in specific states where the sale of Nazi relics was not prohibited. While such a limitation might have been costly at the time, it was certainly not impossible.

But the strongest objection to the request to block the website was related to the refusal to extend to a site operated by a US provider a more restrictive conception of freedom of expression at odds with the "absolutist" vision enshrined in the First Amendment. According to Yahoo!, this decision unjustifiably gave priority to the European understanding of freedom of expression, which embraced a lower standard of protection, thus de facto making this standard applicable at a global level.

The dispute had additional legal consequences, as Yahoo! took action before the US courts to challenge the decision of the High Court of Paris, questioning whether a "foreign" judge had the right to impose a duty to respect a conception of freedom of expression that conflicted with the First Amendment. The US District Court for the Northern District of California accepted Yahoo!'s arguments, finding that the decision by the French was not compatible with the First Amendment, and was thus inapplicable and not subject to enforcement. However, at a later stage, the US Court of Appeals for the Ninth Circuit reversed the ruling at first instance.

This case brings to light at least two critical issues: on the one hand, it demonstrates the inherent conflict between the conceptions of freedom of expression based on the constitutional paradigms of Europe and the United States. On the other hand, it shows that – absent a "common" standard for the Internet or international conventions establishing what level of protection should apply to online speech – the final say is de facto left to the discretion of the courts. But this scenario may give rise to a degree of legal uncertainty, as the legal solution may change depending on the relevant court's discretion. But even more important, the case highlights the increased power wielded by online intermediaries. If, at the very origins of cyberspace, many virtual communities were in competition to attract users, the swift evolution of the Internet led to an oligopolist structure where a few platforms enjoy significant market power. This market power means platforms are able to condition to a significant degree the protection of fundamental rights, including freedom of expression. The *Yahoo! Licra* saga captures this unprecedented growth in the role of online intermediaries and explains why they are more and more frequently considered "private powers."

3 Internet Access and Net Neutrality

3.1 Introduction

At the dawn of the Internet, cyberspace was imagined as free from government interference, belonging to the people and for the people. However, the immense developments that characterized it over the years – from the ARPANet to on-demand services such as Netflix and Spotify – resulted in a very different digital environment. The Internet became an increasingly relevant component of the economy and, more generally, of people's lives. The range of services that are offered on the Internet is of such magnitude that access to the system is essentially unavoidable since in the digital space individuals satisfy a broad spectrum of needs fundamental to the development of the person. This importance has recently been amplified by the epidemiological emergency of COVID-19, which made clear how much the Internet is needed for the exercise of the activities of daily life. The growing importance of the Internet has given rise to a wide-ranging debate, nationally and internationally, about whether or not to identify a real fundamental right of individuals to access the World Wide Web.

At the height of nationwide lockdowns due to the COVID-19 pandemic, up to 1.6 billion children were affected by school closures, causing the largest mass disruption of education in modern history. Yet even before schools shuttered their doors, one in five school-age children (three to seventeen years old) was out of school, and even children in schools were not necessarily learning, with 617 million children and adolescents worldwide failing to reach minimum proficiency levels in reading and mathematics. To address these gaps, more than 90 percent of the world's education ministries have adopted some type of remote learning policy, and stakeholders have sought to "reimagine education" by harnessing technology.

However, 2.2 billion, or two-thirds of children and young people aged twenty-five years or less, do not have Internet access at home, according to the "How Many Children and Youth Have Internet Access at Home" report, a joint project by UNICEF and the International Telecommunication Union. Using the latest available household survey data, the report finds significant inequities between countries, regions, wealth groups and urban–rural settings. For example, only 5 percent of children and young people in West and Central Africa have Internet access at home compared to the 33 percent global average. Differences are starker yet between rich and poor countries, with only 6 percent of children and young people in low-income countries having Internet access compared to 87 percent in high-income countries.

In light of the above, this chapter aims to scrutinize whether there should be a stand-alone human right to Internet access and what the forms of justification for it would be. It explores the notion of the right to Internet access both from a societal and a legal perspective. Section 3.2 offers a concise theoretical background of the right to Internet access. Section 3.3 looks at the concept from both the international and the national law perspective (3.3.1) and briefly analyzes how the main ordinary domestic laws started to consider the right to Internet access as a stand-alone right, in particular, the Brazilian and the Italian experiences. Section 3.4 briefly considers the main academic opinions for and against the codification of the right to Internet access, specifically the example of social media. Finally, Section 3.5 delves into one specific aspect of the right to Internet access, namely net neutrality, and examines a case study from the Court of Justice of the European Union (ECJ): the Telenor's Judgment.

3.2 The right to Internet access

It is indisputable that Internet is an essential resource in modern digital life. The importance of Internet access and of having an Internet connection during the numerous lockdowns in response to the COVID-19 pandemic has led to discussions about establishing new rights or provisions to ensure the right to access the Internet.

However, the right to Internet access has been discussed by regulators and scholars for some time: the first proposals to include such a right in constitutions or in human rights conventions can be traced back to the first decade of the 21st century. In particular, in May 2011, Frank La Rue, the United Nations (UN) Special Rapporteur, published the "Report on the Promotion and Protection of the Right to Freedom of Opinion and Expression." In this document, after analyzing the impact of the Internet on the contemporary world, in particular on the Arab Spring protests, La Rue explored key trends and challenges to the freedom of expression through the Internet, pointing out how the Internet can be a tool that can also foster the realization of a range of human rights.

> The Special Rapporteur is thus concerned that without Internet access, which facilitates economic development and the enjoyment of a range of human rights, marginalized groups and developing States remain trapped in a disadvantaged situation, thereby perpetuating inequality both within and between States. As he has noted previously, to combat situations of inequality it is critical to ensure that marginalized or disadvantaged sections of society can express their grievances effectively and that their voices are heard. The Internet offers a key means by which such groups can obtain information, assert their rights, and participate in public debates concerning social, economic, and political changes to improve their situation. Moreover, the Internet is an important educational tool, as it provides access to a vast and expanding source of knowledge, supplements or transforms traditional forms of schooling, and makes, through "open access" initiatives, previously unaffordable scholarly research available to people in developing States. Additionally, the educational benefits attained from Internet usage directly contribute to the human capital of States. (La Rue 2011, 7).

Policymakers took these issues into consideration. There are many initiatives across the globe that are interested in the creation and promotion of Internet bills of rights. For instance, as discussed in Section 3.3.1, Brazil considered implementing its own comprehensive legal statute on Internet governance, including individual rights. At the European policy level, the European Union's *Digital Agenda* foresees a code (compilation) of digital rights, summarizing existing user rights in the European Union in a clear and accessible way. In March 2012, the Council of Europe adopted its *Internet Governance Strategy for 2012–2015*, building further on its 2011 *Declaration on Internet Governance Principles* and on its 2011 *Recommendation on the Protection and Promotion of the Universality, Integrity, and Openness of the Internet*. Lastly, in 2022, the Commission proposed a *Declaration on Digital Rights and Principles for a Human Centred Digital Transformation*. The declaration aims to put people at the center, to foster solidarity and inclusion, freedom of choice, participation in the digital public space, safety, security and empowerment, and sustainability. The goal is also to underline that those rights and freedoms should be equally respected online as they are offline. In the Declaration's second chapter, "Solidarity and Inclusion," the Commission recognizes that "everyone should have access to technology that aims at uniting, and not dividing, people. The digital transformation should contribute to a fair society and economy in the Union." In doing so, it commits to realizing a range of activities associated with connectivity, digital education and digital public services.

These positions underline how the right to Internet access raises at least two primary concerns. The first aspect is about the exercise of rights and interests of various kinds. Among these rights and interests, it is worth mentioning the expression of one's thoughts, the right to criticize and report on facts of public interest, as well as the right to associate and protest. The right to Internet access seems to be instrumental to the exercise of the aforementioned freedoms but also to education, work and health, and to the possibility of making public administration efficient by also making it easier for the citizen to relate to it. The difficult recognition of the right of access to the Internet as having its own autonomy is subject to the fact that the creation of a new human right under international human rights law is not an automatic process. Instead, there are essentially two ways in which it can occur: either the right is derived from the doctrine, or the right is originated by a justificatory argument that no existing right alone can adequately protect the important interests in question. In the context of international law, the right to Internet access has been derived from the broader dimension of the right to freedom of expression, as discussed further in Section 3.3. Moreover, the debate at the national level, in particular in the Italian case, has also been largely influenced by the conception of the right to Internet access as in the orbit of other rights.

Second, the Internet is not something that can be taken for granted. Even the Internet has its own physicality – that is, routers, cables, antennas, Internet exchange points and data centers – and is by no means safe from interests of different kinds, both public and private and ranging from the desire for control of the web for commercial purposes to the desire to play a hegemonic or monopolistic role, to the possibility of conditioning, limiting or blocking its use by citizens or representative segments of various minorities.

Therefore, in light of the above, the next section will consider how these two positions are balanced and transposed into international and national laws. Notably, it seeks to determine whether a stand-alone positive right to Internet access exists. If it does, it will be necessary to impose positive obligations on firms and states to ensure access. The right to access the Internet would then require the specification of state duties on two dimensions. The first set would aim to make the Internet affordable to those who do not have their own Internet access, entailing a dimension of social assistance. The second set would aim to ensure that access to the Internet is meaningful; this is the case of net neutrality, which will be further considered in Section 3.5. This requires ensuring that Internet access is not limited to only some parts of the Internet and that it is not offered in ways that manipulate or exclude individuals.

3.3 The right to Internet access between international and national law

The Internet is a necessary precondition for the exercise of several rights. In fact, the inability (total or partial, infrastructural or cognitive and social) to access the Internet, to connect to it, potentially leads to a new form of social discrimination. However, due to the global nature of the connection there may be an overlap between national and international norms, not only on regulatory aspects but also in the protection of fundamental rights and freedoms. Hence, the first part of this chapter will try to answer a specific question: is there a need for a "new" right to Internet access, and on what basis and at what level?

> Fundamental rights are awarded through the state's constitution, and their enforceability through (not only) constitutional courts embodies the quintessence of constitutionalism: limiting government and ensuring that rights and freedom protected by the constitution are not "drained" by the possible abuse of power. Instead, human rights are those rights that each human being should have, and which are protected by virtue of global or regional international law through covenants or conventions (but not always by courts). (O. Pollicino 2020, 264)

Given this background, we should consider whether the right to Internet access can be considered an autonomous right in international law or if it is just a medium for the enjoyment of other fundamental rights and freedoms such as freedom of expression. As was anticipated, the UN Special Rapporteur encouraged states to take steps to protect access to the Internet:

> Where the infrastructure for Internet access is present, the Special Rapporteur encourages States to support initiatives to ensure that online information can be accessed in a meaningful way by all sectors of the population, including persons with disabilities and persons belonging to linguistic minorities (§87).

The Organization for Security and Co-operation in Europe adopted a similar approach in a 2011 report, where it stressed that "everyone should have a right to participate in the information society and states have a responsibility to ensure citizens' access to the Internet is guaranteed."

These examples underline the interest of international law in Internet access not as an autonomous right but as a tool that becomes part of, or even boosts, some democratic freedoms already enjoyed by individuals. Therefore, the right to access to the Internet is not a fully autonomous human right under international law. Internet access is often connected to civil and political rights, *representing their digital projection*, and is not treated as an autonomous, independent right. Therefore, despite these provisions, the Report does not expressly qualify Internet access as a human right per se. Instead, it stresses the point that Internet access allows citizens to enjoy other human rights via the Internet.

Moreover, there is another reason why the right to access the Internet, as construed within these documents, cannot be framed as a human right in a strict sense. One of the main principles of international law relies on *pacta sunt servanda*, meaning that states do not create the rule. Still, they agree to be part of agreements, namely, treaties and other sources of international law (see Article 38 ICJ Statute). Hence, states create written agreements, from which general or particular obligations enshrine establishing rules expressly recognized by the contracting states. As seen above, the justification for the derivation of new human rights is either doctrinal or stand-alone. However, the stronger dimension of derivation is when the new human right finds support in the practice of states. Thus, human rights need to be inserted in treaties to enjoy international protections, and from the treaty they derive their enforcement.

Even though there have been some attempts to reach an international agreement, as will be discussed, neither the documents mentioned hereby can be considered to have the value of an international agreement. In other words, it is still not possible to speak of international recognition of Internet access as an autonomous right. However, as Section 3.3.1 demonstrates, states have adopted several approaches to limit the "digital divide" at the national level.

Another piece of this puzzle can be found in some attempts that have been promoted particularly in the context of the Internet Governance Forum – a multi-stakeholder event organized early and globally by United Nations Economic and Social Council (UNECOSOC). The event aims to discuss hot topics related to Internet governance; it does not aim to bring about agreements that bind these actors to certain norms. However, the *Contract for the Web* was launched at the event in 2019, proposed by one of the fathers of the World Wide Web, Tim Berners-Lee. The Contract aims to bring governments, companies, civil society and web users together to build a roadmap to make the Internet a tool that serves humanity and is a public good for everyone, everywhere.

The Contract is built on a broad and growing network of supporters from companies, civil society and – purportedly – governments, many of which had already helped in the challenging drafting process of the nine principles outlined in the document. Each of these three groups commits to three of the nine principles. So, for instance, governments that sign the Contract promise to "keep all of the Internet available, all of the time," which includes a prohibition on cutting off Internet access unless this is consistent with human rights law. Correspondingly, citizens that become supporters are obliged to act "so that everyone

feels safe and welcome online." Principle 5 calls on private companies to "respect and protect people's privacy and personal data from building online trust." Like previous advocacy documents, however, the Contract lacks legal enforceability.
The impact of the Contract is disputed; it seems to be more an instrument of awareness rather than one with a strong policy impact. This view may be confirmed by looking at similar examples. Considering the relevant case law of the European Court of Human Rights (ECtHR), when the judges have had to face cases connected to the restriction of a right to Internet access, they had no doubts about including the latter within the scope of application of Article 10 of the European Convention on Human Rights, meaning, once again, depriving the right to Internet access of autonomy and reading it together with other rights – in this case, freedom of expression. For instance, these aspects clearly emerged in ECtHR, *Ahmet Yıldırım* v. *Turkey* (Appl. no. 3111/10), judgment, 18 December 2012, and ECtHR, *Kalda* v. *Estonia* (Appl. no. 17429/10), judgment, 19 January 2016.

3.3.1 National initiatives on Internet access regulation

Leaving aside consideration of the international difficulties in recognizing the right to Internet access and its autonomy, the main question is whether, under the perspective of inquiry offered by comparative constitutional law, the right to access could be qualified as an autonomous fundamental right. There are some examples of a *strictu sensu* codification of Internet access at the legal level. In the following, we will consider some of the main ones.

The first example, from Brazil, is the Marco Civil da Internet (MCI). Passed in 2014, the MCI is considered the Brazilian Internet Bill of Rights. This legislation was the result of public debates between the Ministry of Justice, the Labor Party, the opposition, non-governmental organizations, activists and scholars. It aims to give citizens, the government and organizations rights and responsibilities regarding the Internet. It codifies ten principles developed by the country's Internet Steering Committee in the constitution, including network neutrality, freedom of expression and privacy, to define and grant solid civil rights for citizens both online and off. These principles represent a set of goals for government, business and society online, providing the framework for a law grounded in the three pillars of net neutrality, privacy and freedom of expression. As scholars underline,

> The Internet Bill of Rights translates the principles of the Brazilian Constitution to the online world. It is a victory for democracy and stands in stark contrast to other recently passed laws in countries like Turkey or Russia, which expanded governmental powers to interfere with the Internet. Brazil's law is an example for countries willing to acknowledge the importance of the web in facilitating both development and a rich and open public sphere. (Souza 2018, 44)

Considering, then, the European experiences, one of the first Member States to include the right to access the Internet in its constitution was Greece. Article 5 of the Constitution was amended as follows:

> All persons have the right to participate in the Information Society. Facilitation of access to electronically transmitted information, as well as of the production, exchange, and diffusion thereof, constitutes an obligation of the State. (Greek Constitution, Article 5 (2))

Another example is the Portuguese Constitution, whose Article 35 was amended in 2005 to include protection of Internet access:

> 1. Every citizen shall possess the right to access to all computerized data that concern him, to require that they be corrected and updated, and to be informed of the purpose for which they are intended, all as laid down by law … 6. Everyone shall be guaranteed free access to public-use computer networks, and the law shall define both the rules that shall apply to cross-border data flows and the appropriate means for protecting personal data and such other data as may justifiably be safeguarded in the national interest. (Portuguese Constitution, Article 35)

Moreover, in 2021, Law No. 27/2021 of 17 May approved the Portuguese Charter of Human Rights in the Digital Age, which establishes a set of innovative standards regulating the digital environment. One of the main features of the Charter is the vertical and horizontal nature of its norms, that sets forth rights and duties which apply both to relations between the state and citizens and to relations exclusively between private individuals. The provision of new rights will undoubtedly increase the compliance of private entities and the number of complaints submitted by users and entities which protect their rights. The Charter also addresses the right to net neutrality, ensuring the absence of discrimination regarding the transmission and reception of content via the Internet.

Italy adopted its "Dichiarazione dei Diritti di Internet" (Internet Bill of Rights) in 2015. The Bill, consisting of fourteen articles, is an exclusively political document with no legal effect. The purpose of the Declaration seems to be of a predominantly cultural nature: it is to urge the Italian government and the Parliament to commit themselves to the principles laid down in the Bill. When it comes to regulating the Internet, the idea is that the government and Parliament should conform to the provisions of the Bill.

> 1. On the Internet, the fundamental rights of every person as recognized by the United Nations, the Charter of Fundamental Rights of the rights of the European Union, the national constitutions and international declarations on the subject.
> 2. These rights must be interpreted in such a way as to ensure their effectiveness in the Network dimension.
> 3. The recognition of rights on the Internet must be based on full respect for the dignity, freedom, equality and diversity of every person, which constitute the principles on the basis of which the balance with other rights is met. (Article 1, Italian Internet Bill of Rights)

An interesting example is the Italian experience, in which two constitutional amendments were proposed in order to expressly enshrine as a fundamental right in the constitution the right to access to the Internet. As mentioned, in 2015 two constitutional bills – no. 1317 and no. 1561 – were introduced in the Italian parliament. The former bill called for the incorporation into the constitution of Article 21-*bis* explicitly protecting the right to Internet access. That provision was placed immediately after Article 21, which protects freedom of speech, in Title I of Part I relating to "civil rights." This is the text of the proposed Article 21-bis amendment:

> Everybody has the right to access to the Internet, without any discrimination, through tools that are technologically adequate and able to remove any obstacle of an economic or social nature. (Article 21-*bis*)

Then, with regard to the second bill, it was proposed to add a new Article (34-*bis*) to the constitution in Title II relating to "social rights" immediately after the provision (Art. 34) protecting the right to education. According to the proposed Article 34-*bis*:

> Everybody has the right to access to the Internet, in a neutral way, and without discrimination and through technologically adequate means. The State promotes the conditions according to which the Internet is effectively protected as a "place" in which the human being develops his/her person and where the rights and duties of social, political and economic solidarity are exercised. (Article 34-*bis*)

The two proposed provisions, despite their apparent similarity, are structurally very different. Even if the intent in both cases is to allow an autonomous right to access to the Internet emerge in the constitution, in the first case the proposed Article 21-*bis* is considering the right in question as belonging to the category of civil rights and, in particular, as being closely connected to the freedom of expression (in its negative dimension), whereas in the second case the proposed Article 34-*bis* is taking into consideration the social (positive) dimension of the right.

This brief overview of the state initiatives aimed at providing the provision of an autonomous right to Internet access has served as a practical example to witness, on the one hand, the attention of state actors and, on the other, attempted emancipation from the scope of protection of freedom of speech.

However, it is clear that the constitutional codification of a "new" right does not exclude other paths by which new rights could be afforded constitutional relevance. More precisely, as will also be explained in the next chapter, the process of constitutional judicialization of the protection of new rights should be taken into consideration. In particular, the constitutional courts seem to be able to define the risk of potential clashes that may encroach upon the adequate protection of fundamental rights between interconnected legal systems.

However, neither the European Court of Human Rights (ECtHR) nor the ECJ has explicitly derived a right to Internet access, based on which individuals may compel states to provide Internet access by way of legal action. Instead, they protect the enjoyment of Internet access and online content against interferences by invoking the freedom of expression and information under Article 10 of the European Convention on Human Rights and Article 11 of the EU Charter of Fundamental Rights, respectively.

> Any restrictions on the operation of websites, blogs or any other Internet-based, electronic or other such information-dissemination system, including systems to support such communication, such as Internet service providers or search engines, are only permissible to the extent that they are compatible with paragraph 3. Permissible restrictions generally should be content-specific; generic bans on the operation of certain sites and

> systems are not compatible with paragraph 3. It is also inconsistent with paragraph 3 to prohibit a site or an information dissemination system from publishing material solely because it may be critical of the government or the political social system espoused by the government. (ECtHR, application no 3111/10, *Ahmet Yıldırım v. Turkey*, ECtHR, 18 December 2012, §30)

As Chapter 7 will explore in more detail, in 2009 the French Constitutional Court (Conseil constitutionnel) issued a judgment in the landmark *Hadopi* case, which concerned the right of access to the Internet specifically in terms of a corollary of freedom of expression and communication on the Internet. It is useful to clarify since Hadopi is now an administrative authority in charge of the control and sanctioning of copyright infringements via peer-to-peer networks. It originally had the power to disconnect users from the Internet in case of repeated copyright infringements via peer-to-peer systems. In this context, the Conseil recognized the freedom of Internet access but not a right to Internet access. In this sense, the right to Internet access was defined specifically in terms of a corollary of freedom of expression and communication on the Internet. In other words, this right was not framed as an autonomous one but was linked to freedom of expression.

The right to Internet access is important not only because it facilitates equality in exercising freedom of expression, but also because it has become key for the full realization of a wider range of civil, economic, political, social and cultural rights. Lack of Internet access leads to rights deprivation for individuals. These hybrid forms of deprivation – both digital and physical – underpin the case for the right to Internet access as a stand-alone right in international law. The universal scope of this right is not controversial. However, there are still several different visions of this right and its justification, which makes it difficult to envisage protection on the level of international law.

3.4 The right to Internet access: Do we really need it?

The previous paragraphs illustrated some of the initiatives at national and international levels on the right to Internet access. However, it is still not clear why it seems so important to incorporate such a right in national or international bills of rights.

According to arguments in favor of granting such protection, the need to make the Internet (access) a fundamental right is deemed important in the face of pressure from the public and private actors to control (online) speech. The right to Internet access requires the state to provide widespread, homogeneous and affordable coverage of the national territory with broadband so that the claimant, wherever he or she resides, can surf the net at speeds suitable for participating in "onlife" communities. Therefore, whoever controls access to the Internet can indirectly impact a variety of human activities, which may also constitute the exercise of human rights, sometimes with strong repercussions in the offline realm. More than others, this right is the demonstration of the relation between the relevant stakeholders of the digital world.

Between those actors there is a peculiar pyramid that Jack Balkin describes with the famous expression "free speech is a triangle" (Balkin 2018). In particular, considering the example of social media platforms, it is indisputable that they have attained a central position between the state and the speakers/publishers, and, even if they are private, they are equipping themselves with rules, institutions and courts. The right to Internet access is also correlated to the activity of the Internet service provider (ISP) and, in particular, the connectivity provider.

Meanwhile, digital platforms are in a critical position as the means through which public discourse is conducted: it has been said that social media sites are where elections are won or lost. For instance, as published in a Pew Research Center report, more than eight in ten US adults (86 percent) get their news from a smartphone, computer or tablet "often" or "sometimes," including 60 percent who say they do so often.

Such platforms played a crucial role during the COVID-19 pandemic. The centrality of those platforms is well witnessed by the role they played during lockdowns when providers, such as Zoom, became essential for almost every activity of our lives. However, exercising what has been defined as functional sovereignty, the provider can decide whether or not to provide access.

> More than ever in these months of lockdown, many millions of people in Europe and worldwide have been forced to rely on an Internet connection to work, study, buy food and communicate with their loved ones. At the same time, lack of access to the Internet, for geographical, economic or social reasons, has proved to be a major cause of marginalisation. … COVID-19 has made something that was already clear glaringly obvious: digitalisation will not wait. …
> Access to the Internet must be recognized as a new human right. The European Parliament is ready for this challenge. (Sassoli 2020)

In August 2021, the Taliban took control of the Afghan capital of Kabul and immediately took control of social media as well. Facebook, Twitter and TikTok have been put in a tricky position: dozens of pro-Taliban accounts sprang up on Twitter, and within twenty-four hours, together they had racked up more than half a million views. In a situation where even states are trying to figure out whether to officially recognize the Taliban as Afghanistan's rulers, the companies have no clue whether to allow their presence or bar the group online. It is evident that the presence of a group, an opinion or a voice on social media is essential to make that group, opinion or voice part of the public discourse; this is true for the Taliban as well.

This holds even more true if one considers what has happened during the war in Ukraine in 2022. This war has been fought on the field and in cyberspace via daily cyberattacks from Ukraine and Russia. In this context, together with civilians and cities, it has been crucial to protect the critical infrastructure and grant Internet access. For instance, Ukrainian telecom workers have been mounting a heroic effort to keep their fellow citizens connected, working around the clock to maintain the availability of these services.

In light of the above, protecting access to the web also means *protecting the enjoyment of digital rights and fundamental freedoms online*. This threat is even more urgent than in the recent past since there is a growing need to preserve and maintain the Internet's very nature. Moreover, these developments towards control and censorship bring us back to the very first function of human rights, that is, to serve as a shield for the individual against the unnecessary use or abuse of power by a state. The right to Internet access can be a safeguard capable of reducing the social and digital divide.

> Internet coverage in the European Union (EU) is impressive, standing at 100 %; however, numbers on de facto usage (85 %), broadband take-up (78 %), users with at least basic digital skills (58 %), next-generation access coverage providing at least 30 Mbps (86 %) and 5G readiness (21 %) cloud the picture. In rural areas, 10 % of the households are not covered by any fixed network and 41 % are not covered by next-generation access technology capable of reaching 30 Mbps. Some 8.4 % of those EU residents who had a fixed broadband subscription did not receive the minimum of 10 Mbps approximately necessary for ensuring the functionality of basic services in 2020. The proportion of these people ranged from 23.3 % in Italy to 7.8 % in Slovenia and 0.3 % in Greece. Currently, there are no official, EU-wide, and up-to-date reports on the contract compliance of Internet service providers (ISPs), but there are strong indications that ISPs are not delivering the speeds advertised. The significance of these circumstances does not only lie in the economic implications but also in the severe consequences for the individual and society. People without adequate Internet access are missing out on means of participation and opportunities that have become part of everyday life. Countless contributions have been published on socioeconomic inequalities relating to access to, use of, or impact of ICTs, known as the digital divide(s). (Mildebrandt 2021, 1)

At the same time, there are some arguments against the recognition of the right to the Internet.

First, some scholars argue against considering the technical issues as material for a human rights approach. This first counterargument sees the Internet merely as a technology, not as a means for threats or the realization of other situations *de iure* and de facto. Therefore, according to the "moral doctrine" of human rights, the latter are guaranteed to people in all countries and cultures simply because they are human. Hence, in this context, technology is just a means, not a right itself.

If we consider technology and the Internet as capable of being emancipated from other rights, this would mean not allowing the right in question to have an added constitutional value or to be enforced independently of other freedoms, such as freedom of speech.

The second counterargument follows the same approach. According to this approach, *technology is seen as an enabler of rights, not as an inherent right*. Since treaties and constitutions did not guarantee the right to access a printing press, a typewriter or a telephone, no right to the Internet should be introduced.

The third argument is about human rights inflation in general and questions the actual enforceability of this right. If not taken with adequate care, there is a risk of fragmentation and balkanization of human rights, which means that in a globalized field such as the digital one, the constant increase of human rights is seen as an issue from the perspective of providing a high level of protection everywhere. Consequently, inflation of rights could then diminish the value of other existing rights. The inclusion of new rights in the international human rights framework is only justified if there is a substantial added value to the protection offered by existing rights and when there is a consensus that a high level of protection is strictly necessary.

From a practical point of view, it may be argued that the need for such action has not been sufficiently demonstrated and that a more detailed analysis is necessary. Moreover, the effectiveness and efficiency of a right to Internet access in securing social and economic participation might be challenged. Additionally, universal service provisions (Articles 84-92 of the EECC) and provisions granting individual remedies in case of mal- and non-performance (as per Article 4(4) of the Open Internet Access Regulation) may already sufficiently address the need for connectivity and protection against backsliding by national legislators.

This last aspect is also emphasized by the Council of Europe:

> Any measure taken by State authorities or private-sector actors to block, filter or remove Internet content … must, in particular, be prescribed by a law which is accessible, clear, unambiguous, and sufficiently precise to enable individuals to regulate their conduct. They must at the same time be necessary for a democratic society and proportionate to the legitimate aim pursue. (Council of Europe 2018, 1).

By looking at the arguments presented above, one may think that the inclusion of the right to Internet access can be provided by other rights and by working on the flexibility of other existing rights. Nonetheless, some scholars are discussing the opportunity to integrate the concept of the right to Internet access into social inclusion as established by Articles 25, 26, and 36 of the Charter of Fundamental Rights of the European Union. However, it is deemed crucial to work for the emancipation of the right to Internet access from the constitutional destiny of free speech, as well as from the applicability of other existing freedoms. Only in this way would the right to access to the Internet be independent of the possible decrease of protection that freedom of expression can experience when the relevant playing field shifts from the world of atoms to the world of bits.

Beyond the recognition of the Internet as a legitimate object of protection, another aspect that must be taken into consideration is net neutrality.

3.5 Net neutrality

The recognition of Internet access as a new right cannot be considered detached from the recognition and protection of one of its corollaries: the neutrality of the net. This is the principle whereby online data traffic cannot be discriminated against, and no management policies are allowed to slow down, restrict or block data traffic for commercial reasons. Net neutrality has been discussed by scholars and policymakers since the early days of the network. In simple terms, it is the translation of the end-to-end technical principle into legal principles. The numerous definitions formulated in both academics and institutions oscillate between the interest of edge providers in distributing their services and content without any restrictions whatsoever from broadband providers and that of end users to make free use of the Internet.

> Net neutrality is the idea that Internet service providers like Comcast and Verizon should equally treat all content flowing through their cables and cell towers. That means they shouldn't be able to slide some data into "fast lanes" while blocking or otherwise discriminating against other material. In other words, these companies shouldn't be able to block you from accessing a service like Skype, or slow down Netflix or Hulu, in order to encourage you to keep your cable package or buy a different video-streaming service. (Wired 2020)

Without such recognition, both the effectiveness of the right and the need for online equality would be irreparably compromised. Suppose the right to access to the Internet can be considered as a means for the exercise of other interests. In that case, net neutrality is among the elements that guarantee its effectiveness.

In this sense, net neutrality is also a principle to protect users, with critical importance from the point of view of competition in digital markets and concerning the circulation of content. This topic has interested the European Commission since the first decade of the 21st century. In 2011, it was the subject of the "Communication from the Commission to the European Parliament, the Council, the Economic and Social Committee and the Committee of the Regions" (COM(2011) 222 final). This communication resulted from "The open Internet and net neutrality in Europe" consultation, conducted between 30 June and 30 September 2010. This document clarified the need to adopt legal measures to preserve net neutrality in order to prevent predatory behavior. Once again, the protection of the digital environment was second to the protection of other interests, such as market competition.

> The essence of net neutrality and the issues underpinning the debate concern first and foremost how best to preserve the openness of this platform and to ensure that it can continue to provide high-quality services to all and to allow innovation to flourish while contributing to enjoyment of and respect for fundamental rights, such as freedom of expression and freedom to conduct business. … However, the fact that some operators, for reasons unrelated to traffic management, may block or degrade legal services (in particular Voice over IP services) which compete with their own services can be considered to run against the open character of the Internet. Transparency is also an essential part of the net neutrality debate. Obtaining adequate information on possible limitations or traffic management enables consumers to make informed choices. These issues of traffic management, blocking and degradation, quality of service, and transparency need to be addressed. (Communication from the Commission to the European Parliament, the Council, the Economic and Social Committee and the Committee of the Regions, 2011)

Another vital add-on at the European level is EU Regulation 2015/2120, also known as the "Open Internet Access Regulation." The Regulation on Open Internet Access aims to safeguard equal and non-discriminatory treatment of Internet traffic. It promotes the quality of Internet access services through transparency measures and regulatory supervision and therefore provides for meaningful Internet access. If net neutrality is considered a tool to increase the state's positive obligations to ensure the realization of fundamental rights, such as freedom of expression, the need for visibility and state commitment can also be applied to the consideration of Internet access as a fundamental right.

If access to the Internet finds only implicit recognition in Article 3(1) of that Regulation, net neutrality, on the other hand, is explicitly regulated in paragraph 3 of the same article. Paragraph 1 enshrines the right of users to access and disseminate information and content. A description of positive actions corresponds to the conceptualization of the right to access online content and services. Paragraph 2 states that neither the agreements between Internet access service providers and users nor the business practices adopted by providers of services may restrict the right referred to in paragraph 1, namely the enjoyment of the Internet. Moreover, paragraph 3 states:

> Providers of Internet access services shall treat all traffic equally, when providing Internet access services, without discrimination, restriction or interference, and irrespective of the sender and receiver, the content accessed or distributed, the applications or services used or provided, or the terminal equipment used. (EU Regulation 2015/2120, Article 3 para. 3)

The ECJ has assessed the practices of so-called zero-rating as possible violations of net neutrality and has spoken of the principle ruled by Article 3 para. 3 as a measure to protect the rights of users online. A zero-rating practice occurs when a provider applies a price of zero to the data traffic associated with a particular application or class of applications (and the data do not count towards any data cap in place on the Internet access service). For example, suppose an Internet access service does not charge a user for the data used to access a piece of a specific music streaming application or all music streaming applications. In that case, the ISPs are zero-rating those applications. This case needs further explanation.

Judgment in Joined Cases C-807/18 and C-39/19 Telenor Magyarország Zrt. v Nemzeti Média- és Hírközlési Hatóság Elnöke

Telekom, the applicant, is an information and communications technology undertaking that had been offering its end customers an add-on option in the form of a free "zero tariff" option called "Stream On," which allowed data volume consumed by audio and video streamed by Telekom's content partners (i.e., Spotify, Netflix, etc.) not to be counted toward the data volume included in the basic package. By activating the "Stream On" tariff option, the end customer had to accept bandwidth being limited to a maximum of 1.7 Mbit/s for video streaming, irrespective of whether content partners or other providers streamed the videos, and once that data volume was used up, the transmission speed would be reduced. The Federal Agency for Electricity, Gas, Telecommunicications, Post and Rail Networks, Germany, found that the tariff option concerned did not comply with the obligations arising from Article 3(3) of EU Regulation 2015/2120 since it was accompanied by a reduction in the data transmission speed for video streaming to a maximum of 1.7 Mbit/s. Hence, the Federal Agency prohibited Telekom from limiting bandwidth for video streaming covered by that tariff option and from using terms to reduce bandwidth in contracts concluded with both content providers and end customers.

The Fővárosi Törvényszék (Budapest High Court, Hungary) referred the matter to the European Court of Justice for a preliminary ruling in order to ascertain how to interpret and apply Article 3(1) and (2) of Regulation 2015/2120.

In its judgment of 15 September 2020, the court, sitting as the Grand Chamber, interpreted for the first time Regulation 2015/2120. About the first question, the court's finding was that, while interpreting Article 3(2) of Regulation 2015/2120, read in conjunction with Article 3(1) of that regulation, Article 3(1) provides that the rights it safeguards for end users of Internet access services are intended to be exercised "via their Internet access service" and that Article 3(2) requires that such a service does not entail any limitation of the exercise of those rights. In addition, it follows from Article 3(2) of Regulation 2015/2120 that the services of a given provider of Internet access services must be assessed in light of that requirement by the national regulatory authorities. The court found that a "zero tariff" option, such as that at issue in the main proceedings, draws a distinction within Internet traffic, on the basis of commercial considerations, by not counting towards the essential package traffic to partner applications. Consequently, such a commercial practice does not satisfy the general obligation of equal treatment of traffic, without discrimination or interference, laid down in Article 3(3) of Regulation 2015/2120.

The court clarified: "it must be found, first of all, that an agreement by which a given customer subscribes to a package whereby once the data volume included in the tariff purchased has been used up, that customer has unrestricted access only to certain applications and services covered by a 'zero tariff,' is liable to entail a limitation of the exercise of the rights set out in Article 3(1) of Regulation 2015/2120. Whether such an agreement is compatible with Article 3(2) of that regulation must be assessed on a case-by-case basis, in the light of the parameters set out in recital 7 of that regulation. Next, such packages, which fall within the scope of a commercial practice within the meaning of Article 3(2) of Regulation 2015/2120, are, in the light of the cumulative effect of the agreements to which they may lead, liable to increase the use of certain specific applications and services, namely those which may be used without restriction on a 'zero tariff' once the data volume included in the tariff purchased by customers has been used up, and are, accordingly, liable to reduce the use of the other applications and services available, having regard to the measures by which the provider of the Internet access services makes that use more difficult, if not impossible. Lastly, the greater the number of customers concluding subscription agreements to such packages, the more likely it is that, given its scale, the cumulative effect of those agreements will result in a significant limitation of the exercise of end users' rights or even undermine the very essence of end users' rights, a situation expressly referred to in recital 7 of Regulation 2015/2120" (see §43-44-45).

In the second place, as regards the interpretation of Article 3(3) of Regulation 2015/2120, the court found that to make a finding of incompatibility with that provision, no assessment of the effect of measures blocking or slowing down traffic or the exercise of end users' rights is required. Article 3(3) does not lay down such a requirement to assess whether the general obligation of equal and non-discriminatory treatment of traffic in that provision has been complied with. Lastly, noticing that the limitation on bandwidth was solely on account of the activation of the zero tariffs option, the court held that the exceptions provided for management measures could not be taken into consideration since, according to Article 3(3), such actions could not be based on commercial strategies pursued by the Internet access provider.

3.6 Conclusions

The right to Internet access is a solid and much-needed guarantee for the democratic dimension of human lives, both in the bit and in the atomic dimensions. The right to Internet access manifests itself in the inclusion of the person in the social and political process, because bandwidth shrinks the distances between remote locations, resets age differences to zero and levels out unequal physical conditions: in short, it makes equal those who otherwise would not be due to their different backgrounds, fostering the active participation of citizens in the information society. Internet access can also be considered an unprecedented tool to revitalize the democratic dialogue between representative and represented – a crucial characteristic of representative democracy.

This chapter explored the notion of the right to Internet access both from a societal and legal perspective and from an international and national one. The discussion of the different approaches to this right leads to the conclusion that an international recognition of the right to Internet access as a stand-alone right is still lacking. This recognition is also at the core of the doctrinal debate around the right to Internet access. On the balance of those arguments, the instrumental case for deriving the right to Internet access as a human right in international law appears stronger than those arguments that would advise against it.

Second, the necessity of seeing the right to Internet access as separate from freedom of expression must be underlined, since this approach is not capable of comprehending a broader range of inequalities that are perpetrated by unequal Internet access for a wider range of civil, political, economic, social and cultural rights. Along these lines, there is also a part of Italian doctrine that reads the right to access the Internet precisely in light of paragraph 2 of Article 3 of the Italian Constitution, which enshrines the principle of substantive equality.

This is why the specific aspect of net neutrality deserved attention, that is, to further support the idea of Internet access as a tool for diminishing inequalities. Internet access is therefore functional to substantive equality because, by acting as a lever capable of removing material and economic obstacles to the full development of the person, it becomes an opportunity for the effective exercise of fundamental freedoms. In this context, the Telenor's judgment was examined in depth because it elevates net neutrality to a legal standard for the protection of end users, as the court noted, while at the same time it also provides protection for the freedom and competitiveness of digital markets. Hence, net neutrality, as an expression of the principle of equality in the digital context, stands as a safeguard of an open, effective connection, equal and neutral, and contributes to the prominence of Internet access as a right of end users.

Net neutrality and the right to Internet access are treated as means to achieve broader goals, such as fairness in the commercial protection of end users. Nevertheless, codification on a fundamental level may better reflect the Internet's unmatched significance for the individual and effectively contribute to eliminating the digital divide. As a fundamental right, on the one hand, Internet access will allow individuals to exercise their claims and rights directly; on the other hand, it will raise awareness and state sensitivity to these topics. In the end, the very legal interest protected by the right to access the Internet is the inclusion of the person in the social, economic and political life that increasingly takes place in the digital realm. It is difficult to say whether this will be explicitly recognized as a fundamental right, at least in the short term. It is more likely that the issue will be regulated starting from concrete needs, such as, once again, eliminating the digital divide, one of the many targets of public policies such as the Recovery and Resilience Facility and the Digital Education Action Plan.

Part II
Freedom of Expression

4 Freedom of Expression and the Internet

4.1 Introduction

The previous chapters have given an overview of how the Internet has developed in recent decades and brought changes to our lives and societies, and how, therefore, the law has had to be rethought in light of the digital and Internet revolution. The present and the following chapters will address how the spread of the Internet has impacted and transformed a specific fundamental right: *freedom of expression*. The development of electronic means of expression has restructured the world of communication and given rise to new legal issues and dilemmas concerning not only the need to foster freedom of expression as much as possible in the contemporary age, but also the need to balance its protection with that of other potentially conflicting fundamental rights or democratic values.

In general, freedom of expression represents a key value for contemporary Western democracies. First and foremost, it is a fundamental individual right with which all people are naturally endowed. Being able to express one's personal ideas and personal opinions, as well as to decide how to convey those ideas and thoughts (e.g., by speaking, writing, through art, music, satire, etc.) allows us, as humans, to fully participate in social life and to project outside of us our system of values as well as our own personality. In this sense, freedom of expression is directly connected to the concept of human dignity. However, freedom of expression is valuable not only from an individual perspective, but also from a collective point of view. By allowing people to discuss issues among themselves and to express their doubts, concerns and criticisms, it is possible to ensure the full protection and promotion of democratic values as well as to foster general societal progress.

It is evident that the Internet has revolutionized the way freedom of expression is exercised and enjoyed nowadays. Social networks and social media, in particular, have given us a platform on which to express our messages and views and deliver them to our families, friends, acquaintances and the general public. In other words, the Internet has given us all an "electronic voice" through which we can produce content to share it with the entire world. Nonetheless, the situation is complicated. First, it is necessary to take into account that our freedom of expression across the Internet is necessarily privately filtered by those same platforms that offer us a space to talk. Social networks and social media set the rules concerning the ways we can express ourselves across the Internet, and through the use of algorithms they are capable of influencing the material reach of content. Second, the exercise of freedom of expression can sometimes result in an assault on others' fundamental rights or democratic values, and the Internet has greatly amplified such a risk.

This chapter thus focuses on the notion of freedom of expression and on how such a freedom has been impacted by the development of the Internet. Section 4.2 offers a brief theoretical background concerning the reasons why freedom of expression is so important for contemporary democracies and how such a freedom has been dealt with within historical human rights law documents. Section 4.3 addresses the constitutional legal framework around freedom of expression on the two sides of the Atlantic, looking at the US First Amendment, on the one hand, and at European fundamental rights documents, on the other hand. Section 4.4 looks at how the US Supreme Court (4.4.1), the European Court of Human Rights (4.4.2) and the Court of Justice of the European Union (4.4.3) have interpreted such a right in the context of their respective jurisdictions, and how they have dealt with the increasing role of the Internet with respect to its enjoyment.

4.2 The origins of freedom of expression

Freedom of expression is a pillar of democratic society. Without the possibility to express opinions and ideas freely, it would not be possible to promote the exchange of views, the right to inform or even the promotion of civil and political rights.

Freedom of expression encompasses two different dimensions: an "active" and a "passive" one. Whereas the "active" dimension consists precisely of the freedom to express one's thoughts and opinions and spread information, the "passive" dimension refers to people's right to "be informed." This second aspect of freedom of expression and information, which is particularly relevant within the European legal landscape, also encompasses a right to be informed in a pluralistic and trustworthy manner. Monistic and/or low-quality information (think, for instance, of so-called fake news) can deeply affect the public debate and the opportunities for people to develop their own ideas and thoughts. This will inevitably impact also on a country's democratic processes, since polluted and unsatisfying information will be reflected in the results of democratic elections. For this reason, whereas liberal approaches, such as that characterizing traditional US legal theory, advocate for a "negative" protection of freedom of expression, in the sense that the government should never regulate speech, a different, "democracy-based" approach argues the need for the law to positively intervene to avoid concentration and to foster more diverse, wide-ranging and trustworthy media coverage.

The central role of freedom of speech, expression and information can find its philosophical justifications in a range of theories and principles that have been deeply explored especially within the Anglo-American tradition. Such theories can be classified as follows: (a) justification from *democracy*; (b) justification from *social contract*; (c) justification from the *pursuit of the truth*; and (d) justification from *individual autonomy*. The first three theories tend to look at the "public" dimension of freedom of expression, whereas the fourth one focuses more on its individual dimension. Of course, within any given legal context, the role of these philosophical perspectives is variously mixed and accepted.

According to the "justification from democracy" theory, freedom of expression is necessary and fundamental for the proper functioning of democracies. The possibility of conveying and receiving ideas is what allows citizens to successfully carry out their duties, responsibilities and prerogatives; therefore free speech, and especially political speech, requires extra protection. According to the "justification from social contract" theory, political institutions are somehow justifiable in terms of an actual or hypothetical agreement among all members of the relevant society. In this framework, the free dissemination of speech and information helps citizens be more aware of social and political issues, so that further decisions concerning the "social contract" can be taken more conscientiously and successfully. The "justification from the pursuit of truth," which is today preponderant in the United States, argues that the search for truth is based on a process of trial and error and thus requires uninhibited discussion. According to this approach, states should avoid regulating speech since, when opposing ideas and opinions conflict, the best idea or thought is bound to win. Finally, a more individualistic approach considers freedom of expression as benefitting the needs of individual autonomy, well-being and self-respect. The possibility of expressing oneself must thus be regarded as a fundamental and personal right of the individual as such.

Freedom of expression has long been central to domestic and international human rights law. Article XI of the Declaration of the Rights of Man and of the Citizen, adopted in 1789 during the French Revolution, contained the first modern definition of such a right: it declared that "the free communication of ideas and opinions is one of the most precious of the rights of the man" and that "every citizen may, accordingly, speak, write, and print with freedom," although the law might define some responsibilities when such a right is abused.

In the 20th century, especially following World War II and the establishment of the United Nations, a range of international documents and treaties began setting global standards for countries to comply with when addressing the protection of their people's fundamental human rights and liberties. Within these texts, freedom of expression always plays a central role because of its relevant importance in the building of truly democratic societies. Article 19 of the Universal Declaration of Human Rights (1948), for instance, states that "everyone has the right to freedom of opinion and expression" and that this right includes not only freedom to hold opinions without interference but also that to "seek, receive and impart information and ideas through any media and regardless of frontiers." Similarly, art. 19 of the International Covenant on Civil and Political Rights (ICCPR) of 1966 protects freedom of expression while recognizing the possibility to limit this right to protect reputation, national security or public order, public health or morals.

Thus, the right to freedom of expression has found extensive protection in the framework of constitutional democracies. In particular, the US and European approaches to this right are interesting examples of differing models.

4.3 Freedom of expression across the ocean

Freedom of expression is a constitutional pillar on both sides of the Atlantic. However, Europe and the United States protect this right in very different ways, as has been underlined by the rise of the Internet and the consolidation of new actors operating in the digital environment. Looking at the US constitutional framework, we can see how the succinct wording of the First Amendment gives rise to very extensive protection of free speech:

> Congress shall make no law respecting an establishment of religion, or prohibiting the free exercise thereof; or abridging the freedom of speech, or of the press; or the right of the people peaceably to assemble, and to petition the Government for a redress of grievances.

This provision imposes a prohibition on Congress from adopting any law that may entail a restriction on free speech. Moreover, it must be stressed that, although the First Amendment only refers to Congress, this provision must be read together with the Fourteenth Amendment, which, through the so-called equal protection clause, states that such constitutional limitations on the actions of Congress are applicable also to state governments (*Gitlow v. New York*, 268 US 652, 1925). It is worth noting that there is no mention in the text of the First Amendment of the possibility to impose restrictions necessary to protect other fundamental rights. The First Amendment thus seems to protect free speech as an *absolute right* that does not tolerate any restriction or interference: furthermore, the US Supreme Court has adopted a similar stance in relation to speech on the Internet.

The absolute nature of free speech under the US First Amendment is absent within the European legal framework, where freedom of expression can more easily be subject to public interference and limitation. However, this different approach does not affect the fundamental role played by freedom of expression in the European landscape. Freedom of expression is protected by many different legal frameworks: first, at the international level, freedom of expression is enshrined in the European Convention on Human Rights (ECHR); second, at the EU level, it is enshrined in the Charter of Fundamental Rights of the European Union (CFREU); third, all national constitutions recognize at a domestic level such a right. In the context of Europe, one of the first texts that mentioned freedom of expression was the French Declaration of the Rights of Man and of the Citizen. Since the end of the 18th century, therefore, freedom of expression has developed to become a cornerstone of democracy and pluralism.

The very nature of the right to freedom of expression in Europe can be appreciated by focusing on the text of the ECHR, which protects the right not only to impart information but also to receive it "without any public interference and regardless of frontiers."

While the right to information primarily relates to the media, as relayers of information and opinions to the public, it also entails the public's right to be adequately informed, especially where public interests are involved. This passive dimension is inherently linked to the individual's right to be exposed to a diverse and trustworthy information ecosystem. However, if disinformation practices become pervasive and systemic, they may de facto distort the very foundations of public discourse and impair individuals' ability to freely exercise their political rights in an informed manner. In other words, access to information sources is not just a matter of "quantity" but also of "quality" relating to the information that users read and share online.

Article 10 ECHR, in contrast to the First Amendment, is very clear in rejecting the view that free speech is an absolute right. By contrast, this provision has a bipartite structure. On the one hand, it attaches to freedom of expression the value of a human right:

> Everyone has the right to freedom of expression. This right shall include freedom to hold opinions and to receive and impart information and ideas without interference by public authority and regardless of frontiers. This article shall not prevent States from requiring the licensing of broadcasting, television or cinema enterprises.

It is worth noting that the scope of freedom of expression encompasses a broad range of rights applicable both to passive actions (holding opinions and ideas, receiving information) and to active actions (imparting information). As has been noted by commentators, art. 10 ECHR thus protects "several freedoms of speech."

On the other hand, unlike the First Amendment, art. 10 ECHR highlights that the exercise of the rights it protects carries with it duties and responsibilities and may thus be subject to interferences that are necessary, in a democratic society, to meet certain pressing social needs:

> The exercise of these freedoms, since it carries with it duties and responsibilities, may be subject to such formalities, conditions, restrictions or penalties as are prescribed by law and are necessary in a democratic society, in the interests of national security, territorial integrity or public safety, for the prevention of disorder or crime, for the protection of health or morals, for the protection of the reputation or rights of others, for preventing the disclosure of information received in confidence, or for maintaining the authority and impartiality of the judiciary.

Contracting states can thus legitimately impose restrictions on freedom of expression, provided that the criteria set forth under art. 10(2) ECHR are respected. There are three relevant fundamental criteria. First, any measure restricting or limiting freedom of expression and information must be foreseen and regulated by law prior to its implementation.

Given that the ECHR applies to a wide range of jurisdictions with very different legal traditions, the ECtHR has adopted a notion of "law" that is autonomous and not formal, meaning that it may include acts and statutes not formally referred to as "laws" within the relevant jurisdiction. The notion of "law," for the purpose of art. 10, is therefore a substantive notion and may even encompass, to a certain extent, case law and law in practice (*Kruslin v. France*, 11801/85). Along these lines, the potential restriction of speech rests on a case-by-case analysis.

Second, any measure must be specifically aimed at protecting one of the legitimate aims enlisted within art. 10(2). Such a list is a *numerus clausus* (closed number), meaning that contracting states are not allowed to impose any restriction, limitation or penalty on freedom of expression for a reason or aim that is different from those already considered by the provision (*Stoll v. Switzerland*, 69698/01).

Third, the restriction must be "necessary in a democratic society," meaning that the state's intervention must be justified by a pressing social need and that intervention must be proportionate to such a need.

With respect to the third criterion, most notably, the ECtHR has focused on the possible restrictions envisaged by contracting states that can give rise to so-called chilling effects, that is, possible imbalances resulting from the adoption of measures that excessively circumscribe the legitimate exercise of rights protected by constitutions and by the ECHR (see, *ex multis*, *Goodwin v. the United Kingdom*, 17488/90).

The prohibition on the abuse of rights completes this constitutional framework. Art. 17 provides a general upper limit for the exercise of fundamental rights, stating that "nothing in this Convention may be interpreted as implying for any State, group or person any right to engage in any activity or perform any act aimed at the destruction of any of the rights and freedoms set forth herein or at their limitation to a greater extent than is provided for in the Convention." In other words, the exercise of a right or freedom set within the Convention cannot be of such a nature as to destroy others' fundamental rights or freedoms. If this concept is applied to the freedom protected within art. 10, then that means that certain forms of speech will not be tolerated in a democratic society because they amount to an "abuse of rights" and put at risk other values enshrined within the Convention. An example of this is represented by certain forms of hate speech (see Chapter 6).

The approach adopted by the ECHR is also reflected within art. 11 CFREU. The possibility of imposing limitations on such a freedom, although not explicitly mentioned in art. 11, is nonetheless possible under art. 52(1):

> Any limitation on the exercise of the rights and freedoms recognised by this Charter must be provided for by law and respect the essence of those rights and freedoms. Subject to the principle of proportionality, limitations may be made only if they are necessary and genuinely meet objectives of general interest recognised by the Union or the need to protect the rights and freedoms of others.

The measures and limitations envisaged by art. 52, nonetheless, must comply with the principle of necessity and pursue objectives of general interest recognized by the Union, or the protection of the rights and freedoms of others.

In addition, in a manner similar to art. 17 ECHR, the CFREU also prohibits the abuse of rights, which consists of the "destruction of any of the rights and freedoms recognized in this Charter or at their limitation to a greater extent than is provided for herein" (art. 54).

The European scenario is thus different from the US system for at least two reasons. The first one concerns the degree of protection. The reach of constitutional protection for freedom of expression is more limited in Europe, as there is no provision carving out a sphere of protection as broad as that provided by the First Amendment. Europe is also different due to the lack of a unique constitutional architecture. Whereas in the United States the First Amendment is the sole and "sacred" point of reference, the European model cannot be explained or understood unless the EU system is combined with that of the ECHR, and unless the decisions of the respective courts are read in light of the reciprocal influence and integration between the relevant principles under each system.

As the next sections will bring to light, while free speech is "the paramount right within the American constellation of constitutional rights," the same cannot be said with regard to European law, especially when considering the case law of the ECJ and of the ECtHR. The metaphor of the marketplace of ideas, developed by Justice Oliver W. Holmes in his famous dissenting opinion for *Abrams v. United States* (250 US 616, 1919), analyzed below, does not seem to fit well with the EU framework of rights protection.

4.4 Freedom of expression in action

The different approaches to freedom of expression and information that characterize the US and European paradigms can be fully understood by taking a look at the case law of the US Supreme Court, on the one hand, and of the European courts (ECtHR and ECJ), on the other hand. Although the formulas implemented by the First Amendment and by European constitutional sources are visibly different at first glance, interpretation of the law has been critical in the building of freedom of expression jurisprudence on both sides of the Atlantic.

Throughout the 20th century, and especially in the years following World War I and the spread of the "red scare" about Communism, the US Supreme Court, having to balance the values of free speech with social security issues, reframed and developed its jurisprudence on the First Amendment. Although the First Amendment was written at the end of the 18th century, it was not until the end of the 1910s that its scope of action started being defined as it is today. Similarly, the decisions rendered from the 1970s onward by the European courts, and especially by the ECtHR, have had a fundamental role in giving art. 10 ECHR (and art. 11 CFREU) an effective content. In particular, the ECtHR, throughout the second half of the 20th century, has set and defined a range of criteria meant to clarify the conditions for the imposition of measures restricting or limiting people's freedom of expression. It is thus through the analysis and confrontation of the case law and jurisprudence of these courts that the gap between the United States and Europe truly emerges.

4.4.1 The US Supreme Court

The extensive protection of free speech rights in the United States as enshrined in the First Amendment emerges especially when looking at the Supreme Court's decisions. In *Schenck v. United States* (249 US 47, 1919), Justice Holmes developed the "clear and present danger" doctrine for the first time, which has so far been the test for assessing public powers' ability to restrict freedom of speech. According to this test, speech may be subject to restrictions and limitations if it is capable of giving rise to imminent dangers and risks given its specific context. In Holmes's words:

> The question in every case is whether the words used are used in such circumstances and are of such a nature as to create a clear and present danger that they will bring about the substantive evils that the United States Congress has a right to prevent. It is a question of proximity and degree. When a nation is at war, many things that might be said in time of peace are such a hindrance to its effort that their utterance will not be endured so long as men fight, and that no Court could regard them as protected by any constitutional right.

Justice Holmes dissented, however, in a famous opinion joined by Justice Louis Brandeis, in the already mentioned case of *Abrams v United States* (250 US 616, 1919). The US Supreme Court has embraced the well-known metaphor of the "free marketplace of ideas." This metaphor is closely linked to a particular concept of liberal democracy, in which the role of the state is minimal. According to Justice Holmes:

> Persecution for the expression of opinions seems to me perfectly logical. If you have no doubt of your premises or your power, and want a certain result with all your heart, you naturally express your wishes in law, and sweep away all opposition. To allow opposition by speech seems to indicate that you think the speech impotent, as when a man says that he has squared the circle, or that you do not care wholeheartedly for the result, or that you doubt either your power or your premises. But when men have realized that time has upset many fighting faiths, they may come to believe even more than they believe the very foundations of their own conduct that the ultimate good desired is better reached by free trade in ideas – that the best test of truth is the power of the thought to get itself accepted in the competition of the market, and that truth is the only ground upon which their wishes safely can be carried out.

These cases concerned the constitutional review under the First Amendment of the provisions of the Espionage Act 1917 and the Sedition Act 1918, which provided for the prosecution of certain speech acts during the historical period of World War I. The most important legacy of these opinions is the assumption that freedom of speech can only be limited when its exercise is likely to create a clear and present danger. Outside this scope, there is a "marketplace of ideas" where opinions and thoughts may achieve consensus by virtue of their true or authoritative content.

US constitutional legal theory is also characterized by the general refusal of "content discrimination," that is, the imposition of restrictions on free speech simply based on the messages or ideas conveyed, or upon its subject matter or content. Content discrimination can encompass both "subject-matter" discrimination (where discussion of a specific topic is in some way limited) and "viewpoint discrimination," which, by silencing a specific point of view, is perceived as being especially egregious. Regulation, in order to be constitutional, must in general avoid being "content-based" and only be "content-neutral" (e.g., it could regulate the time and place of a speech).

When a content-based or viewpoint-based regulation is enacted, the Supreme Court may uphold it only if it overcomes a "strict scrutiny" test, that is, a high form of constitutional review based on which a law restricting freedom of speech must achieve a compelling government interest and be narrowly tailored to that interest or be the least speech-restrictive means available to the government. For instance, the 1998 Child Online Protection Act (see below) was quashed by the Supreme Court precisely because, although aimed at protecting children from pornography, it put in place measures that were not considered to be the least restrictive available (*Ashcroft v. ACLU*, 535 US 564, 2002). Conversely, in *Holder v. Humanitarian Law Project* (561 US 1, 2010) the Supreme Court upheld a federal law prohibiting the provision of service, training and "expert advice or assistance" to foreign terrorist organizations, considering it to have overcome the strict scrutiny test. Regulation that is not content-based or viewpoint-based is generally subjected to less restrictive tests, that is, the "intermediate scrutiny" and the "rational basis" tests.

In some cases, the Supreme Court has made a distinction between "high value" and "low value" speech. Whereas the former identifies speech gravitating around matters of public concern (public discourse), the second encompasses speech categories such as obscenity, libel, commercial speech and child pornography. In general, when "low value" speech is regulated, the Supreme Court does not apply the "strict scrutiny" test.

A picture of the US approach to free speech can be obtained by applying these principles to certain specific areas of the law. As far as defamation law is concerned, the decision taken in *New York Times v. Sullivan* (376 US 254, 1964) is one of the leading cases. The core issue was whether the use of false or defamatory statements by the press against public figures was protected by freedom of expression. The US Supreme Court pointed out that statements made with actual malice or reckless disregard are beyond the protection of freedom of speech (more specifically, freedom of the press) and can therefore trigger liability for the author: otherwise, where these criteria are not met, no limit can be imposed on public debate. With respect to hate speech (see Chapter 6), leading cases such as *Brandeburg v. Ohio* (395 US 444, 1969), the judicial saga of *Skokie (Smith v. Collin*, 439 US 916, 1978) and *R.A.V. v. City of Saint Paul* (505 US 377, 1992) have built a legal framework setting a very high threshold for the possibility of constraining hate speech. Only incitement to violence (not incitement to discrimination) may be punishable, and only in the case where that incitement leads to a "clear and present danger" of violence actually being committed.

The United States stands out as a free speech bastion within the new digital ecosystem as well. This approach is the result of the broader constitutional protection afforded by the First Amendment to the US Constitution. This stance emerges from the value frame adopted by the Supreme Court, which has been inclined since the very first judgments in this area to highlight the unprecedented libertarian dimension of the Internet. From the outset, in the eyes of the US Supreme Court, the Internet has offered new fora and spaces for free speech, which must be viewed through different lenses and with reference to different categories from those applied to traditional media. This constituted the basis for the choice, in *Reno v. ACLU* (521 US 844, 1997), to borrow the metaphor of the "free marketplace of ideas."

The judgment, which dates back to 1997 and thus preceded *Ashcroft v. ACLU*, came as a response to the first attempt by the US government to limit access to online content prohibited for minors. This intervention was caused by concerns about the fact that it was impossible to replicate online the zoning and age verification systems used in the real world to prevent minors from gaining access to prohibited material. For this purpose, the Communications Decency Act was approved in 1996 to prevent the circulation of, notably, "indecent" and "patently offensive" content. However, the Supreme Court struck down some of its provisions, arguing that said restrictions were excessively vague and indeterminate and did not pass the strict scrutiny test to which, according to the Supreme Court, any limitation of freedom of speech must be subject. In other words, the restrictions on free speech did not remain within the limits of what was strictly necessary in order to achieve the goal pursued, namely the protection of minors.

The judgment recognized the technological discontinuity and the new sociotechnological developments that the Internet entails and resisted the temptation to extend to the web the case law on radio and television broadcasting, which would have represented a form of resistance against what was then a new technology. The justices emphasized the reasons why the regulatory regime for radio and television could not be transferred *sic et simpliciter* to the Internet. For instance, television was originally a scarce resource calling for public regulation. Moreover, with specific reference to the protection of minors, the justices noted that, whereas the Internet required minors to take "affirmative steps" to access obscene material, television and radio entail a passive exposition to content, be it indecent or not. In other words, whereas radio and television could not adequately protect the listener from unexpected content, the Internet made such risk more remote.

Most importantly, the decision makes explicit reference to the notion of the marketplace of ideas, underscoring that the Internet represents an invaluable asset for the fostering of such marketplace:

> The dramatic expansion of this new marketplace of ideas contradicts the factual basis of this contention. The record demonstrates that the growth of the Internet has been and continues to be phenomenal. As a matter of constitutional tradition, in the absence of evidence to the contrary, we presume that governmental regulation of the content of speech is more likely to interfere with the free exchange of ideas than to encourage it. The interest in encouraging freedom of expression in a democratic society outweighs any theoretical but unproven benefit of censorship.

Following the Supreme Court's judgment in *Reno v. ACLU*, further attempts were made by US authorities to regulate the circulation of content considered harmful to minors. However, none of these attempts successfully passed muster before the Supreme Court. 1998 saw the enactment of the Child Online Protection Act, which took account of some of the indications provided in *Reno*. However, according to the Supreme Court, the definition of "material that is harmful to minors," which was based on a generic reference to the standards of the reference community, did not comply with the criteria of legitimacy that restrictions on freedom of expression must respect. The outcome was similar in the third and last chapter of the battle between the US government and the Supreme Court concerning the prohibition from the Internet of obscene content harmful to minors, which concerned the Child Pornography Prevention Act. In this case too, according to the Supreme Court, the restrictions introduced to prohibit the dissemination of pictures of children engaging in sexual acts or in a manner evocative of sexual acts proved to be excessive and to lack the required proportionality. In the view of the court, the scope of the conduct covered by these rules was much broader than that which the legislature could have legitimately regulated to achieve the objective of protecting minors.

Reno v. ACLU is indicative of a recognition of the Internet as an instrument capable of causing an extraordinary expansion of the First Amendment. The Supreme Court did not make any effort to "downgrade" its sensitivity to free speech. On the contrary, it confirmed and reinforced its liberal vision.

More recently, in *Packingham v. North Carolina* (85 USLW 4353, 2017), the Supreme Court addressed another case involving the relationship between the digital dimension and free speech. In 2008, the North Carolina General Assembly enacted a law to prevent registered sex offenders from using commercial social networking websites that allow minors to have accounts. Pursuant to the legislation, there was no need for the state to prove any contact between the registered offender and a minor in order to charge the former, nor was it necessary that access had been made for illicit purposes. Mr. Packingham was thus identified as a user of Facebook and charged with violating the law. The North Carolina Supreme Court supported the conviction, observing that the state had sufficient interest in "forestalling the illicit lurking and contact" of registered sex offenders and their potential future victims, thereby facilitating "the legitimate and important aim of the protection of minors." The US Supreme Court was then required to answer "whether, under this Court's First Amendment precedents, such a law is permissible, both on its face and as applied to the petitioner – who was sentenced based on a Facebook 'post' in which he celebrated the dismissal of a traffic ticket." The US Supreme Court, finding the law unconstitutional, stated:

> While we now may be coming to the realization that the cyber age is a revolution of historic proportions, we cannot appreciate yet its full dimensions and vast potential to alter how we think, express ourselves, and define who we want to be … The forces and directions of the Internet are so new, so protean, and so far reaching that courts must be conscious that what they say today might be obsolete tomorrow.

In other words, it was stated that the court should assess such a matter in a cautious way before limiting application of the First Amendment to the Internet.

Nonetheless, it should be stressed that the US Supreme Court is not completely oblivious to the risks connected to the Internet. In *Elonis v. United States* (575 US 723, 2015) the Supreme Court upheld the conviction of Mr. Elonis, who had posted threats on Facebook to injure his co-workers, his wife, the police, a kindergarten class and the FBI. Confirming that the posts had amounted to "true threats," the Supreme Court thus recognized that content published online may pose some dangers and risks. In particular, the concurring opinion of Justice Samuel Alito is interesting in that he explicitly highlighted how "threats of violence and intimidation are among the most favored weapons of domestic abusers, and the rise of social media has only made those tactics more commonplace."

4.4.2 The European Court of Human Rights

Historically, case law concerning art. 10 ECHR has widely addressed freedom of expression with respect to the offline world.

In its central decision *Handyside v. the United Kingdom* (5493/72), the ECtHR rejected a complaint brought by an editor who had been convicted for having published a schoolbook containing sexually explicit content. The court found that the restrictions imposed on freedom of expression in the case, including the seizure of copies of the book, met the criteria set forth under art. 10(2) ECHR. However, what is notable in this decision is an *obiter dictum* where the court stressed that:

> Freedom of expression constitutes one of the essential foundations of such a society, one of the basic conditions for its progress and for the development of every man. Subject to paragraph 2 of Article 10, it is applicable not only to "information" or "ideas" that are favourably received or regarded as inoffensive or as a matter of indifference, but also to those that offend, shock or disturb the State or any sector of the population. Such are the demands of that pluralism, tolerance and broadmindedness without which there is no "democratic society."

According to the ECtHR, therefore, freedom of expression also encompasses offensive, shocking or disturbing expressions with respect to the state or to any part of the population, and this is necessary to meet the demands of pluralism, tolerance and openness that are necessary in a democratic society. This ruling considerably widens the boundaries of freedom of expression, stating that even those contents that would be considered by society to be shocking or offensive cannot be deprived of protection as free speech acts. Therefore, the level of social approval for an expression cannot be regarded as a criterion justifying protection for it. As a result, this approach seems to support the idea that the more the panorama of ideas and opinions is varied, the more the democratic character of a democracy will benefit.

Although *Handyside* seems to promote a liberal approach to freedom of expression that is somehow similar to that of the US Supreme Court, the following case law of the ECtHR has proven to move in a very different direction. The ECtHR has in many cases upheld limitations and restrictions to freedom of expression.

In the leading case of *Sunday Times v. the United Kingdom* (App. No. 6538/74), the ECtHR found for the first time that art. 10 ECHR had been violated. In 1972 the *Sunday Times* published articles about the settlement negotiations with respect to a famous case concerning the so-called thalidomide children. The case had arisen from the collateral effects of a drug that had been marketed as a sedative for pregnant women. However, use of the drug, which contained a component called thalidomide, proved to have severe side effects and in many cases caused serious birth defects. The *Sunday Times* criticized the negotiation procedures and was eventually ordered not to publish any further articles on the topic since this would amount to the offence of contempt of the court. In this case, the court held that such an injunction was prescribed by prior law and aimed at protecting the legitimate aim of "maintaining the authority and impartiality of the judiciary." However, the court held that the restriction did not respect the third criterion set by art. 10(2) ECHR, since it was not "necessary in a democratic society." According to the court, the thalidomide case represented "a matter of undisputed public concern" such that the press should be granted ample freedom to discuss it. The public had a right to be informed about the developments and critical aspects of the negotiations. In addition, the ECtHR reviewed the prohibited article and found it to be moderate and balanced. Therefore, the court concluded that the injunction did not satisfy the criterion of proportionality. This case clearly shows the role of art. 10 ECHR as an additional layer of control protecting freedom of expression in Europe.

The case of *Jersild v. Denmark* (15890/89) is also of particular importance in the field of freedom of expression. The applicant was a journalist sentenced in Denmark for having produced video footage of interviews with the members of an organization of young racists ("Greenjackets") in which they offend and insult black people, which was broadcast on TV. Although Mr. Jersild had clearly dissociated himself from their statements and had rebutted some claims made by the young extremists, he was convicted for aiding and abetting the dissemination of such thoughts and views. The ECtHR found that Denmark had failed to comply with the criterion of proportionality. First, the purpose of the documentary was considered a key element to take into account: the footage aimed at exposing, analyzing and explaining who the Greenjackets were and at inquiring into the origins of such an extremist organization, rather than at disseminating its ideas. Second, the court noted that the program that had broadcast the documentary was known as profoundly serious and its target was generally composed of a well-informed public, so that the risk of the audience misunderstanding the footage's goal was limited. Most notably, *Jersild* clarified the importance of journalism's role as a "public watchdog" of democracy, whose duty is that of imparting information and ideas of public concern (including the existence of a potentially dangerous group). In this sense, *Jersild* shows how journalists enjoy a higher degree of freedom of expression when reporting others' ideas and views.

The central role of the press as the watchdog of democracy was confirmed once more in March 2022, when the ECtHR delivered its decision in the case of *OOO Memo v. Russia* (2840/10). The applicant was the founder of an online media outlet that had been condemned for having published an article defaming the executive authority of the Volgograd Region. The court recognized that an infringement of art. 10 ECHR had taken place: notably, according to the judges, the measures adopted against the applicant did not pursue a "legitimate aim" as requested by para. 2 of that provision. The Russian government had submitted that the measure had meant to protect "the reputation and rights of others"; however, the Strasbourg court held that, since the supposedly defamed actor was a public institution, which should be subject to the public's strict scrutiny, it could not invoke the protection of art. 8 on the right to privacy with respect to the present case. The judgment states:

> The Court considers that bodies of the executive vested with State powers are essentially different from legal entities, including public or State-owned corporations, engaged in competitive activities in the marketplace as the latter rely on their good reputation to attract customers with a view to making a profit and the former exist to serve the public and are funded by taxpayers. To prevent abuse of powers and corruption of public office in a democratic system, a public authority's activities of all kinds must be subject to the close scrutiny not only of the legislative and judicial authorities but also of public opinion.

The case is particularly notable because, for the first time, the court referred to the notion of SLAPPs (strategic lawsuits against public participation), that is, to those groundless legal actions, promoted by powerful individuals or companies, whose only goal is to intimidate journalists.

OOO Memo v. Russia is also in line with another key topic of ECtHR case law on art. 10, that is, the high degree of protection accorded to political speech. According to the ECtHR case law, not all forms of speech and expression are on the same level. Most notably, the ECtHR has introduced a distinction between political and commercial speech. Whereas contracting states enjoy a broader margin of appreciation in imposing limitations on the latter, restrictions are less tolerable when rights to political speech are at stake. Thus, for instance, the court declared in *Incal v. Turkey* (22678/93) that "while precious to all, freedom of expression is particularly important for political parties and their active members," since "they represent their electorate, draw attention to their preoccupations and defend their interests." Additionally, artistic and literary speech, including satire, are also subject to a higher degree of protection. In this respect, an important decision is also that represented by the 2021 judgment of *Dickinson v. Turkey* (25200/11), where the judges unanimously held that Turkish criminal actions against a British artist who had made a satirical collage "insulting" the Turkish Prime Minister were in violation of art. 10.

These cases indicate that the protection granted to freedom of expression by art. 10 should in principle be interpreted broadly as covering even those expressions that do not make a significant contribution to public opinion and/or have disturbing content. However, it must be stressed once again that the ECtHR has often adopted a flexible approach allowing for limitations to freedom of expression. In contrast with the trend in the US Supreme Court, the advent of the Internet has further extended the scope for such limitations, provided that the conditions laid down in art. 10(2) ECHR have been met by national legislation. Although the court has repeatedly held that the regime set by art. 10(2) ECHR must be construed narrowly, the Internet brought an increase in the number of cases involving restrictions on the right to freedom of expression. While the "relative," rather than "absolute," status of the fundamental rights protected by the Convention is nothing new, this element has been particularly stressed in cases involving the Internet. In particular, in the view of the ECtHR, the Internet has contributed to amplifying the threats posed by the exercise of freedom of expression.

This specific point emerged, for the first time, in *Editorial Board of Pravoye Delo and Shtekel v. Ukraine* (33014/05), which concerned the topic of freedom of the press:

> The risk of harm posed by content and communications on the Internet to the exercise and enjoyment of human rights and freedoms, particularly the right to respect for private life, is certainly higher than that posed by the press. Therefore, the policies governing reproduction of material from the printed media and the Internet may differ. The latter undeniably have to be adjusted according to technology's specific features in order to secure the protection and promotion of the rights and freedoms concerned.

The 2021 judgment of *Sanchez v. France* (45581/15) also suggests caution on the part of the court with respect to online freedom of expression. In that case, the court upheld the sentence to a pecuniary sanction inflicted upon a local politician for failing to promptly delete unlawful hate comments against Muslim people that had been written by third users under a post he had published on Facebook.

Unlike the US Supreme Court in *Reno*, the assumption behind the reasoning of the ECtHR is that the Internet is likely to give rise to new problems for the protection of fundamental rights and that the measures applicable to traditional media will not work effectively in the new digital environment. A new balance must therefore be sought between freedom of expression and other constitutional rights. In a nutshell, since the Internet has given rise to unprecedented legal issues, restrictions on freedom of expression should be more broadly accepted. Whereas the US Supreme Court presumes that content regulation, and hence control over speech, is not beneficial, the European approach is more skeptical as it takes into consideration dangers to other rights and, therefore, assumes the need to apply corrective measures that may limit the exercise of freedom of expression.

Nonetheless, it is interesting to note that, precisely for this reason, *Stoll v. Switzerland* (69698/01) concluded that the duties of journalists have become more demanding in the digital age. According to the court, since journalists' freedom of expression is specifically protected provided that they act "in good faith and on accurate factual basis," the compliance with journalistic ethics "takes on added importance" in a world where information increasingly relies on the Internet and the digital ecosystem.

In *K.U. v. Finland* (2872/02), the ECtHR highlighted the non-absolute nature of protection for certain fundamental rights on the Internet. The case concerned the dissemination of the personal data of a minor by an anonymous individual who had posted an online advertisement in which he claimed to be interested in starting a sexual relationship. When the applicant filed a complaint with the local court, there were no legal grounds under domestic law to force an Internet service provider (ISP) to disclose the personal data of the person who had created the online account. The domestic legislation had thus failed to strike a balance between the right to data protection and other interests. The ECtHR stated:

> Although freedom of expression and confidentiality of communications are primary considerations and users of telecommunications and Internet services must have a guarantee that their own privacy and freedom of expression will be respected, such guarantee cannot be absolute and must yield on occasion to other legitimate imperatives, such as the prevention of disorder or crime or the protection of the rights and freedoms of others

> ... [I]t is nonetheless the task of the legislator to provide the framework for reconciling the various claims which compete for protection in this context.

The ECtHR only adopted a stricter approach when the limitations imposed on freedom of expression were excessive in comparison with the aim pursued. For instance, this was the case in *Ahmet Yıldırım v. Turkey* (3111/10), when the Strasbourg court concluded that Turkey had violated art. 10 ECHR by imposing a disproportionate restriction on Internet access. With reference to criminal proceedings against the owner of a website on which expressions insulting Ataturk's memory had been posted, an administrative authority imposed a block on the entire Google Sites service in order to prevent access to the site in question, without first considering whether a less far-reaching measure could have been ordered. The applicant, who owned a website on which his academic works were published and who was affected by the extension of the blocking order, alleged a violation of his right to freedom of expression. The Strasbourg court noted that the blocking of a website falls within the legitimate restrictions that contracting states may adopt in accordance with art. 10(2) ECHR, but only upon condition that such a restriction meets the requirements referenced therein. In this case, a strict legal framework defining the scope of the ban was lacking, and there was no provision for judicial review. A similar decision was also taken in *Cengiz and Others v. Turkey* (48226/10 and 14027/11).

The approach of the ECtHR has proven to be extremely cautious. On the one hand, the court's opinion is that art. 10 ECHR is violated whenever the restrictions to freedom of expression do not fulfil the conditions set forth under art. 10(2) ECHR. On the other hand, the Strasbourg court concedes that freedom of expression is not an absolute right, or a right that must be protected more than other rights. Moreover, given the risks that the Internet entails, there are more grounds for limiting the right to freedom of expression online than there are in the non-digital context.

The cautious approach of the ECtHR can also be examined in the field of copyright. In the *Pirate Bay* case (*Neij and Sunde Kolmisoppi v. Sweden*, 40397/12), the applicants were the owners of a well-known online platform providing users with links to download copyrighted materials illegally through peer-to-peer systems. They had been convicted under a Swedish law that criminalized copyright infringements but objected that this constituted a violation of their right to freedom of expression. The ECtHR ruled the complaint inadmissible, as the restriction imposed fulfilled the conditions laid down by art. 10(2) ECHR and was thus proportionate to the legitimate aim pursued. Similarly, in *Ashby Donald and others v. France* (App. No. 36769/08) the ECtHR found that the applicants' conviction for copyright infringement committed by unlawfully reposting photographs on the Internet for commercial purposes did not amount to a violation of art. 10 ECHR. As in the *Pirate Bay* case, the court was of the opinion that there are reasons to afford states a wide margin of appreciation with respect to interference meant to guarantee the interests of rights holders.

The precautionary approach of the ECtHR toward online freedom of expression also emerges in *Delfi AS v. Estonia* (64569/09), a landmark decision of the Grand Chamber, which, as will be further highlighted in Chapter 5, had to deal for the first time with a complaint concerning liability for comments published by third parties on an online news portal. The Strasbourg court ruled that the finding of the Estonian courts, according to which *Delfi* was liable for defamatory and hateful comments published on it, had amounted to a justified and proportionate restriction on the portal's freedom of expression. The court stressed in particular how the balancing process must be changed in relation to the Internet, which constitutes a new medium:

> Therefore, the Court considers that because of the particular nature of the Internet, the "duties and responsibilities" that are to be conferred on an Internet news portal for the purposes of Article 10 may differ to some degree from those of a traditional publisher as regards third-party content.

Regarding such a complex framework, it must nonetheless be stressed that the "relative" (rather than "absolute") consideration paid to the fundamental rights enshrined in the ECHR does not constitute an invention of the ECtHR following from the impact of new digital technologies. The balancing of fundamental rights has been the task of the ECtHR since it was created. However, the digital environment where fundamental rights can be enjoyed has led the ECtHR to adopt an approach that further underscores the relative nature of the protection of fundamental rights, thus justifying restrictions that most likely would not have been tolerated in the physical world.

In any case, it must be stressed that the ECtHR still grants high value to freedom of expression. For instance, in December 2021 the Strasbourg court delivered the decision for the case of *Standard Verlagsgesellschaft mbH v. Austria (no. 3)* (39378/15), where it confronted the question whether a news portal offering the possibility to post anonymized comments could be ordered to disclose personal data about those who posted those comments in the case where this may be essential to bring action against them for defamation. In that case, the court concluded that the disclosure of those data would inherently infringe the news portal's freedom of expression by stifling the publication of comments thereon: therefore, the imposition of such an order should be subject to a careful balancing of proportionality.

4.4.3 The European Court of Justice

Moving from Strasbourg to Luxembourg, the question arises with respect to how the ECJ has addressed the challenges of online freedom of expression, and thus of how the EU standard of protection concerning freedom of expression compares with that of the ECHR.

As already clarified, as far as freedom of expression is concerned, the ECtHR decides whether the conduct of domestic authorities complies with the standard of protection established by art. 10 ECHR. In other words, the ECtHR addresses cases as a constitutional court in the context of the Council of Europe. However, it is necessary to stress that such a parameter was established when the Convention entered into force in 1950. Therefore, when dealing with applications where the use of new technologies is at issue, the Strasbourg court grounds its assessment on a parameter which was drafted in the analog era.

In contrast, the ECJ delivers its judgments on this matter mostly in the context of preliminary proceedings. The ECJ intervenes when a court must apply EU law to the case it faces but is unsure about the right interpretation. In such cases, therefore, a crucial role is played by the domestic courts that refer questions to the ECJ. Such a difference leads the ECJ to play de facto a role as a fundamental rights adjudicator.

However, given the historical origins of the European Union as a fundamentally market- and economy-driven supranational body, the ECJ has in many instances taken a perspective focusing more on the protection of the (digital) Single Market rather than a human rights perspective such as that of the ECtHR. Nevertheless, this does not mean that freedom of expression has not been taken seriously into account in the judgments of the ECJ. By focusing on the ECJ's case law, it is possible to assess that the right to free speech has been balanced with other fundamental rights that enjoy protection in the EU framework. More specifically, the case law in the field of copyright protection reveals the crucial role of freedom of expression in the reasoning of the ECJ.

Copyright is enshrined as a fundamental right in the Charter, which expressly protects intellectual property under art. 17(2). The recognition of such a right in the Charter entails that intellectual property is a competing interest that needs to be taken into consideration when balancing it with other rights such as freedom of expression. Whereas, in the past, freedom of expression was considered an individual fundamental right far from conflicting with property rights such as copyright, the scenario has completely changed nowadays, with the result that economic interests are put in the same position as individual fundamental rights. In the (sister) cases of *Scarlet v. Sabam* (C-70/10) and *Sabam v. Netlog* (C-360/10), the main question was whether the domestic judicial authority could impose an obligation on ISPs to adopt a filtering system in order to detect potential copyright infringements. More specifically, in both cases, the court was required to assess the compatibility of the national measures with EU law, specifically with users' freedom of expression, users' right to data protection and ISPs' freedom to carry out economic activity. As will be outlined more specifically in Chapter 7, the new DSM Copyright Directive, that is, Directive (EU) 2019/790, created the legal regime applicable to ISPs with respect to copyright infringement; in particular, art. 17 has introduced a clause requiring them to make "best efforts" to remove content that violates copyright.

The ECJ considered the adoption of the above-mentioned filtering systems as a disproportionate measure to protect the fundamental right of intellectual property. First, the court observed that the national measure was not proportionate because it hindered the ISPs' right to carry out economic activity pursuant to art. 16 of the Charter. Second, as an ancillary consideration, the court observed that the system also constituted a violation of arts. 8 and 11 of the Charter, thus expressly referring to the rights to data protection and freedom of expression. Similar considerations can be extended to other cases addressed by the ECJ in the field of copyright protection, where matters concerning freedom of expression are still viewed mainly through the lens of economic copyright-related interests.

However, it is necessary to stress that the ECJ also balanced freedom of expression with other constitutional rights. The ECJ has focused on data protection and freedom to conduct business for the purposes of adjudication. In October 2019, the ECJ delivered another fundamental decision with respect to ISP liability. In *Glawis-*

chnig-Piesczek v. Facebook (C-18/18), a case dealing with the dissemination of defamatory content concerning an Austrian politician, the court concluded that when content is determined to be illegal, an ISP may be required to remove all content identical to that recognized as illegal as well as "equivalent" content. This may, as a matter of fact, represent a burdensome duty on ISPs, in part because of the inherent difficulty of identifying "equivalently" harmful content.

Member States still maintain an ample margin of discretion with respect to content regulation, although some recent legislative instruments have introduced significant novelties in this respect (e.g., Directive (EU) 2018/1808 amending the Audiovisual Media Services Directive and the Terrorist Content Online Regulation). The e-Commerce Directive (see Chapter 5) addresses the liability of ISPs without providing any guidance about content regulation. The Directive establishes that ISPs that do not exercise any editorial control over content cannot be considered responsible for any unlawful conduct performed by third parties.

On a different account, the ECJ also addressed the relationship between freedom of expression and information and the right to data protection within the *Google Spain* decision (C-131/12). As mentioned previously, in the European legal context freedom of information does not cover only its active dimension, that is, individuals' freedom to express their own opinions and share information. The passive dimension of such a freedom, meaning the freedom to receive pluralistic, adequate and unpolluted information, is also relevant to the purposes of both art. 10 ECHR and art. 11 CFREU. In *Google Spain*, the Court underscored that the so-called *right to be forgotten*, that is, the right to have one's personal information removed (de-indexed) from a search engine's results page, might be in contrast with the right of the public to be informed. In that specific case, the claimant demanded that Google remove links to an old newspaper article that connected him to a judicial case. The ECJ held that, given that the events described in the article had taken place much earlier, the information it contained had become "inadequate, irrelevant or no longer relevant, or excessive in relation to the purposes of the processing at issue carried out by the operator of the search engine." As a consequence, the court concluded that in such a case the right to data protection, as well as that to the respect of private and family life, should be considered as overriding "not only the economic interest of the operator of the search engine but also the interest of the general public in finding that information upon a search relating to the data subject's name."

However, the court also pointed out that, although the rights to privacy and data protection tend to override, as a general rule, the Internet users' right to access information, there are some cases where the opposite may be true. The ECJ underlined that a different outcome would have taken place if it had appeared, for reasons such as the public role of the person involved, that interference in their personal right was justified by the "preponderant interest of the general public." In other words, the ECJ did not establish an absolute hierarchy between freedom of information and the right to privacy and data protection; on the contrary, what emerges from the decision is that the two should both be deemed highly relevant, and that all conflicts should be assessed on a case-by-case basis so that all the practical and contextual aspects can be carefully evaluated. However, it should be highlighted that in that case the court did not consider the active dimension of freedom of expression, so the right to speak and express one's mind and thoughts was not touched on by the decision.

4.5 Conclusions

Freedom of expression is a pillar of contemporary Western democracies and has become increasingly central to the legal, political and philosophical debate throughout the 20th century, in part as a reaction to the totalitarian experiences that dominated in Europe from the 1920s onward. The possibility to express one's opinions and thoughts is a right of paramount importance from both an individual and a collective point of view. On the one hand, it responds to the need we have, as human beings, to speak our own mind and participate in the public debate, and, from this perspective, it is an essential feature of a legal paradigm respectful of basic values of human dignity. On the other hand, freedom of expression is a precondition for the development of public debate and, therefore, is the oil of democratic discussion and democratic processes.

Nonetheless, the exact scope of freedom of expression differs quite widely on the two sides of the Atlantic. The First Amendment to the US Constitution grants individuals a right to free speech which is almost an absolute, in the sense that the government (both at a federal and at a state level) cannot impose any restrictions, limitations or conditions on the enjoyment of such a right unless it presents a "clear and present danger." Conversely, the European approach, and especially the one inaugurated by the ECtHR, is much more open to public intervention to avoid the spread of discourses whose content might be inherently harmful to people and to a democratic society.

Such a divergence, which is particularly evident when it comes to the regulation of phenomena such as hate speech, as will be further explored in Chapter 6, is also reflected in the terms of the debate on the role of the Internet as a public forum for democratic participation and discussion. Whereas the US Supreme Court, in *Reno v. ACLU*, has highlighted that the Internet represents an extraordinary tool for fostering free speech, the ECtHR, in decisions such as *Editorial Board of Pravoye Delo*, has pointed out the inherent risks of additional harm that characterize online speech as opposed to offline speech, such as its potential viral character. Case law from the ECJ, too, shows how the Internet, as the new ground where the enjoyment of freedom of expression and information takes place, raises issues and concerns with respect to the dissemination of content that infringes or harms others' rights (e.g., copyright and the right to privacy and data protection).

Such preoccupations have rapidly increased throughout the first two decades of the 21st century, and especially at the end of the 2010s. As will be highlighted in the next chapter, this has led EU institutions to rethink the legal framework concerning online freedom of expression and, especially, the role played by Internet intermediaries in the fight against the dissemination of illegal, unlawful or harmful content. With respect to these actors, the EU is seemingly moving from a liberal laissez-faire approach, inspired by US federal law and embodied by the 2000 e-Commerce Directive, to a different model meant to make these actors more responsible for monitoring what is transmitted across their networks.

5 Internet Service Provider Liability

5.1 Introduction

In the early days of the Internet, online providers mainly offered access and hosting services; the Internet was much simpler at the turn of the millennium, with basic applications that did not fully allow users to contribute to and enrich the online landscape.

With the advent of Napster, a famous peer-to-peer online service created in 1999, things began to change: through this service, millions of users began sharing music and could do so without the authorization of rights holders. Although Napster had to close down in 2001 due to bankruptcy caused by lawsuits brought by rights holders, it represented a symbolic starting point of what has been defined the *Web 2.0*: the Internet was no longer a place to surf web pages but had become a channel for the distribution of online content through communities of users. From that moment on, the web became a place to share content and information. This radical transformation of the online environment also affected the role of online intermediaries, especially hosting providers. Moreover, the rise of the information society has led to the consolidation of new business models based on the provision of digital services and the processing of data. These actors have developed new business models extending to the e-commerce marketplace, social media, online payments and other products and services.

According to a definition proposed by the Organization for Economic Co-operation and Development (OECD), "online intermediaries," or "Internet intermediaries," are actors who play a fundamental role in the functioning of the Internet. Most notably, they bring together and facilitate transactions between third parties on the Internet, either by giving access to, hosting, transmitting and indexing content, products and services originated by others or by providing Internet-based services to third parties. The expression is thus a shorthand for a wide range of actors, which, according to the OECD, include Internet service providers (ISPs) and access providers; data processing and web hosting providers (including domain name registrars); Internet search engines and portals; e-commerce intermediaries; Internet payment systems; and participative networking platforms. It is important to stress that the key aspect of online intermediaries is that they are generally positioned in between two or more parties and, more often than not, they are not the actual source of the content, services or products populating their networks and servers. In other words, online intermediaries are generally distinguished from content providers, which, as the name suggests, actually produce the content to be enjoyed by Internet users. As will be underscored below, this has an important impact on the liability regime of online intermediaries for third-party content.

Among the various categories of Internet intermediaries, a special role is played by social media and social network sites. Social media encompass a broad range of Internet-based applications, the main feature of which is that they build on the ideological and technological foundations of the Web 2.0 and allow the creation and exchange of user-generated content (UGC), such as, for example, Wikipedia. Among social media, "social network sites" aim at transposing from the physical to the digital world the set of anthropological relationships (networks) connecting human beings. Websites such as Facebook, Twitter and Instagram have the ultimate goal of hosting and favoring digital social bonds and thus constitute "social network sites."

Online intermediaries raise serious questions and challenges with respect to the online dissemination of illegal and/or harmful content. In particular, the main challenge is that of determining whether and to what extent these actors should be legally (and/or morally) responsible for the spread and the circulation of such content, since, although they do not produce it, they do in fact offer services and spaces necessary for this purpose. Given the variety of services and actors included within the ample notion of "online intermediaries," the legal framework and the duties imposed upon them may vary depending on their degree of intervention in the content, as will be outlined further within this chapter.

This chapter aims to analyze the legal regime of online intermediaries. By comparing the European and the US approaches, it explains the reasons for introducing systems of immunity and exemption of liability of online intermediaries. Section 5.2 examines the evolution of the "safe harbor" doctrine by looking at the introduction of this system in the United States and at its extension in Europe. Section 5.3 examines the legal regime of online intermediaries' liability in Europe. Section 5.4 analyzes the European case law addressing online intermediaries. Section 5.5 focuses on the intersection between the regime of online intermediaries' liability and the field of data protection. Section 5.6 discusses the recent developments in this field and the introduction of a new European system of responsibility by looking at the Digital Services Act proposal.

5.2 The rise and consolidation of the "safe harbor" doctrine

5.2.1 The US system: Section 230 CDA

From a legal perspective, the consolidation and development of the role of online intermediaries has been primarily encouraged by the adoption of a liability exemption regime on both sides of the Atlantic.

In 1996, the United States introduced a provision regulating the liability regime of ISPs. Section 230 of the Communications Decency Act (CDA), as well as the Digital Millennium Copyright Act (DMCA) of 1998 with respect to the field of intellectual property, recognize that online intermediaries are not involved in the creation of content; albeit in different ways, they thus exempt online intermediaries from liability for transmitting or hosting unlawful third-party content.

When the US Congress passed Section 230 of the CDA, the primary aim was to encourage free expression and the development of the digital environment. In order to achieve this objective, they chose to exempt computer services from liability for the unlawful conduct of third-party users. Otherwise, online intermediaries would have been subject to a broad and unpredictable range of cases concerning their liability for editing third-party content since their activities consisted of transmitting and hosting vast amounts of content. In other words, ISPs faced the risk of being considered responsible for the mere existence of illegal material uploaded through or onto their digital infrastructures (such as, for example, defamatory statements or copyrighted content).

Since the lack of legal protection would have negatively affected the development of new digital services in the early days of the Internet, as some cases had already shown at that time, the US policy aimed to encourage online intermediaries to grow and develop their businesses under the protection of the "safe harbor" doctrine and of the "Good Samaritan" clause. Section 230(c)(1) thus introduced the system of a safe harbor for ISPs by ruling that "no provider or user of an interactive computer service shall be treated as the publisher or speaker of any information provided by another information content provider." Therefore, ISPs should be exempted from any editorial responsibility.

Meanwhile, Section 230(c)(2) contains the so-called Good Samaritan clause.

In order to fully understand the significance of such a clause, a reference should be made to the decision that sparked its introduction, that is, the decision rendered by the New York Supreme Court in the *Prodigy* case (1995). Prodigy Services Co. was an early online service provider that had begun employing a software to filter out profanity as a means to attract families. When a user posted defamatory statements about a securities firm named Stratton Oakmont, the latter sued Prodigy for having published those statements.

Although the service provider argued that it was not possible for it to edit all posts and messages uploaded by its users, the court held the ISP liable for defamation. The court underscored that the fact that Prodigy was employing a system to filter out profanity was proof that it was acting as an editor and, therefore, pursuant to press law, Prodigy was to be held accountable for editorial responsibility. In other words, Prodigy lost the case because it had voluntarily chosen to actively remove profanity from its infrastructure. Proponents of the CDA, however, were unsatisfied with such a finding, since they believed that the voluntary removal of "indecent" material by providers was a practice to be encouraged rather than discouraged.

The Good Samaritan clause rules that providers of interactive computer services shall not be held liable on account of "any action voluntarily taken in good faith to restrict access to or availability of material that the provider … considers to be obscene, lewd, lascivious, filthy, excessively violent, harassing, or otherwise objectionable, whether or not such material is constitutionally protected." In other words, pursuant to Section 230, providers are not liable for any content published online by users, but they can nonetheless decide to intervene to remove content they deem inappropriate without the risk of being associated to editors and without therefore incurring any editorial liability.

This provision opened the door to the evolution of the digital environment and still constitutes the basic pillar legitimizing online intermediaries' activities. The liability of online intermediaries in relation to third-party content has always been limited: on the one hand, to foster the development of information society services, thus protecting freedom of economic initiative; and on the other hand, to avoid holding liable actors that do not have effective control over the contents they host.

5.2.2 Secondary liability: Another road?

The approach adopted by the United States is not, in theory, the only viable one. A second option is represented by the introduction of secondary liability for platforms with respect to UGC.

It is possible to underline at least two main advantages linked to this second model. First, it would encourage intermediaries to confront in the most effective way possible illicit behaviors occurring in the digital spaces they administer. Online intermediaries would be compelled to tackle the spread of unlawful content, such as copyright-protected works of art or defamatory material, by preventing or blocking their dissemination. Second, online intermediaries can easily perform this task since they govern the digital spaces where user-generated information flows; in other words, online intermediaries are in the best position to check and monitor the flow of information and data through their services.

Additionally, from the users' standpoint, this system implies that the victim of illicit online conduct may rely on a second entity to obtain compensation. This is especially convenient because, more often than not, identifying (and prosecuting) primary infringers is not an easy task: this is the case, most notably, of primary infringers resorting to anonymizing techniques such as VPN systems or based in foreign jurisdictions where enforcing a judicial order may be difficult. As a result, the possibility of relying on intermediaries as secondary accountable actors is a clear advantage for victims.

Despite these favorable arguments, the institution of a secondary liability regime also leads to negative outcomes. First, it is true that a system of secondary liability can have a positive effect in encouraging online intermediaries to tackle the spread of illicit behaviors online. However, this kind of responsibility could limit their freedom to run their businesses and hinder the development of new digital services. As a result, users' rights would again be affected, since the exercise of fundamental rights and freedoms on the Internet, including freedom of online expression, depends directly on the services offered by online intermediaries. From a competition standpoint, this system may also discourage small actors who do not have sufficient resources to face the risk of liability.

Moreover, the main drawback relates to the fact that online intermediaries would be de facto vested with the power of controlling and limiting the online behavior of users. This might lead to "collateral censorship," which takes place when intermediaries facing dubious cases decide to remove legitimate content to avoid any risk of legal consequences. For instance, if an intermediary were unsure about whether to classify a post as instigation to terrorism, it might decide to remove it just as a precaution. Similar examples, as well as the general resort to filtering systems for online content moderation, show how a secondary liability system could have potential drawbacks for the rights of users, and especially for freedom of expression.

However, these objections derive from a perceived context that does not fully reflect the evolution of the Internet in recent years and, especially, the role of some intermediaries such as social media platforms and search engines. In fact, numerous intermediaries can no longer be perceived as merely passive actors. Social media platforms, for instance, actively engage in the organization and curation of the content appearing on users' feeds, thus potentially contributing to making a specific item viral or uninfluential. Today's social media platforms actively facilitate the distribution of content, thus making the Internet a place where people can create, upload and share content with their online communities. Given such a development, "old-school" rules concerning the liability of intermediaries do not fit perfectly within the current information society since they are still based on a passive idea of the role of online intermediaries.

The services offered by online intermediaries have allowed the digital dimension to acquire a crucial role for the entire society and have empowered individuals to exercise their rights and freedoms in the online environment. Nevertheless, this positive framework of human flourishing is countered by at least three main factors: the dissemination of unlawful content; the private nature of online intermediaries; and the use of automated technologies to perform online content management activities. It is no coincidence that, according to the EU Commission, the relevance of the digital economy, given its diversity and the fast-changing nature of platform ecosystems, raises new policy and regulatory challenges.

Moreover, the development of new technologies, especially those that embed algorithmic systems, has made it even harder to understand the material role those actors play in organizing and selecting content, and therefore raises concerns with respect to users' rights to free speech, privacy and human dignity. Among others, algorithms raise serious concerns in the field of content moderation due to their often unpredictable outcomes. Online platforms, by programming automated decision-making processes, are able to decide how to show and organize online content, following criteria that are often not at all transparent. The outcomes provided by algorithms are based on pre-accepted parameters without the possibility of balancing the different fundamental rights at stake. In other words, algorithms cannot operate a case-by-case analysis, an activity that is at the core of the balancing system of fundamental rights.

As analyzed in this chapter, the EU Commission has issued several proposals to increase the degree of transparency and accountability of online platforms within the framework of the European Digital Single Market Strategy.

For instance, art. 13 of the Digital Services Act proposal of December 2020 expressly requires providers of intermediary services to publish yearly reports on content moderation practices, to include not only figures concerning the contents actioned either autonomously or following Member States' orders or users' flags, but also the number of cases where the provider subsequently reviewed its prior decision.

Article 12 of the same regulation proposal also establishes a duty to adequately inform users about the tools used for content moderation, including information about the adoption of algorithmic decision-making techniques. Transparency requirements are also provided for by Regulation (EU) 2021/784 of April 29, 2021, "on addressing the dissemination of terrorist content online." Article 7(2) of the new regulation, in particular, reads that hosting service providers shall publish yearly transparency reports about the way they implement mechanisms and practices for the moderation of online terroristic content.

5.3 The legal regime of online intermediaries within the EU: The e-Commerce Directive

The starting point to frame the regulation of online intermediaries in Europe is Directive 2000/31/EC, also known as the "e-Commerce Directive," which exempts service providers from liability.

Art. 2(b) defines "service provider" as "any natural or legal person providing an information society service." According to letter (a) of the same article, the notion of "information society service" should be interpreted within the meaning of art. 1(2) of Directive 98/34/EC, as amended by Directive 98/48/EC. However, such provision was subsequently repealed by Directive (EU) 2015/1535 "laying down a procedure for the provision of information in the field of technical regulations and of rules on Information Society services." Currently, the notion of "information society service" is thus defined by art. 1 of the latter directive, according to which the term includes "any service normally provided for remuneration, at a distance, by electronic means and at the individual request of a recipient of services."

The e-Commerce Directive exempts online intermediaries from liability based on their passive role. Thus Recital 42 of the e-Commerce Directive states:

> The exceptions to the liability laid down in this Directive only concern cases where the activity of an information society service provider is limited to the technical process of activating and providing access to a communication network over which information made available by third parties is transmitted or temporarily stored for the sole purpose of making the transmission more efficient. Such an activity is purely technical, automatic and passive, which implies that the information society service provider neither knows nor controls the information transmitted or stored.

Within this framework, the e-Commerce Directive deals specifically with the liability of three types of service providers: (a) mere conduit service providers; (b) caching service providers; and (c) hosting service providers.

Mere conduit services consist either of the transmission in a communication network of information provided by a recipient of the service, or of the provision of access to a communication network (access providers). Mere conduit providers may also engage in the automatic, intermediate and transient storage of the information transmitted, but only when this is strictly necessary for the purpose of the transmission and, in any case, only for the brief time necessary for the transmission. *Caching* services, conversely, operate automatic, intermediate and temporary storage as a means of making the information's onward transmission to other recipients of the service more efficient. Finally, *hosting* providers store information provided by their recipients. Hosting providers include, among others, social network sites and social media.

Pursuant to art. 12, mere conduit providers shall not be held liable for the information transmitted in so far as: (a) they do not originate the transmission; (b) they do not select the recipient of the transmission; and (c) they do not select or modify the information transmitted. When all three conditions are met, mere conduits are not liable for the information they transmit. Article 13 states that caching providers are not liable for the automatic, intermediate and temporary storage of any piece of information to be transmitted across a communication network when such storage is performed for the sole purpose of making the information's onward transmission to other recipients of the service upon their request more efficient. However, this further liability exemption is applicable on condition that (a) the provider does not modify the information; (b) the provider complies with conditions on access to the information; (c) the provider complies with rules regarding the updating of the information, specified in a manner widely recognized and used by industry; (d) the provider does not interfere with the lawful use of technology, widely recognized and used by industry, to obtain data on the use of the information; and (e) the provider acts expeditiously to remove or to disable access to the information it has stored upon obtaining actual knowledge of the fact that the information at the initial source of the transmission has been removed from the network, or access to it has been disabled, or that a court or an administrative authority has ordered such removal or disablement.

Article 14, finally, defines the liability regime of hosting service providers. As defined by the provision, hosting services consist of the storage of information provided by a recipient of the service: in this case, in contrast to caching services, the storage will not necessarily be automatic, intermediate or temporary, nor will it simply serve the purpose of making the transmission of information more efficient. Providers of hosting services are exempt from liability for the information stored at the request of recipients provided that (a) the provider does not have actual knowledge of illegal activity or information and, as regards claims for damages, is not aware of facts or circumstances from which the illegal activity or information is apparent; or (b) the provider, upon obtaining such knowledge or awareness, acts expeditiously to remove or to disable access to the information.

After outlining the responsibilities of service providers, art. 15 establishes a ban on Member States imposing a general obligation on providers to monitor the information they transmit or store, or to actively seek facts or circumstances indicating illegal activity. Member States, in other words, cannot introduce legal obligations for providers to actively undertake monitoring or content moderation activities aimed at reducing the dissemination of unlawful items across the Internet.

This approach, which reconfirms the passive and purely technical perception of the nature of intermediaries that underlies the entire directive, is, however, without prejudice to the possibility for Member States to introduce obligations on them either (a) to inform the competent public authorities of alleged illegal activities undertaken or information provided to the recipients of their services; or (b) to communicate to the competent authorities, at their request, information enabling the identification of recipients of their services with whom they have storage agreements. Moreover, arts. 12–14 are without prejudice to the possibility that, under Member States' law, a court or administrative authority may require the provider to prevent or terminate an infringement.

5.4 European courts and online intermediaries

As outlined in the previous paragraph, the e-Commerce Directive set out the formal legal framework for intermediary liability within the EU. On the one hand, the black-letter rules left some issues unresolved; on the other hand, the system created by the directive was inspired by the functioning of the Internet at the beginning of the new millennium. For this reason, the subsequent work of the Court of Justice of the European Union (ECJ) in interpreting the exact meaning and scope of applicability of arts. 12–15 has been fundamental. To fully understand how the system of liability of online intermediaries works in Europe, therefore, law in action is as important as the text of the law.

The evolution and consolidation of online intermediaries has led to increasing challenges: if the rules defining the liability of online intermediaries made (and still make) sense when faced with subjects that play a completely passive and neutral role with respect to the contents conveyed through their services, the evolution of the structure of the network and the participatory dimension of Web 2.0 have strongly challenged the traditional categories of ISPs, stimulating reflections and rethinking about the current discipline and its adequacy. Over the years, online intermediaries have developed new services based on different business models. Along with traditional Internet access providers and hosting providers, new players offering online services, often referred to as "online platforms," have entered the information market. These include search engines (e.g., Google, Yahoo!), platforms of communication, exchange and access to information (e.g., Facebook, Twitter), cloud computing services (e.g., Dropbox, Google Drive), e-commerce intermediaries (e.g., e-Bay, Amazon) and online payment systems (e.g., PayPal).

As will be shown in the following subsections, the ECJ tried to address these emerging challenges by adapting the interpretation of the e-Commerce Directive to the new technological and digital landscape. Furthermore, some interesting decisions were also rendered by the European Court of Human Rights (ECtHR), which around the mid-2010s had to deal with the complex question of the liability regime of online intermediaries with respect to the dissemination of hate speech. Finally, domestic law has, in some cases, been relevant at a national level to further identify the exact extent of the liability exemption regime: in the Section 5.4.3, therefore, Italian case law will be taken as a case study.

5.4.1 Case law from the European Court of Justice

A turning point within the case law of the ECJ was the 2010 *Google France* case (C-236/08), where the ECJ addressed the issue of the liability of the provider of a referencing service with respect to the unlawful exploitation of keywords by third parties that infringed trademarks. In this case, Google had been sued in France by the owners of distinctive signs who complained that, by selecting keywords identical to trademarks, users were seeing advertisements for counterfeit or imitation products alongside the original products. For instance, Vuitton had found out, at the beginning of 2003, that by typing keywords coinciding with its trademarks (e.g., "Vuitton," "Louis Vuitton" and "LV") within the Google search toolbox, a user would find, under the heading "sponsored links," links to websites selling imitation copies of its products. Moreover, Google had actually offered advertisers the possibility of selecting keywords associated with Vuitton as well as the combination of trademark keywords with other keywords such as "copy" or "imitation."

The ECJ explicitly referred to the rationale behind the liability exemptions provided for by the e-Commerce Directive, recalling that arts. 12–15 should operate with exclusive respect to providers whose activity is "merely technical, automatic and passive" (Recital 42) and who do not know or control the information stored or transmitted. This assessment is made by national courts looking at the characteristics of the services in question. Therefore, the provider can benefit from the exemption of liability provided for by the e-Commerce Directive only in as much as it acts as a neutral provider. It is no coincidence that the boundary of the regime of irresponsibility of service providers coincides with the knowledge of the unlawfulness of the content or activities they host. However, it is not completely clear how the "non-neutrality" of a provider might be ascertained.

The ECJ excluded, for example, that the payment of a fee for the referencing service could be considered sufficient to prove the non-neutrality of a provider. The abstract (and simply potential) awareness of the content and data uploaded by users was considered insufficient. However, in the present case, Google's active contribution could be assessed through other elements, such as its role in drafting the commercial message associated to the incriminated links and the active establishment and selection of keywords to be associated with such links. More generally, the "non-neutrality" of online intermediaries may thus be evaluated by looking at further elements other than the simple existence of a compensation, such as the factual promotion of certain products or services, as is the case when the provider assists the user in the drafting of an advertising message.

In *L'Oréal* (C-324/09), the ECJ provided further elements of interpretation. L'Oréal had brought action against eBay for the sale, through its platform, of a number of products in violation of L'Oréal's trademark rights. Before taking legal action, the firm had sent a letter expressing its concerns about the widespread incidence of transactions made across eBay that infringed its property rights. Moreover, as highlighted by L'Oréal, eBay resorted to advertising and commercial messages and actively referred to links in a manner similar to that of Google. The ECJ confirmed some of the points that had already been addressed in *Google France*: most notably, it clarified that the activity of *assistance*, including the optimization, presentation or promotion of offers for sale, cannot be considered consistent with a neutral and passive nature of the online intermediary.

However, the court also clarified the meaning of art. 14 of the e-Commerce Directive, pursuant to which hosting service providers may be exempted from liability on condition that they do not have actual knowledge of illegal activity or information or awareness of facts or circumstances from which the illegal activity or information is apparent and, upon obtaining such knowledge or awareness, they act expeditiously to remove or to disable access to the illegal information. According to the ECJ, when an online intermediary has not played an active role, it may nonetheless be held liable both when (a) it has conducted an *autonomous investigation* to detect the presence of unlawful content; and (b) when it has *received a notification* from the holder of the relevant rights. In these cases, online intermediaries should be considered as having control over the content they host and may thus be held liable for the presence of illegal items or information. The court also specified that the mere receival of users' notification by the service provider does not necessarily imply that the provider is actually "aware" of the unlawfulness of the information or content. The notification has to be precise and adequately motivated so as to enable the provider to take action to remove the reported content. In this case, the fact that eBay actively organized the display of products to be sold, thus assisting and fostering its clients' transactions, as well as the fact that it had been notified by L'Oréal of the actual existence of transactions infringing the firm's property rights, would reasonably lead to the conclusion that the service provider could not be exempted from liability.

With regard to the distinction between service and content providers, in *Papasavvas* (C-291/13), the plaintiff complained of damage suffered as a result of the publication of certain articles, considered to be defamatory, on the website of a national newspaper. One of the national court's questions was whether the limits on liability laid down in arts. 12–14 of the e-Commerce Directive were applicable to a publisher that had a website where the online version of a newspaper was published. In the present case, the court did no more than confirm the orientation resulting from a reading of Recital 42 of the e-Commerce Directive. Most notably, it clarified that the limits of liability provided for in arts. 12–14 could not apply to the present case since the publisher was aware of the information published on its website, or, in any case, it exercised control over the content it hosted. In other words, in the case in question, the court recognized that the publishing house acted as a content provider and, therefore, was subject to editorial liability.

Another important area of the ECJ's case law concerns art. 15 and, in particular, the limits imposed to injunctions issued by national courts against service providers to counter the proliferation of online copyright infringements. In *Scarlet* (C-70/10) and *Netlog* (C-360/10), Belgian courts required online intermediaries to adopt a preventive filtering system to detect content disseminated in an unauthorized manner and therefore in breach of copyright. Although art. 15 of the e-Commerce Directive does not allow Member States to introduce general monitoring obligations, at the same time it does not prohibit judicial authorities from ordering providers to put an end to specific illegal situations. Moreover, looking at Recitals 45–47 of the e-Commerce Directive, art. 15 does not apply to monitoring obligations in specific cases and, in particular, it allows national authorities, in accordance with their respective laws, to order providers to terminate or prevent an infringement, including by removing the infringing information or disabling access to it. Moreover, the e-Commerce Directive does not affect the possibility for Member States to require service providers, who hold information provided by recipients of their service, to comply with the duty of care that can reasonably be expected, and that is provided for by national law, in order to detect and prevent certain types of unlawful activity.

Consequently, the primary issue in *Scarlet* and *Netlog* concerned the *proportionality* of such filtering systems. On that point, the court noted that the Belgian courts' order to filter the content of the information stored by the recipients of the services upon those providers' servers applied indiscriminately to all users, as a preventive measure, at the provider's sole expense, and without any limitation in time. Therefore, the ECJ deemed such orders contrary to the prohibition of general monitoring laid down in art. 15. In this case, the ECJ reaffirmed that the measures adopted by national authorities and courts must strike a fair balance between the protection of copyright and other fundamental rights that are affected, thus concluding that the orders imposed by the national courts were incompatible with EU law. Such a system would have led, first, to an infringement of the freedom of providers to conduct business. In addition, albeit from a less obvious perspective of balancing the interests at stake, the court emphasized the relevance of the right of freedom of expression, on the one hand, and the right to protection of personal data, on the other, as protected by the Charter of Fundamental Rights.

In *Telekabel* (C-314/12), the ECJ addressed the issue of the imposition of an order by national courts against an online intermediary offering network access services. In particular, the case concerned an access provider whose services allowed users to download and transmit copyright-protected content from a website without having previously obtained the authorization of the rights holders. On that occasion, the national court's question concerned the compatibility with EU law of generally prohibiting an access provider from allowing its subscribers to access a particular Internet site containing content violating copyright, provided that the provider could avoid all penalties by proving that it had taken all reasonable measures to prevent it. The ECJ held that, based on EU fundamental rights law, such injunctions may be in compliance with EU law as long as they do not specify what measures should be taken and if the provider is allowed to avoid penalties by showing that it has taken all reasonable measures. The ECJ also added two conditions: on the one hand, the measures adopted must not unnecessarily deprive Internet users of the possibility of gaining lawful access to the information available; on the other hand, those measures must prevent or, at least, make the unauthorized consultation of protected material difficult and seriously discourage recipients of the service from consulting material in violation of intellectual property rights. These conditions should be assessed by national authorities and courts.

In *Mc Fadden* (C-484/14), the ECJ came to a similar conclusion in a similar case. In that case, a German retailer was offering a free and unsecured Wi-Fi service to attract potential customers to its shop. The main issue revolved around the sharing of a musical work owned by Sony Music and available for download through the network provided by the retailer. According to the ECJ, McFadden was as an access provider and, consequently, its liability regime was framed within the framework of art. 12 of the e-Commerce Directive. The ECJ underscored that, unlike art. 14(1), which contains the conditions upon which hosting service providers might enjoy exemption from liability, art. 12 does not require mere conduit providers to act expeditiously upon obtaining knowledge of illegal information or content and that this is justified by the different activities conducted by the two types of providers. Therefore, the Court argued, rights holders may not claim compensation from an access provider on the ground that the connection to the network was used to infringe their property rights. Nonetheless, the ECJ recognized the possibility for the rights holder to ask the competent national authority to order the service provider to cease the unlawful conduct. However, the court added that that injunction is compatible with EU law only if the provider has the possibility of choosing the technical measures to be taken in order to comply with that injunction, even if that choice is limited to the measure consisting in protecting the Internet connection by means of a password, in so far as the users of that network are required to disclose their identity in order to obtain the requested password and cannot therefore act anonymously.

In the joint decision of *YouTube* (C-682/18) and *Cyando* (C-683/18), published in June 2021, the ECJ dealt again with the interpretation and scope of application of art. 14 of the e-Commerce Directive. In *YouTube*, the plaintiff had brought action against the famous video-sharing platform after a number of videos reproducing singer Sarah Brightman's performances in violation of the plaintiff's proprietary rights were uploaded to the Internet. In *Cyando*, editor Elsevier brought action against the homonymous defendant, who operates a file-hosting and file-sharing platform named "Uploaded," where several protected materials had been uploaded and made available for downloading.

Again, the ECJ confirmed its previous case law on liability exemption for online providers pursuant to the e-Commerce Directive, referring explicitly to cases such as *Google France* and *L'Oréal*. It thus conditioned the exemption from liability on the passive and neutral nature of the platforms' activities. National courts should therefore assess, on a case-by-case basis, whether intermediaries are going beyond the mere provision of a platform. As a second step, if the activity of an intermediary has been qualified as merely technical, automatic and passive, it is for the national court to evaluate whether the conditions set by art. 14(1) for granting exemption from liability have been met. With respect to these conditions, the ECJ adopted a view favorable to the position of hosting service providers. Most notably, according to the court, pursuant to letter (a), the exemption from liability wanes only when the intermediary has "specific" knowledge of illegal activities being carried out or of illegal information being stored. However, such knowledge may not be inferred simply from the fact that an operator of an online content-sharing platform uses automated tools to index uploaded content, nor from the fact that the platform has a search function or uses recommendation algorithms to suggest content to users. In other words, the ECJ in *YouTube and Cyando* clarified that simple activities of automated content curation and curation are not sufficient to give rise to the provider's liability. Moreover, the court also confirmed, referring to *L'Oréal*, that pursuant to letter (b) of art. 14(1), notifications concerning an illegal communication to the public of protected content must contain sufficient information to enable the operator to satisfy itself that that communication is illegal and that removing that content is compatible with freedom of expression. Otherwise, a video-sharing or file-sharing platform will not incur any liability.

Another important development of ECJ case law with respect to ISP liability is the case, already mentioned in Chapter 4, of *Glawischnig-Piesczek v. Facebook* (C-18/18). The case did not deal with copyright infringement but, rather, with defamation, and therefore had to operate a balance between freedom of expression, freedom of conducting business and the right to personal dignity. Eva Glawischnig-Piesczek, an Austrian politician, had been depicted in an article posted on Facebook, together with insulting words. Glawischnig-Piesczek thus demanded that Facebook delete the image and provide data concerning the author of the post. After Facebook refused to do so, Glawischnig-Piesczek brought action against the company, and the Austrian Supreme Court eventually referred some questions to the ECJ concerning the possibility of ordering Facebook to remove the content and the precise extent of the courts' powers. The ECJ, in its judgment, introduced two fundamental principles. First, it concluded that Member States are allowed to issue an order requiring an ISP to remove specific illegal content worldwide. This is, of course, a simple faculty of Member States: the e-Commerce Directive allows them to impose such a worldwide order but does not oblige them to do so. Second, the ECJ also concluded that a removal order may encompass not only content that is identical to that found to be illegal, but also content that is "equivalent" to it. In this respect, the ECJ argued:

> It is important that the equivalent information … contains specific elements which are properly identified in the injunction, such as the name of the person concerned by the infringement determined previously, the circumstances in which that infringement was determined and equivalent content to that which was declared to be illegal. Differences in the wording of that equivalent content, compared with the content which was declared to be illegal, must not, in any event, be such as to require the host provider concerned to carry out an independent assessment of that content. In those circumstances, an obligation such as the one described … on the one hand – in so far as it also extends to information with equivalent content – appears to be sufficiently effective for ensuring that the person targeted by the defamatory statements is protected. On the other hand, that protection is not provided by means of an excessive obligation being imposed on the host provider, in so far as the monitoring of and search for information which it requires are limited to information containing the elements specified in the injunction, and its defamatory content of an equivalent nature does not require the host provider to carry out an independent assessment, since the latter has recourse to automated search tools and technologies.

Overall, the case law of the ECJ on the topic of ISP liability signals the court's awareness of the insufficiency of the e-Commerce Directive vis-à-vis the new technological developments and the new services provided through the Internet. The creation of the requirement of neutrality for the purposes of ensuring the applicability of the "safe harbor" clause helped update the legal framework and set a limit on a liability regime that was excessively permissive toward ISPs. Moreover, the case of *Glawischnig-Piesczek v. Facebook* shows that intermediary liability is a relevant issue not only with respect to the protection of copyright, but also with respect to the protection of other fundamental rights, including that to dignity.

As will be underscored below, such a roadmap was eventually seconded by EU lawmakers, with the introduction of new legal acts as well as with the presentation of the proposal for a "Digital Services Act."

5.4.2 Case law from the European Court of Human Rights

Moving from Luxembourg to Strasbourg, the role of fundamental rights in the field of online intermediaries is also predominant in the case law of the ECtHR, which has repeatedly addressed the issue of the publication of defamatory comments on online platforms.

The first relevant case, *Delfi AS v. Estonia* (64569/09), was decided by the Grand Chamber of the ECtHR in 2015. Delfi, an information portal, had published an article concerning a company, SLK, which had triggered a number of defamatory comments against it. After several weeks, SLK had asked Delfi to remove the offensive comments and claimed compensation for damages. Although Delfi had immediately removed those comments, Estonian courts eventually ordered it to pay compensation. Although the operator of the portal had maintained its extraneousness from the activities carried out by its users, not only did national judges consider those comments defamatory, but they also found the provider's activity not to have been merely technical, automatic and passive. Delfi had therefore filed an application against Estonia to the ECtHR, arguing that the national courts' decision had infringed its right to freedom of expression pursuant to art. 10 of the ECHR.

However, the Strasbourg judges held that the imposition of a fine on the platform was in line with the criteria set out in art. 10(2) ECHR. The restriction of freedom of expression was provided by national law and justified by the purpose of protecting the victim's reputation. Moreover, the measure was considered proportionate, and therefore necessary in a democratic society, to such a legitimate purpose. Such a conclusion was mainly motivated by the insignificant amount of the penalty imposed (approximately €320), as well as by the assessed active role of the platform and by the need to provide effective protection to the defamed company. Interestingly, the court also highlighted that the *medium* used (in this case the Internet) should also be taken into account when operating a balancing test such as that required in the case at hand.

> On this basis, and in particular considering that this is the first case in which the Court has been called upon to examine a complaint of this type in an evolving field of technological innovation, the Court considers it necessary to delineate the scope of its inquiry in the light of the facts of the present case.

If one takes as an example the *Delfi AS* case, one can reflect on what the outcome would have been if it had been decided by the ECJ rather than by the ECtHR. In all probability, the ECJ would have relied on the application of the e-Commerce Directive regime. Indeed, the ECJ generally delivers preliminary rulings based on more specific parameters rather than principles of human rights law. The rules set by the directive, therefore, would have been central to the decision, probably even more than the simple standard of protection established by art. 11 of the Charter. More specifically, as has been pointed out by many commentators, the ECJ most likely would have adjudicated the case based on the system of liability exemptions outlined within arts. 12–14 of the e-Commerce Directive. As a result, the ECJ would have likely assessed the lack of control over third-party conduct rather than focus exclusively on the interference in freedom of expression (as done by the ECtHR): in other words, the court would have investigated the matter not from a human rights-centered point of view, focusing on free speech, but from the point of view of the functioning of the Digital Single Market under the e-Commerce Directive. From this perspective, it has been highlighted by many authors that, if EU law had been applied to that case rather than the ECHR, the outcome might have been radically different.

Nonetheless, in a similar case, the Strasbourg court ruled in a different way. In *MTE v. Hungary* (22947/13), the applicants (MTE, a self-regulatory body of Hungarian content providers, and the news portal Index.hu) had also been held liable for the presence on their portals of offensive and defamatory statements published by pseudonyms against a third company. In this case, contrary to *Delfi*, the ECtHR held that the decision of the national authorities constituted an interference with the platform's freedom of expression, especially considering the fact that the applicants should not be bound by an obligation to monitor comments posted by users who had not been subject to prior moderation. According to the court, the case differed from *Delfi* especially in that the defamatory comments that had given rise to the controversy did not amount to serious forms of hate speech and incitement to violence.

Pihl v. Sweden (74742/14) also dealt with a case of defamation. A blog and an anonymous comment had been posted on the website of a small non-profit organization; considering them to be highly offensive and defamatory, the applicant requested the organization to remove it, which it immediately did. The organization also added a post acknowledging the falsity of the information published and apologizing to the applicant. However, Mr. Pihl, having discovered that the defamatory blog could still be located by searching for his name on the Internet, proceeded to sue the organization. Swedish courts concluded, however, that the organization could not be considered responsible for failing to remove the anonymous comment sooner than it had. Mr. Pihl thus filed a complaint before the ECtHR, alleging that his right to respect for private and family life pursuant to art. 8 ECHR had been infringed. The Strasbourg court, however, having noted that the comment, although defamatory, did not amount to hate speech or incitement to violence, argued that it had to strike a balance between the organization's freedom of expression and the applicant's right to respect for private life. Following that balancing operation, the court ultimately concluded that no violation had taken place; besides, the ECtHR noted that the applicant could avail himself of the right to be forgotten as a means to require search engines to remove the blog post and the comment from the results of search engine queries (see Chapter 11).

A similar case to *Pihl* was that dealt with in *Høiness v. Norway* (43624/14). The ECtHR concluded that the case required a balancing between Ms. Høiness's rights and the freedom of expression of the online forum, which had promptly removed the defamatory content. As a result, the ECtHR evaluated the main features of the case and concluded that no violation of art. 8 had taken place. The 2020 judgment of *Jezior v. Poland* (31955/11), on the other hand, concerned the administrator of a local website who had been held liable for third-party comments: the court, as in *MTE*, concluded that Mr. Jezior's sentence was not proportionate and thus represented a violation of art. 10 ECHR.

In sum, what emerges from the case law of the ECtHR is that, after its first decision in *Delfi*, the Strasbourg judges have gradually become more cautious in deciding whether or not ISPs should be held liable for third-party content. In particular, the importance of the *balancing test* has become increasingly central and important to this end.

5.4.3 National case law: The example of Italy

If, on the one hand, the European courts have played a prominent role in defining the boundaries of online intermediaries' liability, national case law has provided further keys to interpreting the European discipline. For example, it is worth recalling the distinction theorized by the Italian case law between *active* and *passive* hosting providers. On the one hand, passive hosting would preserve those characteristics of neutrality and impartiality with respect to content that the ECJ identified as conditions for the operation of liability exemptions in *Google France*. On the other hand, active hosting is described in such a way as to remind one of the activity of a content provider, the fate of which in terms of liability is therefore shared.

Italian case law on this point held that, when a hosting provider hosts, indexes, optimizes, makes online content searchable and links it to advertising content, it should be considered active and therefore fall out of the exemption of liability (Court of Milan, November 9, 2011). According to other case law, hosting providers should in any case be considered passive and therefore not liable when the performance of the activities does not include any intervention in the content (Milan Court of Appeal, January 7, 2015). However, the distinction between an active hosting provider and a passive hosting provider ceases to be relevant when the provider receives a report from the user. From that moment on, online platforms must take steps to remove the reported content. A further question debated in case law concerns the way in which the user should notify the provider. In particular, according to a part of the case law, notifications sent by the user to the provider must be specific, for example, indicating the URL of the illegal content (Court of Turin, April 7, 2017); according to other case law, however, it is sufficient for the rights holder to indicate some information, thus leaving the proper identification of the content to the provider (Court of Rome, April 27, 2016; Court of Appeals of Rome, April 29, 2017).

The arguments that have served national courts to trace the ridge of responsibility of the active hosting provider can be summarized as follows. First, the active nature of a provider may emerge from the inclusion, among the terms and conditions of service, of clauses suggesting the exercise of a form of control over the information provided by users. In the context of possible copyright violations, for example, the provision of a non-exclusive license for the exploitation of the content published by users on a social network has been considered a sufficient condition to qualify the provider as an active host. Second, the activity of organizing and selecting the information provided by users to maximize profit might also represent evidence of the active nature of the provider: among others, the insertion of promotional messages associated with the content published by users might be relevant to this purpose.

In other cases, national courts have excluded the applicability of liability exemptions to the provider under conditions such as the provision of a search engine that allows users to enter keywords; the indexing and selection of audiovisual content and the display of related content; the provision of a selective removal procedure for reporting content deemed unlawful by users; and the direct uploading, by the provider, of certain content.

The distinction between active and passive hosting providers was finally addressed within the Court of Cassation's decision for the *RTI v. Yahoo!* case (Civil Court of

Cassation, No. 7708/2019). The Italian Supreme Court introduced three criteria meant to guide courts in the assessment of a specific hosting provider as active. First, a hosting provider may be recognized as active when it operates one or more of the following actions on user-generated content: filtering; selection; indexing; organization; cataloging; aggregation; evaluation; use; modification; extraction; promotion. These activities are commonly defined as "interference indexes." Second, the provider must operate as a business when carrying out such operations. Third, courts may consider as evidence of the active nature of the provider the employment of behavior analysis techniques with the purpose of retaining users and making the display of content more appealing to the public. The same decision, moreover, intervened with respect to the question whether or not rights holders should indicate the URL of the illegal content when notifying hosting providers. On this point, the Court of Cassation held that the evaluation of the adequacy of a notification should be made through a case-by-case approach, so that in some cases the URL may be necessary whereas it may not be so in other cases (such as the case of a video identifiable by its title).

Moreover, the Court of Rome also recently highlighted that the evaluation of a provider as active or passive should invest the specific activity carried out by it within the specific case examined, rather than the provider as a whole (Court of Rome, July 12, 2019). In other words, according to the court, the evaluation should be carried out looking at the interplay between the contents or files considered and not looking at the activity and at the general content management practices of the provider.

5.5 Data protection and liability of online intermediaries

In the information society, online intermediaries are increasingly responsible not only for moderating content but also for processing personal data. Although the regime of data is governed by a different framework of liability, there could be some overlap between the legal framework of content regulation and data in the field of online intermediaries. The scope of the e-Commerce Directive does not include "matters relating to information society services covered by Directives 95/46/EC and 97/66/EC." However, already before the adoption of the General Data Protection Regulation (GDPR) and of the e-Commerce Directive itself, in 1997, the Commission had stressed the horizontal nature of ISP liability, which would include copyright, consumer protection, trademarks, misleading advertising, personal data protection, product liability, obscene content and incitement to hatred. Even after its adoption in 2003, the Commission emphasized the general scope of the e-Commerce Directive in relation to third-party content.

Within this framework, the ECJ has had to face various types of cases: (a) users publishing unlawful content (e.g., defamation), thus triggering the e-Commerce Directive; (b) users infringing privacy and personal data rules through the network of online intermediaries, thus triggering Directive 95/46/EC (i.e., the Data Protection Directive, still applicable at the time of the cases that will be examined); and (c) online intermediaries being required to set up filtering systems or to disclose data and information about users who had breached law other than that on privacy or personal data, thus triggering both the e-Commerce Directive and the Data Protection Directive.

An example of the third case is *Promusicae* (C-275/06), in which an organization of producers and publishers of musical and audiovisual recordings (Promusicae) brought action against a commercial company providing Internet access services. Promusicae, in particular, requested the court to order the defendant to disclose information (identity and physical address) about users who had resorted to the services of that access provider to download protected material through a peer-to-peer exchange program. The question referred to the ECJ was whether EU law required Member States to establish, in order to ensure effective protection of copyright, an obligation to disclose certain personal data in the context of civil proceedings. The court noted that Member States are not required to establish such an obligation but, when transposing the relevant directives, they must nevertheless strike a fair balance between the rights at stake, bearing in mind the general principle of proportionality.

Likewise, in *LSG* (C-557/07), the ECJ stressed that the rules of the Enforcement Directive, together with those of Directive 2002/58/EC concerning the processing of personal data and the protection of privacy in the electronic communications sector, do not preclude Member States from imposing an obligation to disclose personal traffic data to private third parties in order to allow civil proceedings to be brought for copyright infringements. Again, the ECJ clarified that such a system is compatible with EU law provided that Member States take care to ensure a fair balance between the different fundamental rights at stake. The same approach was confirmed in *Bonnier Audio* (C-461/10), which held that European legislation protecting privacy does not preclude the application of national legislation that, in order to ensure the enforcement of intellectual property rights, allows an Internet operator to be ordered to disclose to the copyright holder the identity of a user to whom an IP address has been allocated for the purpose of infringing that right.

A case that deserves a particularly careful analysis is *Google Spain* (C-131/12). In this case (which will be analyzed further in Chapter 11), it is possible to notice the overlap between the legal regime of the e-Commerce Directive and that of the Data Protection Directive. In its seminal decision, the ECJ established for the first time what has come to be known as the "right to be forgotten."

Although the ECJ did not consider the question of the liability regime of online intermediaries in this case, the role of search engines in the management of online content is predominant. According to the Data Protection Directive, the term "controller" identifies the natural or legal person who determines the purposes and means of the processing of personal data. Qualifying the operator of a search engine as a controller would have major implications, since it would mean imposing on the provider a series of obligations that are far from irrelevant. However, the ECJ did not apply the rules laid down in the e-Commerce Directive, which would have allowed the search engine to benefit from the exemption of liability. Therefore, the neutral role of online intermediaries is not relevant for data protection law.

The overall picture outlined so far could be subject to further developments in light of the new scope of Regulation (EU) 679/2016, also known as the General Data Protection Regulation. The GDPR, the content of which will be addressed in Chapter 10, has not only revisited the EU legal framework on privacy and personal data protection, ensuring a higher degree of uniformity among the legislations of Member States, but has also clarified that the application of the new regulation should be without prejudice to the rules provided within the e-Commerce Directive, in particular those relating to the liability of online intermediaries. In terms of online intermediary liability, the possibility of applying the regime provided by the e-Commerce Directive would allow platforms to rely on the safe harbor for online content published by third parties in breach of privacy and data protection rules. As a result, the two regimes could thus tend to overlap, whereas, until the adoption of the GDPR, they were conceived separately.

The ECtHR also addressed the role of ISPs at the intersection between freedom of expression, privacy and data protection. The 2021 decision of *Hurbain v. Belgium* (57292/16) concerned the request of a person, G., who in 1994 had been involved in a series of fatal incidents and had thus been convicted, to anonymize the article published by the newspaper *Le Soir* concerning the episode. Based also on the Belgian law on the rehabilitation of offenders, the Belgian courts ordered the newspaper to anonymize the article; thus, Mr. Hurbain, the editor of *Le Soir*, filed a complaint before the ECtHR alleging a breach of art. 10. The ECtHR, in a manner similar to the ECJ, underscored that in the case at hand the main issue was that of balancing G.'s right to privacy with the public's interest to be informed of the incidents and of the identity of those responsible for them. In finding G.'s right to be prominent, the Strasbourg court argued most notably:

> As to the existence of a debate of public interest not diminished by the passage of time … the Court stresses the fact that, by their very nature, archives contribute to a debate of public interest in a different way from an initial publication … In the present case, the Court of Appeal correctly observed that the online publication of the article did not have any value in terms of newsworthiness … It held that, twenty years after the events, the identity of a person who was not a public figure did not enhance the public interest of the impugned article, which merely contributed at a statistical level to a general debate on road safety. The article concerned a series of – admittedly tragic – events whose contribution to a debate of public interest related mainly to the hazards of road traffic and the causes of those hazards. Hence, the Court notes the Court of Appeal's finding that mentioning G.'s full name was not apt, twenty years after the events, to contribute to a debate of public interest.

Just a few months later, in November 2021, the ECtHR delivered the decision for the case of *Biancardi v. Italy* (77419/16). An online newspaper had published an article describing a fight at a restaurant and the criminal proceedings that ensued. The person described therein requested the newspaper to remove and de-index the article: since this was not done immediately, the Italian courts, seised by the person seeking to enforce their right to be forgotten, concluded that the publisher had violated the applicant's right to reputation by leaving the article online for a significant amount of time. Once again, the ECtHR upheld the decision, finding that the balance between the interests at stake had been correctly struck.

The role of ISPs in protecting privacy and data protection, at its intersection with the Internet and freedom of expression, has also been dealt with by some domestic courts. An example is the Italian case of *Google v. Vivi-Down*, concerning the relationship between content management and personal data processing. A video had been published on a video platform owned by Google picturing a boy affected by Down's syndrome being bullied by his classmates. Three Google executives were convicted by the first-instance Court of Milan for the unlawful processing of data pursuant to the Italian so-called Privacy Code (Legislative Decree No. 196/2003): the judgment argued in particular that the provider had not preliminarily informed the uploaders of the video about the relevant law with which they should comply (Court of Milan, April 12, 2010). The Court of Appeal of Milan partially overturned the first instance (Court of Appeal of Milan, December 21, 2012) based on the argument that Legislative Decree No. 196/2003 did not provide for a monitoring obligation of service providers. As recalled by the court, Google had no duty to monitor the content uploaded by users on its systems, nor was there any duty to inform the users about the law with which they should comply. What is interesting to note is that, with respect to the offense of unlawful data processing, the first-instance court approached the issue from a data protection perspective, referring to art. 167 of the Privacy Code, whereas the Court of Appeal considered Google's role as a hosting provider. The Court of Cassation (Criminal Court of Cassation, No. 5107/2014) reiterated the orientation of the Court of Appeal, holding that the service provider had no knowledge of the content and could not therefore be held liable. The criminal offense concerning the processing of data could only be ascribed to the uploaders and could not be extended to the hosting provider.

5.6 Toward a new regulatory framework: The DSA proposal

The European Commission has recently questioned the legal regime of online intermediaries. As clarified in the communication "Online Platforms and the Digital Single Market: Opportunities and Challenges for Europe" (COM/2016/288), one of the Commission's objectives is to ensure that online platforms are responsible for "protecting fundamental values," ensuring transparency and fairness to maintain users' trust and safeguard innovation. This is due to the role of online platforms in providing access to information and content to society and, consequently, due to their impact on users' fundamental rights. As the Commission points out, the role of online platforms entails "wider responsibilities."

Moreover, as stated by the Commission in the communication on "A Digital Single Market Strategy for Europe" (COM/2015/0192), the legal regime of online intermediaries provided by the e-Commerce Directive, based on the dual principle of passivity and the effective intervention of the provider in order to remove content, constitutes a challenge for the fight against illegal conduct on the Internet. The Commission underlined:

> Recent events have added to the public debate on whether to enhance the overall level of protection from illegal material on the Internet. In tandem with its assessment of online platforms, the Commission will analyse the need for new measures to tackle illegal content on the Internet, with due regard to their impact on the fundamental right to freedom of expression and information, such as rigorous procedures for removing illegal content while avoiding the take down of legal content, and whether to require intermediaries to exercise greater responsibility and due diligence in the way they manage their networks and systems – a duty of care.

As will be further analyzed in the following chapters, the Commission decided for some time to intervene with ad hoc measures (e.g., the adoption of the DSM Copyright Directive, the adoption of the Regulation on Online Terrorist Content and the amendment to the Audiovisual Media Services Directive) without modifying the safe harbor principle provided for by the e-Commerce Directive. Nonetheless, the Commission recently changed its approach, especially by presenting in December 2020 a proposal for the adoption of a Digital Services Act (DSA) (COM/2020/825).

Article 1 clarifies the scope and purposes of the proposed regulation. In particular, the Act aims to contribute to the proper functioning of the internal market for intermediary services as well as to set out uniform rules for the creation of a safe, predictable and trusted online environment that is respectful of the rights enshrined within the Charter of Fundamental Rights of the European Union. In order to do so, the DSA sets a new framework for the conditional exemption from liability of providers of intermediary services.

Articles 3–5 and 7 of the DSA shall substitute arts. 12–15 of the e-Commerce Directive, though replicating in fact their content.

> With respect to hosting providers (art. 5), the DSA simply introduces a clause concerning platforms that allow consumers to conclude distance contracts with traders. In particular, if certain information is presented on the platform that leads a consumer to believe that a product or service is being provided directly by the platform or by a recipient working under the platform's authority and control, then that platform's liability exemption will not apply with respect to consumer law. Thus, for instance, if a consumer buying a product from Amazon was led to believe that that product was being sold directly by Amazon, then Amazon would be held liable pursuant to consumer law.

Article 7, in particular, confirms the provision set by art. 15(1) of the e-Commerce Directive, banning the imposition of general monitoring obligations on intermediaries.

A particularly interesting provision that the DSA aims at introducing *ex novo* is art. 6 on *voluntary own-initiative investigations* and legal compliance. In a manner similar to Section 230(c)(2) of the US CDA, that is, the provision setting the so-called Good Samaritan clause, art. 6 states:

> Providers of intermediary services shall not be deemed ineligible for the exemptions from liability referred to in Articles 3, 4 and 5 solely because they carry out voluntary own-initiative investigations or take measures aimed at detecting, identifying, and removing, or disabling access to, illegal content, or take the necessary measures to comply with the requirements of national and Union law, including the Charter and the requirements set out in this Regulation.

In other words, in order to avoid the paradoxical result of discouraging providers from actively fighting against the dissemination of unlawful content across the Internet, the DSA expressly states that the measures adopted for this purpose do not sweep away the merely technical, automatic and passive nature of a provider's activity.

As for the e-Commerce Directive, the DSA also foresees the possibility for national judicial or administrative authorities of the Member States to issue orders to act against specific items of illegal content (art. 8) as well as orders to provide specific items of information about one or more specific individual recipients of the service (art. 9): in such cases, providers must comply expeditiously with the orders. Those orders must, in any case, be consistent with EU law and comply with the formal requirements provided within arts. 8 and 9 themselves.

Although the DSA maintains in the background the liability regime that was developed under the e-Commerce Directive, it introduces significant new due diligence obligations for a transparent and safe online environment. These new obligations are scaled depending on the services offered and upon the dimension of the providers themselves. Therefore, there are four sets of rules that apply respectively to (a) all providers of intermediary services; (b) only hosting service providers; (c) only online platforms; and (d) only very large online platforms (VLOPs) and very large online search engines (VLOSEs).

Pursuant to art. 2, whereas hosting providers, in general, offer services that consist of the storage of information provided by, and at the request of, their recipients, the new category of online platforms represents a subsection of hosting providers that, at the request of the recipients of their services, not only store but also disseminate to the public the uploaded information. In other words, online platforms are meant to be used by individuals to share the information they produce to a potentially unlimited audience. An even smaller subsection of online platforms is that represented by VLOPs, which will be identified by quantitative criteria set within art. 25.

With respect to the system implemented by the e-Commerce Directive, the greatest novelties concern hosting service providers (and online platforms) rather than mere conduits and caching providers.

One of the most important provisions is art. 14, which requires all hosting service providers to implement a notice and action mechanism "to allow any individual or entity to notify them of the presence on their service of specific items of information that the individual or entity considers to be illegal content." Moreover, providers must ensure that measures are taken to enable and facilitate the submission of notices that are sufficiently precise and substantiated. The fundamental role of this new obligation is signaled, in particular, by para. 3 of the provision, which expressly states that, if a notice is sent to the provider through such a procedure, then such a notice shall be considered as giving rise to actual knowledge or awareness of the existence of illegal information or activity. Therefore, the new notice and action mechanism has the effect and purpose of definitely and clearly sweeping away the provider's exemption from liability with respect to that specific content.

In addition to this, art. 19 introduces the notion of "trusted flaggers," that is, entities who (a) have particular expertise and competence for the purpose of detecting, identifying and notifying of illegal content; (b) represent collective interests and are independent from any online platform; or (c) carry out their activities for the purposes of submitting notices in an accurate and objective manner. When a notice pursuant to art. 14 is submitted by a trusted flagger, that notice will need to be processed and decided upon with

priority and without delay. However, art. 19 is applicable to online platforms alone and not to all hosting services providers.
Arts. 20 and 21 also provide measures that online platforms must take to fight against the dissemination of illegal content. On the one hand, art. 20 requires that online platforms take measures against the misuse of their services, such as, for instance, suspending the provision of their services when a recipient has frequently exploited them to publish "manifestly illegal content." Such a suspension should be operated, however, for a reasonable period of time and after having issued a prior warning. On the other hand, art. 21 obliges online platforms to notify the authorities whenever they have any suspicion that a serious criminal offense, involving a threat to the life or safety of persons, has taken place, is taking place or is likely to take place.

With respect to obligations imposed upon very large online platforms, art. 26 states that VLOPs and VLOSEs must operate yearly assessments of systemic risks. Following such risk assessments, they will have to put in place "reasonable, proportionate and effective mitigation measures" (art. 27).

Assessments pursuant to art. 26 should address the following risks: (a) dissemination of illegal content through the services provided; (b) negative effects for the exercise of the fundamental rights to respect to private and family life, freedom of expression and information, the prohibition of discrimination and the rights of the child; and (c) intentional manipulation of their service, with an actual or foreseeable negative effect on the protection of public health, minors, civic discourse, or actual or foreseeable effects related to electoral processes and public security. In operating such a risk assessment, VLOPs and VLOSEs must also consider the effects of recommendation systems and of the automated and algorithmic management of online content.
The mitigation measures to be adopted vis-à-vis such systemic risks may include (a) adapting content moderation or recommender systems, their decision-making processes, the features or functioning of their services, or their terms and conditions; (b) targeted measures aimed at limiting the display of advertisements; (c) reinforcing the internal processes or supervision of any of their activities in particular as regards detection of systemic risk; (d) initiating or adjusting cooperation with trusted flaggers; and (e) initiating and adjusting cooperation with other online platforms through the adoption, for instance, of codes of conduct.

In case they fail to comply with the provisions set within the DSA, providers of intermediary services will be subject to penalties, the amount of which will be determined by the Member States within the framework set by the regulation. Article 42 provides that, when laying down the rules concerning penalties, Member States will have to ensure that these are effective, proportionate and dissuasive.

The introduction of such obligations, and of the connected penalties, might give rise to concerns regarding the risk of collateral censorship to the detriment of users and individuals themselves. The proposal is seemingly aware of such an issue and of the potential implications it might have for fundamental rights such as freedom of expression and information. For this reason, a number of provisions aim at mitigating these risks, especially through the introduction of measures aimed at fostering transparency concerning the activities of providers.

Pursuant to art. 12, for instance, all providers of intermediary services are expected to include within their terms and conditions information concerning any restriction they might impose upon information provided by users and the technical and algorithmic tools employed for content moderation purposes. Moreover, all providers will have to publish transparency reports concerning compliance with the regulation's requirement at least once a year; these reports will have to include, among other things, information about practices and figures of content moderation (art. 13). Transparency obligations vary, again, depending on the nature and dimension of the provider concerned: online platforms and VLOPs, in particular, will have to comply with further and more specific duties and requirements.

In addition, the DSA also envisions some procedural tools aimed at guaranteeing users' freedom of expression and information and at avoiding the removal of legal content by mistake. In particular, art. 17 states that when online platforms decide (a) to remove or disable access to information, (b) to suspend or terminate the provision of their services, in whole or in part, (c) to suspend or terminate the account of a recipient, or d) to restrict the ability to monetize content provided by the recipients of their services, then they will have to provide, for a period of at least six months, an effective internal complaint-handling system.

In case of a complaint, platforms will need to assure users that the new evaluation will not be conducted only through the use of automated tools and will have to allow recipients of their services to contact a human interlocutor. Moreover, if the platform rejects the complaint, recipients will have the possibility of availing themselves of affordable and accessible out-of-court dispute settlement systems before external bodies certified by the Member States.

5.7 Conclusions

Online intermediaries provide users with services and infrastructures that are of critical importance for the functioning of the Internet. Without them, the digital market, as well as digital communication, would not be possible. For this reason, both in the United States and in Europe, lawmakers have chosen to design a liability regime that, by setting a "safe harbor" model, will encourage and foster the development of those infrastructures and services. In the United States, the legal framework set by Section 230 was in many ways pioneering for this purpose and thus inspired the European Union in drafting arts. 12–15 of the e-Commerce Directive in 2000.

This choice was consistent with the technological landscape existing at the turn of the century and was actually successful if one considers the extraordinary worldwide evolution of the digital landscape and the consequent birth of the Web 2.0. Such phenomena, however, are precisely the reason why new challenges emerged with respect to the increasing risks of the online dissemination of unlawful and harmful content by third-party recipients of intermediaries' services. This is the reason why, at least in Europe, European courts, and the ECJ in particular, had to work extensively to define the exact scope of application of the liability exemptions set by the e-Commerce Directive. Particularly relevant in this sense was the decision to exclude from those exemptions all intermediaries whose activity is not merely automatic, technical and passive, a choice that, within the Italian domestic legal framework, was adopted even more extensively by identifying, defining and clarifying the category of "active" (as opposed to "passive") hosting service providers. Moreover, the *Delfi* case and, in a more moderate way, the *MTE* case signal that the ECtHR itself is favorable to recognizing, at least to a certain extent, the liability of intermediaries and portals for the dissemination of content that is potentially harmful to individuals.

It should not come as a surprise, therefore, that in the last few years the European Union has begun moving from a liberal laissez-faire regime to an approach more open to recognizing intermediaries' responsibilities in the spread of illegal, unlawful or harmful content. Recent legislation, with respect to copyright, audiovisual online media services and online terrorism, has introduced a range of obligations that must be complied with by Internet providers. These include, among others, the publication of transparency reports, the assessment of risks and the creation of adequate procedures for the identification of illegal activities taking place through the services they provide. In this sense, the Digital Services Act proposal seemingly confirms such an evolution of European policies. By horizontally reforming the legal regime of online intermediaries, and especially of "online platforms," the DSA will represent an important milestone for the future development of the Digital Single Market.

6 Hate Speech and Disinformation

6.1 Introduction

The rise of the Internet has provided individuals with new avenues for the exercise of freedom of speech, allowing everyone to potentially become a content provider and spread their thoughts across the globe. Nonetheless, new challenges have also emerged. This chapter will focus specifically on two separate, though interconnected, issues: that of hate speech and that of disinformation.

First, the debate around hate speech on the Internet has become increasingly relevant worldwide. Digital communication has greatly enhanced the risks connected to the spread of content dehumanizing and disparaging specific demographic groups that are the victims of violence and discrimination. Between 2016 and 2017, for instance, the Rohingya genocide in Myanmar has been tragically encouraged and strengthened by the resort to hate speech against that minority, echoing through the newsfeeds of Facebook. In a similar way, the Rwandan genocide of 1994 was inflamed through radio messages instigating the massacre of Tutsi people: however, the network effect of the Internet and social networks has made the dissemination and spread of this type of content even more pervasive. Second, the issue of disinformation (and so-called fake news) has led to problematic outcomes with respect to democratic processes and the smooth functioning of society. Thus, for instance, disinformation has been used in many cases to influence foreign (or internal) politics and the outcomes of democratic elections: this has been the case, for instance, in the vote on Brexit in the United Kingdom and the in US presidential elections in 2016. The notorious Cambridge Analytica scandal concerned the use of personal data harvested surreptitiously and then used for purposes of targeted propaganda. Such use of disinformation has led, especially in Europe, to increasing concern about the phenomenon at hand and to the development of legislative tools aimed at containing it.

As described in Chapter 4, Europe's constitutional tradition on freedom of expression, as resulting from art. 10 ECHR within the context of the Council of Europe and from art. 11 CFREU in the context of the EU, recognizes that such liberty encompasses both an active dimension (i.e., freedom to express oneself) and a passive dimension (i.e., freedom to receive information in a pluralistic context). According to the European Court of Human Rights, moreover, this passive dimension of the freedom of expression, in order to guarantee pluralism and tolerance in a democratic society, may require the presence and circulation of shocking, offensive or disturbing opinions (*Handyside v. the United Kingdom*, 5493/72). Along these lines, one could argue that receiving false news or hate speech could also contribute to the full enjoyment of the passive dimension of freedom of expression: such is the idea behind the US "free marketplace of ideas" tenet. Nevertheless, not all forms of online speech enjoy unfettered immunity under the umbrella of art. 10 ECHR. Provided that the requirements of art. 10(2) ECHR are met, state intervention to regulate online speech is in principle possible and the task to reconcile competing claims lies with the legislator. ECHR Contracting States, as well as EU Member States, may thus adopt regulatory measures that are necessary in a democratic society to reduce the spread of false and hateful content.

This chapter is structured as follows. Section 6.2 addresses the topic of hate speech regulation, looking at both the US and European experiences: most notably, it analyzes firstly seminal case law from the US Supreme Court (6.2.1) and from the ECtHR (6.2.2) and, secondly, the legislative measures adopted or foreseen within the European Union to limit the spread of such a phenomenon (6.2.3). Subsection 6.2.4 briefly addresses a different, but connected, issue: that of counter-terrorism and, in particular, the approval of the Terrorist Content Regulation. Section 6.3 discusses the topic of disinformation regulation, focusing both on theoretical questions (6.3.1, 6.3.2) and on the concrete actions taken in recent years by the European Union (6.3.3). Finally, Section 6.4 explores the action taken with respect to online hate speech and disinformation across various jurisdictions, notably Germany, Italy, France, Russia, Singapore and Malaysia.

6.2 Hate speech across the Atlantic

Hate speech has been at the center of legal and political debate throughout the 20th century and has become an even more pressing issue in the aftermath of the worldwide spread of the Internet; hate speech has thrived in cyberspace. However, defining what hate speech is, especially from a legal perspective, is not always an easy task: identifying exactly what hate is and who the relevant target of such hate is can be particularly challenging.

The peculiar aspect of hate speech is that it generally targets specific groups of people, or members of such groups, because of a common feature that is generally linked to some form of discrimination. Hate speech targeting such people may take various forms, including advocacy of hatred; incitement to discrimination; incitement to hatred; incitement to violence; and denial of genocide, of crimes against humanity, or of war crimes.

> In the context of international human rights law, some historical legal instruments expressly foresee the prohibition, or even the criminalization, of certain forms of hate speech, especially with respect to discrimination based on ethnicity and/or religion. Art. 20(2) of the International Covenant on Civil and Political Rights (ICCPR, 1966), for instance, states that "any advocacy of national, racial or religious hatred that constitutes incitement to discrimination, hostility or violence shall be prohibited by law."

Article 4 of the International Convention on the Elimination of All Forms of Racial Discrimination (ICERD, 1965), instead, requires convening states to criminalize (a) all dissemination of ideas based on racial superiority or hatred; (b) incitement to racial discrimination; (c) incitement to acts of violence against any race or group of persons of another color or ethnic origin; and (d) the provision of any assistance to racist activities (including the financing thereof). As far as their scope of action is concerned, it should be noted that the ICERD, as opposed to the ICCPR, does not refer to forms of hate speech based on religious discrimination. However, the two texts also differ in another aspect: whereas the prohibition required by the ICCPR does not necessarily imply an intervention through criminal law (allowing for "simple" civil and/or administrative sanctions), the ICERD especially provides for criminalization.

In the context of the Council of Europe, one of the most important and extensive legal definitions of hate speech is given by the European Commission against Racism and Intolerance (ECRI) General Policy Recommendation No. 15 (CRI/2016/15), adopted in December 2015:

> Hate speech for the purpose of the Recommendation entails the use of one or more particular forms of expression – namely, the advocacy, promotion or incitement of the denigration, hatred or vilification of a person or group of persons, as well as any harassment, insult, negative stereotyping, stigmatization or threat of such person or persons and any justification of all these forms of expression – that is based on a non-exhaustive list of personal characteristics or status that includes "race", colour, language, religion or belief, nationality or national or ethnic origin, as well as descent, age, disability, sex, gender, gender identity and sexual orientation.

Such a definition, of course, is not legally binding per se. National jurisdictions, both within the framework of the Council of Europe and within the framework of the European Union, are in general left free to decide to what extent they wish to impose (or not) bans on cases of hate speech. Nonetheless, the notion of hate speech proposed by ECRI seems to be especially useful in the present context in that it encompasses the wide range of expressive forms that may constitute hate speech, as well as an (open) list of the various grounds on which hate speech may be based.

Be that as it may, hate speech has become an increasingly relevant target of regulation in Europe within many jurisdictions. Such openness to the proscription of such a phenomenon is reflected in the case law of the ECtHR. As will be highlighted in the following subsection, this represents a peculiar trait that distinguishes the system on the eastern side of the Atlantic from the US legal system, where the supremacy of the First Amendment, as interpreted by the federal Supreme Court, does not allow for general bans on hate speech.

6.2.1 Hate speech in the US First Amendment case law

The First Amendment, within the US constitutional framework, limits the space for federal and state governments to impose restrictions on free speech. Speech regulation in the United States is still deeply connected to the "clear and present danger" test developed by Justice Oliver W. Holmes in the subsequent decisions of *Schenck* and *Abrams v. United States*, as well as to the notion of the free marketplace of ideas. Additionally, First Amendment jurisprudence is especially hostile toward "content discrimination" and "viewpoint discrimination": content-based or viewpoint-based regulation must overcome a "strict scrutiny" test, unless it targets "low value" speech (see Chapter 4). Low value speech also encompasses, among others, so-called fighting words (*Chaplinsky v. New Hampshire*, 315 US 568, 1942), that is, "those personally abusive epithets which, when addressed to the ordinary citizen, are, as a matter of common knowledge, inherently likely to provoke violent reaction" (*Cohen v. California*, 403 US 15, 1971). Low value speech, including fighting words, may thus be more easily subjected to speech regulation, including, to a certain extent, content-based regulation.

In *Beauharnais v. Illinois* (343 US 250, 1952), the Supreme Court upheld the conviction of a man who had distributed leaflets calling for applications for membership in the "White Circle League of America, Inc." and portraying depravity, criminality, unchastity and lack of virtue of black citizens in such a way as to expose them to "contempt, derision, or obloquy." In this case, the court recognized the applicant's conduct as a form of "public libel" and, therefore, as a form of low value speech not subject to the "clear and present danger" test. As a result, the First Amendment had not been violated. However, *Beauharnais v. Illinois* was short-lived, since the subsequent decision of *Brandenburg v. Ohio* (395 US 444, 1969) led to its substantial overcoming. In this case, a Ku Klux Klan (KKK) leader, together with other members of the KKK, had made derogatory remarks about black and Jewish people during a rally staged on television, in front of a number of reporters, for which he was eventually convicted. The Supreme Court, however, reversed the sentence, highlighting that Brandenburg had rejected the argument that the KKK should take matters into its own hands and stating that criminalization of advocacy of the use of force or advocacy of the violation of the law may be in compliance with the First Amendment only in as much as it is "directed to inciting or producing imminent lawless action and is likely to incite or produce such action." As a result, *Brandenburg* abandoned the public libel scheme and fundamentally reintroduced, with respect to hate speech, the "clear and present" danger test.

Another critical case within American constitutional law with respect to hate speech proscription is represented by the *Skokie* judicial saga. This decision is particularly relevant because it underscored the relationship between hate speech and fighting words: the courts held implicitly that, if an instance of hate speech were to be recognized as "fighting words," then it would amount to low value speech and would thus not be subjected to the strict scrutiny test of the "clear and present danger" test. In that case, the organization of a march in which participants wore Nazi uniforms and displayed swastikas was not recognized as such and could not, therefore, be subject to restrictions: rejecting the Nazis' request to march in the Jewish-inhabited village of Skokie (in the suburbs of Chicago) had amounted to a violation of the First Amendment. In *R.A.V. v. City of Saint Paul* (505 US 377, 1992), the Supreme Court took another step forward. The petitioner had been sentenced for having set fire to a cross in front of a house where an African American family had recently moved in, an act that is traditionally linked to threats from the KKK. The Supreme Court overturned the decision and declared the local statute, pursuant to which R.A.V. had been convicted, unconstitutional. Although the court recognized that the statute prohibited, per se, only "fighting words" discriminating on the basis of "race, colour, creed, religion or gender," it nonetheless revisited the traditional interpretation of low value speech, concluding that even low value speech cannot be subjected to prohibitions that are only moved by a viewpoint discriminatory rationale. In the subsequent decision of *Virginia v. Black* (538 US 343, 2003), concerning Virginia's cross-burning statute, the Supreme Court accepted that such a ban might be consistent with First Amendment case law if it criminalizes an act of intimidation amounting to true threat (i.e., a statement "where the speaker means to communicate a serious expression of an intent to commit an act of unlawful violence to a particular individual or group of individuals").

All in all, the described case law sheds a light on the very high threshold that the First Amendment, as interpreted by the Supreme Court, sets for state and federal governments to impose restrictions on hate speech. Hate speech as such cannot be considered as a case of low value speech and, therefore, cannot be prohibited; otherwise, the government would be putting in place a regulation vitiated by viewpoint discrimination. Ultimately, in the wake of decisions such as *Brandenburg* and *Virginia v. Black*, hate speech may be prohibited, without violating the First Amendment, only when it amounts to fighting words, when it is very likely to cause "imminent lawless action" or when it constitutes a "true threat," and, following *R.A.V.*, when such regulation is not clearly based on viewpoint discrimination. The simple utterance of discourses that are disparaging of certain groups of people may not be criminalized nor prohibited, as also highlighted in the memorable words of *Matal v. Tam* (582 US, 2017):

> The Government has an interest in preventing speech expressing ideas that offend. And, as we have explained, that idea strikes at the heart of the First Amendment. Speech that demeans on the basis of race, ethnicity, gender, religion, age, disability, or any other similar ground is hateful; but the proudest boast of our free speech jurisprudence is that we protect the freedom to express "the thought that we hate."

6.2.2 Hate speech in the case law of the ECtHR

As outlined previously in Chapter 4, freedom of expression and information within the ECHR system does not represent an absolute right: in fact, pursuant to art. 10(2), it may be subject to "formalities, conditions, restrictions or penalties" when such measures are provided by the law and when it is necessary in a democratic society to pursue a legitimate aim such as "the protection of the reputation or rights of others." Based on such provision, the ECtHR has developed a case law open to the imposition of restrictions and penalties on hate speech.

At the same time, art. 17 ECHR, concerning the abuse of rights, has often played an important role too. In some cases, the court held that specific forms of hate speech were so egregious that they could not be protected by the safeguards and conditions set by art. 10. In these cases, in other words, once the court had assessed that the applicant had violated art. 17, it would not proceed to evaluate the case to find out if the conditions foreseen by art. 10(2), most notably the principle of proportionality, had been respected; it simply recognized the validity of the Contracting State's intervention. The choice of the court to rely on art. 17 to deliver its decisions on hate speech is generally based on the careful evaluation of the gravity and danger posed by the specific contents expressed and on an analysis of the environment and time of those speech acts. Nonetheless, some clear patterns emerge by looking at the case law: in particular, art. 17 has been consistently applied in cases of Holocaust denial, antisemitism and Islamophobia.

With respect to Holocaust denial, two cases are especially relevant historically. In *Lehideux and Isorni v. France* (24662/94), the applicants had tried to initiate, through an advertisement on *Le Monde*, a debate on the historical figure of Marshal Philippe Pétain, whom they presented in a positive way, and had been convicted for defending a Nazi collaborationist and perpetrator of crimes against humanity. The ECtHR Grand Chamber reversed their sentence, namely because it held that the debate on the person of Pétain did "not belong to the category of clearly established historical facts – such as the Holocaust – whose negation or revision would be removed from the protection of Article 10 by Article 17." Although it acquitted the applicants, therefore, the court stated that, since the Holocaust is historically a clearly established fact, its denial is not worthy of being protected by art. 10. This approach was later confirmed in the case of *Garaudy v. France* (65831/2003), where the Strasbourg court declared the inadmissibility of the complaint of an applicant who had been sentenced for publishing a book that denied Hitler's "final solution" and the use of gas chambers in Nazi concentration camps.

With respect to antisemitism, the court declared the inadmissibility of the applications both in the case of *Pavel Ivanov v. Russia* (35222/04), where the applicant had published a series of articles in his newspaper calling for the exclusion of Jewish people from social life in Russia, and in the case of *M'bala M'Bala v. France* (25239/13), where a comedian had been sentenced for an offending sketch against Jewish people and for having offered the stage and paid homage to the well-known revisionist Robert Faurisson. As regards Islamophobia, a central case was that of *Norwood v. the United Kingdom* (23131/03), where a member of the British National Party had displayed, from November 2001 to January 9, 2002, a large poster of the Twin Towers burning, accompanied by a crescent and star in a prohibition sign and by the words "Islam out of Britain – Protect the British People." The court declared Norwood's application inadmissible, underscoring that the identification of Islam with the terrorist attack on the Twin Towers represented a particularly dangerous allegation (especially in the aftermath of 9/11).

Whenever art. 17 is not deemed applicable, the court has to evaluate the matter at hand through the lens of art. 10 ECHR. In this sense, legal scholarship has underscored that the court has adopted what could be defined as a "two tiers approach":

depending on the type of hate speech being analyzed, the court will apply either the "guillotine" provision of art. 17 or art. 10. In the second case, the ECtHR has to consider if the imposition of restrictions on freedom of expression complies with the criteria set in art. 10(2). Whereas the requirement of prior provision by the law and the requirement of the legitimate aim do not generally pose relevant challenges (in particular, the court generally recognizes that hate speech bans aim at protecting "the reputation or rights of others"), the main issue is usually represented by the proportionality test. The analysis, which must be made on a case-by-case basis, generally takes into account a whole set of factors, including purpose of the speech; content of the speech; context of the speech (including the status and role in society of the speaker and of the target of the speech, as well as the time and place of the speech and the audience); medium used and potential for dissemination and harm; and nature and seriousness of the penalty or restriction imposed by the state.

The application of such criteria is evident in the 2012 case of *Vejdeland v. Sweden* (1813/07), the first case in the history of the ECtHR to deal with homophobic speech. The applicants had been convicted for entering a high school and distributing leaflets, putting them also inside students' lockers, containing serious allegations against homosexuals and "homosexual propaganda." Although it declared the application admissible, the court found the measure to be consistent with the conditions set by art. 10(2). The ECtHR noted that, with respect to content, the leaflets contained very "serious and prejudicial allegations" that could not be considered valuable input for initiating a public debate. Additionally, the court underscored the young age of the audience and the fact that, since the leaflets had been put inside their lockers, the students had been made a captive audience, meaning they could not avoid exposure to the possibly harmful material.

With respect to homophobic speech, in 2020 the court delivered its judgment in the case of *Beizaras and Levickas v. Lithuania* (41288/15). The applicants were a homosexual couple and LGBTQIA+ activists. After posting a photo on Facebook of them kissing, they received many insults and threats, including "Burn the faggots," "into the gas chamber with the pair of them," "you should be exterminated," "I would shoot every single one of them" and others. The applicants, together with an LGBTQIA+ association (LGL), filed a complaint with the Prosecutor General's Office to initiate criminal proceedings against the authors of the comments, as art. 170(2) of the Lithuanian Criminal Code criminalizes the act of ridiculing or inciting discrimination against a group of people or a member of a group of people on grounds of their sexual orientation. The Prosecutor, however, refused to initiate the pre-trial investigation. The applicants, therefore, filed an application with the ECtHR alleging a violation of art. 14 (non-discrimination) in conjunction with art. 8 (right to respect of private and personal life) as well as a violation of art. 13 (right to an effective remedy). The court ultimately gave reason to the applicants, recognizing that their rights had indeed been infringed. In the same year, the court also delivered the decision of *Lilliendahl v. Iceland* (29297/18), where it upheld the conviction of the applicant who had published derogatory homophobic comments online.

With respect to hate speech on the Internet, the most important decision is represented by *Delfi AS v. Estonia*, which has been extensively addressed in Chapter 5. In that case, the court underscored the following:

> Defamatory and other types of clearly unlawful speech, including hate speech and speech inciting violence, can be disseminated like never before, worldwide, in a matter

> of seconds, and sometimes remain persistently available online … Bearing in mind the need to protect the values underlying the Convention, and considering that the rights under Articles 10 and 8 of the Convention deserve equal respect, a balance must be struck that retains the essence of both rights. Thus, while the Court acknowledges that important benefits can be derived from the Internet in the exercise of freedom of expression, it is also mindful that the possibility of imposing liability for defamatory or other types of unlawful speech must, in principle, be retained, constituting an effective remedy for violations of personality rights.

As highlighted in Chapter 5, decisions subsequent to *Delfi* proved to be less open to recognizing liability of Internet service providers for the dissemination of harmful content such as defamatory posts. Nonetheless, *MTE v. Hungary*, *Pihl v. Sweden*, *Høiness v. Norway* and *Jezior v. Poland* all stressed that, in such cases, the balancing between the ISPs' right to freedom of expression and freedom to conduct business and the pursuit of the protection of the rights and dignity of others should take into account whether the contested speech represented an egregious form of hate speech.

6.2.3 Tackling hate speech at the EU level

From a hard law point of view, the main relevant legislative instrument within the European Union is currently Framework Decision 2008/913/JHA "on combating certain forms and expressions of racism and xenophobia by means of criminal law," which first required Member States to introduce criminal provisions against hate crimes and hate speech on grounds of "race, colour, religion, descent or national or ethnic origin." In particular, art. 1(1) requires Member States to criminalize (a) the public incitement to violence or hatred directed against a group of persons or a member of a group of persons by reference to one of the protected grounds (also through the public dissemination of tracts, pictures or other material); (b) the public condonement, denial or gross trivialization of genocide, crimes against humanity and war crimes committed against groups of persons by reference to one of the protected grounds; and (c) the public condonement, denial or gross trivialization of the Holocaust and of Nazi crimes.

Framework Decision 2008/913/JHA thus represents an exception to the general absence of competence of the European Union in the context of criminal law. Such an exception was justified based on art. 29 of the pre-Lisbon Treaty on European Union (TEU). In its current text the provision, which was subsequently transposed within art. 67(3) of the Treaty on the Functioning of the European Union (TFEU), expressly reads:

> The Union shall endeavour to ensure a high level of security through measures to prevent and combat crime, racism and xenophobia, and through measures for coordination and cooperation between police and judicial authorities and other competent authorities, as well as through the mutual recognition of judgments in criminal matters and, if necessary, through the approximation of criminal laws.

The express reference to the EU's efforts to jointly fight against "racism and xenophobia" justifies the adoption of a Framework Decision harmonizing Member States' laws on racist and xenophobic crimes and hate speech. However, it is evident that the TFEU provision does not allow for further harmonization of criminal law, most notably with respect to hate crimes and hate speech based on different grounds of discrimination (e.g., sex, gender, gender identity, sexual orientation, disability, etc.).

With an awareness that hate speech can deter discriminated and vulnerable categories from expressing their opinions and beliefs, and therefore from actively participating on an equal footing in the democratic process, the European Commission anticipated in its Communication on a European Democracy Action Plan (EDAP, COMM/2020/790) the will to present an amendment to art. 83(1) TFEU. This provision allows EU institutions to "establish minimum rules concerning the definition of criminal offences and sanctions in the areas of particularly serious crime with a cross-border dimension." In December 2021, through its Communication on "a more inclusive and protective Europe" (COMM/2021/777), the Commission followed up on this suggestion and presented a proposal for amending the provision to include hate speech and hate crime in the list of so-called EU crimes. The proposal, in particular, highlights the importance of the amendment in the context of the digital age, where online hate speech has increasingly become a cross-border issue.

In the meantime, the EU also adopted a self-regulatory instrument, that is, the 2016 Code of Conduct for Countering Illegal Hate Speech Online. The text of the Code of Conduct was drafted jointly by the Commission together with a number of information technology (IT) companies (including Facebook, Microsoft, Twitter and YouTube). It refers to art. 1(1)(a) of Framework Decision 2008/913/JHA for the purposes of defining what hate speech is (i.e., public incitement to violence or hatred directed against a group of persons or a member of such a group defined by reference to race, color, religion, descent or national or ethnic origin). Other grounds of discrimination thus seem to fall outside its scope of action. The Code of Conduct states that IT companies recognize that they share "a collective responsibility and pride in promoting and facilitating freedom of expression throughout the online world" and are thus determined to counter illegal hate speech, perceived as a threat to those who speak out for freedom, tolerance and non-discrimination and as having a chilling effect on democratic discourse. The main goal is to offer an efficient guideline to IT companies and to provide them with an instrument to share best practices.

To this purpose, these actors have agreed with the EU Commission a set of public commitments, aiming not only at ensuring effective review mechanisms to assess whether user-generated content amounts to illegal hate speech but also at clarifying and warning users about the contrariety of hate speech to the law and to their guidelines and conditions. IT companies also committed to cooperate among themselves and with the Member States to support counter-speech and other tools necessary for the fight against hate speech. From this perspective, the Code of Conduct also considers particularly relevant the role of civil society organizations in order to achieve successful results: for instance, these organizations may act as "trusted reporters" of unlawful content posted online. Furthermore, IT companies and the European Commission agreed to assess the public commitments of the Code of Conduct, and the impact of the Code itself, on a regular basis, as well as to "further discuss how to promote transparency and encourage counter and alternative narratives."

The Code of Conduct thus endorses, ideally, a model of voluntary compliance, consistent with an approach based on self-regulation of the platforms involved. Such an approach is founded on the perspective that state authorities should not intervene to impose on private IT companies the pursuit of countering online hate speech. Digital platforms should be moved to take action in such a direction not under the threat of legal sanction, but for positive reasons. Nonetheless, vis-à-vis the imminent adoption of the Digital Services Act (DSA) (which has been discussed in Chapter 5) and the proposal to amend art. 83(1) TFEU to include hate speech among the so-called EU crimes, it appears that the EU institutions are gradually moving from a self-regulatory perspective to a gradually co-regulatory (if not regulatory) one.

According to the Council's Assessment for the period 2016–2019, the Code of Conduct had helped achieve quick progress in hate speech moderation, with an increase in the swift review (in 2016, the content reviewed by IT companies within twenty-four hours amounted to 40 percent; the figure had increased to 89 percent by 2019) and removal of hate speech content (in 2016, of the content reviewed by IT companies, only 28 percent of it had been removed; in 2019, it was 72 percent), and in doing so it had contributed to the increase in trust between IT companies, civil society organizations and Member States' authorities. In 2020, 90 percent of hate speech notifications had been assessed within twenty-four hours and 71 percent had led to content removal; in 2021, however, the figures dropped, with 81 percent of content being reviewed within twenty-four hours and an average removal rate of 62.5 percent.
It has been noted, however, that data supplied by these documents are in many ways ambiguous, especially because of the gaps in information concerning the methodology employed and the types of content flagged as hate speech. Moreover, the Commission adopted speed and rate removal as the only indicators of the success of the Code of Conduct; little information is actually given about the quality of the review. The increase in the removal rate may also imply an increase in accidental removal of content that is not actually hate speech.

6.2.4 Tackling terrorist content in the EU: The TERREG Regulation

An issue that is inherently different but strictly connected to the phenomena of disinformation and hate speech is that of online terrorist content. The present subsection will thus give a brief outline of the measures recently adopted by the European Union within this field, looking especially at Regulation (EU) 2021/784 "on preventing the dissemination of terrorist content online" (TERREG, or TCO, Regulation). As suggested by the title, the goal of the regulation is to minimize the dissemination of "terrorist content," that is, content that (a) incites the commission of terrorist offences, "where such material, directly or indirectly, such as by the glorification of terrorist acts, advocates the commission of terrorist offences, thereby causing a danger that one or more such offences may be committed"; or (b) solicits a person or a group of persons to commit or contribute to the commission of a terrorist offence (art. 1(7)).

To this purpose, the notion of "terrorist offences" that can be the object of the incitement or solicitation is given by art. 3, letters (a) to (i) of Directive (EU) 2017/541 "on combating terrorism." These include the following intentional acts, committed with the aim of (a) seriously intimidating a population; (b) unduly compelling a government or an international organization to perform or abstain from performing any act;

or (c) seriously destabilizing or destroying the fundamental political, constitutional, economic or social structures of a country or an international organization:

(a) attacks upon a person's life which may cause death;
(b) attacks upon the physical integrity of a person;
(c) kidnapping or hostage-taking;
(d) causing extensive destruction to a government or public facility, a transport system, an infrastructure facility, including an information system, a fixed platform located on the continental shelf, a public place or private property likely to endanger human life or result in major economic loss;
(e) seizure of aircraft, ships or other means of public or goods transport;
(f) manufacture, possession, acquisition, transport, supply or use of explosives or weapons, including chemical, biological, radiological or nuclear weapons, as well as research into, and development of, chemical, biological, radiological or nuclear weapons;
(g) release of dangerous substances, or causing fires, floods or explosions, the effect of which is to endanger human life;
(h) interfering with or disrupting the supply of water, power or any other fundamental natural resource, the effect of which is to endanger human life;
(i) illegal system interference, as referred to in art. 4 of Directive 2013/40/EU of the European Parliament and of the Council in cases where art. 9(3) or point (b) or (c) of art. 9(4) of that Directive applies, and illegal data interference, as referred to in art. 5 of that Directive in cases where point (c) of art. 9(4) of that Directive applies.

Pursuant to art. 3, Member States shall have the power to issue a removal order requiring hosting providers to remove terrorist content or to disable access to terrorist content: in doing so, the requesting authority shall give the provider all necessary information concerning the content to be removed or the access to which must be disabled. In particular, the URL should be explicitly provided. Hosting service providers receiving such an order will have to comply as soon as possible and, in any event, within one hour. In case a provider cannot comply, it shall inform the Member State's relevant authority.

Competent authorities of the Member States may decide that a hosting service provider is "exposed to terrorist content" (art. 5). Such a decision, which must be notified to the provider to become effective, should be based on objective factors, such as the fact that the intermediary has received at least two final removal orders in the last twelve months. Following such a decision, the provider will have to comply with a range of requirements, aimed at fostering preventive action against the dissemination of terrorist content. Most notably, providers that are "exposed to terrorist content" must include within their terms and conditions, and apply consistently, specific provisions addressing the dissemination of terrorist content to the public. Moreover, they will have to take "specific measures" against such a phenomenon.

For instance, providers exposed to terrorist content should equip themselves with the appropriate technical and human resources to expeditiously moderate terrorist content online. They should also develop easily accessible and user-friendly mechanisms for people to report or flag the existence of unlawful terroristic content. In doing so, the regulation requires that special consideration is given to fundamental rights and freedoms, such as freedom of expression and information, respect for private life and protection of personal data, as well as non-discrimination. The implementation of these specific measures will have to be reported to the Member State's competent authorities, who may issue a decision to order the application of further measures.

Member States' authorities may be requested by a provider to revoke its classification as being "exposed to terrorist content": in this case, the authority shall adopt a reasoned decision.

In order to foster the safeguarding of individuals' fundamental rights vis-à-vis providers, arts. 7 and 8 provide for transparency obligations, such as the publication of yearly reports. Moreover, competent authorities themselves have to publish yearly reports on the subject. Arts. 9 and 10 provide respectively for the establishment of remedies and of internal complaint mechanisms. Finally, providers who fail to comply with the obligations set forth by the regulation may be subject to pecuniary penalties pursuant to art. 18.

6.3 Online disinformation

The phenomenon of so-called fake news is not a new one. Throughout history, various famous hoaxes have taken place around the world. In 1835, six articles were published in the New York newspaper *The Sun* describing the discovery of life on the moon (the so-called Great Moon Hoax); on April Fool's Day in 1957, the BBC broadcast video footage showing the harvesting of spaghetti from spaghetti trees growing in Italy (the so-called Spaghetti-tree Hoax). In both cases, the hoaxes were able to deceive, at least in the beginning, a great part of the population. Although such episodes are little more than innocuous (and to a certain extent colorful) pranks, the ability of falsehood to spread across a population may in some cases lead to more serious issues. False information may, for instance, have a serious impact on political elections and, therefore, on a democratic society as a whole; it could, moreover, be used as a means to encourage acts of violence or to support hate speech discourses.

Falsehood per se should not be prohibited: a government-imposed ban on false content would imply, de facto, the imposition of state-sponsored truth. Giving the state the power to be the only judge of truth would be contrary not only to the free marketplace of ideas doctrine of the United States but also to the basic tenets of European constitutional principles. However, as has been argued by scholarship, the enunciation and dissemination of falsehood could amount to a performative action, meaning that, in some cases, lying in a specific manner or context could entail the commission of a prohibited conduct. For example, lying in the context of a judicial proceeding generally constitutes perjury.

In the context of the digital age, legislative concerns about online disinformation have become more and more pressing within many jurisdictions. The European Union itself, as will be seen below, has taken steps to fight the spread of "information disorder" across the Internet. Vis-à-vis the new communication media offered by the Internet, virtually every user is able to become an editor and to spread and share false information. As a result, if one considers the phenomenon from an aggregate perspective, the potential for harm to constitutional principles and values has become greater and greater in the contemporary age. Most notably, the use of Cambridge Analytica data to spread "fake news" across social media during the 2016 US presidential election and the Brexit referendum vote has shown how falsehood may have become increasingly dangerous and "performative" when applied in greater scale to the Internet.

6.3.1 Defining disinformation

An essential point that must be discussed when debating legal action against online disinformation concerns the identification of what "disinformation" actually means. Falsity on the Internet can take many forms and aspects, some of which may be benign and some of which may be particularly harmful for society.

A popular classification that has been proposed distinguishes seven levels of false content, or information disorder:

a. Satire or parody: artistic forms where the intention to cause harm is generally absent but that are potentially capable of fooling the audience;
b. False connection: refers to situations where headlines, visuals or captions do not support the content (e.g., clickbait newspaper title);
c. Misleading content: refers to the misleading use of information to frame an issue or an individual;
d. False context: genuine content is shared together with false contextual information;
e. Imposter content: consists of the impersonation of genuine sources (e.g., forging the logo of a trustworthy newspaper to make fake news appear more reliable);
f. Manipulated content: refers to situations where genuine information or imagery is manipulated to deceive the public;
g. Fabricated content: the content is completely false and generally made to deceive and do some kind of harm.

The legal response that may be adopted varies depending on the type of false content addressed. Thus, for instance, satire and parody represent essential examples of freedom of expression that should be protected within a democratic society: the ECtHR has in many cases underscored the importance of protecting such artistic forms, which can serve as effective tools for participation in public and political discourse. Conversely, fabricated content may pose some threat and could eventually lead to harmful consequences; states may thus decide to implement legal strategies to fight the spread of this type of content.

Moreover, the activity of disseminating false information and information disorder can have different motivations. In some cases, false or misleading information is spread by individuals who are unaware of its nature, in which case it is "misinformation." In other cases, the dissemination of false information or "fake news" is intentional and designed to cause harm, in which case it is "disinformation." Disinformation can be produced to achieve various results, such as making money, influencing domestic or external politics, or causing trouble just for the sake of it. Disinformation content is often picked up and additionally spread by individuals who are unaware of its falsehood: in this sense, with respect to the same content, a person may be producing disinformation while another person may simply be spreading misinformation. A third category may also be identified, consisting of "malinformation": in this case, however, the information per se is genuine but, as in the case of disinformation, it is disseminated with the specific purpose of harming (e.g., when Russian agents hacked into the emails from the Democratic National Committee to attack Hillary Clinton's presidential campaign).

The extraordinary spectrum of instances and examples of falsehood on the Internet has led the EU's High-Level Group on fake news and online disinformation (HLEG) to reject the popular and vernacular notion of "fake news," which it considers to be fuzzy and overreaching. Moreover, the term "fake news" has been appropriated by some politicians and supporters, who have used it to dismiss information they consider disagreeable; as such, the term has become misleading and potentially dangerous itself. Rather, the choice has been to focus on the notion of disinformation, which actually constitutes a true threat to democracies when dealing with information disorders. As stressed by the HLEG:

> Current debates about "fake news" encompass a spectrum of information types. This includes relatively low-risk forms such as honest mistakes made by reporters, partisan political discourse, and the use of click bait headlines, to high-risk forms such as for instance foreign states or domestic groups that would try to undermine the political process in European Member States and the European Union … In this report, we focus specifically on problems associated with disinformation. We define it as false, inaccurate, or misleading information designed, presented and promoted to intentionally cause public harm or for profit. The risk of harm includes threats to democratic political processes and values, which can specifically target a variety of sectors, such as health, science, education, finance and more. It is driven by the production and promotion of disinformation for economic gains or for political or ideological goals, but can be exacerbated by how different audiences and communities receive, engage, and amplify disinformation. Misinformation, defined as misleading or inaccurate information shared by people who do not recognize it as such, is not our focus.

The decision to focus on disinformation, that is, only on those types of false information that are disseminated with the specific goal of causing harm, is sensible from a freedom of expression standpoint, in that it respects the principle of proportionality that is inherently necessary for the purposes of regulating speech.

As highlighted many times throughout the previous chapters (see, notably, Chapter 4), both the ECHR and the CFREU allow for the imposition of restrictions and limitations on freedom of expression but only when this is "necessary in a democratic society." Therefore, the regulation of disinformation inherently requires an inquiry of at least three parameters: the content's factual truth; the intent and strategic goals associated with the content's generation and initial sharing; and the harm caused by the content's release into the public sphere.

6.3.2 EU policies against disinformation

The challenge of tackling disinformation campaigns has been firstly framed in recent years as a question of foreign policy. The concern first emerged on the EU agenda at a European Council meeting in March 2015, where the High Representative was invited to design an action plan to address ongoing Russian disinformation campaigns. This call ultimately resulted in the establishment of the East Strategic Communication Task Force (East STRATCOM) of the European External Action Service. The duties of the Task Force included supporting a close dialogue with EU neighboring countries, strengthening the media environment in the Eastern Partnership region, reporting on and exposing disinformation trends and narratives, and raising awareness on disinformation coming from Russia. From a foreign policy perspective, the creation of a "Counter-Disinformation Coalition" was also recommended, composed of an informal group of "like-minded governments and non-governmental groups."

The European Union, however, took further action at a later stage, when evidence of the influence of disinformation practices on democratic discourse and processes became widespread in many Western countries. Upon mandate by the European Parliament, the European Commission launched a number of actions "to verify the possibility of legislative intervention to limit the dissemination and spreading of fake content." Finally, in April 2018, the Commission published its Communication on Tackling Disinformation (COM/2018/236), promoting a "European approach" to tackle the phenomenon, with a clear eye set on the then upcoming European elections of May 2019. The Commission's Communication, among other sources, drew important insights from the findings of the HLEG, set up in January 2018 to develop an EU strategy and composed of forty experts representing social media platforms, media organizations, academia, journalists and civil society organizations. Consistently with the European constitutional framework, the HLEG's report assumed that any intervention to fight disinformation should not impair or interfere with the fundamental rights and freedoms at stake, including most notably freedom of expression and freedom of the (pluralistic) press. The HLEG also adopted a definition of the term "disinformation," deemed preferable to the fuzzier and misleading expression "fake news": most notably, "disinformation" identifies "false, inaccurate, or misleading information designed, presented and promoted to intentionally cause public harm or for profit."

Accordingly, the response to the multifaceted nature of disinformation practices was the design of a "multidimensional approach" in order to adequately frame the complexity of the phenomenon, as well as to consider the diverse range of stakeholders involved. Combining both short-term and long-term solutions, recommendations for the following actions were promoted:

> (1) a legal and regulatory effort to enhance the transparency of online news, including on data practices; (2) an educational effort to promote digital media literacy; (3) a technical effort to develop tools that empower readers and journalists and allow them to engage in positive public discourse; (4) a cultural effort to preserve and enhance the diversity and

sustainability of the European news media ecosystem; and finally (5) an effort to keep promoting research on and monitoring of disinformation in Europe.

Subsequently, in December 2018, the EU Action Plan against Disinformation (JOIN/2018/36) was issued, following the European Council's call to "protect the Union's democratic systems and combat disinformation, including in the context of the upcoming European elections" and building on existing initiatives. The Action Plan laid down actions to be taken by the Commission and the High Representative, assisted by the European External Action Service and in cooperation with Member States and the European Parliament. The Plan recognizes the need to combat disinformation in order to preserve the democratic process and maintain citizens' trust in institutions, setting out a strand of actions coordinating EU institutions and the Member States. Namely, the Action Plan provides for a coordinated response to disinformation grounded upon four pillars:

(i) improving the capabilities of Union institutions to detect, analyse and expose disinformation; (ii) strengthening coordinated and joint responses to disinformation; (iii) mobilising private sector to tackle disinformation; (iv) raising awareness and improving societal resilience.

In December 2020, also following the outbreak of the COVID-19 pandemic, the Commission also published the EDAP Communication, confirming its previous position and the need to enhance European efforts to fight the phenomenon of disinformation. On the one hand, the Commission stated that it would work to improve EU and Member States' capacity to counter disinformation, while also introducing new obligations and fostering accountability for online platforms and empowering citizens to make more informed decisions.

In parallel to the abovementioned initiatives, industry efforts, also supported by the European Commission, resulted in the signing of a Code of Practice on Disinformation in October 2018 by major online platforms, who committed on a voluntary basis to a set of standards to counter disinformation practices in different fields of action. The Code of Practice is a short and composite instrument, introduced by a Preamble echoing the alignment with the Communication on Tackling Disinformation, and composed of a statement of purpose and fifteen commitments that may be summarized in the following five main fields: (a) scrutiny of the placement of advertising (to demonetize online purveyors of disinformation); (b) auditing of political advertising and issue-based advertising (with a view to making sure that political adverts are clearly identified by the users); (c) integrity of services (aimed at identifying and closing fake accounts and using appropriate mechanisms to signal bot-driven interactions); (d) empowering consumers (aimed at diluting the visibility of disinformation by improving the findability of trustworthy content and by making it easier for users to discover and access different news sources representing alternative viewpoints); and (e) empowering the research community (aimed at granting researchers access to platforms' data that are necessary to continuously monitor online disinformation).

Despite the Commission's initial positive endorsement of the Code of Practice in its follow-up report to the Communication on Disinformation, the subsequent baseline report on the implementation of the Code submitted by the signatories highlighted its unsatisfactory results. Once more, in the January 2019 intermediate targeted monitoring reports covering Google, Facebook and Twitter, the Commission expressed its concerns about the platforms' failure to take their commitments seriously. Generally, the Commission signaled little progress and a lack of detailed assessments by the platforms specifically in the areas of scrutiny of ad placements, political and issue-based advertising, and integrity of their services.

More recently, the 2020 assessment of the Code of Practice (SWD/2020/180) found that some steps forward had indeed been taken. However, in the wake of the COVID-19 pandemic and the "infodemic" that accompanied it, the assessment also concluded:

> However, this overall assessment highlights that, in order to ensure a complete and consistent application across platforms and Member States, the Code should be further improved in several areas by providing commonly-shared definitions, clearer procedures, more precise commitments as well as transparent key performance indicators and appropriate monitoring, all taking into account applicable regulatory frameworks. Further efforts should also be made to broaden the participation to other relevant stakeholders, in particular from the advertising sector.

As a result, in May 2021 the Commission presented guidance to strengthen the Code of Practice on Disinformation (COM/2021/262), following which an Assembly was called to review the 2018 document with the purpose of transforming it into a stronger instrument. The Strengthened Code of Practice on Disinformation resulted from a process of co-regulation and it was released in June 2022. Signatories will have six months to implement the commitments and measures they have signed up to. A fundamental point of the Strengthened Code is that it will aim to become a code of conduct within the scope of the DSA (see Chapter 5) with a view to mitigating the risks stemming from disinformation for very large online platforms. As to its content, the new Code contains commitments to:

a. Broaden participation to include new actors beyond the big platforms;
b. Cut financial incentives for spreading disinformation by ensuring that purveyors of disinformation do not benefit from advertising revenues;
c. Cover new manipulative behaviors such as fake accounts, bots or malicious deep fakes;
d. Empower users with better tools to recognize, understand and flag disinformation;
e. Expand fact-checking in all EU countries and all its languages, while making sure fact-checkers are fairly rewarded for their work;
f. Ensure transparent political advertising by allowing users to easily recognize political ads thanks to better labeling and information on sponsors, spend and display period;

g. Better support researchers by giving them better access to platforms' data;
h. Evaluate its own impact through a strong monitoring framework and regular reporting from platforms on how they are implementing their commitments;
i. Set up a Transparency Centre and Task Force for an easy and transparent overview of the implementation of the Code, keeping it future-proof and fit for purpose.

6.4 A comparative overview of domestic legislations

The issues of hate speech and disinformation have been variously addressed by numerous national jurisdictions that are aware of the increasing relevance of such phenomena in the context of the contemporary digital age. The present section addresses the legal developments in some chosen European and extra-European jurisdictions. In particular, the first three subsections deal with the legal experiences of Germany, France and Italy, all of which have addressed (or tried to address) these issues through different means and perspectives, notwithstanding membership of the European Union. The last subsection focuses on legislative measures adopted by the Russian Federation, by Singapore and by Malaysia.

6.4.1 Germany

In June 2017 the German Bundestag passed the German Network Enforcement Act (NetzDG), which has been fully operational since January 2018, against the backdrop of the intention to counter both hate speech and "fake news," which were increasingly surfacing in public discourse in the preceding years. Four years later, in June 2021, the text was amended; among other things, the amendment extended the scope of action of the NetzDG, initially limited to social networks, to video-sharing platforms as well, as a means to comply with the new requirements set by Directive (EU) 2018/1808 (see Chapter 8). As far as hate speech and disinformation regulation is concerned, the relevant part of the Act is represented by art. 1, which, as of June 2021, is composed of fourteen sections.

Section 1 defines social networks as profit-oriented providers of telecommunication services that operate platforms designed to allow their users to share or make accessible to the public any type of content. Pursuant to Section 2(1), a social network that has more than two million registered users in Germany and receives more than one hundred notices of illegal content in a calendar year is placed under an obligation to draw up six-monthly transparency reports, which must be public, easily identifiable, directly accessible and constantly available, on the management of such notices. Section 2(2) indicates the content that such transparency must include. Section 3 provides that social networks must establish a procedure to handle complaints regarding illegal content, which must be effective and transparent. This may represent the most important part of the law.

Pursuant to art. 1, section 3, of the NetzDG, the procedure must ensure that the providers of social networks:

1. Take immediate note of the complaint and check whether the content reported in the complaint is unlawful and subject to removal or whether access to the content must be blocked;
2. Remove or block access to content that is manifestly unlawful within twenty-four hours of receiving the complaint; this term does not apply if the social network has reached an agreement with the competent law enforcement authority on a longer period for deleting or blocking any manifestly unlawful content;
3. Remove or block access to all unlawful content immediately, this generally being within seven days of receiving the complaint; the seven-day time limit may be exceeded if: (a) the decision regarding the unlawfulness of the content is dependent on the falsity of a factual allegation or is clearly dependent on other factual circumstances (in such cases, the social network can give the user an opportunity to respond to the complaint before the decision is rendered; or (b) the social network refers the decision regarding unlawfulness to a recognized self-regulation institution within seven days of receiving the complaint and agrees to accept the decision of that institution;
4. In the case of removal, retain the content as evidence and store it for this purpose within the scope of Directives 2000/31/EC and 2010/13/EU for a period of ten weeks;
5. Immediately notify the person submitting the complaint and the user about any decision, while also providing them with reasons for its decision.

The NetzDG also requires social network providers to name a person authorized to receive complaints in Germany and indicate a contact for law enforcement (section 5). At the same time, the Act sets hefty fines in case of systematic failure of the complaints management procedure, even if the offense is not committed in Germany, of up to five million euros, which may amount to up to fifty million euros in reference to section 2(1).

The amendment of June 2021, apart from extending the scope of application of the Act to video-sharing platforms (defined in a manner consistent with the amended Audiovisual Media Services Directive, on which see Chapter 8), introduced the obligation for social network providers to establish an appeals procedure (section 3b) and introduced the possibility to resort to out-of-court bodies for arbitration. Moreover, the Federal Office of Justice has been vested with additional supervision powers (section 4a).

It is important to note that the Act does not define "disinformation" nor "hate speech," although the fight against such phenomena was its main pillar. The NetzDG, rather than introduce new legal categories, refers to twenty-one already existing provisions contained within the German Criminal Code, which are thus made applicable to the context of social networks and video-sharing platforms. These provisions include, among others, "incitement to hatred"; "dissemination of depictions of violence"; "forming terrorist organisations"; "distribution of child pornography"; "insult" and "defamation"; "defamation of religions, religious and ideological associations in a manner that is capable of disturbing the public peace"; "violation of intimate privacy by making photographs"; and "threatening the commission of a felony." Social networks and video-sharing providers are thus required to remove content that amounts to such criminal conduct.

The NetzDG has been considered a controversial measure for a range of reasons, including its alleged incompatibility with the framework established by the e-Commerce Directive and the foreseen impact on fundamental rights, most notably freedom of expression.
While, as shown throughout Chapter 5, the e-Commerce Directive establishes a shield from liability for Internet intermediaries when they react "expeditiously" upon obtaining knowledge or awareness of illegal activity on their platform, it is unclear whether the Directive allows for Member States to specify the terms of this "expeditious" time frame. In this sense, the NetzDG may be perceived as not being consistent with the EU law's goal of cross-border harmonization. The reference to swift removal (within twenty-four hours) of "manifestly illegal" content raises concerns with regard to the risk of over-removal of content, especially because the context-sensitive evaluation of whether or not to remove a specific item is left to business-driven private parties. Furthermore, the longer term of seven days for all other content may lead to overenforcement, since it is evident that the assessment of its illegal character may not be easy. The UN Special Rapporteur on freedom of opinion and expression also raised a number of concerns regarding the NetzDG's compliance with art. 19 of the ICCPR.

With respect to disinformation, the NetzDG is not expected to significantly impact state-sponsored disinformation campaigns. Contrary to what has happened in other countries, the effects of disinformation and "fake news" coming from foreign states appear to be mitigated by the high level of trust in public media.

6.4.2 Italy

Italy made two attempts to legislate disinformation practices. The first proposal, the so-called DDL Gambaro ("Provisions to prevent the manipulation of online information, to ensure transparency on the web and to encourage media literacy") was presented in February 2017 and followed Resolution 2143 (2017) of the Parliamentary Assembly of the Council of Europe, titled "Online media and journalism: challenges and accountability," stating:

> The line between what could be considered a legitimate expression of personal views in an attempt to persuade readers and disinformation or manipulation is frequently crossed. The Assembly notes with concern the number of online media campaigns designed to misguide sectors of the public through intentionally biased or false information, hate campaigns against individuals and also personal attacks, often in a political context, with the objective of harming democratic political processes.

Following the many critiques it received, the DDL Gambaro was never discussed in Parliament. A second draft law, the DDL Zanda-Filippin ("General rules on social networks and to combat the dissemination of illegal content and fake news on the Internet"), was presented a few months later and relied significantly on the model of the recently adopted German NetzDG. However, the DDL Zanda-Filippin was also short-lived and never made it to parliamentary debate.

Additionally, at the beginning of 2018, the then Ministry of Interior, together with the Chief of Police, launched the operational protocol for the "Fight Against the Diffusion of Fake News through the Web" with an eye especially on facing that year's upcoming national elections. This tool, originally available on the Postal Police's website (a unit of the Italian State Police investigating cybercrime), denominated the "red button," was intended to allow citizens to directly report false content. This instrument, however, was also short-lived: the red button alert system was unavailable shortly after its launch.

Later actions in this field have proven to be more cautious and responsible. Regardless of the failure of legislative interventions, in the wake of much alarm following allegations of undue influence on the constitutional referendum of December 2016 and concerns for the then upcoming national and European elections, the Italian independent administrative authority responsible for the communications sector, AGCOM, took on a key role. In 2017, AGCOM undertook a range of studies with a view to updating its traditional policies on media and communications. A technical working group to safeguard "pluralism and fairness of information on digital platforms" was established to encourage and promote self-regulation of online platforms and the exchange of good practices, with its first technical report covering disinformation strategies and the chain of fake content. The increased awareness is demonstrated by the range of studies launched in the fields of disinformation, online news consumption, their application to the specific electoral context, as well as the publication of monthly reviews on online disinformation patterns. Following the approach of the 2018 electoral period, a shift toward an increasingly comprehensive and integrated approach is noticeable, supported by the choice to draw under the umbrella of AGCOM's competence the diverse aspects linking mass communications and technology.

AGCOM also took action with respect to the phenomenon of online hate speech by issuing in 2019 a "Regulation on respect for human dignity and the principle of non-discrimination in relation to hate speech" (Resolution 157/19/CONS). Pursuant to art. 4 of the Regulation, providers of audiovisual and radio video services that are subject to the jurisdiction of Italy are called on to ensure respect for human dignity and the principle of non-discrimination and must oppose all forms of instigation to violence and hatred toward groups of people or members of such groups defined with reference to sex, racial or ethnic origin, religion, disability, age, sexual orientation, gender identity and any other characteristic or personal situation. In this respect, the Authority promotes, coordinates and directs the development of codes of conduct by identifying forms of co-regulation, supervision and verification of activities of providers of audiovisual media services or video-sharing platforms (art. 9). With regard to video-sharing and very large online search engines (VLOSEs) platforms, the Regulation also requires that they submit to AGCOM a trimestral report on the monitoring carried out for the identification of hate content, including the procedures and verification systems they have put in place (art. 9(4)).

In March 2021, Italian Deputy Laura Boldrini, who during her presidency at the Chamber of Deputies had already presided over the "Jo Cox" Commission on phenomena related to hate, intolerance, xenophobia and racism, presented a draft law aimed at introducing "new measures for preventing and fighting the dissemination of manifestations of hate through the Internet" (DDL Boldrini). Apart from expanding the scope of action of arts. 604-*bis* and 604-*ter* of the Italian Criminal Code, with a view to extending the criminal provisions on hate speech and hate crimes to the grounds of sex, gender, sexual orientation, identity gender and disability (in a manner similar to the well-known DDL Zan), the DDL Boldrini aims at introducing a duty for Internet service providers to establish a notice-and-action procedure, as well as a duty, for providers receiving more than one hundred notifications each year, to produce six-monthly reports concerning their moderation activities. The Italian Data Protection Authority, moreover, would be vested with new powers to sanction providers not complying with such duties. Further measures foreseen by the DDL Boldrini include the right, also for minors, to require the shadowing, removal or blocking of data about or images of them from the Internet, as well as the introduction of educational curricula in schools concerning the phenomenon of online hatred and violence and aiming at fostering more responsible use of the Internet. However, the DDL Boldrini has not yet been discussed in Parliament, nor has it yet been calendarized for discussion.

6.4.3 France

Against the background of serious concerns about disinformation-driven meddling in the presidential elections of 2017, in March 2018 a proposition to combat the manipulation of information was introduced in the French National Assembly. The two proposals, an ordinary and a framework law (*loi organique*), met significant opposition in the French Parliament, where, regardless of the accelerated procedure triggered by the government, they faced two successive failures in the Senate. The Acts were finally approved in November 2018 and promulgated after a preliminary constitutionality review.

The ultimate goal of the ordinary law "on information manipulation" (Loi No. 2018-1202 *relative à la lutte contre la manipulation de l'information*) was to address those attempts at deliberate information manipulation by combating the massive and rapid dissemination of false news via digital tools (including the spread pipes of social networks and media under the influence of a foreign state). The law was divided into several parts that respectively set provisions imposing transparency duties on platforms; specify the pand VLOSEs owers of the French public audiovisual regulatory authority (i.e., the Authorité de regulation de la communication audiovisuelle et numérique (ARCOM), formed at the beginning of 2022 from the merger of the Conseil supérieur de l'audiovisuel (CSA) with the Haute Autorité pour la diffusion des œuvres et la protection des droits sur l'Internet (HADOPI)); impose Arts. of cooperation on platforms; and promote media literacy in the educational framework. A crucial part of the law deals with the electoral period, designated as three months prior to an election, with a view to protecting the fairness of elections and the integrity of votes.

With respect to the electoral period, the law establishes, first of all, a transparency obligation on platforms to report sponsored content and publish the source and amount of the payments received.
Second, it establishes proceedings ("*action judiciaire en référée*") to end the dissemination of false information on online public communication services. In this short emergency proceeding, the judge will assess the falsehood grade of such news by looking at whether (a) it is obvious; (b) it is disseminated massively and artificially; and (c) it leads to the disturbance of public peace or of the integrity of an elec-

tion. Judicial authorities have the power to order the deletion of content within forty-eight hours from their reporting, requiring a judge's rapid decision on the truthfulness of the contested information and proof of the author's intent to manipulate public opinion.
Third, duties of transparency and cooperation are imposed on platforms, including an obligation to set measures to tackle false news and its spread. ARCOM is vested with the task of monitoring compliance with such duties; ARCOM may also prevent, suspend or interrupt the broadcasting of television services controlled by or under the influence of a foreign state and affecting the fundamental interests of the nation. Specifically, ARCOM can refuse the conclusion of an agreement for the purpose of broadcasting a radio or television service if the broadcasting of that service involves a "serious risk of violating human dignity, the freedom and property of others, the pluralistic nature of the expression of currents of thought and opinion, the protection of children and adolescents, the protection of public ords of national defence or the fundamental interests of the Nation, including the proper functioning of its institutions" and similarly where the dissemination of the service, by its very nature, would constitute a violation of the law.

Three questions ("*questions préalables*") were referred before the Conseil constitutionnel for a preliminary review of constitutionality (No. 2018-773). These questions mainly concerned the vagueness of the scope and increased powers conferred on the administrative authority, as well as on judges hearing the emergency procedure. The referring senators pointed to "the weaknesses inherent in texts drafted in a hurry, without prior assessment of and VLOSEs the real gaps or deficiencies in our current legislation and regulations" and to "the dangers of infringements of freedom of expression." In its decisions, the Conseil constitutionnel validated the two laws' conformity with the French Constitution, subject to a reservation of interpretation.

One issue concerned the definition of "false information" and the summary proceedings provided by art. 1, which were allegedly incompatible with freedom of expression, defense rights and the right to a fair trial. While the Conseil recognized the essential role that online public communication services play in participation in a democratic society and expression of ideas and opinions, it also admitted that they can cause "massive and coordinated manipulation because of their multiplicity and the particular ways in which their content is disseminated." According to the Conseil, the provision is strictly proportionate to the law's objective of guaranteeing a clear democratic debate and is respectful of the principle of the fairness of elections, due to the limited time frame in which such provisions apply (namely, the designated pre-election period). Nevertheless, the Conseil clarified that the definition of "false information" may only include information whose falsehood can be shown in an objective fashion and excludes opinions, parodies, partial inaccuracies and exaggerations. Moreover, both the misleading character and the consequences on the fairness of voting must be "manifest," and the judge hearing the case may only order the least invasive measures.

The second set of contested provisions concerned the powers granted to the CSA (today ARCOM), extended to the Internet. The Conseil concluded that the grounds for refusing an agreement are not imprecise but noted that the decisions of the CSA could always be challenged before the administrative judicial authorities, so as to ensure the right to an effective remedy. Nor did the Conseil deem the stricter control over media services subject to the control or influence of a foreign state to be contrary to the principle of equality before the law, since it admitted that certain media services may "indeed be the source of destabilisation attempts orchestrated by a foreign power."

The new law was met with criticism within the National Assembly as well as among commentators. Although the law was said to have no impact on journalistic activities, the Syndicate National des Journalistes, the first trade union organization representative of the journalistic profession, labeled it as "liberticide." Criticisms concerned aspects such as the necessity of the law; the broadness of its applicability, which could lead to judicial overload; and the conformity of cooperation duties with EU law (and especially with the prohibition of general monitoring obligations pursuant to art. 15 of the e-Commerce Directive). With respect to the last point, and with a view to ensuring the compatibility of the law with European standards, France attempted to delineate a general framework to regulate social networks, starting with the fight against online hate speech and relying on voluntary cooperation.

Under the new framework, judges are called on to make a very delicate assessment about the falsehood of news disseminated in the pre-electoral period. An example of this difficult application is demonstrated by the first decision applying the law delivered by the Paris Tribunal de grande instance in May 2019. The proceedings involved the request for removal of a tweet posted by the Minister of Interior, who allegedly described facts in an inaccurate way. Recalling the Conseil constitutionnel's interpretive indications, the Paris Tribunal held that the conditions set by it had not been met. First of all, the Minister's tweet, regardless of the tone, depicted an event that had indeed occurred. Second, the requirement of the "artificial or automated" nature of the false information disseminated, according to the explanatory memorandum of the draft law, only refers to content that is sponsored by third parties and that is promoted by means of automated tools. Third, the risk of altering the fairness of the upcoming European Parliament elections had not been met because, while recognizing that the language was exaggerated, the tweet had been immediately contested. Clarifications and an accurate description of the event was reported by several newspapers and the Minister himself recognized the inappropriateness of the terms used. The Paris Tribunal thus dismissed the action and the request to take down the tweet.

With respect to online hate speech, in June 2020 France approved a law "aiming at fighting hateful content on the Internet" (Loi No. 2020-766 *visant à lutter contre les contenus haineux sur internet*). The law, commonly known as Avia Law from the name of its proponent, originally provided for a range of new powers for national administrative authorities, including ARCOM, and modified many aspects of Loi No. 2004-575 *pour la confiance dans l'économie numerique* (implementing the e-Commerce Directive) in order to introduce new obligations and duties upon hosting providers. For instance, art. 1(2) of the law obliged hosting providers to remove content such as hate speech, incitement to terrorism, non-consensual pornography and child pornography within twenty-four hours, under the penalty of a criminal sanction. However, the French Conseil constitutionnel, vested by senators with a range of *questions préalables*, struck down most of the provisions and thus significantly watered down the Avia Law. The resulting text of the law mainly aims at simplifying the notification procedure for users to flag unlawful content such as hate speech; raising the penalty for hosting providers' failure to comply with an order by the administrative authority to remove content constituting incitement to terrorism, apology of terrorism or child pornography; the introduction within the Education Code (*Code de l'éducation*) of provisions concerning the education of children in schools with respect to the issue of online hate speech and online violence; and the introduction, within ARCOM, of an observatory concerning online hatred (*observatoire de la haine en ligne*).

6.4.4 The cases of Russia, Singapore and Malaysia

The previous subsections have addressed domestic legislation concerning disinformation and hate speech with respect to major EU jurisdictions, notably Germany, Italy and France. The present subsection will briefly address the initiatives of some case studies taken from non-EU countries, notably the Russian Federation, Singapore and Malaysia, and comment on emerging trends concerning the development of anti-disinformation and anti-hate speech policies across the globe.

In March 2019, the Russian Federation passed a new piece of legislation addressing "fake news" (but dealing with some forms of hate speech as well), consisting of two Acts. The first Act (Law No. 31-FZ) allows the Federal Service for Supervision of Communications, Information Technology and Mass Media (Roskomnadzor) to take action upon the lodging of claims, either by the State Prosecution *ex officio* or prompted by a third-party complaint, thus endowing the Roskomnadzor with broader legal grounds to tackle "fake news." Accordingly, where such "unreliable, socially significant information" is disseminated by an online mass media outlet, the editors are notified by the Roskomnadzor and ordered to remove the offending content; subsequently, restrictions on access to the website may be ordered if the editors fail to delete it. The second Act (Law No. 27-FZ) establishes a form of administrative liability for the distribution over the Internet of information expressing "any obscene form, insulting human dignity and public morals, clear contempt for society, the state, official state symbols of the Russian Federation, the Constitution of the Russian Federation or bodies of state authority of the Russian Federation", with the possibility that such content will be blocked. Of course, in case the dissemination qualifies as a criminal offence, criminal law shall apply.

A decision, which raised concerns within the media and journalistic community about the expansion and strengthening of propaganda in Russian media outlets, came under the eye of the EU General Court (Case T-262/15, *Kiselev v. Council*). The judgment concerned a request for annulment of restrictive measures that had been established by the Council of the EU concerning some acts of the Russian government aimed at destabilizing Ukraine. The applicant, who had been targeted with a decision of the Russian Collegium for Media Complaints (PCMC) for failing to comply with journalistic standards, and who was also the Head of the Russian Federal State news agency Rossiya Segodnya and a crucial figure in the government propaganda supporting the deployment of Russian forces in Ukraine, challenged the restrictive measures issued by the Council, claiming, inter alia, that his right to free speech had been violated.

However, the previous PCMC decision against the applicant had found that he had indeed engaged in propaganda during the broadcasting of a program, presenting the events during the Ukrainian crisis in a way described as "biased and contrary to the journalistic principles of social responsibility, harm minimization, truth, impartiality and justice, in order to manipulate Russian public opinion through disinformation techniques." The General Court thus confirmed the Council's entitlement to consider the activity as propaganda, justifying the adoption of restrictive measures against the applicant.

The main, almost unanimous, criticisms of the Russian legislation refer, firstly, to the vagueness and broadness of definitions and terms used to identify either "unreliable information" or the offenses against state symbols through which free speech may be limited. Along these lines, legislation formally addressing illegal or undesirable content on online platforms is used to further legitimize online censorship. Secondly, the law does not provide a stage for judicial review: decisions to block information lie principally with prosecutors, in such a way as to reverse the presumption of innocence. Thirdly, there is an evident lack of proportionality in the obligation to restrict access to the entire website in case of failure to delete the contested content. Fourthly, serious concerns have been raised with respect to the targeting of online media outlets and journalists' activity, which should play an essential role in any democratic society. Finally, the provision of high fines that may be awarded directly to individuals, more than just a deterrent, may cause "clear collateral spillover censorship," forcibly silencing speech.

Human rights concerns, in this respect, are even more significant in the wake of the Russian attack on Ukraine which took place on February 24, 2022. On the one hand, in March 2022 the Duma approved a series of amendments to the Russian "fake news legislation," including an increase in the penalties provided therein (e.g., those who spread information "with the artificial creation of evidence of the accusation … based on political, ideological, racial, national or religious hatred or enmity" may face up to ten years' imprisonment, or up to fifteen years if their actions lead to "grave consequences"). On the other hand, Russia's choice to leave the Council of Europe on March 16, 2022, implies that Russian citizens will no longer be able to rely on the ECtHR for the protection of their fundamental rights.

In Singapore, in April 2019 the government introduced an Act on "the protection from online falsehoods and manipulation," following the establishment and work of a dedicated Parliamentary Committee. In its final report, the Committee had concluded the necessity of a calibrated government intervention, providing legislative and non-legislative mutually reinforcing measures to tackle the serious phenomenon of deliberate online falsehoods.

The resulting Singaporean law thus aims at (a) preventing the communication of false statements in Singapore and enabling measures to be taken to counteract the effects of such communication; (b) suppressing the financing, promotion and other support of online locations that repeatedly communicate false statements of fact in Singapore; (c) enabling measures to be taken to detect, control and safeguard against coordinated inauthentic behavior and other misuses of online accounts and bots; and (d) enabling measures to be taken to enhance disclosure of information concerning paid content directed toward a political end. The eighty-one-page-long bill establishes a number of duties for Internet users and intermediaries, coupled with criminal penalties.

Section 7, in particular, prohibits the communication of false statements of fact, on penalty of a fine or of imprisonment for up to five years (penalties are doubled if the statements originate from inauthentic online accounts or bots). This conduct becomes criminally relevant to the extent that it is "likely" to cause detriment to certain public interests listed in section 7(1)(b). A statement qualifies as false, pursuant to section 2(2), "if it is false or misleading, whether wholly or in part, and whether on its own or in the context in which it appears." The following sections criminalize the conducts of "making or altering bots for communication of false statements" and of "providing services for communication of false statements": these actions are considered to be crimes independently of the fulfilment of public interests, although sanctions are doubled if a public interest is affected. Sections 10 and 11 endow Ministers with new powers, such as that of ordering "Directions" to individuals communicating false statements that put public interests at risk.
Part 4 is addressed to Internet intermediaries, who are subjected to the duty to communicate ministerial corrections to all end users in Singapore and, in some cases, to orders to block access to content. Part 5 provides the possibility for the Minister to "declare an online location," and label it as such, as a source from which three or more different false statements have originated, and which may be, under certain conditions, blocked or disabled.

The Singaporean bill has been widely criticized as "Orwellian" and as establishing a "Ministry of truth." The main criticism points to the significant chilling effects on freedom of expression and the fact that it may result in a "clean-up of the Internet." It is also noteworthy that the government itself cannot be held responsible for the same conduct that is regulated by the bill.

The main issues identified include the lack of clear definitions, such as that of what constitutes a "false statement of fact" under section 7; the allocation of powers in the process of determining the facts and the restricted availability of courts; and the proportionality of the consequences attached to the finding of falsehood. Nevertheless, some find that the Singaporean intervention is likely to meet the thresholds for speech restrictions under international law standards. Whereas Singapore is not a signatory to the ICCPR, the UN Special Rapporteur on freedom of expression, under the materially similar tone of the Universal Declaration of Human Rights, expressed concerns about the incompatibility with international human rights standards, as it "confers on select executive officials excessive authority to restrict, censor and punish online expression it designates as 'false', with limited opportunity for appeal." It awards virtually "unfettered discretion" to Ministers to qualify and restrict speech they disagree with as "false statements of fact," based on an overly broad definition of falsehood. Further concerns address the lack of independent review of the Minister's assessments, the possible shutdown of platforms and websites that contribute to democratic dialogue, and deterrence from seeking judicial review against a Minister before the High Court. The Singaporean government's response to the UN Special Rapporteur essentially claims that the criticisms are based on a misconception of the bill.

In 2018, Malaysia passed the Anti-Fake News Bill, which entered into force in April 2018. The law was drafted amid the exposure of a corruption scandal concerning the then Malaysian prime minister and was allegedly intended to shield him from press coverage of the scandal. After the elections determined a governmental change, a Repeal Bill, approved in August 2018, was promoted by the Malaysian House of Representatives but was later rejected by the Senate. Nevertheless, according to the Federal Constitution of Malaysia, the Senate would not be able to stop the bill a second time if it were to be re-tabled and reapproved: this happened in October 2019.

The Anti-Fake News Bill criminalized the acts of publishing, printing, distributing, circulating or disseminating any fake news or publication containing fake news; the provision of financial assistance used to commit or facilitate the commission of such offenses; as well as any form of abetting. Penalties included fines or imprisonment for up to ten years, or both. Section 2 of the bill defined "fake news" as including "any news, information, data and reports, which is or are wholly or partly false, whether in the form of features, visuals or audio recordings or in any other form capable of suggesting words or ideas." Furthermore, the bill established a duty to remove any publication containing fake news, and the right to a judicial remedy to any affected person. The addressee of a removal order could petition the court to have the order set aside, but only in those cases where the government did not consider the publication to be "prejudicial or likely to be prejudicial to public order or national security."
Additionally, it is noteworthy that the territorial scope of application of the bill was not limited to Malaysia but intercepted any fake news concerning Malaysia or a Malaysian citizen.

On March 11, 2021, the government of Malaysia issued the Emergency (Essential Powers) (No. 2) Ordinance 2021, in the wake of the COVID-19 pandemic, with a special eye on the risks connected to the "infodemic." In great part, the ordinance replicates the content of the Anti-Fake News Bill and has thus been widely criticized at an international level, both by scholars and by civil society organizations.

6.5 Conclusions

Within Europe, the issues of disinformation and hate speech on the Internet are attracting increasing attention, and new self-regulatory and co-regulatory strategies are being developed to face them. On the one hand, as far as hate speech is concerned, both the Council of Europe system, notably through the case law of the ECtHR, and the European Union have proven to be especially open to the possibility of imposing restrictions, penalties and punishments to quash its dissemination. Quite the opposite approach has been, and continues to be, taken by the United States. With respect to disinformation, on the other hand, the European Union has been at the forefront in the fight against its dissemination, especially through the adoption of the self-regulatory instrument of the Code of Practice on Disinformation, strengthened in June 2022.

Nonetheless, hate speech and disinformation have also been addressed by many national lawmakers at the domestic level. While these phenomena are to be taken seriously, and lawmakers' concerns have legitimate grounds, the appropriateness of regulatory intervention in the digital sphere, and the forms this assumes, is far from settled and will continue to animate public and academic discussions in the coming years. Any consideration in the field cannot fail to deal with the central role of ISPs (see Chapter 5). While self-regulatory tools are more easily designed and flexible, issues concerning their effectiveness and transparency are often lamented. On the other hand, top-down regulatory models have to face the dilemma of the tension with freedom of expression. The appropriateness of responses is thus, in practice, a matter of nuance.

A common issue concerning most of the legislations analyzed here concerns the lack of clarity and the difficulties connected to the identification of a threshold defining when a specific piece of disinformation or hate speech may be harmful or illegal. Accordingly, the importance of providing a judicial stage of review is crucial to ensure a fair assessment of the case and to mediate between the various voices involved.

What appears to be widely supported internationally is the promotion of measures such as the often cited initiatives to support independent media and qualitative journalism, fact-checking activities, as well as important educational efforts promoting media and digital literacy, which certainly constitute less intrusive measures, relying on individuals' and society's resilience. However, it must be noted that these initiatives are long-term investments whose concrete benefits may take time. Furthermore, for any of these measures to produce meaningful impact, trust in institutions and in the media must be restored. Accordingly, the promotion of open and free speech reliant upon pluralistic values to support the circulation of information across the Internet may contribute more to the democratization of the digital public sphere than paternalistic or policing interventions.

7 Copyright in the Digital Age

7.1 Introduction

Copyright represents a fundamental incentive to literary, artistic and scientific expression by giving the authors of works and the producers of other subject matter (e.g., performances, broadcasting, fixations of films, etc.) both an economic right, meaning that they can profit from the sale or commercialization of those products, and, in most jurisdictions, a "moral" right, meaning that authors are fully recognized as the original creators of their works. Digital technologies have made copyright infringement a more and more frequent phenomenon by reducing enormously the costs and time necessary for the reproduction and circulation of content. Today, creating and sharing a copy of a book, a movie or a musical album only takes a few seconds. The Internet also allows one to transfer files across the world at no cost.

One of the most famous examples of copyright infringement via the Internet took place at the turn of the millennium in the case of Napster, a US-based service provider created in 1999. Napster offered a decentralized, peer-to-peer service that allowed users to share files among themselves. Most notably, the system was typically used to illegally search for and share MP3 music files. Unsurprisingly, Napster was soon flooded with lawsuits for contributory and vicarious copyright infringement under the US Digital Millennium Copyright Act (DMCA) and eventually had to file for bankruptcy in 2002. The case of Napster is just one example of the emerging issues for copyright in the context of the digital age. Copyright enforcement has become an increasingly relevant issue vis-à-vis the development of the Internet and of online services, including social media, social networks and file-sharing services.

In this context, moreover, copyright regulation and copyright enforcement can enter into conflict with freedom of expression: on the one hand, copyright potentially represents a limit to the possibility of reusing or disseminating protected material, even for artistic or educational purposes; on the other hand, copyright enforcement could easily translate into the excessive removal of lawful content (especially when it is based consistently on the use of strict filtering algorithms). Copyright regulation and copyright enforcement must therefore be carefully balanced with freedom of expression to ensure that both interests are effectively protected.

This chapter will address the evolution of Internet copyright law in the context of the European Union. Section 7.2 will deal with the historical InfoSoc Directive of 2001 and will look at the new rights developed under that Act (7.2.1), with a special eye on the notion of "communication to the public" of works as interpreted by the case law of the ECJ (7.2.2). Section 7.3 will introduce the DSM Copyright Directive of 2019, which revolutionized the Union legal framework concerning copyright in the context of the Digital Single Market. Most notably, whereas subsection 7.3.1 will briefly outline the new rules on exceptions and limitations to copyright, subsection 7.3.2 will focus on the content of art. 17, which regulates the liability regime of online content-sharing service providers. Article 17, in particular, has been at the center of a recent controversy initiated by the Republic of Poland, which sought to annul its core provisions (7.3.3). Section 7.4 will outline how the Court of Justice of the European Union and the European Court of Human Rights have framed the debate on copyright as a fundamental right of constitutional standing at the intersection with users' freedom of expression and ISP liability. Finally, Section 7.5 will turn to domestic law, addressing how some jurisdictions have adopted specific administrative models for copyright enforcement: in this context, the section will compare most notably the Italian and French experiences.

7.2 The birth of a "pan-European" Internet copyright law: InfoSoc Directive

The EU copyright legislation is composed of eleven Directives and two Regulations, which harmonize essential rights of authors and performers, producers and broadcasters. By setting harmonized standards, EU law reduces national discrepancies, ensures the level of protection required to foster creativity and investment in creativity, promotes cultural diversity and ensures better access for consumers and businesses to digital content and services across Europe. While the history of copyright law in the European Union dates back to the early days of the European Economic Community, this field of law gained real significance only after legislation started being enacted in the late 1980s and early 1990s.

The whole idea of a "pan-European copyright law" with respect to the digital environment was first introduced through Directive 2001/29/EC "on the harmonisation of certain aspects of copyright and related rights in the information society," the so-called InfoSoc Directive, which established a horizontal discipline for copyright protection. In contrast to earlier directives that dealt with specific – mostly technology-driven – issues, such as computer software, databases, and satellite and cable television, this directive sought to harmonize the main rights and limitations in a largely technology-neutral way. The main goal of the Directive, as stated in Recital 4, was to foster creativity and growth of the European creative industries:

> A harmonised legal framework on copyright and related rights, through increased legal certainty and while providing for a high level of protection of intellectual property, will foster substantial investment in creativity and innovation, including network infrastructure, and lead in turn to growth and increased competitiveness of European industry, both in the area of content provision and information technology and more generally

across a wide range of industrial and cultural sectors. This will safeguard employment and encourage new job creation.

7.2.1 The rights over works and other subject matter: Content, limitations and exceptions

As suggested by its title, the InfoSoc Directive addresses the legal protection of copyright and related rights in the framework of the internal market, with particular emphasis on the information society. In this sense, it grants a series of rights to:

a. Authors, with respect to their works;
b. Performers, with respect to the fixations of their performances;
c. Phonogram producers, with respect to their phonograms;
d. Producers of the first fixations of films, with respect to the original and the copies of their films; and
e. Broadcasting organizations, with respect to the fixations of their broadcasts, be they transmitted by wire or over the air (including by cable or satellite).

Most notably, the Directive sets important rights at arts. 2, 3 and 4.

Article 2 on reproduction rights provides that authors, performers, phonogram producers and broadcasting organizations have the exclusive right to authorize or prohibit the reproduction, by any means and in any form, of their works or other subject matter, be such reproduction direct or indirect and be it temporary or permanent.

Article 3 concerns the right of communication to the public of works and of making available to the public other subject matter. According to para. 1, authors have an exclusive right to authorize or prohibit any communication to the public of their works, be such a communication by wire or by wireless means. In particular, such a rule encompasses all acts of communication to the public that allow members of the public to access those works from a place and at a time individually chosen by them. In other words, the publication of a work on an Internet website in such a way that people may gain access to that work at any time and from any place (e.g., through their laptop) shall be in violation of art. 3, unless the author was in favor of such a publication. Para. 2 extends the same right to performers, phonogram producers, producers of the first fixations of films and broadcasting organizations: in this case, these people hold the exclusive right to authorize or prohibit the making available to the public of their respective subject matter. Moreover, as underscored by para. 3, acts of communication to the public or of making available to the public do not exhaust the rights holders' rights: therefore, even when a work has been communicated to the public, the author shall still maintain its copyright over that work.

Finally, art. 4 concerns distribution rights and is applicable in particular to authors with respect to their works and the copies thereof. Authors shall have the exclusive right to authorize or prohibit any form of distribution, including sale, of such works and copies. In this case, para. 2 states that the distribution right can be exhausted if and only if the first sale or other transfer of ownership of that object is made within the Union directly by the rights holder or with their consent.

Article 5 sets the rules concerning the limitations and exceptions applicable to copyright and related rights: pursuant to para. 5, however, these limitations and exceptions "shall only be applied in certain special cases which do not conflict with a normal exploitation of the work or other subject matter and do not unreasonably prejudice the legitimate interests of the rightholder." First, para. 1 rules that temporary acts of reproduction may be exempted from the right set by art. 2 if they comply with the following criteria:

a. The act of reproduction is transient or incidental;
b. The act of reproduction is an integral and essential part of a technological process;
c. The sole purpose of the act of reproduction is either (a) a transmission in a network between third parties by an intermediary, or (b) a lawful use; and
d. The act of reproduction does not have any independent economic significance.

Additionally, paras. 2 and 3 respectively identify a series of cases where Member States may introduce limitations and exceptions to the right provided for by art. 2 and a series of cases where Member States may introduce limitations and exceptions to both rights provided for by arts. 2 and 3.

Pursuant to Art. 5(2), art. 2 on reproduction rights may be subjected to limitations and exceptions in the following cases: (a) in respect of reproductions on paper or any similar medium, effected by the use of any kind of photographic technique or by some other process having similar effects, with the exception of sheet music, provided that the rights holders receive fair compensation; (b) in respect of reproductions on any medium made by a natural person for private use and for ends that are neither directly nor indirectly commercial, on condition that the rights holders receive fair compensation which takes account of the application or non-application of technological measures aimed at protecting copyrighted material to the work or subject matter concerned; (c) in respect of specific acts of reproduction made by publicly accessible libraries, educational establishments or museums, or by archives, which are not for direct or indirect economic or commercial advantage, without prejudice to the exceptions and limitations provided for in the recent DSM Copyright Directive (see *infra*); (d) in respect of ephemeral recordings of works made by broadcasting organisations by means of their own facilities and for their own broadcasts; the preservation of these recordings in official archives may, on the grounds of their exceptional documentary character, be permitted; (e) in respect of reproductions of broadcasts made by social institutions pursuing non-commercial purposes, such as hospitals or prisons, on condition that the rights holders receive fair compensation.

Art. 2 on reproduction rights and art. 3 on the right of communication to the public of works and on the right of making available to the public other subject matter may be subjected to limitations and exceptions in the following cases enlisted within Art. 5(3): (a) use for the sole purpose of illustration for teaching or scientific research, as long as the source, including the author's name, is indicated, unless this turns out to be impossible and to the extent justified by the non-commercial purpose to be achieved, without prejudice to the exceptions and limitations provided for in the DSM Copyright Directive; (b) uses, for the benefit of people with a disability, which are directly related to the disability and of a non-commercial nature, to the extent required by the specific disability, without prejudice to the obligations of Member States under Directive (EU) 2017/1564 of the European Parliament and of the Council; (c) reproduction by the press, communication to the public or making available of published articles on current economic, political or religious topics or of broadcast works or other subject matter of the same character, in cases where such use is not expressly reserved, and as long as the source, including the author's name, is indicated, or use of works or other subject matter in connection with the reporting of current events, to the extent justified by the informatory purpose and as long as the source, including the author's name, is indicated, unless this turns out to be impossible; (d) quotations for purposes such as criticism or review, provided that they relate to a work or other subject matter which has already been lawfully made available to the public, that, unless this turns out to be impossible, the source, including the author's name, is indicated, and that their use is in accordance with fair practice, and to the extent required by the specific purpose; (e) use for the purposes of public security or to ensure the proper performance or reporting of administrative, parliamentary or judicial proceedings; (f) use of political speeches as well as extracts of public lectures or similar works or subject matter to the extent justified by the informatory purpose and provided that the source, including the author's name, is indicated, except where this turns out to be impossible; (g) use during religious celebrations or official celebrations organised by a public authority; (h) use of works, such as works of architecture or sculpture, made to be located permanently in public places; (i) incidental inclusion of a work or other subject matter in other material; (j) use for the purpose of advertising the public exhibition or sale of artistic works, to the extent necessary to promote the event, excluding any other commercial use; (k) use for the purpose of caricature, parody or pastiche; (l) use in connection with the demonstration or repair of equipment; (m) use of an artistic work in the form of a building or a drawing or plan of a building for the purposes of reconstructing the building; (n) use by communication or making available, for the purpose of research or private study, to individual members of the public by dedicated terminals on the premises of establishments referred to in paragraph 2(c) of works and other subject matter not subject to purchase or licensing terms which are contained in their collections; (o) use in certain other cases of minor importance where exceptions or limitations already exist under national law, provided that they only concern analogue uses and do not affect the free circulation of goods and services within the Community, without prejudice to the other exceptions and limitations contained in art. 5.

Finally, para. 4 states that, when Member States provide for an exception or limitation to the right of reproduction (i.e., an exception or limitation to art. 2) in one of the cases indicated in the lists contained in paras. 2 and 3, they may also "provide similarly for an exception or limitation to the right of distribution as referred to in art. 4 to the extent justified by the purpose of the authorised act of reproduction."

7.2.2 The notion of "communication to the public" and the intervention of the ECJ

The rights introduced by arts. 2, 3 and 4 of the InfoSoc Directive were designed at the very beginning of the digital revolution, when the Internet was much different from what it is today: in particular, at that time, the key role that intermediaries would play in the circulation of copyrighted works or subject matter was not yet evident. Likewise, hosting providers were quite basic compared with those that emerged in the aftermath of the Web 2.0 era. The idea that, by creating new channels for the dissemination of content, hosting providers could – albeit indirectly – contribute to copyright infringement was still alien to lawmakers and courts.

Today, the system developed by the InfoSoc Directive has become outdated vis-à-vis the consequences brought by the digital revolution. In particular, the notion of "communication to the public" has come to play an increasingly pivotal role in the contemporary context. EU lawmakers eventually found that the time was ripe for modernizing the legal framework applicable to copyright. In fact, many legal issues had come up in the absence of crystal-clear provisions about whether the rights conferred upon copyright holders by the InfoSoc Directive could be enforced vis-à-vis ISPs. Most notably, important issues concerned hosting providers whose services could be used by users for the unlawful dissemination of copyrighted materials. Once again, it was up to the ECJ to provide some answers.

In *Svensson v. Sverige AB* (C-466/12), the court held that the owner of a website could, without the authorization of the copyright holders, redirect Internet users to copyrighted works that were already freely available on another site. In the specific case, the applicants were journalists who wrote freely accessible press articles, the hyperlinks to which were supplied to the users of the respondent's news-monitoring service. Against this background, the judgment interpreted the notion of "communication to the public" in light of two criteria. First, the ECJ noted that in order for a communication to the public to occur there must be an "act of communication": this concept has to be construed broadly in order to ensure a high level of protection for copyright holders. In addition, the work in question must be communicated to a public, that is, to "an indeterminate number of potential recipients." Such a reference implies that the requirement is met when it comes to "a fairly large number of persons."

However, in the view of the ECJ, the communication has to be directed at a new audience, or a new "public," that had not been taken into account by the original copyright holder. In *BestWater International* (C348/13), the ECJ further specified that whenever, and as long as, a work is freely available on the hyperlinked website, it must be presumed that when the copyright holders authorized the communication, they took into account all Internet users as the potential public. The mere fact that a protected work, which is freely available on an Internet site, is inserted on another website via a hyperlink using the technique of "transclusion" ("framing"), as happened in the case at hand, could not be described as an act of "communication to the public," to the extent that the work in question was not transferred to a new public nor communicated following a specific technical mode that is different to the original communication.

Another remarkable decision was taken by the ECJ in the *GS Media* case (C-160/15). According to the court, in order to assess whether a website link giving access to a work posted online without the authorization of the rights holder amounts to a communication to the public, it must first be determined whether the links are provided for a reason other than financial gain by someone who did not know, and could not reasonably have known, that the linked-to publication was unauthorized. If so, the link is not a communication to the public. On the one hand, the ECJ affirmed the principle by which a communication to the public requires both an act of communication and a new public; on the other hand, it called for an individual assessment to be applied on a case-by-case basis. In the specific case, by applying such an individualized assessment, the ECJ reached the following conclusions: where a person who is not acting for profit publishes a link to a work available online without the consent of the rights holder, it is necessary to take account of the fact that the person does not know, or cannot reasonably know, that the work has been published without authorization. Under these circumstances, the individual is not in full knowledge of the consequences of their conduct in giving access to a work unlawfully posted on the Internet, so there is no act of communication. By contrast, where the person knew or ought to have known that the link provided access to a work published illegally online (e.g., because they received prior notification about it) or provides a link to circumvent restrictions that limit access to a work, the provision of that link would constitute a communication to the public.

It follows from these conclusions that, where hyperlinks are posted for profit, the person posting the links should carry out the necessary checks to ensure that the linked-to work has not been illegally published: therefore, a presumption that the posting of the link has been done with full knowledge of the protected nature of the work and the possible lack of consent to its online publication applies in such cases.

7.3 The new DSM Copyright Directive

In April 2019, Directive (EU) 2019/790 was passed, which contains provisions "on copyright and related rights in the Digital Single Market and amending Directives 96/9/EC and 2001/29/EC" (DSM Copyright Directive). The new legislation complemented the previous legal framework with some important new provisions, also taking into account the case law of the ECJ on such matters.

For instance, art. 15(1) expressly requires Member States to extend the protection set by arts. 2 (reproduction right) and 3(2) (making available to the public other subject matter) to the publishers of press publications with respect to the online use of their press publications by information society service providers. However, the article specifies that such a provision shall not apply to (a) private or non-commercial uses of press publications by individual users; (b) acts of hyperlinking; or (c) use of individual words or very short extracts of a press publication.

Most importantly, the DSM Copyright Directive introduced new rules concerning both the modernization of the system of limitations and exceptions (7.3.1) and the introduction of a new regulation for "online content-sharing service providers," including most notably art. 17 (7.3.2).

7.3.1 The new rules on limitations and exceptions

Title II of the new DSM Copyright Directive is dedicated to the introduction of "measures to adapt exceptions and limitations to the digital and cross-border environment." It is interesting to underscore that, pursuant to art. 7, any contractual provision contrary to the exceptions newly introduced by arts. 3, 5 and 6 shall be unenforceable.

Articles 3 and 4 both concern the topic of text and data mining: whereas art. 3 is specifically focused on text and data mining that occurs for the purposes of scientific research, art. 4 sets a more general framework for these activities. Thus, art.

3(1) states that Member States shall provide for an exception to a range of copyright-related rights concerning works and other subject matter, including databases. This exception shall apply, in particular, to the "reproductions and extractions made by research organisations and cultural heritage institutions in order to carry out, for the purposes of scientific research, text and data mining of works or other subject matter to which they have lawful access." In other words, three criteria must be met in order for the exception under art. 3 to apply:

a. The reproduction or extraction must be made either by research organizations or by cultural heritage institutions;
b. The reproduction or extraction must be made in order to carry out text and data mining for the purposes of scientific research;
c. The text and data mining operated through such reproductions or extractions must concern works or other subject matter that are lawfully accessible.

In doing so, research organizations and cultural heritage institutions can make and retain copies of the works and other subject matter used for the purposes of scientific research, provided they store such copies with an appropriate level of security. Rights holders are allowed to apply measures to ensure the security and integrity of the networks and databases where the works and other subject matter is stored. In any case, Member States shall work in the direction of fostering the definition of agreed best practices.

Article 4 envisages an additional exception to a range of copyright-related rights concerning works and other subject matter, including databases and computer programs. In this case, the exception applies more generally to "reproductions and extractions of lawfully accessible works and other subject matter for the purposes of text and data mining," so that it is applicable irrespective of the actors putting in place the text and data mining activities and irrespective of their purposes. However, the retainment of those reproductions and extractions is allowed only as long as is necessary: when those works, databases, computer programs or other subject matter are no longer necessary, reproductions and extractions must be eliminated; nor is the possibility of making copies mentioned, as was the case in art. 3. Moreover, in this case, rights holders retain the right to expressly reserve the use of works and other subject matter. By exercising this right "in an appropriate manner," the exception set by the article shall be waived; furthermore, such a clause is fully coherent with the general provision set by art. 7(1), which, in declaring unenforceable all contractual provisions contrary to the exceptions provided in arts. 3, 5 and 6, expressly leaves out art. 4.

Article 5 requires Member States to provide an exception or limitation to copyright-related rights in order to allow the digital use of works and other subject matter for the purposes of "digital and cross-border teaching activities." Such exceptions or limitations, however, are applicable only to those situations where:

a. Such a use is made for the sole purpose of illustration for teaching;

b. Such a use is limited to the extent justified by the non-commercial purpose to be achieved;
c. Such a use takes place under the responsibility of an educational establishment, on its premises or at other venues, or through a secure electronic environment accessible only by the educational establishment's pupils or students and teaching staff;
d. Such a use is accompanied by the indication of the source, including the author's name, unless this is impossible.

Article 6, finally, introduces an exception that Member States must introduce with respect to a range of copyright-related rights concerning works and other subject matter, including databases and computer programs, for the purpose of allowing the creation of copies, in any format or medium, that are aimed at preserving cultural heritage. In particular, the new exception shall apply when:

a. The copies are made by cultural heritage institutions;
b. The works or other subject matter subject to copy are permanently in the cultural heritage institutions' collections;
c. The copies are made for purposes of preservation;
d. The copies are made and stored to the extent necessary for such preservation.

7.3.2 Online content-sharing service providers and the "value gap" provision of art. 17

Apart from the introduction of new limitations and exceptions to copyright-related rights, the new DSM Copyright Directive directly tackled the matter of the role of ISPs in the acts of illegal communication to the public of works and of illegally making available to the public other subject matter. In this respect the Directive introduced a specific legislative framework for online content-sharing service providers, defined as follows by art. 2(6):

> "Online content-sharing service provider" means a provider of an information society service of which the main or one of the main purposes is to store and give the public access to a large amount of copyright-protected works or other protected subject matter uploaded by its users, which it organises and promotes for profit-making purposes. Providers of services, such as not-for-profit online encyclopedias, not-for-profit educational and scientific repositories, open-source software-developing and-sharing platforms, providers of electronic communications services ..., online marketplaces, business-to-business cloud services and cloud services that allow users to upload content for their own use, are not "online content-sharing service providers" within the meaning of this Directive.

Article 17 is one of the most important provisions of the Directive, since it introduces a new regulatory framework for these specific ISPs. Article 17 has been referred to as the "value gap" provision: the expression "value gap" refers to the fact that video-sharing and content-sharing platforms undercompensate rights holders for streams of user-uploaded videos containing copyrighted material. The new rules aim to strike a new balance between the competing (albeit not necessary conflicting) interests of rights holders, online content-sharing service providers and users.

Most notably, art. 17 introduces an obligation for online content-sharing service providers to obtain authorization from rights holders for the content uploaded on their websites. Paragraph 1 clarifies the situations where an online content-sharing service provider is performing an act of communication to the public of works or of making available to the public other subject matter: such acts occur whenever the provider gives the public access to such works and subject matter as uploaded by its users.

With respect to this point, the ECJ's decision in the joint cases of *YouTube* (C-682/18) and *Cyando* (C-683/18) (see Chapter 6) seems to be particularly interesting. While interpreting existing national provisions in light of the InfoSoc Directive, the ECJ noted that when users make protected content available to the public illegally on a video-sharing platform (or a file-hosting and -sharing platform), the simple provision of video-sharing or content-sharing services does not constitute a form of "communication to the public" of that content pursuant to art. 3 of the InfoSoc Directive, unless the provider, other than merely making the platform available, actually contributes to giving access to such content to the public in breach of copyright. The ECJ thus implicitly acknowledged that art. 17 of the Copyright Directive, as opposed to the previous art. 3 of the InfoSoc Directive, contains a genuinely new provision, on the basis of which online content-sharing service providers perform an act of communication to the public or make available to the public *ipso iure* whenever the circumstances provided by para. 1 are in place.

On such occasions, consistently with art. 3 of the InfoSoc Directive, the online content-sharing service provider must obtain authorization from the rights holders; this can be done, for instance, by concluding a licensing agreement. Paragraph 2 clarifies that, when such authorization is obtained, the authorization shall also cover acts of communication to the public or of making available to the public carried out by users provided that those acts comply with one of the following conditions:

a. They are not performed on a commercial basis;
b. They do not generate significant revenues.

Paragraph 3 clarifies that, when such obligations and criteria are complied with, then the online content-sharing service provider will be exempted from any liability for the acts of communication to the public of works or of making available to the public other subject matter. This exemption shall thus be applicable irrespective of the rules set by art. 14(1) of the e-Commerce Directive: this means that the provider shall not have to comply with the conditions set within that provision (i.e., absence of knowledge or awareness and expeditious action to remove the contested contents). Having obtained authorization shall thus be considered sufficient to presume that the uploading of those contents by users is in compliance with the law.

However, it may well be possible that an online content-sharing provider cannot obtain authorization from the rights holders; in this case, art. 17(4) applies. In such cases, the providers must comply with other requirements in order to escape liability for the illegal communication to the public of works or the illegal making available to the public other subject matter. In particular, a safe harbor mechanism similar to that established for the e-Commerce Directive applies. Online content-sharing service providers, therefore, must demonstrate that:

a. They made best efforts to obtain authorization;
b. In accordance with high industry standards of professional diligence, they made best efforts to ensure the unavailability of specific works and other subject matter for which the rights holders have provided the service providers with the relevant and necessary information;
c. They acted expeditiously, upon receiving a sufficiently substantiated notice from the rights holders, to disable access to, or to remove from their websites, the notified works or other subject matter, and made best efforts to prevent their future upload in accordance with point (b).

Pursuant to para. 5, in determining whether the service provider has complied with its obligations under para. 4, and in light of the principle of proportionality, elements such as (a) the type, the audience and the size of the service and the type of works or other subject matter uploaded by the users of the service; and (b) the availability of suitable and effective means and their cost for service providers shall be taken into account.

Not every online content-sharing service provider is subject to all these requirements to escape liability: the DSM Copyright Directive takes into account especially the dimensions of such providers. Pursuant to para. 6, when it comes to new online content-sharing service providers whose services have been available to the public in the Union for less than three years and that have an annual turnover below ten million euros, the conditions under the liability regime are limited to compliance with point (a) and to acting expeditiously, upon receiving a sufficiently substantiated notice, to disable access to the notified works or other subject matter or to remove those works or other subject matter from their websites. Where the average number of monthly unique visitors of such service providers exceeds five million, calculated on the basis of the previous calendar year, the providers of content-sharing services shall also demonstrate that they have made best efforts to prevent further uploads of the notified works and other subject matter for which the rights holders have provided relevant and necessary information.

As outlined in para. 7, the cooperation between online content-sharing service providers and rights holders shall not result in the prevention of the availability of works or other subject matter uploaded by users, which do not infringe copyright and related rights, including where such works or other subject matter are covered by an exception or limitation. Therefore, there is an explicit obligation to prevent over-blocking mechanisms. Additionally, Member States shall ensure that users are able to rely on existing exceptions or limitations to copyright when uploading and making available content generated by users on online content-sharing services such as quotation, criticism, review or their use for the purpose of caricature, parody or pastiche.

As provided by para. 8, the application of these provisions shall not lead to a general monitoring obligation, in accordance with art. 15 of the e-Commerce Directive.

At the same time, this paragraph also establishes some measures to safeguard transparency and protect users. Specifically, online content-sharing services shall provide rights holders, at their request, with adequate information on the functioning of their practices under para. 4 and, where licensing agreements have been concluded, information on the use of content covered by such agreements. In addition, providers shall make available an effective and expeditious complaint and redress mechanism to users of their services in the event of disputes over the disabling of access to, or the removal of, works or other subject matter uploaded by them.

Para. 9 also contains some further important substantial and procedural guarantees aimed at protecting users' freedom of expression:

a. First, it requires that online content-sharing service providers put in place an effective and expeditious complaint and redress mechanism for users to challenge the disabling of access to, or the removal of, works or other subject matter;
b. Second, rights holders are required to justify their requests for disabling access to, or removing, their works or other subject matter;
c. Third, decisions taken by the service provider against user-generated content must be subject to human review;
d. Fourth, Member States must ensure the availability of out-of-court redress mechanisms for the settlement of disputes: such mechanisms will have to enable disputes to be settled impartially and shall not deprive the user of the legal protection afforded by national law;
e. Content-sharing service providers must inform their users in their terms and conditions that they can use works and other subject matter under exceptions or limitations provided for in Union law.

Moreover, para. 9 explicitly states that "the Directive shall in no way affect legitimate uses, such as uses under exceptions or limitations provided for in Union law, and shall not lead to any identification of individual users nor to the processing of personal data," except in accordance with Union privacy and data protection law.

Finally, para. 10 sets some rules to foster cooperation between the Commission, Member States and stakeholders with a view to discuss best practices. In particular, the Commission was tasked with the duty to issue guidance on the application of the provisions set within art. 17, and most notably para. 4. Consistently with this provision, on June 4, 2021, the European Commission issued its guidelines on art. 17. The guidelines, most notably, contain practical indications of the main provisions of art. 17 to help market players comply with the relevant national legislation in their implementation.

7.3.3 The case of Poland v. Parliament and Council on the annulment of art. 17

Article 17 has been at the center of an important controversy before the ECJ. Soon after the DSM Copyright Directive was passed, the Republic of Poland brought an action before the court, claiming that art. 17(4)(b) and (c) infringed art. 11 CFREU on freedom of expression (Case C-401/19, *Poland v. Parliament and Council*). As a result, Poland requested the ECJ to annul those letters or, alternatively, should the court consider that art. 17(4)(b) and (c) could not be severed from the rest of the article's provision, to annul art. 17 in its entirety. In fact, with respect to the admissibility of Poland's request, the ECJ held that the annulment of the sole letters (b) and (c) would end up changing substantially the legal regime set for online content-sharing providers, creating a system more favorable to the latter in a manner not consistent with the ultimate aim of the Directive. A partial annulment, since it would alter substantially art. 17, therefore was not possible. In other words, letters (b) and (c) could not be severed. However, the court concluded that art. 17 in its entirety was in principle severable from the remainder of the Directive. The provision is the only one concerning the regulation of those specific ISPs. The ECJ thus had to evaluate whether to annul art. 17 in its entirety.

According to the Republic of Poland, requiring online content-sharing service providers to make their "best efforts" both to ensure the unavailability of specific protected content for which the rights holders have provided the relevant and necessary information (letter (b)) and to prevent the protected content that has been the subject of a sufficiently substantiated notice from those rights holders from being uploaded in the future (letter (c)) would entail a particularly serious interference with the right to freedom of expression and information of users. The preventive review of content inherently required of the providers carries with it the risk that lawful content will be blocked. Additionally, the regime created by art. 17 would necessarily lead to the implementation of algorithms automatically detecting unlawful content: the use of these systems, apart from the inherent risk of contributing to the over-removal of content, could be problematic especially from the point of view of transparency.

Ultimately, the ECJ had to decide whether art. 17 created a legal regime that correctly balanced the two main interests at stake: freedom of expression, on the one hand, and the protection of copyright and related rights, on the other. With respect to the latter, the ECJ also noted that the specific regime established by letters (b) and (c) would only apply in the case where an online content-sharing service provider is not able to obtain authorization from rights holders. Besides, it is the right of rights holders not to give their authorization nor to conclude licensing agreements for the use of their works: it would not be possible to oblige them to do so.

The ECJ agreed with Poland's view that the liability regime established by art. 17 requires online content-sharing service providers not only to act expeditiously to remove the illegal content, but also to make best efforts to prevent infringements from occurring or reoccurring, thus inherently imposing an obligation to carry out a prior review of content. In practice, this would inevitably translate into the use of algorithmic systems for moderation. As a result, the ECJ recognized that art. 17 entailed a limitation to freedom of expression as protected by art. 11: therefore, the court had to evaluate whether that interference was justified or not.

In so doing, the ECJ stressed that the provision should be interpreted in accordance with the general principle of interpretation by which an EU measure must be interpreted, as far as possible, in such a way as not to affect its validity and in conformity with primary law as a whole and, in particular, with the provisions of the Charter. Thus, if the wording of secondary EU law, such as is the DSM Copyright Directive, is open to more than one interpretation, preference should be given to the interpretation that renders the provision consistent with primary law. In particular, the ECJ underscored that the "best efforts" clause, as highlighted by the Parliament and the Council, is intended to ensure that the obligations imposed can be adapted to the particular circumstances of the various online content-sharing service providers and also to the development of industry practices and of available technologies. As a result, requiring providers to put in place their "best efforts" should be interpreted in the sense that the duty of content review is to be calibrated to the specific service provided and to the technological tools at the disposal of the industry.

Moreover, the court generally underscored that art. 17(4)(b) and (c) should be interpreted in light of the other paragraphs of the article itself. Thus, in particular, the ECJ underscored that the first subparagraph of art. 17(7) expressly states that the "cooperation between online content-sharing service providers and rightholders shall not result in the prevention of the availability of works or other subject matter uploaded by users, which do not infringe copyright and related rights, including where such works or other subject matter are covered by an exception or limitation" of those rights. According to the decision, the unambiguous wording of this sentence is not limited to requiring online content-sharing service providers to make their "best efforts" but prescribes a specific result to be achieved. In other words, whereas the wording of art. 17(4)(b) and (c) implies that service providers must do their best but could be exempted from liability even if their attempt to prevent the uploading of illegal content fails, the wording of art. 17(7) obliges them to actually achieve a specific goal: that is, avoiding the unjustified removal of content that does not infringe copyright or related rights. Furthermore, the third subparagraph of art. 17(9) states that the DSM Copyright Directive "shall in no way affect legitimate uses, such as uses under exceptions or limitations provided for in Union law."

Finally, the ECJ had to establish whether the provision contained within art. 17(4)(b) and (c) is actually proportionate to the purpose of protecting copyright and related rights. For this reason, the court had to find out, first of all, whether the same purpose could have been achieved through a less intrusive mechanism. In this sense, the ECJ held that the liability mechanism referred to in art. 17(4) "is not only appropriate but also appears necessary to meet the need to protect intellectual property rights." The judges evaluated the alternative mechanism proposed by the Republic of Poland, under which only the obligations laid down in point (a) and the beginning of point (c) of art. 17(4) would be imposed on online content-sharing service providers, concluding that it would not be as effective in terms of protecting intellectual property rights. Second, the court had to evaluate whether the new liability system would affect excessively the essence of freedom of expression. The ECJ ultimately held that this was not the case, because the paragraphs subsequent to para. 4 set some important guarantees aimed at protecting freedom of expression; moreover, a more ample reading of the DSM Copyright Directive suggests that art. 17 should be interpreted in such a way as to fully protect freedom of expression as well as copyright and related rights. Against this backdrop, the ECJ concluded that:

> Member States must, when transposing Article 17 of Directive 2019/790 into their national law, take care to act on the basis of an interpretation of that provision which allows a fair balance to be struck between the various fundamental rights protected by the Charter. Further, when implementing the measures transposing that same provision, the authorities and courts of the Member States must not only interpret their national law in a manner consistent with that provision but also make sure that they do not act on the basis of an interpretation of the provision which would be in conflict with those fundamental rights or with the other general principles of EU law, such as the principle of proportionality.

7.4 Copyright and freedom of expression in the case law of the European courts

As shown by the case of *Poland v. Parliament and Council*, copyright regulation and enforcement stands at the crossroads between two widely debated issues. On the one hand, copyright calls to the forefront the role of ISPs, such as online content-sharing service providers, in detecting and preventing the unauthorized circulation of works and other subject matter. On the other hand, a central issue is that of balancing between freedom of expression and copyright enforcement. At least initially, the ECJ focused especially on the first issue, whereas the case law of the ECtHR dealt more with the relationship between freedom of expression, as protected under art. 10 ECHR, and copyright enforcement. However, as a consequence of the Treaty of Lisbon, which gave the Charter of Fundamental Rights of the European Union (CFREU) the same legal value as the treaties, recent decisions of the ECJ have also begun to center the debate on the need to balance between competing fundamental values and rights, notably copyright and freedom of expression.

Despite the different judicial techniques and mandates, the judgments by both the ECJ and the ECtHR in this field rely on the assumption that copyright amounts to a fundamental right and enjoys the same rank as freedom of expression and other competing rights. This assumption is not always taken for granted at a domestic level: at that level, some commentators have claimed that the (administrative) enforcement of copyright interferes excessively with users' free speech. Such criticism seems to be based on the alleged (but undemonstrated) prevalence of individual human rights (such as freedom of speech) over economic rights (such as copyright).

Copyright has, nonetheless, a constitutional stance within Europe. Thus, in the view of the ECJ, copyright falls within the scope of the protection granted to the right to property, and most notably within the scope of intellectual property rights (art. 17(2) CFREU). Similarly, the ECtHR refers to the right to property as safeguarded by Protocol No. 1 to the Convention. The key question, however, is whether and how the digital circulation of works and other subject matter protected by copyright or related rights affects the balance between copyright and freedom of expression.

In the context of the ECJ, two landmark decisions were the twin judgments of *Scarlet* (C-70/10) and *Netlog* (C-360/10). In those cases, the references for a preliminary ruling, promoted by two Belgian courts, aimed at assessing the compatibility with EU law of a judicial order imposing the adoption by intermediaries of a filtering system to prevent users from committing copyright infringements via peer-to-peer systems. The ECJ found that such a mechanism would have triggered a variety of violations of EU law. The court noted that the injunction would have required the relevant service providers to actively monitor almost all data relating to users in order to prevent future infringements of intellectual property rights. As such, these measures were found to constitute an obligation of general monitoring prohibited under art. 15 of the e-Commerce Directive. Furthermore, the ECJ also held that the imposition of such a measure would not be compatible with some fundamental rights protected by the CFREU. First, the order would fail to strike a fair balance between copyright enforcement (art. 17(2)) and freedom to conduct business (art. 16), by disproportionately affecting the latter because of the high costs entailed by such filtering measures. Second, the ECJ found that such injunctions would have undermined both the users' right to personal data (art. 8) and their freedom of information (art. 11), since the adoption of filtering systems would have implied monitoring on the side of service providers with respect to the communications exchanged between users. Both judgments clearly specify that copyright and intellectual property rights, though being (also) economic in nature, must nonetheless be balanced with other competing rights and interests.

Similar nuances also emerged in *Telekabel Wien* (C-314/12), where the ECJ noted that enforcement measures directed to Internet intermediaries pursuant to art. 8(3) of the InfoSoc Directive are compatible with EU law and with the relevant fundamental rights (namely, users' freedom of information and ISPs' freedom to conduct business) as far as they conform with the pivotal principle of proportionality.

Additionally, the ECJ has handed down other notable rulings that have affected the role of intermediaries in a variety of respects. In particular, the ECJ adopted a perspective through which ISPs should be regarded as "facilitators" of copyright enforcement. Notably, in the two seminal judgments of *Google France* (C-236/08) and *L'Oréal* (C-324/09), the ECJ developed for the first time a distinction that many domestic courts would later accept and bring to further consequences in their respective jurisdictions. Specifically, the court made it clear that the application of the liability exemptions provided for in the e-Commerce Directive is conditional on the requirements set forth in Recital 42 thereof, that is, the "merely passive, automatic, and technical" nature of the service operated by the provider (see Chapter 5). This reasoning made it possible for the ECJ and for domestic courts adjudicating to draw an important distinction between so-called active providers and merely passive providers, thus depriving the former of the benefits of the liability exemptions. This specific case law, in other words, gave rise to a *tertium genus*, that is, a new category of ISP that, albeit in the absence of a general obligation to monitor content, could not enjoy the liability exemptions of the e-Commerce Directive. This hybrid legal regime, however, may sometimes lead to a lack of clarity on the practical distinction between active and passive providers. Therefore, such a determination is often left to the discretion of judges.

The regulation of the role of intermediaries as enforcement "facilitators" was further developed by the ECJ through *Eva Glawischnig-Piesczek v Facebook Ireland Limited* (C-18/18), where, in a case concerning defamatory content, the Luxembourg judges held that a court injunction ordering a hosting provider to take down content identical or equivalent to a piece of information already assessed by a court as illegal was compatible with EU law. The ECJ thus made it clear that the absence of a general obligation of monitoring is not affected, provided that the assessment of the illegal nature of certain content or information is not vested in the relevant provider.

Moving from Luxembourg to Strasbourg, the ECtHR, though having had fewer chances than the ECJ to address the relationship between copyright and freedom of expression, has nonetheless set some well-established principles and trends.

First, the ECtHR has generally adopted, with respect to this subject, a perspective mainly focused on the dimension of fundamental rights. Most notably, the court stresses the equal footing of freedom of expression with other possibly competing rights, including copyright. The European Convention on Human Rights (ECHR) does not provide for a hierarchy of the human rights it protects: accordingly, although it represents a distinguishing feature of any liberal democracy, free speech does not automatically prevail over other rights. This statement is also applicable to rights such as copyright that are often believed to have a different nature since they are recognized as "economic rights." Even if there is no doubt that free speech still preserves its pivotal value as "watchdog of democracy," it would be misleading to infer from such qualification that economic rights possessing the same rank cannot be protected in a way resulting in an interference with freedom of expression. The key element, in this respect, is once again represented by proportionality.

Second, with respect to the role of ISPs, the Strasbourg court has handed down some landmark judgments, starting from the case of *Delfi AS v. Estonia* (64669/09, see Chapter 5), stressing the human rights implications inherently attached to the role (and regulation) of ISPs. At the same time, the judgment is notable also for the warnings contained within the dissenting opinion of Justices Sajó and Tsotsoria, according to whom, although the measures adopted by the Estonian authorities in that case might have been proportionate, *Delfi* could ultimately trigger serious chilling effects for freedom of speech since it may lead to the imposition of additional pressure on ISPs:

> The technological infrastructure behind digital communication is subject to less visible forms of control by private and public regulators, and the Court has just added another such form to this panoply. Governments may not always be directly censoring expression, but by putting pressure and imposing liability on those who control the technological infrastructure (Internet service providers, etc.), they create an environment in which collateral or private-party censorship is the inevitable result … Because A is liable for someone else's speech, A has strong incentives to over-censor, to limit access, and to deny B's ability to communicate using the platform that A controls. In effect, the fear of liability causes A to impose prior restraints on B's speech and to stifle even protected speech … These technological tools for reviewing content before it is communicated online lead (among other things) to: deliberate overbreadth; limited procedural protections

(the action is taken outside the context of a trial); and shifting of the burden of error costs (the entity in charge of filtering will err on the side of protecting its own liability, rather than protecting freedom of expression).

It thus may not come as a surprise that the subsequent decisions of *MTE v. Hungary, Pihl v. Sweden, Høiness v. Norway* and *Jezior v. Poland* (see Chapter 5) showed a slight change of direction, although keeping the principles expressed in *Delfi* valid in the background.

7.5 The administrative enforcement of copyright: The examples of Italy and France

Across European domestic jurisdictions, national administrative authorities have played an important role in the enforcement of copyright. The resort to administrative enforcement, though generally effective, has nonetheless led in some cases to critiques concerning the legitimacy of such actors, as well as the effects of administrative enforcement upon conflicting interests. Two relevant examples are, in this respect, that of the Italian AGCOM Regulation for the enforcement of copyright and the French HADOPI law.

In the case of Italy, in 2013 AGCOM issued the "Regulation for the enforcement of copyright on electronic communication networks" (Resolution No. 680/13/CONS), which came into force in March 2014. The AGCOM Regulation defines a public enforcement procedure to tackle copyright infringements occurring via electronic communications networks. This procedure does not focus on the conduct of uploaders, but rather aims to end violations of copyright by requiring ISPs to comply with orders issued directly by AGCOM on the basis of a preliminary legal assessment. The procedure also covers copyright infringements occurring in the context of audiovisual media services.

The procedure consists of two phases. The first phase, carried out by the Media Services Directorate, consists of a preliminary investigation that can be initiated only upon request of the rights holders or their legal successors. The Directorate can either dismiss the request or send a kick-off communication to the service providers, the website manager, the web page manager and the uploader (if identified). The piece of content may thus be removed on a voluntary basis. Otherwise, the parties involved can submit defensive briefs and documents.

The second phase consists of the issuance by AGCOM, in case of need, of orders to the ISP involved. The orders can be of two kinds. Selective removal orders require the relevant hosting providers to take down a piece of content and are viable when the relevant website is hosted by a server located in Italian territory. If, on the contrary, copyright infringements are hosted by a server located abroad, AGCOM has no power to impart such orders; therefore, it will issue an order to disable access to the unlawful content by the mere conduit providers, so that such content is prevented from being available in Italian territory. Both selective removal and disabling access orders must be complied with on penalty of administrative fines. The orders adopted by AGCOM can be appealed before the Administrative Court of the Lazio Region (TAR del Lazio).

The system designed by the AGCOM Regulation is thus based on the role of ISPs as "facilitators" of copyright enforcement. The decision of AGCOM to implement an ad hoc regulation for the public enforcement of copyright online has attracted considerable criticism by scholars and Internet activists. In particular, from the standpoint of constitutional law, criticisms focused on the issue of striking a fair balance between the protection of the legitimate economic interests of rights holders and users' freedom of expression, as well as on the actual constitutional legitimacy of the AGCOM Regulation with respect to art. 21 of the Constitution. Another critical point concerns the alleged lack of judicial review over the orders given by AGCOM to ISPs. According to art. 17 of the Regulation, any order adopted by AGCOM can be appealed before the competent administrative tribunal (i.e., that of the Lazio Region): an open question, however, is whether this solution undermines the uploaders of content subject to orders of removal, given that those orders are directed to ISPs and not to them.

In France, a form of administrative copyright enforcement was designed by the controversial "HADOPI law" (Loi No. 2009-669 *favorisant la diffusion et la protection de la creation sur internet*). Through this law, which created the Haute Autorité pour la diffusion des oeuvres et la protection des droits sur l'Internet (HADOPI), the French government tried to establish a public enforcement procedure aimed at countering the problem of online piracy, and most notably of illegal file-sharing. This procedure had a somewhat different target than the AGCOM Regulation, as it mainly addressed the sanctioning and punitive side of infringements. The first approved version of the HADOPI law provided for a punitive/deterrent notification system for copyright infringement, based on the rationale of a graduated response grounded on the "three strikes rule." According to this mechanism, after two warnings sent within six months to an Internet subscriber violating copyright rules and identified by the tracking of the respective IP address, HADOPI was entitled to impose a sanction in case of a third violation; this could entail the suspension of the Internet access contract for up to one month. The additional penalty of disconnection was imposed in the most serious cases. Moreover, the law introduced a presumption of liability affecting users who were served with three notices within eighteen months.

The law was subjected to a preliminary review by the Conseil constitutionnel (No. 580-2009), which resulted in the modification of the original text. The Conseil constitutionnel highlighted that access to the Internet amounted to a fundamental freedom protected under art. 11 of the French Declaration of the Rights of Man and of the Citizen:

> The free communication of ideas and opinions is one of the most precious of the rights of man. Every citizen may, accordingly, speak, write, and print with freedom, but shall be responsible for such abuses of this freedom as shall be defined by law.

Thus the Conseil inherently found the three strikes system partially unconstitutional under two profiles. First, the fact that the law vested HADOPI, an independent administrative authority, with sanctioning powers was considered a violation of the principles of the separation of powers and legality. Second, the reversal of the burden of proof on subscriber users who had been served with three warnings within eighteen months was considered to be at odds with individuals' right to defense and with the principle of the presumption of innocence. Following the Conseil constitutionnel's ruling, the law was revisited, and the sanctioning powers were accordingly transferred to the judicial authority. The administrative authority remains in charge of the notification procedure: at the end of this phase, it may dismiss the case or send to the judicial authority a notification of the violation for the adoption of a fine up to a maximum of 1,500 euros. The additional penalty of disconnection from the Internet was eventually repealed in 2013. From a constitutional law standpoint, the HADOPI saga is very well known in the context of the debate on the existence of a right to access to the Internet, whereas the attention of scholars on the profiles concerning the administrative enforcement of copyright has proven to be more limited.

However, it is important to stress that the Conseil clarified that vesting the power to impose penalties in an administrative authority does not per se infringe the principle of separation of powers nor the rule of law, provided it "is accompanied by statutory measures designed to ensure the protection of constitutionally guaranteed rights and freedoms." The French law, however, did not meet such a requirement, as the power it granted to an administrative authority such as HADOPI was not limited to specific categories of individuals and could be used to restrict freedom of expression for the entire population. Broad content-based restrictions on freedom of expression of this nature should, instead, be adopted by a court of law. The reason why the Conseil struck down the relevant provisions of the HADOPI law, therefore, ultimately lies with the lack of proportionality of the associated measures, rather than with the choice to grant HADOPI the power to impose penalties for copyright infringements.

A comparison between the Italian model and the French can be made with respect to the different degree of involvement of ISPs. While, pursuant to the AGCOM Regulation, the administrative authority is vested with the power to give ISPs the order to remove content or to disable access to a website, the HADOPI scheme provides that the penalty of temporary suspension of Internet services is imposed directly on the uploaders of illegal content. Additionally, both the French Conseil's experience and the Italian one reveal the role played by proportionality in the context of copyright enforcement: the AGCOM Regulation ultimately aims at creating a balanced system whereby the different interests (most notably, the interests of rights holders and ISPs) are taken into account.

7.6 Conclusions

In the European constitutional system, copyright represents a fundamental right worthy of protection. As such, balancing issues may arise when the enforcement of copyright entails a limitation on other fundamental rights, such as freedom to conduct a business and freedom of expression. As also suggested by the Italian and French experiences, it is necessary to develop proportionate legislative frameworks capable of ensuring that all the interests at stake are effectively protected.

In this context, the digital revolution and the increasingly central role of the Internet and ISPs in the circulation of protected works have required an update of copyright law at the supranational level of the EU as well. The DSM Copyright Directive represents a response to the new technological scenario, where contents can be copied and distributed at limited cost and within limited time frames. The goal of art. 17, by introducing a liability system for ISPs that is more protective of rights holders, was to guarantee effective protection to copyright as an essential human and economic right. At the same time, as underscored by the ECJ, such a provision should be interpreted and understood through the principle of proportionality: the "best efforts" clause, based on which ISPs may be able to enjoy an exemption from liability comparable to a "safe harbor" position, should be applied in such a way as to avoid both the risk of overburdening ISPs with costs and that of pushing providers to remove excessive amounts of content or disable access to the Internet, in violation of users' freedom of expression and freedom to access the Internet.

8 Audiovisual Media Services

8.1 Introduction

Following their emergence in the second half of the 19th century, mass media have become increasingly essential channels for communication. As such, throughout the 20th century, radio and television have been subject to regulation addressing various aspects and points including frequency licensing, content, advertising and so forth.

Digitization and the Internet have brought a revolution also with respect to the provision of audiovisual programs traditionally transmitted through radio and, especially, television. As will be seen below, such a revolution within mass media is reflected also in the development of the law. In particular, a shift took place in the first decade of the new millennium from a regulatory framework dealing simply with traditional broadcasting to new legislation encompassing all new forms of communication used for the provision of audiovisual services. On the one hand, regulation of the audiovisual market has had to address the development and spread of on-demand ("non-linear") services that have transformed the way programs are transmitted and enjoyed by the public. On the other hand, social media and social networks have given individuals new opportunities to share videos and audiovisual material. The latter point is especially important since it creates a strict connection between the regulation of the audiovisual market and the governance of user-generated content (see Chapter 5). European lawmakers have intervened to address this developing situation and, in 2018, created a new innovative legal framework designed for the specific ISP category of video-sharing platform service providers.

The present chapter offers an outline of the current EU legislation applicable to this field, that is, Directive 2010/13/EU (Audiovisual Media Services Directive) as lastly amended by Directive (EU) 2018/1808. Section 8.2 discusses the historical development of the Directive, highlighting in particular the progressive shift from the previous framework of the so-called Television without Frontiers Directive to the Audiovisual Media Services Directive and the subsequent introduction, in 2018, of the new fundamental notion of "video-sharing platform services." Section 8.3 addresses the central "country-of-origin" principle characterizing the Directive, as well as the connected rules on jurisdiction. Section 8.4 concerns the regulation of content set within the Directive, considering most notably the rules on audiovisual commercial communication (8.4.1), those on harmful content and the protection of minors (8.4.2) and those aimed at fostering some important public interests (8.4.3). Section 8.5 discusses the regulation for the promotion and prominence of European works, focusing in particular on on-demand Internet-based services. Finally, Section 8.6 focuses specifically on the new duties and obligations of video-sharing platform services.

8.2 From broadcasting to audiovisual media services

The history of the harmonization of media law at the European level began in 1989 with the approval of Directive 89/552/EEC "on the coordination of certain provisions laid down by law, regulation or administrative action in Member States concerning the pursuit of television broadcasting activities," commonly known as the Television without Frontiers Directive (TVWFD). As suggested by this denomination, the purpose of the TVWFD was to create a common broadcasting area in line, on the one hand, with the typical economic goals of the European Communities (i.e., the pursuit of a closer Union between European peoples and states, with a view to fostering the socioeconomic progress and the quality of life of European citizens) and, on the other hand, with the principle of freedom of expression. The Preamble of the TVWFD expressly stated:

> This right [i.e., the right to free movement of all services] as applied to the broadcasting and distribution of television services is also a specific manifestation in Community law of a more general principle, namely the freedom of expression as enshrined in Article 10 (1) of the Convention for the Protection of Human Rights and Fundamental Freedoms ratified by all Member States … for this reason the issuing of directives on the broadcasting and distribution of television programmes must ensure their free movement in the light of the said Article.

The TVWFD was based on the principle of mutual recognition, a typical regulatory strategy employed by the European Communities from the mid-1980s onward with respect to the introduction of internal market measures. Moreover, the TVWFD was based on the principle of the country of origin, meaning that broadcasters should comply with the normative framework of the Member State from which their services originated. This meant that, as long as broadcasters complied with national laws and regulations concerning the provision of their services, they would be able to export their programs to other Member States. The Directive, nonetheless, indicated a set of basic common rules that Member States had to transpose within their domestic legal frameworks. These rules included, among other things, provisions concerning advertising as well as the promotion of "European works" (see below).

The TVWFD was subjected to a first revision in 1997 (Directive 97/36/EC) and to a second one in 2007 (Directive 2007/65/EC). It was on this second occasion that EU lawmakers changed the title of the Directive itself to the Audiovisual Media Services Directive (AVMSD). A few years later, Directive 2010/13/EU finally repealed Directive 89/552/EC, as amended throughout the previous years, and codified in a more organic way the rules on audiovisual media services that had been developed over the previous twenty years. With respect to the media in the context of the European Union, therefore, the legislative framework currently in force is represented by Directive 2010/13/EU, that is, the codified version of the AVMSD. More recently, Directive (EU) 2018/1808 (Refit) introduced some important new amendments, which will be discussed further below.

The terminological shift from "Television without Frontiers" to "Audiovisual Media Services" is not merely a formal transition. The adoption of this new wording suggests that EU lawmakers in 2007 were aware of how the development of digital technologies would revolutionize the media market itself. Whereas with traditional television, based on analog technology, each frequency only allowed for the transmission of a single sequence of sounds and images, digital technologies make it possible to funnel multiple programs through the same frequency, thus allowing for multiple show schedules as well. Moreover, this contributes to a considerable reduction in the risk of technical interferences. As a result, with the same spectrum of frequencies available, digital technologies allow for a vast increase in the number of potential television networks. In this context, a whole new set of tools for the transmission of audiovisual content have been developed. Hence, art. 1(1)(a) AVMSD introduced the notion of "audiovisual media service" (AVMS), which refers to

> a service as defined by Articles 56 and 57 of the Treaty on the Functioning of the European Union, where the principal purpose of the service or a dissociable section thereof is devoted to providing programmes, under the editorial responsibility of a media service provider, to the general public, in order to inform, entertain or educate, by means of electronic communications networks within the meaning of point (a) of Article 2 of Directive 2002/21/EC; such an audiovisual media service is either a television broadcast as defined in point (c) of this paragraph or an on-demand audiovisual media service as defined in point (g) of this paragraph.

First, through this definition, the new AVMSD widens its scope of action to include both "linear" services, which are dedicated to the simultaneous availability of programs traditionally broadcast by television networks on the basis of a program schedule; and "non-linear" or "on-demand" services, which are provided "by a media service provider for the viewing of programmes at the moment chosen by the user and at his individual request on the basis of a catalogue of programmes selected by the media service provider" (art. 1(1)(g)).

> Pursuant to art. 1(1)(b), "programme" refers to "a set of moving images with or without sound constituting an individual item, irrespective of its length, within a schedule or a catalogue established by a media service provider, including feature-length films, video clips, sports events, situation comedies, documentaries, children's programmes and original drama."

Second, in contrast to "television broadcasting" (see art. 1(a) TVWFD), AVMS, pursuant to art. 1(1)(a)(i) AVMSD, can be transmitted through all sorts of "electronic communications networks." This also means that the scope of application of the AVMSD includes content that can be enjoyed through a plurality of different terminals (e.g., other than a television, users of AVMS can enjoy such services through a computer, tablet or smartphone).

Article 1(1)(a)(i) AVMSD, when referring to "electronic communications networks," makes an explicit reference to point (a) of art. 2 of Directive 2002/21/EC. In fact, this Directive was repealed in 2018 by Directive (EU) 2018/1972 "establishing the European Electronic Communications Code (Recast)." Therefore, in order to understand what systems are included within the notion of "electronic communications networks," it is currently necessary to refer to art. 2(1) of the latter act, pursuant to which the term refers to transmission systems "which permit the conveyance of signals by wire, radio, optical or other electromagnetic means, including satellite networks, fixed (circuit- and packet-switched, including internet) and mobile networks, electricity cable systems, to the extent that they are used for the purpose of transmitting signals, networks used for radio and television broadcasting, and cable television networks, irrespective of the type of information conveyed."

Such an ample notion of AVMS could, nonetheless, open up some interpretive issues concerning the delimitation of the scope of action of the AVMSD. Most notably, what is the difference between audiovisual content provided on demand through a non-linear system and audiovisual content published and disseminated across social networks? For this reason, lawmakers set some important conditions to define the exact scope of the term. In particular, the provision makes reference to two elements. On the one hand, the services must be provided "in order to inform, entertain or educate" the general public. On the other hand, and this is precisely the most relevant point, providers of AVMS retain "editorial responsibility" for the content they offer to the public.

Pursuant to art. 1(1)(c), editorial responsibility means, for the purposes of the AVMSD, "the exercise of effective control both over the selection of the programmes and over their organization either in a chronological schedule, in the case of television broadcasts, or in a catalogue, in the case of on-demand audiovisual media services." However, the AVMSD stresses that editorial responsibility does not necessarily entail liability for the content or the services provided.

The requirement of editorial responsibility thus makes a clear distinction between the notion of AVMS providers and that of hosting providers within the meaning of the e-Commerce Directive. Therefore, social media and social networks were not subjected, initially, to the rules set out within the AVMSD, since their regulation was outlined within art. 14 of Directive 2000/31/EC. This changed in part in 2018, when the AVMSD was amended to include a new regulation on video-sharing platforms.

8.3 The AVMSD Refit and the new notion of video-sharing platform services

Following the Commission's Communication on "A Digital Single Market Strategy for Europe" (COM/2015/192), where the Commission underscored the need for a revision of the audiovisual market regulation, as well as of the regulation of platforms, to face the new challenges of digitization in the 21st century, Directive (EU)

2018/1808, the AVMS "Refit" Directive, established further rules concerning the regulation of AVMS providers while developing at the same time a new legal framework for video-sharing platform service providers. Recital 1 of the Directive underscores precisely how video clips and user-generated content have become more and more popular across the Internet, as have video-on-demand (VODs) services and video-sharing platform (VSP) providers: such a convergence of media thus required a new legal framework "to reflect developments in the market and to achieve a balance between access to online content services, consumer protection and competitiveness."

The new art. 1(1)(aa) AVMSD thus reads:

> "Video-sharing platform service" means a service as defined by Articles 56 and 57 of the Treaty on the Functioning of the European Union, where the principal purpose of the service or of a dissociable section thereof or an essential functionality of the service is devoted to providing programmes, user-generated videos, or both, to the general public, for which the video-sharing platform provider does not have editorial responsibility, in order to inform, entertain or educate, by means of electronic communications networks within the meaning of point (a) of Article 2 of Directive 2002/21/EC and the organisation of which is determined by the video-sharing platform provider, including by automatic means or algorithms in particular by displaying, tagging and sequencing.

The first, fundamental distinction between AVMS and VSP services is that, in contrast to the former, the latter are not under the editorial responsibility of their providers. Moreover, apart from "programs," VSPs may provide user-generated videos (i.e., pursuant to art. 1(1)(b), "a set of moving images with or without sound constituting an individual item, irrespective of its length, that is created by a user and uploaded to a video-sharing platform by that user or any other user"). Therefore, VSP providers are also, in practice, hosting providers within the meaning of art. 14 of the e-Commerce Directive (see Chapter 5). As a result, the legal regime of VSP providers, following Directive (EU) 2018/1808, is today a combination of both the e-Commerce Directive and the AVMSD.

Nonetheless, the AVMSD sets an important condition for defining whether a specific ISP should fall within the category of VSP providers. The provision specifically states that, in order for a provider to be identified as such, the goal of providing programs or user-generated videos must be the "principal purpose of the service or of a dissociable section thereof or an essential functionality of the service" itself. As a result, the rules concerning VSP providers may be applicable both to platforms purely dedicated to the sharing of videos (e.g., YouTube) and to other social media and social network platforms: however, in the latter case, such rules will only apply if the social media or social network platform is recognized as featuring video-sharing as an "essential functionality."

With respect to social media (and thus to social networks), Recital 4 expressly states that social media services, such as VSPs, should be included in the scope of the AVMSD because they compete for the same audiences and revenues as AVMS and because they have a considerable impact "in that they facilitate the possibility for users to shape and influence the opinions of other users." However, Recital 5 clarifies the extent to which social media should be subject to the provisions of the AVMSD: "While the aim of Directive 2010/13/EU is not to regulate social media services as such, a social media service should be covered if the provision of programmes and user-generated videos constitutes an essential functionality of that service."

However, the meanings of "principal purpose" and "essential functionality" are not entirely clear and have thus been the subject of debate.

With respect to "principal purpose", the issue is not a new one. The 2010 text of the AVMSD already stated, in art. 1(1)(a)(i), that an AVMS provider was such only in as much as its "principal purpose" was the provision of "programs" to the public. In the 2015 judgment of *New Media Online GmbH v. Bundeskommunikationssenat* (C-347/14), the ECJ was called on to establish whether the video section of the website page of a newspaper could be recognized as an AVMS. The court held that the videos provided through such a section could be qualified as "programs" under the AVMSD when they represented journalistic reports that were not linked to news already published in textual form upon the website and that, therefore, did not constitute an accessory of such news. A service consisting of the provision of a video, within the context of an electronic version of a newspaper, should not be automatically excluded from the scope of action of the AVMSD; rather, the latter applies when the "service as such has content and form which is independent of that of the journalistic activity of the operator of the website at issue, and is not merely an indissociable complement to that activity."

More recently, in the 2018 judgment of *Peugeot Deutschland GmbH v. Deutsche Umwelthilfe* (C-132/17), the ECJ held that a channel used to disseminate brief video adverts, and hosted by an online platform such as YouTube, should not be qualified as offering an AVMS, since, for the purpose of the AVMSD, an "audiovisual commercial communication" constitutes an AVMS only when it is part of a wider activity aimed at informing, entertaining or educating the public.

As regards the notion of "essential functionality," Recital 5 of Directive (EU) 2018/1808, in clarifying to what extent social media services should be affected by the AVMSD (and, in particular, by the new provisions on VSPs), states that the provision of programs and/or user-generated videos could be considered to constitute an essential functionality "if the audiovisual content is not merely ancillary to, or does not constitute a minor part of the activities of that social media service." To further clarify this principle, the Commission delivered in 2020 a Communication containing guidelines on the practical application of the essential functionality criterion (2020/C 223/02).

On the one hand, the Commission first clarifies that audiovisual content should be considered ancillary to the activities of the service where it is exclusively an accessory to an underlying activity or functionality provided by the platform concerned. This could be the case, for example, of videos uploaded exclusively with a view to supporting economic transactions (e.g., videos showing particular goods or services meant to be sold): this case may thus include, for example, e-commerce platforms where users show videos of a product they want to sell while in use. On the other hand, audiovisual content is to be considered a "minor part" of the activity of the service whenever, based on quantitative and/or qualitative considerations, it appears that it plays an insignificant role in the overall economy of the service.

In general, when assessing a certain service, particular attention should be given to whether the audiovisual content is instrumental for the commercial success or positioning of the service on the market. However, the essential functionality requirement should not be interpreted in the sense that the absence of the audiovisual content would make the service not able to function or continue to be provided. The Commission also clarifies that Member States should also pay particular attention to the users' perspective and, in particular, to the degree of their exposure to audiovisual content when accessing the relevant services.

Relevant indicators that national authorities should consider include, namely, (1) the relationship between the audiovisual content and the main economic activity or activities of the service; (2) the quantitative and qualitative relevance of the audiovisual content available on the service; (3) the monetization of, or revenue generation from, the audiovisual content; and (4) the availability of tools aimed at enhancing the visibility or attractiveness of the audiovisual content. These indicators, however, should not be applied cumulatively: in particular, the absence of one or more of them should not automatically lead to the conclusion that the service is not a video-sharing platform.

Finally, art. 1(1)(aa) specifies another feature characterizing VSPs, that is, the fact that their providers determine the organization of the programs and user-generated videos provided by the service, including by automatic means or algorithms, in particular by displaying, tagging and sequencing. In order words, VSPs are typically subject to activities of "content curation" operated by the providers, which may put such activities in place through the use of specific artificial intelligence tools such as recommender systems.

8.4 The "country-of-origin" principle and the rules on jurisdiction

An essential feature of the TVWFD was the "country-of-origin" principle, which was based in turn on the principle of mutual recognition. These general rules, which are in line with the treaties' regulation of the freedom to provide services, are also present within the AVMSD. Thus, the provider of an AVMS shall be subject only to the legislation of its country of origin and shall not have to comply with a plurality of different laws across Europe.

The country-of-origin system entails, in turn, two corollaries: on the one hand, Member States enjoy exclusive jurisdiction over the AVMS providers established in their territory; on the other hand, Member States also have an inherent obligation to surveil those same providers' effective compliance with the rules (home country control). As a means to foster the protection of the interests of the users of AVMS, art. 5(1) says that providers should inform them of the relevant information, including the Member State having jurisdiction over them and the competent authority or national body.

The country-of-origin principle, together with its corollaries, are codified within art. 2 AVMSD; most notably, art. 2(1) rules that "each Member State shall ensure that all audiovisual media services transmitted by providers under its jurisdiction comply with the rules of the systems of law applicable to audiovisual media services intended for the public in that Member State." The following paragraphs specify the general rules concerning jurisdiction.

As a general rule, jurisdiction over a media service provider follows from the establishment of the provider in a specific Member State. For this purpose, a provider shall be deemed to be established within a specific Member State when it has its head office in that Member State and the editorial decisions (i.e., decisions that are taken regularly for the purpose of exercising editorial responsibility and that are linked to day-to-day operations) about the AVMS are taken in that Member State (art. 2(3)(a)).

However, in some cases, the head office and the place where editorial decisions are taken may be different. In that case, the Member State of establishment shall be deemed to be that where "a significant part of the workforce is involved in the pursuit of the programme-related audiovisual media service activity operates"; if a significant part of the workforce operates in both states, the state of establishment shall be that where the head office is; if a significant part of the workforce operates in neither of those states, the place of establishment shall be identified based on the Member State where the provider "first began its activity in accordance with the law of that Member State, provided that it maintains a stable and effective link with the economy of that Member State" (art. 2(3)(b)). Finally, if a provider has its head office in a Member State but editorial decisions are taken in a third country (or vice versa), the provider shall be deemed to be established within the Member State concerned, provided that a significant part of the workforce operates there (art. 2(3)(c)).
If a provider is not established within a Member State under the meaning of art. 2(3), it shall nonetheless be deemed to be under the jurisdiction of a Member State if (a) it uses a satellite up-link situated in that Member State; or (b) if it uses the satellite capacity appertaining to that Member State (art. 2(4)). In all other cases, arts. 49–55 of the Treaty on the Functioning of the European Union (TFEU) apply (art. 2(5)).

To help prevent controversies, para. 5b requires Member States to keep a list of the providers that are under their jurisdiction, indicating on which criterion their jurisdiction is based. The list, as well as any update to that list, shall be communicated to the Commission, which has to ensure, in turn, that the Member States' lists are available in a centralized database accessible to national regulatory authorities or bodies. In case of inconsistencies, the Commission shall contact the relevant Member States to find a solution. Moreover, in case Member States do not agree among themselves with respect to which of them should have jurisdiction pursuant to paras. 3 and 4, they shall bring the matter without undue delay to the attention of the Commission, which may require the European Regulators Group for Audiovisual Media (ERGA) to provide an opinion within fifteen working days.

Whereas art. 2 AVMSD focuses on the regulation of jurisdiction, art. 3 concerns more specifically the principle of mutual recognition, stating, in para. 1, that "Member States shall ensure freedom of reception and shall not restrict retransmissions on their territory of audiovisual media services from other Member States for reasons which fall within the fields coordinated by this Directive." Provisional derogations from this principle are possible where an AVMS provided by a provider under another Member State's jurisdiction "manifestly, seriously and gravely" violates the prohibition to provide programs containing incitement to violence or hatred, or the rules concerning the protection of minors (see below), or if it "prejudices or presents a serious and grave risk of prejudice to public health" (art. 3(2)). Provisional derogations, pursuant to para. 3, are also possible when an AVMS provider "manifestly, seriously and gravely" violates the prohibition to provide programs containing public provocation to commit a terrorist offense (see below) or if it "prejudices or presents a serious and grave risk of prejudice to public security, including the safeguarding of national security and defence."

Additionally, since the AVMSD allows Member States to adopt more detailed or stricter rules than those set by the Directive itself, art. 4 provides that, when a Member State (a) has adopted more detailed or stricter rules "of general public interest" and (b) assesses that a media service provider under the jurisdiction of another Member State directs its services wholly or mostly toward its territory, it may request the Member State having jurisdiction over the provider to address any problems arising from such a situation. Upon receiving a substantiated request, the Member State having jurisdiction will require the AVMS provider to comply with the requesting Member State's rules of general public interest and regularly inform that Member State about the steps taken. In doing so, "both Member States shall cooperate sincerely and swiftly with a view to achieving a mutually satisfactory solution."

Finally, with respect to VSP providers, the relevant provision is represented by art. 28a AVMSD. Pursuant to para. 1, "a video-sharing platform provider established on the territory of a Member State within the meaning of art. 3(1) of Directive 2000/31/EC shall be under the jurisdiction of that Member State." In other words, with respect to these specific providers, the AVMSD refers to the legal framework of the e-Commerce Directive, according to which "Each Member State shall ensure that the information society services provided by a service provider established on its territory comply with the national provisions applicable in the Member State in question which fall within the coordinated field." Jurisdiction, generally, is thus based on the rule of the establishment of the provider itself. Evidently, since AVMSD explicitly states that VSP providers do not have editorial responsibility over their services, the issue of the conflict between the place where the head office is established and the place where editorial decisions are taken, characterizing AVMS providers, is not relevant in this case.

In case para. 1 is not applicable, the VSP provider shall nonetheless be deemed to be established within a Member State if (a) it has a parent undertaking or a subsidiary undertaking that is established on the territory of that Member State; or (b) it is part of a group and another undertaking of that group is established on the territory of that Member State (art. 28a(2)). Paragraphs 3 and 4 specify the applicable rules to determine which Member State should have jurisdiction in such cases. In the case of VSP providers, Member States must also compile a list of those that fall under their jurisdiction. The Commission shall keep a database accessible to national regulatory authorities or bodies. The identification of the Member State having jurisdiction over a platform is especially relevant since that Member State shall have the duty to decide whether the provision of audiovisual content is an essential function of the service provider pursuant to art. 1(1)(aa).

8.5 The rules on content

The AVMSD sets a range of rules concerning the content of AVMS with a view to building an audiovisual market fully respectful of Union values and principles. The present section will address some of these rules. In particular, the first subsection will provide an outline of the rules concerning audiovisual commercial communication, with specific attention to the rules that are applicable to non-linear services; the second subsection addresses the rules concerning the regulation of harmful content, in particular content that may impair the physical, mental or moral development of minors and content constituting hate speech or public provocation to commit a terrorist offense; finally, the third subsection indicates some other rules set for the pursuit of publicly relevant interests.

8.5.1 The rules on audiovisual commercial communication

The AVMSD contains a range of provisions concerning audiovisual commercial communication, defined by art. 1(1)(h) as

> images with or without sound which are designed to promote, directly or indirectly, the goods, services or image of a natural or legal person pursuing an economic activity; such images accompany, or are included in, a programme or user-generated video in return for payment or for similar consideration or for self-promotional purposes. Forms of audiovisual commercial communication include, inter alia, television advertising, sponsorship, teleshopping and product placement.

The AVMSD sets a differentiated regime for linear and non-linear services. As highlighted by Recital 79, although adopting specific rules applicable to on-demand AVMS would not be justifiable nor would it make sense, "nevertheless all audiovisual commercial communication should respect not only the identification rules but also a basic tier of qualitative rules in order to meet clear public policy objectives." A set of qualitative rules, acting as forms of content regulation, thus apply to both linear and on-demand services; however, the former are also subject to quantitative rules setting, in particular, a limit of duration for the transmission of commercial communication. The reason behind this distinction is, clearly, determined by the type of service provided itself, since on-demand systems allow consumers ample choice of the content they are exposed to, whereas, in the case of traditional broadcasting, such a choice is much more restricted.

As concerns qualitative rules, the most important provision is represented by art. 9(1). The norm presents a list of essential limitations to audiovisual commercial communication, which can be grouped within three major classes. The first one includes basic rules concerning the way commercial communications are presented as well as their contents. Such rules apply horizontally to all private actors providing AVMS where they host advertising and include:

a. The prohibition of surreptitious audiovisual commercial communication;
b. The prohibition of the use of subliminal techniques;
c. The prohibition of content affecting the protection of individuals' fundamental rights and dignity. In particular, pursuant to letter (c), audiovisual commercial communication must not (i) prejudice respect for human dignity; (ii) include or promote any discrimination based on sex, racial or ethnic origin, nationality, religion or belief, disability, age or sexual orientation; (iii) encourage behavior prejudicial to health or safety; or (iv) encourage behavior grossly prejudicial to the protection of the environment.

The second group includes rules concerning the advertising of specific types of products. Most notably:

a. The advertising of cigarettes and other tobacco products, including electronic cigarettes and refill containers, shall be prohibited;
b. The advertising of alcoholic beverages must not be aimed specifically at minors nor shall it encourage immoderate consumption of such beverages;
c. Advertising of medical products and medical treatment available only on prescription in the Member State having jurisdiction over the provider shall be prohibited.

Finally, art. 9(1) provides for the protection of minors:

a. Audiovisual commercial communication must not cause physical, mental or moral detriment to minors; most notably they must not (i) directly exhort minors to buy or hire a product or service by exploiting their inexperience or credulity; (ii) encourage them to persuade their parents or others to purchase the goods or services being advertised; (c) exploit the special trust minors place in parents, teachers or other persons; or (d) unreasonably show minors in dangerous situations.

Directive (EU) 2018/1808 extended these provisions to VSP providers: art. 28b(2) currently provides that "Member States shall ensure that video-sharing platform providers under their jurisdiction comply with the requirements set out in art. 9(1) with respect to audiovisual commercial communications that are marketed, sold or arranged by those video-sharing platform providers."

Paragraph 2 extends to on-demand services the rules set by art. 22, which, with respect to television advertising and teleshopping of alcoholic beverages, rules that: (a) it may not be aimed specifically at minors or, in particular, depict minors consuming these beverages; (b) it shall not link the consumption of alcohol to enhanced physical performance or to driving; (c) it shall not create the impression that the

consumption of alcohol contributes towards social or sexual success; (d) it shall not claim that alcohol has therapeutic qualities or that it is a stimulant, a sedative or a means of resolving personal conflicts; (e) it shall not encourage immoderate consumption of alcohol or present abstinence or moderation in a negative light; (f) it shall not place emphasis on high alcoholic content as being a positive quality of the beverages.
Paragraphs 3 and 4, moreover, envisage the possibility of fostering the use of co-regulation and self-regulation to reduce the exposure of minors to audiovisual commercial communication concerning alcoholic beverages and to reduce their exposure to audiovisual commercial communication emphasizing the positive quality of the nutritional aspects of foods and beverages "containing nutrients and substances with a nutritional or physiological effect ... of which excessive intakes in the overall diet are not recommended."

Finally, arts. 10 and 11 respectively are dedicated to the regulation of sponsored AVMS or programs and to the regulation of product placement, whereas Chapter VII provides a range of provisions for television advertising and for teleshopping. Chapter VII, therefore, does not apply in general to audiovisual commercial content transmitted by non-linear services or by VSPs. An exception is represented by art. 22, on the advertising and teleshopping of alcoholic beverages, whose content is extended to all forms of audiovisual commercial communication (except for sponsoring and product placement) by art. 9(2). Chapter VII also provides for some quantitative rules for the broadcast of audiovisual commercial communication.

8.5.2 The regulation on harmful content: Notably, the protection of minors and the prohibition of hate speech and terrorist content

The AVMSD sets some important rules aiming to protect minors from AVMS that are potentially harmful to them. As highlighted in the previous subsection, a range of provisions on audiovisual commercial communication are dedicated to this purpose, with a view to reduce the exposure of minors to advertising encouraging the consumption of unhealthy foods and beverages, including alcohol, taking advantage of their young age, or capable of putting them in distress.

At the same time, the Directive also contains measures governing the content of the programs provided. In its original text, Directive 2010/13/EU indicated such rules within its art. 27, the only provision of Chapter VIII, expressly dedicated to the "protection of minors in television broadcasting." This positioning suggested that the criteria required therein were only applicable to the case of linear AVMS services. Directive (EU) 2018/1808 repealed art. 27 and substituted it with art. 6a, the latter falling within Chapter III about "provisions applicable to all audiovisual media services." Today, therefore, both linear and non-linear services must comply with those requirements.

In particular, para. 1 states that Member State shall take appropriate measures to ensure that AVMS that may impair the physical, mental or moral development of minors are only made available in such a way as to ensure that minors will not normally hear or see them. In order to do so, providers of AVMS may, for instance, set limitations on the time of broadcast or adopt age verification tools; in any case, the measures adopted by AVMS providers must be proportionate to the potential harm of the program, so that "the most harmful content, such as gratuitous violence and pornography, shall be subject to the strictest measures." Moreover, para. 3 requires AVMS providers to provide sufficient information to viewers about a transmission that could impair the physical, mental or moral development of minors; an ad hoc system, to describe the potentially harmful nature of the content of an audiovisual media service, shall thus have to be developed and adopted.

Paragraph 2, focusing on minors' rights to privacy and data protection, states that their personal data, collected or otherwise generated by the providers (as well as through the implementation of measures such as age verification), "shall not be processed for commercial purposes, such as direct marketing, profiling and behaviourally targeted advertising."

Art. 6a also envisages the possibility for Member States and the Commission to encourage, respectively, the use of co-regulation concerning the transmission of "sufficient information" about the potential harmfulness of content transmitted (cf. para. 3) and the exchange of best practices on co-regulatory codes of conduct for the purpose of fulfilling the requirements provided by the article. Moreover, self-regulatory tools are also encouraged. However, part of the legal literature on this topic has highlighted that the high reliance on co-regulation and self-regulation could ultimately reduce the actual effectiveness of rules on the protection of minors.

The AVMSD also sets some relevant rules aimed at protecting vulnerable and discriminated categories of people. A particularly relevant provision in this sense is art. 6 of the Directive dedicated to the prohibition of hate speech. The original text of the article, as set out in 2010, ruled that AVMS should not contain any incitement to hatred "based on race, sex, religion or nationality." In a manner similar to Framework Decision 2008/913/JHA (see Chapter 6), therefore, the Directive only considered some specific grounds of discrimination, most notably those ascribable to the category "racism and xenophobia" pursuant to art. 67(3) TFEU.

Directive (EU) 2018/1808 significantly modified the content of art. 6. The current text of the provision, apart from underscoring the "obligation of Member States to respect and protect human dignity," extends the mentioned prohibition to "incitement to violence or hatred directed against a group of persons or a member of a group based on any of the grounds referred to in art. 21 of the Charter." The new text thus extends significantly the scope of action of the prohibition, since art. 21(1) reads as follows:

> Any discrimination based on any ground such as sex, race, colour, ethnic or social origin, genetic features, language, religion or belief, political or any other opinion, membership of a national minority, property, birth, disability, age or sexual orientation shall be prohibited.

Additionally, Directive (EU) 2018/1808 also introduced a new prohibition concerning content consisting of the public provocation to commit a terrorist offense as set out in art. 5 of Directive (EU) 2017/541 (see Chapter 6).

Article 6(2) specifies that the measures taken for the purposes of the prohibition of hate speech and terrorist content shall be "necessary and proportionate and shall respect the rights and observe principles set out in the Charter." It seems evident that, among the rights that should be balanced with the need to fight the transmission of programs and services containing such harmful content, there should be freedom of expression and information. Moreover, the reference to the principles of necessity and proportionality is reminiscent of the criteria set by the European Convention on Human Rights, and thus by the Charter of Fundamental Rights of the EU, with respect to the imposition of limitations upon such freedom (see Chapter 4).

As will be highlighted below, Directive (EU) 2018/1808 also introduced similar provisions with respect to VSP providers.

8.5.3 Other rules for the pursuit of public interests

The AVMSD also provides for other rules aimed at pursuing publicly relevant interests with respect both to the content provided by AVMS providers and to its form.

As to the form of content, art. 7, most notably, concerns the requirement that audiovisual services are made "continuously and progressively more accessible to persons with disabilities." Providers, therefore, shall have to take appropriate measures for this purpose and inform the relevant national authorities on a regular basis about their implementation. In turn, from December 19, 2022, and every three years thereafter, Member States are expected to submit reports to the Commission about the state of advancement of accessibility measures for persons with disabilities. To help with the pursuit of the goal of accessibility for persons with disabilities, art. 7(3–5) provides that Member States shall (a) encourage media service providers to develop accessibility action plans (to be communicated to the national authorities or bodies) in respect of continuously and progressively making their services more accessible to persons with disabilities; (b) designate a single, easily accessible including by persons with disabilities, and publicly available online point of contact for providing information and receiving complaints regarding any accessibility issues; and (c) ensure that emergency information, including public communications and announcements in natural disaster situations, which is made available to the public through audiovisual media services, is provided in a manner that is accessible to persons with disabilities.

Art. 7a, meanwhile, provides that Member States may take measures to ensure the appropriate prominence of AVMS "of general interest." This provision does not set an obligation on Member States to adopt such measures, nor does it indicate what may be included within the notion of "general interest": therefore, the implementation of art. 7a may vary greatly from Member State to Member State. However, Recital 25 of Directive (EU) 2018/1808 suggests explicitly that, at the least, "media pluralism, freedom of speech and cultural diversity" should be included among the possible goals relevant to the "general interest":

> Directive 2010/13/EU is without prejudice to the ability of Member States to impose obligations to ensure the appropriate prominence of content of general interest under de-

> fined general interest objectives such as media pluralism, freedom of speech and cultural diversity. Such obligations should only be imposed where they are necessary to meet general interest objectives clearly defined by Member States in accordance with Union law. Where Member States decide to impose rules on appropriate prominence, they should only impose proportionate obligations on undertakings in the interests of legitimate public policy considerations.

As will be highlighted below, the principles of pluralism and, especially, of "cultural diversity" are also at the basis of the Directive's regulation on the prominence of European works.

Further provisions provide for the television broadcast of content of public interest: thus, for instance, arts. 14–15 lay down the rules for exclusive rights and short news reports, whereas art. 28 sets the right to reply pursuant to which "any natural or legal person, regardless of nationality, whose legitimate interests, in particular reputation and good name, have been damaged by an assertion of incorrect facts in a television programme must have a right of reply or equivalent remedies."

8.6 Promotion and prominence of European works on non-linear services

The AVMSD sets a range of provisions aimed at guaranteeing the promotion and prominence of European works. Such a discipline has a long history and dates back to the TVWFD, whose art. 4 already required Member States to "ensure where practicable and by appropriate means, that broadcasters reserve for European works … a majority proportion of their transmission time, excluding the time appointed to news, sports events, games, advertising and teletext services." To this purpose, art. 5 provided for a system of quotas concerning the amount of time to be dedicated to the broadcast of European works.

Since the beginning, the rules on the promotion and prominence of European works in the audiovisual market sought to pursue two goals: on the one hand, the economic (and protectionist) goal of helping the European-based audiovisual industry develop and flourish; on the other hand, the cultural purpose of ensuring the production and dissemination of programs and services expressing the many and diverse cultures present on European territory. This second, cultural, goal became more and more relevant, as confirmed by Recital 69 of Directive 2010/13/EU, which, with respect to the extension of the rules on the prominence of European works, stated:

> On-demand audiovisual media services have the potential to partially replace television broadcasting. Accordingly, they should, where practicable, promote the production and distribution of European works and thus contribute actively to the promotion of cultural diversity. Such support for European works might, for example, take the form of financial contributions by such services to the production of and acquisition of rights in European works, a minimum share of European works in video-on-demand catalogues, or the attractive presentation of European works in electronic programme guides.

The goal of fostering cultural diversity is consistent with art. 167(1) of the TFEU, pursuant to which "the Union shall contribute to the flowering of the cultures of the Member States, while respecting their national and regional diversity and at the same time bringing the common cultural heritage to the fore."

The notion of "European works", pursuant to art. 1(1)(n) AVMSD, includes (i) works originating in Member States; (ii) works originating in European third states party to the European Convention on Transfrontier Television of the Council of Europe; and (iii) works co-produced within the framework of agreements related to the audiovisual sector concluded between the Union and third countries fulfilling the conditions defined in each of those agreements.

For the purposes of the cases *sub* (i) and (ii), those works are considered to be European works if "(i) they are made by one or more producers established in one or more of those States; (ii) the production of the works is supervised and actually controlled by one or more producers established in one or more of those States; (iii) the contribution of co-producers of those States to the total co-production costs is preponderant and the co-production is not controlled by one or more producers established outside those States."

The AVMSD sets different rules for the prominence of European works, depending on the types of services provided: in particular, whereas art. 13 sets the rules for on-demand AVMS, arts. 16–17 address television services.

Prior to the reform of Directive (EU) 2018/1808, art. 13 (i.e., the transposition of art. 3i previously introduced by Directive 2007/65/EC) required on-demand AVMS providers to promote European works and, to this effect, introduced the notion of "prominence" as a principle that should guide the presentation of such works within their catalogues. Nonetheless, the absence of a clear definition of what prominence was led to the uneven implementation of art. 13 across the various Member States: in a mapping of the measures adopted by the relevant state authorities, the European Audiovisual Observatory highlighted that provisions to foster the prominence of European works across non-linear services had been introduced by the relevant authorities or bodies in nineteen cases out of thirty-one (and only ten authorities made specific reference to prominence). To help ensure a more efficient regulation, Directive (EU) 2018/1808 introduced within art. 13 a system of quotas. Para. 1 requires Member States to ensure that media service providers of on-demand AVMS under their jurisdiction secure at least a 30 percent share of European works in their catalogues and ensure prominence of such works.

Additionally, para. 2 recognizes the possibility that Member States may require media service providers to contribute financially to the production of European works (including via direct investment as well as via contributions to national funds); such a requirement may be imposed both on those providers that are under their jurisdiction and on those providers that, though established in another Member State, target audiences in their territories. In any case, the obligation to contribute financially must be "proportionate and non-discriminatory." Paragraph 3 clarifies that "the financial contribution shall be based only on the revenues earned in the targeted Member States"; moreover, when the Member State under whose jurisdiction the media service provider is established wants to impose such financial obligations on that provider, it shall have to take into account any financial contributions imposed by targeted Member States.

The rules just described, nonetheless, shall not apply to media service providers with a low turnover or a small audience (art. 13(6)): in such a way, the AVMSD aims to protect small and medium-sized businesses from excessive regulatory burdens. Additionally, "Member States may also waive such obligations or requirements where they would be impracticable or unjustified by reason of the nature or theme of the audiovisual media services."

As mentioned above, arts. 16 and 17 provide for similar rules on European works with respect to television programs. In particular, art. 16(1) provides that "broadcasters reserve for European works a majority proportion of their transmission time, excluding the time allotted to news, sports events, games, advertising, teletext services and teleshopping," whereas art. 17 requires that broadcasters reserve at least 10 percent of their transmission time, excluding the time allotted to news, sports events, games, advertising, teletext services and teleshopping, or alternatively, at the discretion of the Member State, at least 10 percent of their programming budget, for European works created by producers who are "independent of broadcasters."

8.7 The rules on video-sharing platform services: Focus on article 28b

As mentioned above, Directive (EU) 2018/1808 introduced, within the AVMSD, Chapter IX-A on video-sharing platform services. Consumption of audiovisual content through such platforms has increased significantly in the last years, thus requiring an intervention to update the AVMSD to address the new challenges brought by the increased role of these new actors. The previous sections have already analyzed the notion of VSPs pursuant to art. 1(1)(aa), as well as the rules on jurisdiction set by art. 28a. The present section will focus on the *new duties* introduced by Directive (EU) 2018/1808 with respect to this category of actors.

First, it is essential to underscore once again how the current legal regime applicable to VSPs is a combination of the rules provided by the e-Commerce Directive and the new rules of the AVMSD. Art. 28a(5) expressly states that "Article 3 and Article 12 to 15 of Directive 2000/31/EC shall apply to video-sharing platform providers." This means that the rules on liability for third-party content set by the e-Commerce Directive, and especially the "safe harbor" system (see Chapter 5), are fully applicable to VSPs. In other words, the regime of liability exemption, as well as the prohibition on general monitoring obligations, still survives as a general background rule when dealing with VSPs.

On top of those provisions, however, art. 28b AVMSD introduces some new duties and obligations for providers of VSPs. Most importantly, para. 1 rules that, without prejudice to arts. 12–15 of the e-Commerce Directive, VSPs shall have to take the appropriate measures to protect:

a. Minors from programs, user-generated videos and audiovisual commercial communications that may impair their physical, mental or moral development (cf. art. 6a on AVMS providers);
b. The general public from programs, user-generated videos and audiovisual commercial communications containing incitement to violence or hatred directed against a group of persons or a member of a group based on any of the grounds referred to in art. 21 of the Charter (cf. art. 6(1)(a) on AVMS providers);
c. The general public from programs, user-generated videos and audiovisual commercial communications containing content the dissemination of which constitutes an activity that is a criminal offence under Union law, namely public provocation to commit a terrorist offense as set out in art. 5 of Directive (EU) 2017/541 (cf. art. 6(1)(a) on AVMS providers), offenses concerning child pornography as set out in art. 5(4) of Directive 2011/93/EU of the European Parliament and of the Council, and offenses concerning racism and xenophobia as set out in art. 1 of Framework Decision 2008/913/JHA (see Chapter 6).

Paragraph 2, meanwhile, extends to VSP providers the general principles on audiovisual commercial communication laid down within art. 9(1) with respect to AVMS providers. In particular, such principles must always be complied with when the audiovisual commercial communications are marketed, sold or arranged by the VSP provider; however, when they are not marketed, sold or arranged by them, VSP providers must nonetheless "take appropriate measures" to comply with those requirements.

Paragraph 3 clarifies the meaning of "appropriate measures," stating that their adequacy shall be determined

> in light of the nature of the content in question, the harm it may cause, the characteristics of the category of persons to be protected as well as the rights and legitimate interests at stake, including those of the video-sharing platform providers and the users having created or uploaded the content as well as the general public interest.

In other words, "appropriate measures" refers to measures that are proportionate to the risk of harm and that take into account and balance the various interests of the parties involved.

Paragraph 3 indicates a list of possible measures that may be adopted by VSP providers to comply with paras. 1 and 2:

> (a) including and applying in the terms and conditions of the video-sharing platform services the requirements referred to in paragraph 1; (b) including and applying in the terms and conditions of the video-sharing platform services the requirements set out in Article 9(1) for audiovisual commercial communications that are not marketed, sold or arranged by the video-sharing platform providers; (c) having a functionality for users who upload user-generated videos to declare whether such videos contain audiovisual commercial communications as far as they know or can be reasonably expected to know; (d) establishing and operating transparent and user-friendly mechanisms for users of a video-sharing platform to report or flag to the video-sharing platform provider con-

> cerned the content referred to in paragraph 1 provided on its platform; (e) establishing and operating systems through which video-sharing platform providers explain to users of video-sharing platforms what effect has been given to the reporting and flagging referred to in point (d); (f) establishing and operating age verification systems for users of video-sharing platforms with respect to content which may impair the physical, mental or moral development of minors; (g) establishing and operating easy-to-use systems allowing users of video-sharing platforms to rate the content referred to in paragraph 1; (h) providing for parental control systems that are under the control of the end-user with respect to content which may impair the physical, mental or moral development of minors; (i) establishing and operating transparent, easy-to-use and effective procedures for the handling and resolution of users' complaints to the video-sharing platform provider in relation to the implementation of the measures referred to in points (d) to (h); (j) providing for effective media literacy measures and tools and raising users' awareness of those measures and tools.

Among these potential measures, particularly relevant is the establishment of a transparent and user-friendly mechanism for users to report or flag the presence of prohibited content, as well as the creation of a system through which users may be informed about the processing of their reports and flags. Moreover, as a means to guarantee the rights of minors and to protect them from content that might impair their physical, mental or moral development, the Directive suggests adopting age verification systems and providing for parental control systems. On the part of Member States, the use of co-regulation may be encouraged.

To a certain extent, the system introduced by Directive (EU) 2018/1808, based on which the traditional safe harbor system is maintained but combined with the introduction of duties and obligations meant to help fight the presence of harmful or illegal content online, seems to have anticipated that envisaged by the Digital Services Act proposal (see Chapter 5). Furthermore, like the Digital Services Act (DSA), art. 28b(7) sets an important procedural guarantee for the uploaders of content. Pursuant to that provision:

> Member States shall ensure that out-of-court redress mechanisms are available for the settlement of disputes between users and video-sharing platform providers relating to the application of paragraphs 1 and 3. Such mechanisms shall enable disputes to be settled impartially and shall not deprive the user of the legal protection afforded by national law.

Of course, apart from these out-of-court redress mechanisms, users may also avail themselves of national courts.

8.8 Conclusions

The shift from the TVWFD to the 2018 AVMSD is a clear signal of the impact of digitization on the contemporary information system. Digital technologies have brought with them new systems and tools for the transmission of content and programs. These systems have become increasingly relevant and have required a progressive amplification of the scope of action of the European regulation of the audiovisual market, with an expansion first toward non-linear audiovisual media services and subsequently toward video-sharing platform services. This expansion, in turn, has required EU lawmakers to adapt their legal strategies to the various technologies involved.

More specifically, with respect to the reform operated by Directive (EU) 2018/1808, the introduction of art. 28b seems to be consistent with other developments of EU law in the context of the regulation of freedom of expression. In particular, as happened within legislative acts such as the DSA proposal, the Terrorist Content Online Regulation, and the DSM Copyright Directive, the system introduced by the new provision focuses on holding intermediary actors more responsible for the contents they host. Although such a solution is consistent with the pursuit of a safer digital environment, it may also lead to potential counter-effects, such as the over-regulation of online speech.

Part III
Privacy and Data Protection

9 The Right to Privacy and Data Protection

9.1 Introduction

The evolution of the digital society has shed light on the relevance of data in daily life. Algorithms, automated decision-making systems and artificial intelligence are becoming more pervasive, providing new opportunities for the private sector and even for the performance of public tasks. The possibilities raised by automated technologies have led to the definition of data as the driving force of the fourth industrial revolution. These systems are not just drivers of economic growth. Their implementation by public and private actors is increasingly influencing individuals' private lives. The digital environment, by shortening the distance between what is digital and what is real, is exposing private matters to the public sphere. Such interference can be initiated by citizens, businesses and states alike. In these frameworks, data, meaning personal and non-personal information about individuals, cities, governments and, more broadly, the whole world, have been collected on a massive scale in the last ten years. For instance, data was the leading add-on that made artificial intelligence one of the most popular commodities globally. As a matter of fact, greater computing power and greater amount of data facilitated the transition from a purely static logic to a statistical one. Neural networks have become standard tools in machine learning. However, all this has been possible thanks to the increase in the quality and the quantity of available personal and non-personal data.

These tools are contributing to changes in the relationship between digital and physical identity, as well as that between individuals.

> Rapid technological developments and globalisation have brought new challenges for the protection of personal data. The scale of the collection and sharing of personal data has increased significantly. Technology allows both private companies and public authorities to make use of personal data on an unprecedented scale in order to pursue their activities. Natural persons increasingly make personal information available publicly and globally. Technology has transformed both the economy and social life and should further facilitate the free flow of personal data within the Union and the transfer to third countries and international organisations, while ensuring a high level of the protection of personal data. (Cons. no. 6 GDPR)

Thus, while new digital technologies have multiplied opportunities for the exercise of freedom of expression and freedom of association, they have also increased opportunities for conflict with other rights, especially the protection of privacy, personal identity and personal data. As will be discussed more fully in Chapter 12, the protection of personhood in the digital world is mostly anchored in the data protection framework, which encapsulates interests already deemed worthy of protection in the past, such as the protection of personal identity and privacy. Therefore, in order to explore issues related to these new technological challenges, it is necessary to reconstruct the origins of the concept of privacy and its evolution in the projection of personal identity and personal data protection.

This chapter, hence, will analyze the evolution and the concepts of privacy and data protection by looking at the legal, judicial and, in part, the academic development of these two milestones. Section 9.2 frames the theoretical conceptualization of the right to privacy and data protection, whereas Subsection 9.2.1 focuses more on the legal stigmatization of these two rights. Section 9.3 examines the judicial consolidation of the evolution of privacy, in particular from the atomic to the digital world, by looking at the elaborations of US judges. Sections 9.4 and 9.5 observe the evolution of the right to privacy and data protection from a European perspective by considering the case laws of the European Court of Human Rights (ECtHR) (9.4.1) and the European Court of Justice of the European Union (ECJ) (9.5.1) in order to understand how they have interpreted such rights, and how they have influenced their evolution while addressing the new challenges of the digital world.

9.2 The right to privacy and to data protection

Privacy is a social value, meaning that it is beneficial to society as a means by which the equal treatment of citizens is promoted. Privacy enhances the individual's interest in protection, but in a collective dimension, that is, as a member of a social group. Hence, historically privacy is connected with the notions of liberty, dignity and control of one's information, whereas data protection is about protecting any information relating to an identified or identifiable natural (living) person, including name, date of birth, photographs, video footage, email address and telephone number.

The origins of the right to privacy are to be found in the US doctrine whose nucleus is to exclude interference in one's private life by others. This conception of privacy was first elaborated in an 1890 *Harvard Law Review* article ("The Right to Privacy") by Samuel Warren and Louis Brandeis, two distinguished American jurists, as the right to be let alone, translating into a subjective prerogative that then appeared to be little more than a whim of the bourgeoisie, accustomed to worldliness, to lead a free existence outside the spotlight of the tabloids. Warren and Brandeis emphasized the need for the legal system to provide adequate safeguards to defend the person against interference resulting from new technologies, such as photography and printing. The attention of the two jurists was directed at the regulations in force to verify the existence of a basis for the protection of confidentiality. This anchor was actually identified in a series of jurisprudential decisions that, while using rules designed to protect proprietary rights, in applying them betrayed the intent to protect aspects relating to the personal dimension. They proposed the example of a letter received by mistake from a person other than the recipient: none of the rules designed to protect property rights could be usefully invoked to prevent the publication of the content. On the contrary, it is the right to privacy that lays the foundations for the protection of the personal sphere. Ultimately, it is the right of every individual to possess and control their own person, free from all restraint or interference by others. As well said by Judge Cooley in the decision *Union Pacific Railway Co. v. Botsford*, the right to privacy is "the ... right of complete immunity, to be let alone."

However, this concept, when translated into the European *acquis*, acquired a very different interpretation than the "right to be let alone" as framed by the two American scholars. In Europe, these rights are basically two "sister" souls. The right to privacy and data protection consists of the right of the person to whom the data refer to exercise control, including active control, over such data, extending from access to rectification. Both are *critical safeguards* to protect the individual and to ensure the enforcement of substantive and procedural safeguards.

Hence, privacy and data protection, though connected, are commonly recognized all over the world as two separate rights. In particular, as will be further explained, in Europe, the Charter of Fundamental Rights of the European Union (CFREU, also known as the Nice Charter) protects these two rights under two different articles. The distinction is not merely indicative. Thanks to this division, European lawmakers recognize the right to data protection as an independent fundamental right that is considered separate from the right to privacy. Under this provision, everyone has the right to the protection of their own personal data. Such data must be processed fairly for specified purposes and on the basis of the concerned person's consent or some other legitimate basis laid down by law. Moreover, everyone has the right to access the data collected and the right to have it rectified.

On the one hand, privacy represents *negative freedom*, that is to say, the freedom not to suffer interference in one's private life. Through this right, it affirms the right to respect for one's private and family life, one's home and one's communications. For this reason, privacy is often identified as the possibility to exercise control over the flow of one's own information. On the other hand, the right to data protection has different premises. It is *positive freedom*, understood as the right to informational self-determination, that is, the choice of a subject to self-define themself. However, this is not a given since this understanding results from a developing process. For this reason, having provided at least a theoretical frame of what these two rights are, the next section will delve into a more legal definition of the right to privacy and data protection.

9.2.1 The right to privacy and the right to data protection: A legal definition

The right to privacy, as mentioned, was the doctrinal creation of two scholars, and, over the years, it penetrated into national and international documents. For instance, the right to privacy is included in the Universal Declaration of Human Rights adopted by the United Nations General Assembly on December 10, 1948. The Declaration, in Article 12, states:

> No one shall be subjected to arbitrary interference with his privacy, family, home, or correspondence, nor attacks upon his honor and reputation. Everyone has the right to protect the law against such interference or attacks. (Article 12)

Moreover, the International Convention on Civil and Political Rights, which was added to the Declaration in 1966, protects the right to privacy under Article 17 according to a similar formula. In these first statements, the right to privacy seems to be anchored to the guarantees provided for *habeas corpus*.

Hence, even though the right to privacy has been recognized in international documents including the Universal Declaration of Human Rights, it should not be forgotten that privacy and data protection do not enjoy the same legal status across the globe. These two rights are not protected in the same way, as can be seen in comparing the European and US experiences in this field. Although the right to privacy has been the result of a progressive maturation in North America, it has followed its own path in Europe. Even within the European framework, the way in which this right has emerged has not been homogeneous.

During the initial stages, the Council of Europe adopted a proactive approach to the development of the positive dimension of the right to privacy; the European Union, on the other hand, first perceived personal data as a resource for ensuring the broad circulation of data within the Internal Market.

The Universal Declaration of Human Rights was echoed by the European Convention on Human Rights (ECHR) adopted by the Council of Europe in Rome in 1950. Article 8 establishes the right to respect for private and family life:

> Everyone has the right to respect his private and family life, home, and correspondence. There shall be no interference by a public authority with the exercise of this right except such as is by the law and is necessary in for a democratic society in the interests of national security, public safety, or the economic well-being of the country, for the prevention of disorder or crime, for the protection of health or morals, or for the protection of the rights and freedoms of others. (Art. 8 ECHR)

Even in this formula, the concept of privacy has scarce autonomy, and it is identified through a negative wording. Concerning the first aspect, privacy is conceived together with other guarantees, such as the freedom of domicile and correspondence, to which the sphere of private and family life is de facto linked. Regarding the second aspect, corresponding to the second paragraph of Article 8, the ordinary guarantees of fundamental rights in democratic systems are simply extended to the right to privacy (a general prohibition of interference by public authorities, which can be suspended in case of limitations provided for by law and justified by the pursuit of specific purposes according to the standard of a democratic society).

In the European experience, unlike the Council of Europe, the (former) European Economic Community (EEC) did not follow the same path, although before 1995, at the time Directive 95/46 ('Data Protection Directive') was adopted, some Member States had already enacted legislation on data protection (i.e., France). The EEC approach was driven mainly by economic considerations relating to the harmonization of rules on the free flow of data in the internal market. The Data Protection Directive focused on the free movement of personal data, considered as a crucial asset for the internal market. Therefore, the protection of personal data did not immediately capture the attention of the European institutions as a fundamental right.

However, these considerations should not lead us to conclude that the EU had entirely undermined fundamental rights, including the right to privacy and the protection of personal data, for the sake of the fundamental economic freedoms enshrined in the EU Treaties. In particular, the influence of the Council of Europe's framework is certainly not extraneous, at least in the reasoning of the ECJ before the adoption of the CFREU. Although, as already explained, the Data Protection Directive was inspired by the economic dimension of the European Community, it was the first instrument to harmonize data protection rules at the EU level by establishing general principles applicable to the processing of personal data. The path toward the constitutionalization of the protection of personal data has been closely linked to the evolution of the European Union's own identity in more recent times. As noted above, in the last decade, thanks to the proclamation of the CFREU in 2000 and its entry into force in 2009, the EU has been progressively yet decisively emancipated from the economic vocation that characterized the first fifty years of its existence. At the same time, the Treaty of Lisbon revolutionized the EU architecture as a precursor to its adherence to the ECHR, thus bringing the EU closer to a 'constitutional-like' system. As was noted in the previous section, the Charter protects these rights with two different provisions.

> Article 7: Respect for Private Life and Family Life
> Everyone has the right to respect for his or her private and family life, home and communications.

> Article 8: Protection of Personal Data
> 1. Everyone has the right to the protection of personal data concerning him or her.
> 2. Such data must be processed fairly for specified purposes and on the basis of the consent of the person concerned or some other legitimate basis laid down by law. Everyone has the right of access to data which has been collected concerning him or her, and the right to have it rectified.
> 3. Compliance with these rules shall be subject to control by an independent authority.

These two provisions are the cornerstones of these two rights at the European level. Compliance with these rules shall be subjected to control by an independent authority. The recognition of a constitutional right to data protection in the EU Charter has to be considered highly relevant for several reasons. Since data protection explicitly covers values that are not at the core of privacy, such as the requirements of *fair processing*, *consent* and *legitimacy*, it provides more comprehensive protection for individuals. As the literature explains, privacy as framed by art. 7 is related to the protection of the private sphere to safeguard individuals' dignity. At the same time, data protection can be considered a "bureaucratic" right that protects the data by demanding compliance from those who process personal data with procedural and substantial safeguards.

What is privacy? Privacy relates to the control over personal information. Accordingly, privacy protects the individual against unlawful and excessive use of power from both private and public actors. The increasing availability and exchange of information are facilitating invasive marketing and discriminatory practices that evade current anti-discrimination laws. In addition, private information may be used in ways that have not been authorized and may be considered objectionable. Privacy protects the fundamental political value of a democratic constitutional state, as it guarantees individuals freedom of self-determination, the right to be different and the autonomy to engage in relationships, freedom of choice, and autonomy as regards sexuality, health, personality building, social appearance and behavior.

What is data protection? The role of data protection is to provide safeguards for individuals while allowing them to maintain control of their data. In this sense, data protection represents the "positive" side of the right to privacy against interference with the individual freedom to be left alone. Without rules governing the processing of personal data, individuals could not rely on guarantees protecting their privacy and autonomy against the discretionary processing of personal information. Without accountability and transparency safeguards, it is not possible to mitigate the asymmetry of power and the effects of automated decisions not only on fundamental rights but also on democratic values.

In this sense, privacy is as a tool of opacity and data protection is a tool of transparency. Privacy acts as a tool of opacity in that it protects the autonomy, liberty and private life of the individual against interference by the state and private actors. Consequently, data protection prescribes the conditions and rules for the legitimate processing of data. Hence, data protection provides individuals with a level of control over their own data and the way in which those data are used. Thus, data protection has a *precise target* that is distinct from privacy concerns and aims at organizing the fair processing of personal data by both public and private actors.

The theoretical and legal elaboration of the right to privacy and the right to data protection have also been shaped by courts, which have been called to stretch the boundaries of these concepts to answer technological challenges.

9.3 The judicial consolidation of the right to privacy

Historically, Western traditions have tended to link privacy to individual autonomy and liberty. As mentioned previously, the constitutional recognition of privacy rights has led to the creation of a sphere of personal freedom and self-determination. Moreover, human rights have empowered individuals by recognizing their liberties and prerogatives from an international law point of view. However, privacy is not an *absolute right*. It needs to be balanced with other interests, including freedom of expression, which, as already mentioned, enjoys primary protection in the United States.

However, since there is no legal bridge between these two concepts, it has been left to jurisprudence to identify the most appropriate balance. The US Constitution itself, by offering no explicit recognition, confirms this "indirect" consideration of the right to privacy, which emerges in the Fourth Amendment, which is limited to protecting citizens from unjustified searches and seizures. Both the First Amendment, which protects the confidentiality of one's beliefs (privacy of beliefs), and the Fourteenth Amendment, which sets out the due process of law clause, have served the purpose of ensuring an adequate right to privacy. The expansive capacity of the right to privacy thus turned out to be directly proportional to the capacity of the courts to read its foundation in the mesh of principles that are also very different from each other. As anticipated above, the right to privacy has been shaped by judicial interpretations and, as a matter of fact, there are many examples of decisions that demonstrate how this right was interpreted by the courts, within and beyond the boundaries set out by Warren and Brandeis.

Some examples: *Meyer v Nebraska* 262 US 390 (1923); *Griswold v Connecticut* 381 US 479 (1965); Roe v Wade 410 US 113 (1973); Kelley v Johnson 425 US 238 (1976); *Cruzan v Director, Missouri Department of Health* 497 US 261 (1990); *TransUnion LLC v. Ramirez*, 141 S. Ct. 2190 (2021). As early as 1891, in Union Pacific Railway v Botsford (*Union Pacific Railway Co. v. Botsford,* 141 US 250 (1891)), the Court articulated some of the basic reasoning that can be considered the basis of the "right to privacy", as it exists today. After this decision, Courts recognized the existence of the right to privacy, giving to some constitutional provisions articulated interpretations. Accordingly, some provisions of the Constitution's Bill of Rights protect privacy in a relatively narrow sphere.

A very influential decision is *Whalen v Roe* (429 US 589 (1977)). This case involved the New York State Controlled Substances Act of 1972. N.Y. Pub. Health Law scheduled all controlled substances and required a centralized filing system of all prescriptions written for controlled substances that had the potential for abuse. The district court ruled that the Act was unconstitutional. However, the Supreme Court reversed the judgment and found that the law did not violate privacy rights. In doing so, the right to privacy was defined as follows: "[it] involve[s] at least two different kinds of interests. One is the individual interest in avoiding disclosure of personal matters, and another is the interest in independence in making certain kinds of important decisions." Although the court found a fundamental right to privacy embedded in various Constitutional amendments, the applicability of this right is limited, being non-uniformly defined. In the case at stake, the Supreme Court found that there was a constitutionally protected zone of privacy that included the interest in avoiding disclosure of personal matters and the interest in independence in making important personal decisions. The court held that since the Act established limited access to the lists, it ensured protection from disclosures.

Hence, the nature of the right to privacy under the lens of the US courts' interpretation is diffuse and decentralized. The concept of privacy in US jurisprudence is rather a static one, referring to the idea of being let alone and of not suffering unwanted intrusions. This idea allowed for the emergence of the "theory of trespass," related to the very first concept of privacy. This theory is best understood by examining the Olmstead case.

In *Olmstead v. United States,* 277 US 438 (1928), the US Supreme Court considered whether the use of wiretapped private telephone conversations, obtained by federal agents without prior judicial authorization and subsequently used as evidence, constituted a violation of the defendant's rights under the Fourth and Fifth Amendments. The US Supreme Court held that neither the Fourth nor the Fifth Amendment rights of the recorded parties had been violated. The grounds for this interpretation were mainly two. First, the conversations were conducted voluntarily between the parties. Second, wiretapping was not considered to constitute a "search and seizure" since this term involved an "actual physical examination of one's person, papers, tangible material effects, or home." The right to privacy of the citizen was not infringed, the reason being that his private sphere was preserved. There was no entry into the defendants' houses. As a result, by adopting an external perspective, the US Supreme Court did not consider the right to privacy to have been violated in relation to the use by public actors of technology – namely, wiretapping – that was quite new at the time. Nonetheless, this example is significant namely because it conceived of privacy rather statically. Moreover, it is a privacy anchored in things rather than in people. Olmstead's privacy was considered intact because no physical intrusion into the places he frequented took place.

Then, in *Katz v. United States*, 389 US 347 (1967), the Supreme Court considered a situation involving the transmission of gambling information over the telephone to clients in other states. Federal agents used an eavesdropping device situated close to a public phone booth specifically in order to gather such information. Based on the recordings, the court found that the right to privacy of Mr. Katz, the convicted, was violated on the basis that, even if he was using public telephones, he had a general right to privacy. As a demonstration of what was said about the fragmented nature of this right, the court found that "the Fourth Amendment protects people, not places. What a person knowingly exposes to the public, even in his own home or office, is not a subject of Fourth Amendment protection." Hence, in contrast to the previous case, this case recognized a broader right to privacy.

This shift is deemed crucial, since, on its basis, the Supreme Court envisaged a new space for privacy, distinguished from the physical trespass in one's life but opening it to a wider sphere of private existence. Therefore, the Fourth Amendment guarantees one's right to be secure in one's person, house, papers and effects against unreasonable searches and seizures. The definition of searches has two major approaches: the trespass doctrine focused on protection of private places against physical intrusion, and the privacy doctrine protecting people's privacy.

Fourth Amendment of the US Constitution:

> The right of the people to be secure in their persons, houses, papers, and effects, against unreasonable searches and seizures, shall not be violated, and no warrants shall issue, but upon probable cause, supported by oath or affirmation, and particularly describing the place to be searched, and the persons or things to be seized.

In light of the above, it is possible to conceptually define the trespass doctrine as the property-based approach adopted by the Supreme Court that implied an emphasis on the right on property. If the interpretation in *Olmstead v. United States* emphasized that electronic eavesdropping did not violate property rights and did not impact a person, home, paper or effect as stated in the Fourth Amendment, the Supreme Court addressed this problem differently in *Katz*. This decision, as mentioned, gave value to privacy and focused on protecting people, not places. The "privacy doctrine" gives a broader interpretation of privacy protection, implying that what a person seeks to preserve as private, even in the public sphere, may be protected by the Fourth Amendment. It established a twofold requirement for determining the area of protection for determining whether a person had an expectation of privacy and whether this expectation may be recognized as reasonable. In Katz's case, the doctrine was applied as follows: as Katz entered a public telephone booth, closed the door and paid for telephone services, his right to keep his conversation private was constitutionally protected. Then, the physical trespass doctrine interprets the Fourth Amendment as protection against unreasonable searches as involving physical intrusion in places protected by privacy rights. The overcoming of this approach, which occurred in Katz, anchors the protection to people, not places, implying the actions performed in public places under the reasonable expectation of a person to keep them private may be the subject of protection under the Fourth Amendment.

Therefore, another distinctive feature of the US conception of privacy is the "reasonable expectation" enjoyed by individuals. Hence, a person is afforded protection when the person has manifested an actual (subjective) expectation of privacy and, second, when the expectation is one that society is prepared to recognize as "reasonable." This latter aspect recalls what was previously noted: the social value of privacy.

To sum up, the court in *Katz* set aside the very limited approach used in *Olmstead* by adopting an internal perspective. Even if the electronic devices did not penetrate the house, the citizen was enjoying a reasonable expectation of privacy that his conversation was not being listed to and, moreover, recorded. Reading together the results of this interpretation, the right to privacy seems to be connected to a *reasonable expectation of privacy*, not only when the individual is protected by the wall of their house, but also in public. This concept is interesting if we think of the increasing presence of technology, where the boundaries between private and public are overall very thin. Hence, these decisions are examples of how technologies can alter expectations of privacy. The expectation in *Katz* would amount to nothing when compared with the technology used in the information society. As a result, this is particularly significant since it shows how the technological dimension has a strong influence on judicial protection of fundamental rights, resulting in a change in the case law of the US Supreme Court from an external to an internal perspective.

Being very much related to the intrusions in private life, it is no surprise that the US Supreme Court adopted its frame for protection in response to the development of new digital technologies. This concept will be explained by considering two case laws. In particular, the lack of any clear stipulation within the legislation or the Constitution has allowed the US Supreme Court to identify the most appropriate principle for protecting privacy. Furthermore, its conception is very much related to accessing information rather than providing subjects with control over their data.

The *Katz* reasonable expectation of privacy test has been criticized frequently because the subjective expectation of privacy was inevitably assessed by applying an objective criterion: had the individual exposed the thing to the public? And the assessment of the objective reasonableness of a privacy expectation was inherently dependent on the evaluation of the expectation as legitimate. Nonetheless, the Supreme Court in *Katz* moved beyond the trespass doctrine. Under these circumstances, it is possible to identify a clash between the US and European perspectives. When looking at privacy and data protection, the approach followed by the US Supreme Court has been quite different from that of the European courts. It has been characterized by the so-called third-party doctrine, in which any person who voluntarily gives information to third parties, including Internet service providers, has no reasonable expectation of privacy.

This interpretation was solidly applied by the US Supreme Court at least until *Unites States v. Jones* (565 U. S. (2012)) and *Carpenter v United States* (585 US (2018)).

United States v. Jones involved an arrest for drug possession after police had used a tracker without judicial approval for one month. The primary question was therefore whether the warrantless use of a tracking device to monitor the defendant's movements on public streets violated the Fourth Amendment. The US Supreme Court rejected the government's argument concerning the lack of reasonable expectation of privacy and upheld the judgment of the lower court, holding that the use of a GPS tracking device on the defendant's vehicle without a warrant constituted an unlawful search under the Fourth Amendment. Even more importantly, in this case, Justice Sonia Sotomayor stressed the need to reconsider the premise that an individual has no reasonable expectation of privacy in relation to information voluntarily disclosed to third parties:

> This approach is ill suited to the digital age, in which people reveal a great deal of information about themselves to third parties in the course of carrying out mundane tasks. People disclose the phone numbers that they dial or text to their cellular providers; the URLs that they visit and the e-mail addresses with which they correspond to their Internet service providers; and the books, groceries, and medications they purchase to online retailers. (Justice Sotomayor's Opinion in *US v. Jones*)

Therefore, this decision has led to the emergence of the so-called mosaic theory. Before this decision, the Supreme Court addressed violations of the Fourth Amendment by looking at the specific individual step within the investigation. By contrast, the approach adopted in this case results in a focus on the governmental activity as collective or aggregate behavior when reviewing compliance with Fourth Amendment safeguards. In other words, when small pieces of information are collected, there should not be any problem as a warrant should only be required for bulk surveillance. Any given piece within a mosaic cannot reveal the overall picture without adding the other tiles. It is only the aggregation of the tiles that enables the full picture to be established.

This theory was further challenged in *Carpenter*. This case concerned four men arrested by the police for a series of armed robberies. The FBI accessed transactional records, including geo-location, from the telephone of one of the men and discovered that Mr. Carpenter was responsible for aiding and abetting a robbery that affected interstate commerce. The defendant claimed a violation of his Fourth Amendment rights due to failure to obtain a warrant. Therefore, the question was whether a warrantless search and seizure of mobile telephone records violates the Fourth Amendment. The majority ruled that the government violated the petitioner's right to privacy when it accessed his location data without a warrant since it invaded his reasonable expectation of privacy. Hence, to access this information, it is necessary to obtain a search warrant to avoid infringing Fourth Amendment rights.

However, the US Supreme Court did not subject the use of data and the infringement of privacy to safeguards since the system is still based on a narrow notion of a reasonable expectation of privacy. Such a liberal judicial approach to digital privacy is evident in the field of free speech. This is a general trend, which can be described as a decision to favor economic freedoms over fundamental rights, or better, to focus only on the vertical dimension of fundamental rights in the digital world rather than the horizontal one.

However, although interesting, this case did not amount to a revolutionary interpretation of the American conception of the right to privacy. Even if the traditional approach was finally applied to digital technologies, the court did not go beyond it. There are no vast concerns regarding the new challenges raised by new digital technologies and the digital world. In the US framework, privacy and data protection seem to be locked in a judicial frame of complete trust in digital technologies. The US Supreme Court did not subject the use of data and the infringement of privacy to safeguards since the system is still based on a narrow notion of a reasonable expectation of privacy.

The European approach is very different, as the next sections will explain . The concept of privacy is very much adapting to the risks and challenges posed by digital tools to privacy and other fundamental rights and freedoms.

9.4 The evolution of privacy and data protection in Europe

While the US legacy does not explicitly mention privacy or data protection, protection of both rights is explicitly established at the constitutional level in Europe. The right to privacy and the right to data protection are both protected within the CFREU. Besides this, a crucial role has been played by the ECHR: the inclusion of the right to private and family life in the category of rights protected by the ECHR marked the establishment of a first bond for the contracting states, obliging them to adequately protect the right to privacy according to the paradigm indicated in art. 8. Of crucial significance is the presence of the ECtHR in Strasbourg, the competent body to ensure compliance with the ECHR, subject to the exhaustion of the parties concerned of the internal remedies provided by national law. The Strasbourg court, thus, like the US Supreme Court, was able to develop a copious jurisprudence to include under the protection of art. 8 ECHR situations and cases that are very different from each other but are united by the underlying interest in protecting the "negative" dimension of the right to privacy.

Article 8 ECHR represents the crystallization of privacy as independent from data protection. This is a key aspect to be observed in the bigger picture of technological evolution. This latter aspect gave rise to a positive component of the right to privacy. This claim, originally focused exclusively on the negative dimension of confidentiality (as theorized by Warren and Brandeis), was enriched with a "positive" component that corresponds to what is commonly described as data protection.

Privacy is no longer reduced to a negative meaning but also incorporates a positive dimension. This second meaning of privacy is closely linked to personal data and the right to process them correctly. Hence, the foundations of a second meaning are to be found in the processing of personal data. This aspect leads to the need for data to be processed in compliance with a body of principles and rules that ensure the protection of the individual and their personality. However, this process, which led to the identification in the Charter of Nice of two different provisions, did not happen by itself, but thanks to a long transition. The first step in this evolution is to be found in the Convention on the protection of individuals with respect to the automated processing of personal data, also known as Convention n. 108/1981 or the Strasbourg Convention. The merit of this document was to first introduce the need for positive and procedural protection of personal data: namely, it included terminology such as "automated processing" and "personal data."

However, as noted above, a critical role has been played by the ECtHR. Similarly, to the transatlantic development of privacy, also under the framework of the Council of Europe, the judicial bodies became the voice of the adaptation of the legal systems to the needs and challenges of society, in particular with regard to digitalization.

9.4.1 The evolution of privacy and data protection under the case law of the ECtHR

The first technological case that stimulated the creativity of the ECtHR occurred at the end of the 1980s. In *Klass v. Germany* (5029/71), the applicants challenged a German law that authorized the state to intercept correspondence between lawyers and their clients. First, the court was called to determine whether telephone conversations fall within the scope of art. 8 ECHR; second, it had to ascertain whether this system amounted to surveillance and whether the state had adopted adequate and effective guarantees against abuse. However, the technology observed here is, as we saw in the *Katz* decision, very different from the one that processes a massive quantity of personal and non-personal data. For this reason, the court was later called to update the interpretation given in *Klass v. Germany*. It did so in *Leander v. Sweden* (9248/1981), where the court was called to decide whether information collected by the state and retained in secret files may be used for employment vetting purposes for reasons of national security, and whether an individual has the right of access to such files under arts. 8 and 10 ECHR. The ECtHR clarified that the collection and processing of personal data must be included within the scope of art. 8 ECHR:

> It is uncontested that the secret police-register contained information relating to Mr. Leander's private life. Both the storing and the release of such information, which were coupled with a refusal to allow Mr. Leander an opportunity to refute it, amounted to an interference with his right to respect for private life as guaranteed by Article 8(1).

In other cases as well, the ECtHR acknowledged that the protection of personal data also includes the protection of private and family life, which enjoys express protection in the ECHR. For instance, a link can be identified with the case of *S and Marprer v UK* (30562/04 and 30566/04), where the Grand Chamber of the ECtHR recognized that the protection of personal data is of fundamental importance for an individual in order to fully enjoy the right to respect for private and family life.

The court, well aware that privacy is not an absolute right, frequently refers to the "proportionality test," namely, the balance between public interest and individual rights, but also those principles that allow for the storage of personal data, provided that this is relevant and not excessive compared with the purposes for which the data were collected. The ECtHR found that even the mere storing of data relating to the private life of individuals amounts to an interference with the intention of art. 8. The subsequent use of the stored information has no bearing on that finding. However, in order to determine whether the personal information involves any private-lives aspect as defined in art. 8, the court examines the specific context in which the information at issue has been recorded and retained, the nature of the records, the way in which these records are used and processed and the results that may be obtained.

This paradigm has been applied by the court in several cases. For instance, in *M.M. v UK* (24029/07), the Strasbourg judges ruled on violations of art. 8 and found violations on the excessive duration of data collection in relation to the applicant's criminal record. Because the applicant's criminal record was not updated after five years, her application for a job was rejected.
The applicant argued that the retention of the caution data violated the applicant's right to respect for her private life under art. 8(1) of the Convention because it had affected her ability to secure employment in her chosen field; second, she argued that the retention of the caution data on the criminal record for a prolonged period was disproportionate and illegitimate.
The court decided that the storage of information relating to an individual's private life and the release of that information fell within the scope of art. 8(1) and that the United Kingdom had violated art. 8 of the Convention. The criminal records were found to be personal data under the Council of Europe's Data Protection Convention. While acknowledging that there was a public interest in having a comprehensive record of all cautions, convictions, warnings, reprimands, acquittals and other information, the court found that the actual system at issue infringed art. 8. The court observed that an open-ended collection of criminal record data is not legitimate, in part because it lacked a statutory framework defining the purposes for the mandatory disclosure of the records. The court was critical of the fact that no distinction was made on the basis of the nature of the offense, the time that had elapsed since the offense took place (in this case almost twelve years) or the relevance of the data to the employment being sought.

Another issue that has been addressed by the ECtHR is access to personal data in cases involving the absence of mechanisms for obtaining details about incidents that may have caused harm to health or concerning the existence of parental relationships. In *Z. v. Finland* (22009/1993), the ECtHR found that art. 8 ECHR was violated by the disclosure of personal data. In this case, the defendant had appealed against his conviction for manslaughter and related offenses for deliberately subjecting women to the risk of being infected by him with the HIV virus. The applicant, Z, had been married to the defendant and was infected by him with HIV. Z's doctors had been required to give evidence about her medical condition in spite of their, and her, objections to the disclosure of this information, and the police seized her medical records, including laboratory tests and information about her mental state. Those data – which are highly sensitive – had no relevance to the case, and they had been disseminated during a public hearing.

Another example of the active interpretative role of the ECtHR involves cases concerning the interception of communications and surveillance. As we saw for the US courts, also in Europe this topic captured the attention of the Strasbourg judges, who were called to ascertain whether national laws in this area provided for clear and precise limits to the scope as well as the type of restrictions affecting freedom of communication. In particular, the ECtHR's reasoning has focused on exceptions that, according to art. 8(2) ECHR, legitimize interference with the right to private and family life. In the past, the ECtHR held art. 8 ECHR to have been violated by national measures that allowed the judicial authorities to monitor the content of correspondence and telephone conversations with no obligation to inform the interested parties concerning the measures adopted. An example is *Zakharov v Russia* (47143/06). This case addressed the compatibility with art. 8 of the ECHR of a mobile communications interception system. The ECtHR concluded that art. 8 had been breached since national law did not establish adequate safeguards against the risk of abuse and arbitrary interference in the private lives of citizens. The Strasbourg court also noted that risk also resulted from the limitation to the right to challenge the legitimacy of these measures only to applicants who were able to demonstrate an actual interception. It was not possible to meet this condition given the lack of a notification system or any possibility of accessing data relating to the operations carried out in a given case.

A landmark case in this regard is *Big Brother Watch and Others v. The United Kingdom* (App nos. 58170/13, 62322/14, and 24960/15). This decision represents a "judicial saga" that interested in prima facie the First Section of the ECtHR, and, secondly, the Grand Chamber, after a referral made by the applicants in 2019.

This decision relates to the *bulk interception regime* conducted by many states, in this case the United Kingdom. A system of surveillance was revealed in 2013 by former US National Security Agency employee Edward Snowden, who leaked information that demonstrated that the United States and other governments use a wide range of techniques to spy on people at home and abroad. The UK had a mass surveillance program that allowed it to acquire enormous amounts of personal information without a person's consent or knowledge, including both the content and metadata of communications. This case, because of its importance, deserves a closer look.

Big Brother Watch and Others v. The United Kingdom

In *Big Brother Watch and Others v. The United Kingdom*, the first decision was delivered in 2018 by the Frist Section of the European Court of Human Rights. The case was brought before the court by sixteen organizations and individuals, including the UK non-governmental organization Big Brother Watch, against the UK government. The allegations pertained to, inter alia, the breach of the right to privacy (art. 8), together with violations of freedom of expression (art. 10). As mentioned, they were, at least in part, inspired by the Snowden revelations. The complaint against the UK government focused on three main issues concerning the Regulation of Investigatory Powers Act 2000 (RIPA) (subsequently replaced by the Investigatory Powers Act 2016) regulating the interception of communications: (a) the bulk interception of communications pursuant to section 8(4); (b) the obtaining of communications data from communication service providers under Chapter II; and (c) intelligence-sharing arrangements. Under this Act, the Secretary of State could issue a warrant when it was believed necessary in the interests of national security, for the purpose of preventing or detecting serious crime, or for safeguarding, in circumstances relevant to the interests of national security and the economic well-being of the United Kingdom. In a certificate accompanying the warrant, the Secretary of State must also set out a description of the intercepted material that it considered needed to be examined. It must be noted that, remarkably, not only the intelligence services but also law enforcement authorities may apply for such a warrant. The applicants relied upon the so-called *Weber criteria* (developed by the court in *Weber and Saravia v. Germany no.* 54934/00), meaning the minimum requirements established by the ECtHR that have to be set out in law in order to avoid abuses of power contrary to the "in accordance with the law" and "necessary in a democratic society" conditions of art. 8(2) ECHR.

Having clarified the facts, the First Section of the court found a violation of art. 8 rights in relation to grounds (a) and (b) but considered the intelligence-sharing agreements with foreign governments or intelligence agencies to be Convention compliant. The operation of bulk surveillance was found to constitute an interference. However, the court found that this does not amount to a violation of art. 8 per se (§314). It also asserted that "it is clear that bulk interception is a valuable means to achieve the legitimate aims pursued, particularly given the current threat level from both global terrorism and serious crime" (§386). However, a breach of art. 8 was found in relation to the techniques used by the intercepting authorities: they did not adhere to the prescribed safeguards, and adequate oversight mechanisms were lacking. The applicants contended that the requirement of "reasonable suspicion" introduced in *Zakharov v Russia* should equally be applicable to bulk systems. This claim was rejected as the court reasoned that "bulk interception is by definition untargeted and to require 'reasonable suspicion' would render the operation of such a scheme impossible" (§ 317). The ECtHR here clarified that in so far as the conducting of bulk interception of foreign communications is concerned, the court will pursue its earlier approach laid down in *Weber* that does not concern analysis of whether the system itself is legal vis-à-vis states' obligations under art. 8 but controls if the operation meets the necessary standards. Hence, since mass surveillance of foreign communications was recognized as an indispensable tool for states to safeguard national security, it was considered licit when undertaken in accordance with adequate safeguards and oversight mechanisms.

Unsatisfied by this decision, the applicants referred the question to the Grand Chamber (GC), which ruled on May 25, 2021, that some aspects of the UK surveillance regime violated arts. 8 and 10 of the ECHR. The GC first identified three "fundamental deficiencies" in the UK's interception regime. First, the bulk interception was not authorized by an independent body of the executive (but rather by the Secretary of State). Second, categories of search terms defining the kinds of communications to be examined were not specified. And finally, the use of specific identifiers had not been authorized.

Then, the court pointed out that even if judicial authorization was not necessary for the legality of bulk interception programs, authorization by a body independent from the executive (though not necessarily a judicial one) *is* necessary (§351). For these reasons, the GC found that the UK's bulk interception regime failed to satisfy the "quality of law" requirement, violating art. 8 ECHR (§425–426). Hence, the GC ruled that the UK's acquisition of communications data from communication service providers also breached art. 8 because it was not "in accordance with law." The authorities' access to data retained by communications service providers was not limited to the purpose of combating "serious crime," and access was not subject to prior review by an independent body (§518–522). The GC further ruled, in line with the Chamber's findings, that both the regime's bulk interception of communications *and* the acquisition of data from communications service providers violated art. 10 ECHR because they lacked safeguards in relation to journalistic sources and confidential journalistic material (§456–458, 524–528). Finally, the system of information sharing, through which the UK authorities received material from US intelligence services, did not violate art. 8 or 10 ECHR (§510–514, 515–516). In the court's view, intelligence sharing is permissible provided there are "adequate safeguards" against abuse in place and that the regime is subject to independent oversight and *ex post facto* review (§13).

Leaving aside the arguments that allowed the ECtHR to embrace the protection of personal data within the framework of art. 8 ECHR, it is worth focusing on another interpretative phase based on the shift from offline data processing to online data processing.

The court included the web in the scope of art. 8 in 2007. The digital environment was seen by the ECtHR as another form of threat to the enjoyment of fundamental rights and freedoms. For this reason, it adopted an approach that reinforces the dimension of confidentiality and the protection of personal data in comparison with other rights, as also shown in the case *Editorial Board of Pravoye Delo and Shtekel v Ukraine* (33014/05). The court, in this case, relied on the doctrine of "positive obligations" that demands that Contracting States ensure protection for fundamental rights. However, because of the increasing role vested by private actors in the digital space, this doctrine was applied to them as well.

This step seems critical when considering the digital environment since it leads network operators, which are private subjects, to be involved in the protection of privacy and data through the legal measures that states are required to implement in order to safeguard these fundamental rights.

The role of the ECtHR is just one aspect of the evolution of the right to privacy and data protection in Europe. If the Strasbourg Convention and the ECtHR case law can be considered the first steps toward protecting the right to privacy and personal data in Europe, in recent years the actions of the European Union, and especially the ECJ, have resulted in the consolidation and adaptation of these fundamental rights in the digital domain. In the next section, this framework will be supplemented by the ECJ case law, the judicial activism that has paved the way for the creation of what is considered the EU First Amendment: privacy.

9.5 The right to privacy and data protection in the Union

In the European context, the right to data protection is the protagonist of a regulatory process that began twenty years ago with Directive 95/46/EC. It is part of the purely market-oriented thrusts that wanted to create, even then, a single European area of circulation (and protection) of personal data. As is logical, the Directive had taken on board a cultural, social and legal debate based on a static model of personal data processing, also due to the technology available. The right to privacy received attention from the European Union through the "filter" of the mercantile dimension.

The economic inspiration for this provision can be seen in its title: the Directive is "on the protection of individuals with regard to the processing of personal data and on the free movement of such data." Therefore, the Data Protection Directive, as the first instrument of harmonization at the EU level of the laws in force in the Member States, has built an analytical regulatory framework, where general rules and regulations appear alongside the general principles relating to the processing of personal data.

A further turning point that confirms the complex physiognomy of the right to privacy (on the one hand, confidentiality, on the other, protection of personal data) coincided with the entry into force of the CFREU. Since 2009, the year in which the Lisbon Treaty was applied, this Charter has had the same legal status as the Treaties and therefore that of the primary law of the Union. Although the Charter had already been proclaimed with a non-binding value in 2000 and its content, by express provision of the Preamble, is limited to "reaffirming" the rights deriving from the constitutional traditions and international obligations common to the Member States (including those enshrined in the ECHR), its placement in the primary rank is not without consequences. This operation allowed the ECJ to use the rules entrusted to arts. 7 and 8 of the Charter as parameters to judge the validity of secondary legislation (regulations, directives and decisions) of the Union, as well as to assess the compliance of any transposition provisions adopted by the Member States. Even on a purely symbolic level, the Charter represents the European bill of rights and therefore formalizes the relevance as fundamental rights of the two pillars of privacy.

The phase of the codification of privacy in its further meaning as protection of personal data has not exhausted the evolutionary path of the content of this right and of the relevant legislation. In fact, the Data Protection Directive, despite having marked a turning point at the European level in laying the foundations for a discipline as symmetrical as possible between the Member States, soon proved to be inadequate in the face of the digital revolution in the past two decades.

The last chapter, at least for the moment, of this evolving legal conceptualization of privacy and data protection, has been Regulation (EU) 2016/679 on the protection of natural persons with regard to the processing of personal data and on the free movement of such data (the General Data Protection Regulation, GDPR). Not only has the GDPR influenced other countries to adopt new privacy regulations, but it has also triggered enormous compliance, especially by US companies doing business in

Europe. The GDPR has a significant territorial and extra-territorial scope that covers data processing not only within the European Union and among its consumers but also where data is processed outside Member State territory with respect to EU citizens. Hence, the GDPR regulates how companies, public organizations, governments and businesses can use and process personal data, including data collection, mining, data aggregation or sharing of data.

Therefore, the GDPR marks a new milestone on this journey. As will be seen in the following chapter, the Regulation has revised the rules on personal data as governed by Directive 95/46/EC. The Regulation is part of the reform of the Digital Single Market: a review process of the current legislation that has been launched aimed at raising the level of harmonization between the laws of the Member States. This process, started on the basis of a proposal from the European Commission of January 2012, ended with the approval of the GDPR.

With the reform that led to the approval of the GDPR, the European Union then intended to replace the rigor of the measures that Directive 95/46/EC obliged owners to adopt with a greater degree of flexibility, a direct consequence of a new "risk-based approach." This process, which responds to a more liberal vision of privacy and compliance processes, has as its fulcrum the principle of accountability, that is, empowerment of the owner who processes data. It thus responded to the need to prepare a regulatory framework that would not make compliance on the part of the owners excessively burdensome, without sacrificing the rights of the parties at stake.

This regulatory process has not only involved European legislators but has also been fed by another important player: the ECJ, namely the judicial body within the European Union. Therefore, to understand the process that led to privacy becoming such a cornerstone of European values, it is necessary to discuss some of the case laws that interested the ECJ.

9.5.1 The right to privacy and data protection in the Union under the lenses of the ECJ

The ECJ cases reveal a judicial frame that is focused on modelling a new right to privacy and data protection as a consequence of the legal implications of the Internet. In fact, this dynamic is backed up by a complex process of deterritorialization, denationalization and dematerialization that reflects, inter alia, the jurisdictional issue characterizing the digital revolution. To understand the extent of this interpretation, which will be further examined in the following chapters, we are going to examine three examples.

Bodil Lindqvist v Åklagarkammaren i Jönköping

One of the most important cases that interested the ECJ is *Bodil Lindqvist v Åklagarkammaren i Jönköping* (C-101/01). The case is about Mrs. Lindqvist, who worked as a catechist in the Alseda Parish (Sweden). At the end of 1998, she set up Internet pages on her personal computer in order to allow parishioners preparing for their confirmation to obtain any information they needed. The pages she set up contained information about Mrs. Lindqvist and eighteen of her colleagues in the parish. The pages contained information including their full names, jobs held, hobbies, telephone numbers and medical information on one of her colleagues. She had neither informed her colleagues of those pages nor obtained their consent to process their personal data. In this context, the case has important implications for the posting of personal data on the Internet. The court clearly excluded that the activity conducted by Mrs. Lindqvist could be considered as "a purely household or personal activity." The court interpreted the exception to mean that it covers only activities that are carried out in the course of purely private or family life of individuals, which clearly is not the case here since the activities carried out by Mrs. Lindqvist were of a charitable or religious nature. Through this case, the ECJ clarified that posting personal data on the Internet amounts to processing personal data for the purposes of the Data Protection Directive. The court's finding highlights the fact that Europe's data protection regime is extremely far-reaching.

After this case, the ECJ issued a Grand Chamber ruling in *Promusicae v. Telefónica* (C-275/06). The applicant, Promusicae, was a non-profit organization composed of producers and publishers of musical and audiovisual recordings. They asked the ECJ to order Telefonica, an Internet service provider (ISP), to reveal personal data about its users, since users were allegedly accessing the intellectual property (IP)-protected work of Promusicae clients without permission. The conflicting interests at stake are numerous: if, on the one hand, there is an issue with arts. 7 and 8 of the Charter of Nice, due to the revealing of personal data, on the other hand, there was also a problem of copyright protection under arts. 17 and 47 of the Charter.

The court held that European law does not require ISPs to disclose their subscribers' identities to trade organizations for the purpose of civil litigation against them, but that European law also does not prohibit Member States from imposing such requirements if the legislation sufficiently balances IP and privacy rights. In its ruling, the ECJ appeared to seek a balance between preserving the content industry's ability to protect its intellectual property and maintaining ISP customers' privacy. Interpreting the EU's primary electronic commerce regulations in the context of EU intellectual property law and the privacy rights recognized in the CFREU, the court held that European law alone does not require ISPs to disclose their subscribers' identities to trade organizations for the purpose of civil litigation against the subscribers. The court noted, however, that nothing in the EU directives would prohibit Member States from imposing such requirements on their own.

Lastly, another important case is *LSG-Gesellschaft zur Wahrnehmung von Leistungsschutzrechten GmbH v Tele2 Telecommunication GmbH* (C-557/07). The applicant, LSG, was a collecting society that, like Promusicae, enforced the rights of recorded music producers in their worldwide recordings and the rights of the recording artists in respect of the exploitation of those recordings in Austria. The rights concerned are, in particular, the right to reproduce and distribute the recordings and the right to make them available to the public. Tele2 was an Internet access provider: it assigned to its clients' Internet Protocol Addresses ('IP addresses'). Hence, Tele2 was able to identify individual clients on the basis of their IP addresses. LSG's clients suffered financial loss as a result of the creation of file-sharing systems that make it possible for participants to exchange copies of saved data. In order to be able to bring civil proceedings against the perpetrators, LSG applied for an order requiring Tele2 to send it the names and addresses of the persons to whom it had provided an Internet access service and their IP addresses, together with the day and time of the connection, if known. Tele2 stated that, since it was not an intermediary, it was not authorized to save access data.

The ECJ decided that Community law does not preclude Member States from imposing an obligation to disclose to private third parties personal data relating to Internet traffic in order to enable them to bring civil proceedings for copyright infringement. Community law nevertheless requires Member States to ensure that, when transposing into national law Directive 2000/31/

EC, 2001/29/EC, 2002/58/EC and 2004/48/EC, they rely on an interpretation of those directives that allows a fair balance to be struck between the various fundamental rights involved. Moreover, when applying the measures transposing those directives, the authorities and courts of Member States must not only interpret their national law in a manner consistent with those directives but also must make sure that they do not rely on an interpretation of those directives that would conflict with those fundamental rights or with the other general principles of Community law, such as the principle of proportionality. The ECJ further decided that access providers that merely provide users with Internet access, without offering other services such as email, FTP or file-sharing services or exercising any control, whether *de iure* or de facto, over the services of which users make use, must be regarded as "intermediaries" within the meaning of art. 8(3) of Directive 2001/29/EC.

As will be shown in the following pages, the ECJ explored the impact of technological changes on the level of protection for fundamental rights. The crucial aspect in this respect is not whether limitations are legitimate. Rather, these decisions deal with how new technology affects fundamental rights across jurisdictions. The new right to digital privacy is the result of the attempt made by the ECJ to adopt a judicial frame that is capable of protecting fundamental rights in the world of bits. As will be stressed in the next chapter, the primary question is still whether the existing rules, including but not limited to those with constitutional standing, should constitute an appropriate legal basis for protecting the "new" rights emerging on the Internet, or whether alternatively they should be replaced by new provisions adopted on an ad hoc basis to regulate the consequences of the Internet.

9.6 Conclusions

"Data is the new oil" is one of the most used expressions in the field of data protection. However, it is very misleading. Oil is an exhaustible resource, scarcely available on the planet, increasingly the subject of conflict and difficult to acquire. Data are the opposite and, in general, are progressively growing in quantity and quality, partly due to the use of tools that have decreased the distance between the online and offline worlds, such as the Internet of Things and facial recognition technologies. While the potential of oil is in sharp decline, the prospects of data, on the other hand, are growing and seem to be potentially perpetual. Having this in mind, it became crucial to better protect privacy and data, meaning to put individuals in control of their digital selves. This process, which has global effects, particularly captured the attention of European scholars, policymakers and judges to tailor the borders of these crucial rights, which is the focus of the last part of this book. In this chapter the origins, the evolution and the extent of the right to privacy and the right to data protection were investigated. This analysis adopted a specific angle: the contribution of judicial reasonings to developing the current framework, from both a European and a transatlantic perspective.

At least in the European framework, the focus on "personal data" has constituted a critical premise for the consolidation of a frame of protection that is linked to individuals, the movements of whom directly engage the concept of privacy. In fact, if personal data are not processed correctly, the protection of that essential core of the person, which lies at the heart of the concept of personal identity, will be put at risk. Thus, personal data must be processed in accordance with a body of principles and rules in order to ensure protection for the individual and their personality. It is thus no longer simply privacy but also data protection that is a constitutional pillar of the information society. At the same time, the protection of privacy in the United States is not linked to the individual but rather to a mosaic theory where the individual per se is not relevant without the other parts of the mosaic. In other words, while under the EU framework the focus is on the individual and the protection of personal data, the US approach instead focuses more on the aggregated effects that certain processing can produce for society.

Moreover, the dualist nature of the right to privacy and the right to data protection have contributed to the creation of a legal and judicial space that recognizes the individual as a space of autonomy and self-determination. At the end of the 20th century, the development of new technologies allowed the rise of new business models based on the processing of multiple kinds of information including personal data, which are increasingly collected, organized and processed both by public actors for pursuing public tasks and by business actors for profits.

This chapter has examined the concepts of privacy and data protection by looking at the legal, judicial and, in part, the academic development of these two concepts. It has shown that in the US framework, privacy and data protection seems to be locked in a judicial frame of full trust in digital technologies. Aside from the exceptions mentioned above, there are no concerns regarding the new challenges raised by new digital technologies and the digital world. The US Supreme Court has not subjected the use of data and the infringement of privacy to safeguards since the system is still based on a narrow notion of a reasonable expectation of privacy. The consequence of this has been to demonstrate that, in that framework, the concept of privacy is still bound to an idea of privacy that does not amount to the constitutional protection of a fundamental right. Differently, in Europe, the inclusion of the right to private and family life in the category of rights protected by the ECHR marked the establishment of a first bond for the Contracting States, who are obliged to adequately protect the right to privacy according to the paradigm indicated in art. 8. The Strasbourg court, thus, like the US Supreme Court, was able to develop a copious jurisprudence in which to include under the protection of art. 8 ECHR situations and cases that are also very different from each other.

Moreover, as has been highlighted, the role of the ECtHR is just one aspect of the evolution of the right to privacy and data protection in Europe. In particular, in the last few years, the actions of the European Union, and especially the ECJ, have resulted in the consolidation and adaptation of these fundamental rights in the digital domain. Through legislative intervention, such as Directive 95/46/EC and the GDPR, European legislators have acknowledged that data processing now takes place on a large scale almost constantly. Particularly, the GDPR created a new framework that updated the compliance system by making it more aligned to the two tenets of privacy and data protection, giving more control to the data subjects, and recognizing accountability of those who collect and process personal data, throughout the indispensable recognition of both privacy and data protection has fundamental rights.

10 The General Data Protection Regulation

10.1 Introduction

Rapid technological developments and globalization have brought new challenges for the protection of personal data. The scale of the collection and sharing of personal data has increased significantly. Technology allows both private companies and public authorities to make use of personal data on an unprecedented scale in order to pursue their activities. Natural persons increasingly make personal information available publicly and globally. Technology has transformed both the economy and social life and should further facilitate the free flow of personal data. The path of European data protection has culminated with the adoption of the Regulation (EU) 2016/679, also known as the General Data Protection Regulation (GDPR). As already explained in the previous chapters, this step was the result of a constitutional process that pushed the European Union to abandon its market-oriented approach and adopt a constitutional-oriented strategy.

Even if the leading role given to the right to protection of personal data has been evident since the adoption of Directive 95/46/EC, recently the evolution of digital technology prompted the EU to recognize that the 1995 Data Protection Directive was out of date and needed to be modernized to protect EU citizens. Moreover, since the Directive, as a legislative tool, left each Member State to implement its own national laws to meet its goals, the overall scope of a uniform application of the right to personal data protection was defeated. Directive 95/46/EC has not prevented fragmentation in the implementation of data protection across the Union, legal uncertainty or a widespread public perception that there are significant risks to natural persons, in particular with regard to online activity. Such a difference in levels of protection is due to the existence of differences in the implementation and application of Directive 95/46/EC.

Therefore, recognizing the need to update European legislation in light of technological innovations, in 2012 the European Commission proposed a comprehensive plan to reform the processing of personal data in the EU, culminating in the approval of the GDPR. Analysis of the Regulation makes particularly evident the European Commission's choice of an omnibus approach, involving the creation of a comprehensive regulation directly applicable to each Member State's legal system.

In order to ensure a consistent and high level of protection of natural persons and to remove obstacles to the flow of personal data within the Union, the level of protection of the rights and freedoms of natural persons with regard to the processing of such data should be equivalent in all Member States. Consistent and homogeneous application of the rules for the protection of the fundamental rights and freedoms of natural persons with regard to the processing of personal data should be ensured throughout the Union.

In parallel, on the same day the Regulation was approved, Directives (EU) 2016/680 and 2016/681 were adopted. The first (also known as the "Law Enforcement Directive") relates to the protection of individuals regarding the processing of personal data by competent authorities for the purposes of prevention, investigation, detection and prosecution of criminal offenses or the execution of criminal penalties, and the free movement of such data. The second (also known as the "PNR Directive"), deals with the use of Passenger Name Record (PNR) data for the prevention, detection, investigation and prosecution of terrorist offenses and serious crime. While the Regulation is therefore the *lex generalis* in terms of personal data processing, the two directives deal with two specific aspects, namely the processing of data for the purpose of the prevention and detection of crimes, purposes explicitly excluded from the scope of application of the GDPR.

This chapter aims to illustrate the principles and obligations introduced by the GDPR. Section 10.2 describes the material and territorial scope of the GDPR and the subjects involved (10.2.2). Section 10.3 shows the general principles that have to be respected, while Section 10.4 provides the legal basis and primary obligations. Additionally, the chapter describes the characteristics of data subjects' rights (10.5). Section 10.6 addresses the primary obligations introduced by the GDPR, while Section 10.7 deals with the transfer of personal data, which will be further discussed in Chapter 14. Lastly, Section 10.8 describes the functioning of supervisory authorities and the system of sanctions.

10.2 Material and territorial scope

The GDPR inherited the terminological categories that were introduced by the Data Protection Directive. To understand the subjective and objective scope of application, it is essential to start from some definitions provided in art. 4. Personal data are defined as "any information relating to an identified or identifiable natural person (data subject)." Thus, the natural person who can be identified, directly or indirectly, is considered identifiable. Therefore, a very wide range of information is included.

Examples of personal data are name and surname, the image of a person and their tax code. In the first two examples, the data subject is identified. In the latter case, however, the person can only be identified indirectly, that is, through the association of other data. The IP address could be considered a case study. According to the Article 29 Working Party (WP29), Internet access providers can, using reasonable means, identify Internet users to whom they have assigned IP addresses as they record the date, time, duration and specific IP address in a specific file (opinion no. 4 of June 20, 2007 – WP 136). The ECJ addressed this point in *Breyer* (C-582/14).

While "static" IP addresses are considered personal data, doubts have arisen with respect to the "dynamic" IP address, which varies with each new Internet connection and does not allow univocal and direct identification of the user. The court recognized that the dynamic IP address constitutes personal data as the website operator has legal means that allow the visitor to be identified thanks to the additional information available under the Internet access provider's control.

The GDPR then identifies some special categories of personal data, which include personal data revealing racial or ethnic origin, political opinions, religious or philosophical beliefs, or trade union membership as well as genetic data, biometric data intended to uniquely identify a natural person, and data relating to the health or sexual life or sexual orientation of the data subject. These personal data merit specific protections as their processing could create significant risks for the fundamental rights and freedoms of the data subject. Therefore, under the GDPR, the processing of these particular categories of data is subject to additional precautions and more stringent requirements, as will be explained below; for example, the consent of the data subjects to their processing must be explicit.

Personal data fall within the scope of the GDPR when they are processed. The GDPR defines processing as

> any operation or set of operations which is performed on personal data or on sets of personal data, whether or not by automated means, such as collection, recording, organization, structuring, storage, adaptation or alteration, retrieval, consultation, use, disclosure by transmission, dissemination or otherwise making available, alignment or combination, restriction, erasure or destruction.

It is a deliberately all-encompassing notion that describes almost all operations likely to involve personal data.

10.2.1 Data controller

According to art. 4(7) of the GDPR,

> "controller" means the natural or legal person, public authority, agency or other body which, alone or jointly with others, determines the purposes and means of the processing of personal data; where the purposes and means of such processing are determined by Union or Member State law, the controller or the specific criteria for its nomination may be provided for by Union or Member State law.

The data controller, determining the purposes and the means of the processing, can be considered the governor of the processing of personal data or the "counterpart" of the data subject who collects and processes the personal data. For instance, an employer is the data controller with respect to the personal data of the employees; the educational institution with respect to students' personal data; a social network with respect to users' personal data; and the search engine with respect to personal data contained in the indexed web pages. The WP29 clarified that the data controller is the accountable subject for the processing of personal data. This is why it is important that the data controller is identified not on the basis of a formalistic reading but by virtue of a functionalistic and substantial interpretation. In this regard, the European Data Protection Board (EDPB) clarified that the concept of controller is a functional concept, as it is based on a factual rather than a formal analysis.

With reference to the objective profiles, it is therefore necessary to identify the controller on the basis of the existence of a power of control, which may derive from an explicit and formal attribution of competences (for example, in the event that the law expressly establishes that a subject or an authority has to be identified as the data controller), by an implicit attribution of competences (for example, in the case of the employer who processes the personal data of employees or the publisher who processes the personal data of subscribers) or by a factual influence (for example, where the contractual terms and conditions do not provide for an explicit investiture, but actually attribute a power of lordship to one of the parties on the processing of the data that the counterparty transfers; or in the case of a subject who sends an image to the interested party and can thus dispose of it). This power of control, whatever its source, is embodied in the definition of the purposes and means of the processing, that is, the "why" and "how" of the processing. In order to correctly qualify the parties, the interpreter should look at the specific processing operations in question and understand who determines them, by first considering the following questions: "why is this processing taking place?" and "who decided that the processing should take place for a particular purpose?". While the contribution to the determination of the purposes produces in any case the qualification as controller, the contribution to the definition of the means can be considered decisive only when it pertains to essential elements of the modalities. According to the EDPB, a distinction can be made between essential and non-essential means. "Essential means" are traditionally and inherently reserved to the controller. While non-essential means can also be determined by other subjects, essential means are to be determined by the controller. "Essential means" are means that are closely linked to the purpose and the scope of the processing, such as the types of personal data that are processed, the duration of the processing, the categories of recipients and the categories of data subjects. Together with the purpose of processing, the essential means are also closely linked to the question of whether the processing is lawful, necessary and proportionate. "Non-essential means" concern more practical aspects of implementation, such as the choice of a particular type of hardware or software or the detailed security measures, which may be left to the processor to decide.

Therefore, anyone who decides to process data must consider whether this includes personal data and, if so, consider the obligations that will apply to it according to the GDPR. An actor will be considered a "controller" even if it does not deliberately target personal data as such or has wrongfully assessed that it does not process personal data.

It is not necessary that the controller has access to the data that is being processed. In this context, it should be considered that someone who outsources a processing activity and, in doing so, has a determinative influence on the purpose and (essential) means of the processing (e.g., by adjusting parameters of a service in such a way that it influences whose personal data shall be processed), must be regarded as a controller even though they will never have actual access to the data.

The GDPR also deals with joint controllership. According to art. 4(7) of the GDPR:

> Where two or more controllers jointly determine the purposes and means of processing, they shall be joint controllers.

In broad terms, joint controllership exists with regard to a specific processing activity when different parties determine jointly the purpose and means of this processing activity. Therefore, assessing the existence of joint controllers requires examining whether the determination of purposes and means that characterize a controller is made by more than one party. This assessment should be carried out through a factual, rather than a formal, analysis of the actual influence on the purposes and means of the processing.

The GDPR expressly disciplines this case in art. 26. This provision requires, in compliance with what has already been specified by the EDPB, that the joint controllers determine in a transparent manner, through an internal agreement, their respective responsibilities with regard to compliance with the obligations deriving from the GDPR, with particular regard to the exercise of the rights of the data subjects, and the respective information communication functions. The data subject may in any case act indistinctly against each of the joint controllers for the exercise of their rights.

For instance, a relationship of joint controllership has been recognized by the ECJ in the *Facebook Fanpage* case (C-210/16). The ECJ held that the administrator of a fan page hosted on Facebook, by defining parameters based on its target audience and the objectives of managing and promoting its activities, must be regarded as taking part in the determination of the means of the processing of personal data related to the visitors to its fan page.

As noted by the ECJ in *Facebook Fanpage* (C-210/16), the processing of personal data through statistics of visitors to a fan page is intended to enable Facebook to improve its system of advertising transmitted via its network and to enable the administrator of the fan page to obtain statistics to manage the promotion of its activity. Each entity in this case pursues its own interest, but both parties participate in the determination of the purposes (and means) of the processing of personal data of visitors to the fan page. In this respect, it is important to highlight that the mere existence of a mutual benefit (e.g., commercial) arising from a processing activity does not give rise to joint controllership. If the entity involved in the processing does not pursue any purpose(s) of its own in relation to the processing activity, but is merely being paid for services rendered, it is acting as a processor rather than as a joint controller.

Lastly, it should be recalled that the fact that several actors are involved in the same processing does not mean that they are necessarily acting as joint controllers of such processing. Not all kind of partnerships, cooperation or collaboration imply qualification of joint controllers, as such qualification requires a case-by-case analysis of each processing at stake and the precise role of each entity with respect to each processing. For example, the exchange of the same data or set of data between two entities without jointly determined purposes or jointly determined means of processing should be considered a transmission of data between separate controllers.

10.2.2 Data processor

The GDPR also defines the role of the data processor in art. 4(8) as the

> natural or legal person, public authority, agency or other body which processes personal data on behalf of the controller.

The processor is concretely the entity carrying out the processing of personal data. It can also be identified for the most part on a factual basis rather than on the basis of strict formal requirements. Two conditions have been indicated for qualification as a data processor:

a. on the one hand, the existence of a separate entity with respect to the data controller;
b. on the other hand, the carrying out of personal data processing on the behalf of the data controller.

The extent of the processing activity may vary significantly depending on the context.

The qualification as a processor does not necessarily derive from the subjective otherness with respect to the controller but rests on the activity carried out in practice in a specific context. Indeed, for the same processing activities, an entity can act at the same time as controller and as processor, depending on who is deciding the purposes and the means of the processing. Thus, a hosting provider acts as a processor for the data published by the site operators using its permanent storage services. However, it acts as a controller in the event that it processes that data for its own purposes and for those other than storing content. Similarly, a professional firm that provides accounting and payroll management services.

The EDPB recalls in its "Guidelines 07/2020 on the concepts of controller and processor in the GDPR" that not every service provider that processes personal data in the course of delivering a service is a "processor" within the meaning of the GDPR. The role of a processor does not stem from the nature of an entity that is processing data but from its concrete activities in a specific context.

The nature of the service will determine whether the processing activity amounts to processing of personal data on behalf of the controller within the meaning of the GDPR. In practice, where the provided service is not specifically targeted at processing personal data or where such processing does not constitute a key element of the service, the service provider may be in a position to independently determine the purposes and means of the processing that is required in order to provide the service. In that situation, the service provider is to be seen as a separate controller and not as a processor. A case-by-case analysis remains necessary, however, in order to ascertain the degree of influence each entity effectively has in determining the purposes and means of the processing.

What is relevant, therefore, for the purposes of identifying the processor is the performance of the mandate on behalf and in the interest of the controller. Art. 28 of the GDPR provides that the processing carried out by the processor is governed by a contract or other legal act according to the law that binds the processor to the controller and identifies the subject matter, the duration, the nature and the purposes of the processing, the types of data processed and the categories of data subjects, obligations and rights of the controller, as well as all the instructions of the processing the controller may give to its processor.

10.2.3 Territorial scope

Regarding the territorial scope, the GDPR has a broad application. As the EDPB has clarified in Guidelines 3/2018 on the territorial scope of the GDPR, art. 3 of the GDPR reflects the legislators' intention to ensure comprehensive protection of the rights of data subjects in the EU and to establish, in terms of data protection requirements, a level playing field for companies active in EU markets in a context of worldwide data flows. Art. 3 of the GDPR defines the territorial scope on the basis of two main criteria:

1. the "establishment" criterion, as per art. 3(1).

> Example 1: A car manufacturing company with headquarters in the United States has a fully owned branch office located in Brussels overseeing all its operations in Europe, including marketing and advertisement. The Belgian branch can be considered to be a stable arrangement, which exercises real and effective activities in light of the nature of the economic activity carried out by the car manufacturing company. As such, the Belgian branch could therefore be considered an establishment in the Union, within the meaning of the GDPR.

2. the "targeting" criterion as per art. 3(2).

> Example 2: A start-up established in the United States, without any business presence or establishment in the European Union, provides a city-mapping application for tourists. The application processes personal data concerning the location of customers using the app (the data subjects) once they start using the application in the city they visit, in order to offer targeted advertisements for places to visit, restaurants, bars and hotels. The application is available for tourists while they visit New York, San Francisco, Toronto, Paris and Rome. Since EU-located data subjects' personal data are processed in connection with the offering of the service, it falls within the scope of the GDPR as per art. 3(2).

Where one of these two criteria is met, the relevant provisions of the GDPR will apply to relevant processing of personal data by the controller or processor concerned.

In addition, art. 3(3) confirms the application of the GDPR to the processing where Member State law applies by virtue of public international law.

The EDPB underlines that the application of art. 3 aims at determining whether a particular processing activity, rather than a person (legal or natural), falls within the scope of the GDPR. Consequently, certain processing of personal data by a controller or processor might fall within the scope of the GDPR, while other processing of personal data by that same controller or processor might not, depending on the processing activity.

More specifically, the first criterion is met when the processing of personal data is carried out in the context of the activities of an establishment of a controller or a processor in the Union, regardless of whether the processing takes place in the Union or not. The second criterion is met when the processing of personal data of data subjects who are in the Union is carried out by a controller or processor not established in the Union, where the processing activities are related to:

a. the offering of goods or services, irrespective of whether a payment of the data subject is required, to such data subjects in the Union.

Example 2(a): A website, based and managed in Turkey, offers services for the creation, editing, printing and shipping of personalized family photo albums. The website is available in English, French, Dutch and German and payments can be made in euros. The website indicates that photo albums can only be delivered by mail in France, Benelux countries and Germany. In this case, it is clear that the creation, editing and printing of personalized family photo albums constitutes a service within the meaning of EU law. The fact that the website is available in four languages of the European Union and that photo albums can be delivered by mail in six EU Member States demonstrates that there is an intention on the part of the Turkish website to offer its services to individuals in the Union. As a consequence, it is clear that the processing carried out by the Turkish website, as a data controller, relates to the offering of a service to data subjects in the Union and is therefore subject to the obligations and provisions of the GDPR, as per its art. 3(2)(a).

b. the monitoring of their behavior as far as it takes place within the Union.

Example 2(b): A retail consultancy company established in the United States provides advice on retail layout to a shopping center in France, based on an analysis of customers' movements throughout the center collected through Wi-Fi tracking. The analysis of customers' movements within the center through Wi-Fi tracking will amount to the monitoring of individuals' behavior. In this case, the data subjects' behavior takes place in the Union since the shopping center is located in France. The consultancy company, as a data controller, is therefore subject to the GDPR in respect of the processing of this data for this purpose as per its art. 3(2)(b).

In these cases, the controller or the processor shall designate in writing a representative in the Union as a point of contact necessary to allow the enforcement of the rights of the data subjects and to avoid, at the same time, possible evasive behavior. Nonetheless, according to art. 27, the obligation to designate a representative in the Union does not operate in the case of occasional processing or processing that does not involve large-scale operations relating to particular categories of data or data relating to criminal convictions or crimes and if it is unlikely that the processing poses a risk to the rights and freedoms of natural persons considering the nature, context, scope and purpose of the processing. Furthermore, the appointment obligation does not apply to public authorities and public bodies.

Lastly, the GDPR also applies to the processing of personal data by a controller not established in the Union, but in a place where Member State law applies by virtue of public international law.

10.3 General principles

Art. 5 provides a list of all the general principles applicable to the processing of personal data. This provision is of enormous importance as it summarizes the criteria of the entire discipline of personal data protection. Moreover, the explication of these principles reveals the intentions of European legislators to issue "a charter of individual rights" related to personal data that contains a list of general principles. From a practical point of view, this provision serves as a useful tool for the interpretation of the GDPR: the balancing between data subjects' rights, the areas of application of the various provisions, the exceptions and the limitations can only be fully understood in light of the general principles.

Therefore, the GDPR establishes the principles according to which the processing of personal data must be conducted, in particular:

a. lawfulness, fairness and transparency (the data must be processed in a lawful, correct and transparent way towards the interested party);
b. purpose limitation (the data must be collected for specific, explicit and legitimate purposes, and subsequently processed in a way that is not incompatible with these purposes);
c. data minimization (data must be adequate, relevant and limited to what is necessary with respect to the purposes);
d. accuracy (the data must be accurate and, if necessary, updated);
e. storage limitation (the data must be kept in a form that allows the identification of the data subjects for a period of time not exceeding the achievement of the purposes for which they are processed);
f. integrity and confidentiality (the duties must be treated in such a way as to guarantee adequate security).

However, these requirements must be part of what has been described as the pillar of the GDPR, that is, the principle of accountability. In fact, art. 5(2) establishes that the data controller is required to comply with these principles and is obligated to prove such compliance. Generally, the aim of incorporating the accountability principle into the GDPR and making it a central principle is to emphasize that data controllers must implement appropriate and effective measures and be able to demonstrate compliance. The accountability principle is directly addressed to the controller and, together with the other, more specific rules, makes it necessary to define the different roles of several actors involved in personal data processing activities.

This reflects a dynamic notion of responsibility where the data controller is not only liable but also accountable. According to art. 24, the responsibility of the data controller is assessed taking into account the nature, scope, context and purposes of processing as well as the risks of varying likelihood and severity for the rights and freedoms of data subjects. Accordingly, the controller is required to put in place appropriate technical and organizational measures as well as to implement the principles on data protection both when determining the means of processing and at the time of processing itself. Furthermore, it requires that the guarantees necessary to comply with the obligation of the GDPR and to protect the rights of the data subjects are integrated into the processing.

In this case, it is important to focus on the principles of "privacy by design" and "privacy by default." According to art. 25, the controller is required, both at the time of the determination of the means for processing and at the time of the processing itself, to implement appropriate technical and organizational measures. These include pseudonymization, which is designed to apply data protection principles, as well as data minimization, that have to be implemented in an effective manner in order to meet the requirements and protect the rights of data subjects. Even in this case, the GDPR underlines that such assessment should take into account the state of the art, the cost of implementation and the nature, scope, context and purposes of processing as well as the risks of varying likelihood and severity for rights and freedoms of natural persons posed by the processing. Further, the controller shall implement appropriate technical and organizational measures for ensuring that, by default, only personal data that are necessary for each specific purpose of the processing are processed. This obligation applies to the amount of personal data collected, the extent of their processing, the period of their storage and their accessibility.

10.4 Legal bases

As can be seen from the first two principles set out in the previous paragraph, the scope of the processing of personal data is defined by a legal basis that constitutes justification to process them. The terms "legal basis" and "lawfulness" are used throughout the GDPR to refer to when it is permissible to collect or process personal data. Personal data can only be processed according to a specific legal basis.

Art. 6 is, perhaps, the most important section of the GDPR covering lawful bases for the collection and processing of personal data. One or more valid legal basis is/are required in all cases. There is no hierarchy or preferred option. All processing of personal data should be based on the legal basis that is most appropriate in the specific circumstances of that processing.

10.4.1 Consent

The most well-known and widespread legal basis is the consent of the data subject. This legal basis represents the highest expression of data subjects' autonomy.

The GDPR strengthens the conditions for the expression of consent in order to ensure effective awareness on the part of the data subject. The consent, as also clarified by the EDPB in Guidelines 05/2020 on consent under Regulation 2016/679, should be:

a. freely given, so that four elements have to be analyzed:
   - imbalance of power;
   - conditionality;
   - granularity; and
   - detriment.
b. specific;
c. informed; and
d. an unambiguous indication of the data subject's wishes by which they, by a statement or by a clear affirmative action, signifies agreement to the processing of personal data relating to them.

Therefore, data controllers have to provide clear information to explain the purposes and means of the processing. Furthermore, the controller should be able to demonstrate that the data subject has consented to the processing. As mentioned, when consent concerns the processing of personal data, it must also be explicit.

The EDPB has dedicated detailed guidelines to the characteristics of consent provided for by the GDPR (Guidelines 05/2020 on consent under Regulation 2016/679). Freedom implies real choice and control for data subjects. As a general rule, the GDPR prescribes that if the data subjects have no real choice, feel compelled to consent or will endure negative consequences if they do not consent, then consent will not be valid. If consent is bundled up as a non-negotiable part of terms and conditions, it is presumed not to have been freely given. Accordingly, consent will not be considered to be free if the data subject is unable to refuse or withdraw their consent without detriment.

This requirement is strictly linked to the notion of imbalance between the controller and the data subject. First, the existence of an imbalance of power is important, as it could arise both in the relationship with public authorities and in employment contexts. These circumstances do not necessarily exclude the freedom of consent but are indicative of factual situations in which a conditioning can be presumed according to a higher probability index.

Second, the element of conditionality should be considered. The hypothesis in which the execution of a contract or service is subject to the manifestation of consent to the processing of data that is not necessary for the purposes of the main service is particularly highlighted. In doing so, consent would be forced under the threat of not performing a contract or a service. Furthermore, with the provision of consent to the processing of unnecessary data, the interested party would offer a non-economic "hidden" counterpart to the controller. To verify any hypothesis of unification or subordination, the scope of the relevant contract and the data strictly necessary for its execution must therefore be taken into account.

Another predicate necessary to hold the manifestation of consent free is its granularity, which requires that, in the case of multiple processing for different purposes, the data subject is free to identify which purposes to accept and therefore to give separate consent for each of these. It may thus happen that more consents are collected for the provision of a service.

Lastly, the manifestation of consent is free if no prejudice is feared (detriment). The threat of prejudice extends to a number of different situations in which not only economic variables are relevant. For example, the prejudice may consist in the reduction of the functionality of a service when the data subject has revoked the consent previously given to data processing that is not essential for its performance.

The second requirement of consent is specificity. The consent must be specific as the data subjects must preserve the freedom to choose in relation to each of the purposes of the processing of their data. It is therefore connected to the attribute of granularity and at the same time to the need for consent to be "informed." Specific consent aims to preserve a sufficient degree of control and transparency for the benefit of the interested party.

The principle of informed consent also responds to similar needs: only as such does the consent preserve an effective awareness of the interested party and therefore a capacity for control that can be expressed even in its revocation. Based on art. 5 of the GDPR, the requirement for transparency is one of its fundamental principles, closely related to the principles of fairness and lawfulness. Providing information to data subjects prior to obtaining their consent is essential in order to enable them to make informed decisions, understand what they are agreeing to and, possibly, exercise their right to withdraw their consent. If the controller does not provide accessible information, user control becomes illusory, and consent will be an invalid basis for processing.

The GDPR introduces a new predicate so that consent can be considered free, requiring its unequivocal manifestation, that is, by means of an unequivocal positive statement or action. This attribute is not substantiated in the requirement of the written form – which, however, appears to be the most suitable to satisfy it – but requires deliberate action. What it aims to avoid is completely passive attitudes and behaviors that can be considered suitable to constitute manifestations of consent.

Lastly, it should be noted that consent must be explicit in the event of the processing of particular categories of data. According to the WP29, the methods for expressing consent must be such as to draw the attention of the data subjects to the peculiarity of the situation and the delicacy of the data in question and the choice to consent to their processing.

10.4.2 Other legal bases

In addition to consent, there are other frequently used legal bases that can legitimize the processing of personal data. According to art. 6:

a. the data subject has given consent to the processing of his or her personal data for one or more specific purposes (as analyzed in Section 10.4.1);

b. processing is necessary for the performance of a contract to which the data subject is party or in order to take steps at the request of the data subject prior to entering into a contract;
c. processing is necessary for compliance with a legal obligation to which the controller is subject;
d. processing is necessary in order to protect the vital interests of the data subject or of another natural person;
e. processing is necessary for the performance of a task carried out in the public interest or in the exercise of official authority vested in the controller;
f. processing is necessary for the purposes of the legitimate interests pursued by the controller or by a third party, except where such interests are overridden by the interests or fundamental rights and freedoms of the data subject which require protection of personal data, where the data subject is a child.

The notion of legitimate interest is one of the most challenging issues. This is a concept that cannot be traced back to a precise definition, since it is to be understood as an "open" case including a series of situations in which data subjects could reasonably expect the processing of their personal data, based on their relationship with the data controller. Nonetheless, when relying on legitimate interests, the data controller cannot adversely affect the rights and freedoms of the data subject. Therefore, the data controller cannot always process personal data based on legitimate interest, but only when this use does not disproportionately affect the rights and freedoms of data subjects.

Nevertheless, Opinion 06/2014 on the notion of legitimate interests of the data controller of the WP29 tries to clarify that the concept of "interest" is closely related to, but distinct from, the concept of "purpose." It can be defined as an interest that a controller may have in the processing overall or the benefit that the controller derives – or that society might derive – from the processing. For instance, a company may have an interest in ensuring the health and safety of its staff working at its nuclear power plant. Related to this, the company may have as a purpose the implementation of specific access control procedures that justifies the processing of certain specified personal data in order to help ensure the health and safety of staff. Moreover, an interest must be sufficiently clearly articulated to allow the balancing test to be carried out against the interests and fundamental rights of the data subject. In addition, the interest at stake must also be "pursued by the controller." This requires a real and present interest, something that corresponds with current activities or benefits that are expected in the very near future. In other words, interests that are too vague or speculative are not sufficient. The nature of the interest may vary. Some interests may be compelling and beneficial to society at large, such as the interest of the press to publish information about government corruption or the interest in carrying out scientific research (subject to appropriate safeguards). In the view of the WP29, the notion of legitimate interest could include a broad range of interests, whether trivial or very compelling, straightforward or more controversial.

The examples provided by some recitals of the GDPR certainly help to clarify this particular legal basis. There are hypotheses of legitimate interest, for example, when there are qualified relationships between the data subject and the controller, such as when the first is a customer of the second or employed by them. Cases of legitimate interest occur when the controller carries out processing for fraud prevention purposes or for direct marketing purposes. Furthermore, controllers belonging to an entrepreneurial group or entities connected to a holding may have a legitimate interest in transmitting data within the entrepreneurial group for internal administrative purposes (including the processing of personal data of customers or employees). Likewise, there is a legitimate interest when the controller processes personal data relating to traffic in order to ensure network and information security.

10.5 Data subjects' rights

The GDPR establishes specific rights of data subjects in relation to the processing of personal data. In particular, these rights are important pieces of the puzzle to ensure that data subjects can control the processing of their personal data and react in case of unlawful processing.

As a general guideline, in order to guarantee the exercise of the data subjects' rights, the GDPR states that it is appropriate to provide for procedures aimed at facilitating the exercise by the data subject of the various rights envisaged (Recital 59). These facilitating "modalities" may consist, for example, of organizational or technological means, or special forms on the website, or even through means of direct interaction with the data themselves. In particular, the GDPR requires that where personal data are processed by electronic means, the data controller should also provide the means to forward requests by electronic means. Once the data subject requests the exercise of rights, then the general rule is that the data controller should respond to the request of the data subject "without undue delay and at the latest within one month" and give a reason if the data controller's intention is not to grant such request (Recital 59). Moreover, any refusal to respond to users' requests must be specifically justified.

10.5.1 Right of access

The first right recognized by the GDPR is the right of access (art. 15), which allows the data subject to ascertain the existence of their personal data being processed by the data controller and to acquire every detail in this regard. More specifically, the purpose of the right of access is to make it possible for the data subject to understand how their personal data is being processed as well as the consequences of such processing, and to verify the accuracy of the data processed without having to justify their intention.

The data subjects have the right to obtain from the controller confirmation as to whether or not personal data concerning them are being processed and, where that is the case, access to the personal data. The controller provides a copy of the personal data undergoing processing for free. Nevertheless, it can apply a reasonable fee for further requests, or when there are limits to this right as it could affect the right of others (e.g., privacy). In particular, the controller is required to provide the following information:

a. the purposes of the processing;
b. the categories of personal data concerned;
c. the recipients or categories of recipient to whom the personal data have been or will be disclosed, in particular recipients in third countries or international organizations;
d. where possible, the envisaged period for which the personal data will be stored, or, if not possible, the criteria used to determine that period;
e. the existence of the right to request from the controller rectification or erasure of personal data or restriction of processing of personal data concerning the data subject or to object to such processing;
f. the right to lodge a complaint with a supervisory authority;
g. where the personal data are not collected from the data subject, any available information as to their source;
h. the existence of automated decision-making, including profiling, referred to in arts. 22(1) and (4) and, at least in those cases, meaningful information about the logic involved, as well as the significance and the envisaged consequences of such processing for the data subject.

Moreover, where personal data are transferred to a third country or to an international organization, the data subject has the right to be informed of the appropriate safeguards pursuant to art. 46 relating to the transfer.

10.5.2 **Right to rectification**

The data subject has the right not only to access but also, under art. 16, to request the rectification of inaccurate personal data without undue delay. This also includes the possibility to provide information regarding incomplete personal data.

Specifically, "rectifying" data means replacing incorrect data with the correct information. This can also include correcting an incomplete data set by updating it with the missing information. Thereafter, the controller should contact each recipient to whom the personal data have been disclosed, unless this proves impossible or involves disproportionate efforts. This right is clearly closely related to the accuracy principle set forth in art. 5 of the GDPR.

10.5.3 Right to erasure

Even more importantly, the data subject can ask the data controller to erase their personal data. The right to erasure allows the data subject to obtain the deletion of personal data in the following cases:

a. the personal data are no longer necessary in relation to the purposes for which they were collected or otherwise processed;
b. the data subject withdraws consent on which the processing is based according to point (a) of art. 6(1), or point (a) of art. 9(2), and where there is no other legal ground for the processing;
c. the data subject objects to the processing pursuant to art. 21(1) and there are no overriding legitimate grounds for the processing, or the data subject objects to the processing pursuant to art. 21(2);
d. the personal data have been unlawfully processed;
e. the personal data have to be erased for compliance with a legal obligation in Union or Member State law to which the controller is subject;
f. the personal data have been collected in relation to the offer of information society services referred to in art. 8(1).

However, this right is not restricted to these cases but is subject to other limitations that aim to balance conflicting interests. In particular, the right to erasure does not apply when the processing is necessary for exercising the right of freedom of expression and information. Similarly, the right of erasure cannot be exercised when the stored personal data allow the compliance with a legal obligation established by Union or Member State law to which the controller is subject or for the performance of a task carried out in the public interest or in the exercise of official authority vested in the controller. Moreover, this right cannot be exercised when it conflicts with reasons of public interest in the area of public health in accordance with points (h) and (i) of art. 9(2), as well as art. 9(3), with archiving purposes in the public interest, scientific or historical research purposes or statistical purposes in accordance with art. 89(1). Lastly, the right does not apply when the personal data are necessary for the establishment, exercise or defense of legal claims.

10.5.4 Right to restriction of processing

According to art. 18, data subjects can require data controllers to restrict the processing of personal data when:

a. the accuracy of the personal data is contested by the data subject, for a period enabling the controller to verify the accuracy of the personal data;
b. the processing is unlawful and the data subject opposes the erasure of the personal data and requests the restriction of their use instead;

c. the controller no longer needs the personal data for the purposes of the processing, but they are required by the data subject for the establishment, exercise or defense of legal claims;
d. the data subject has objected to processing pursuant to art. 21(1) pending the verification whether the legitimate grounds of the controller override those of the data subject.

In these cases, the data controller can always process these data for the establishment, exercise or defense of legal claims or for the protection of the rights of another natural or legal person or for reasons of important public interest of the Union or of a Member State.

10.5.5 Right to data portability

The GDPR also introduces the right to data portability under art. 20. This would be a precondition for users in order to rely on an automatic transfer of personal data across different data controllers. In this case, the data subject has the right to receive the personal data they have provided to a controller, in a structured, commonly used and machine-readable format, and the right to transmit, or to ask the data controller to transmit, those data to another controller without hindrance from the controller to which the personal data have been provided. However, this right can be exercised only when the processing is based on consent or a contractual relationship, and when it is carried out by automated means. Even in this case, the GDPR underlines that the right to data portability should not adversely affect the rights and freedoms of others.

10.5.6 Right to object

Furthermore, according to art. 21, the GDPR also provides the possibility to object to and avoid interferences by decisions taken solely by automated means. The data subjects have the right to object, on grounds relating to their particular situation, at any time, unless the processing of personal data is necessary for the performance of a task carried out in the public interest or in the exercise of official authority vested in the controller, or the processing is necessary for the purposes of the legitimate interests pursued by the controller or by a third party. However, the GDPR provides for an exception where such interests are overridden by the interests or fundamental rights and freedoms of the data subject that require protection of personal data, particularly where the data subject is a child. In the case of direct marketing, this right can always be exercised. Once the data subject exercises the right to object, the controller cannot process the personal data in question any longer unless the controller demonstrates compelling legitimate grounds for the processing which override the interests, rights and freedoms of the data subject or for the establishment, exercise or defense of legal claims.

10.5.7 Automated individual decision-making, including profiling

Art. 22 establishes the right, or more precisely the freedom, not to be subject to a decision solely based on automated decision-making that produces legal effects concerning the subject or similarly significantly affects them. Even in this case, the GDPR provides exceptions when the decision:

a. is necessary for entering into, or performance of, a contract between the data subject and a data controller;
b. is authorized by Union or Member State law to which the controller is subject and which also lays down suitable measures to safeguard the data subject's rights and freedoms and legitimate interests; or
c. is based on the data subject's explicit consent.

In particular, in the first and third cases, the data controller shall implement suitable measures to safeguard the data subject's rights and freedoms and legitimate interests, at least the right to obtain human intervention on the part of the controller, to express their point of view and to contest the decision.

In any case, data controllers cannot base their decisions solely on automated decision-making when processing particular categories of personal data. Even in this case, the GDPR provides an exception when the data subject has given explicit consent or the processing is necessary for reasons of substantial public interest, on the basis of Union or Member State law, and the data controller applies suitable measures to safeguard the data subject's rights and freedoms and legitimate interests.

10.6 Obligations under the GDPR

Significant obligations introduced by the GDPR are placed on the side of compliance, as a consequence of the paradigm change determined by adherence to the so-called risk-based approach, driven by the principle of accountability. The GDPR establishes a set of obligations applicable without distinction to data controllers and processors and provides for a series of additional obligations in the presence of personal data processing that involve "high" risks for the rights and freedoms of the data subjects. The reason for this approach is to leave margins of discretion in assessing the level of risk in practice by the controllers and processors and consequently to graduate the obligations.

10.6.1 Records of processing activities

As regards the first set of obligations, art. 30 requires the data controller and processor to keep a record of the processing activities of personal data. This obligation does not apply to companies or organizations with fewer than 250 employees. However, this exemption from the obligation does not apply when (a) the processing may present a risk for the rights and freedoms of the data subject, (b) it is not occasional, or (c) it includes the processing of particular categories of data or personal data relating to criminal convictions and offenses. In the presence of one of the three factors just mentioned, therefore, the obligation to keep a record applies indiscriminately, regardless of the size of the company or organization. Therefore, art. 30 requires the creation and maintenance of records of processing activities, which must reflect the reality of personal data processing and allow the controller to precisely identify, among others, the actors involved (controller, processor, representative, joint controller, etc.) in the data processing; the categories of data processed; the purpose of the processing (what is done with the collected personal data); who has access and who are the recipients of the personal data; how long the personal data is retained; and the technical and organizational security measures that are implemented. Additionally, under art. 30(2), data processors, where appointed, have to keep a record of all categories of activities relating to processing carried out on behalf of a data controller.

Generally, it should be considered that the types of information contained in the records are largely reminiscent of the information that, although related to the individual data subject, must be communicated to the data subjects and that which must be provided to the data subject upon request, for example, for the exercise of their rights. Therefore, it is easy to understand that a proper record should also allow for easier availability of information to be provided in other contexts and for other purposes. In addition, the standard requires that records be kept in written form, including electronic form, but does not impose any formalities.

10.6.2 Security measures related to processing

Art. 32 requires the controller and the processor to implement appropriate technical and organizational measures to ensure a level of security appropriate to the risk. The data controller is required to put in place adequate technical and organizational measures to ensure that processing activities comply with the GDPR. These measures – subject to continuous updating – are defined taking into account the nature, scope, context and purpose of the processing, as well as risks with different probabilities and gravity for the rights and freedoms of individuals. These measures include, among others, pseudonymization and data encryption; the ability to permanently ensure the confidentiality, integrity, availability and resilience of processing systems and services; the ability to promptly restore the availability and access of personal data in the event of a physical or technical incident; and procedures aimed at testing, verifying and evaluating the effectiveness of technical and organizational measures on a constant basis. In assessing the adequate level of security, particular account is taken of the risks deriving from the destruction, loss, modification, unauthorized disclosure or access, accidentally or illegally, to personal data transmitted, stored or otherwise treated: these types of events correspond to so-called data breaches, that is, violations of personal data.

10.6.3 Data breach

In case a data breach occurs, under art. 33, controllers are required to report the violation to the competent supervisory authority within seventy-two hours of the moment they became aware of it, describing the nature of the violation and the essential information to identify it. Particularly, controllers shall at least:

a. describe the nature of the personal data breach including, where possible, the categories and approximate number of data subjects concerned and the categories and approximate number of personal data records concerned;
b. communicate the name and contact details of the data protection officer or other contact point where more information can be obtained;
c. describe the likely consequences of the personal data breach;
d. describe the measures taken or proposed to be taken by the controller to address the personal data breach, including, where appropriate, measures to mitigate its possible adverse effects.

Moreover, under art. 34, when the personal data breach is likely to result in a high risk to the rights and freedoms of natural persons, the controller shall report the personal data breach to the data subject without undue delay. It should be noted that under art. 34, the communication is mandatory when the breach "is likely to present a high risk to the rights and freedoms of the data subjects, in order to enable them to take the necessary precautions" (Recital 85). The communication to the data subject shall describe in clear and plain language the nature of the personal data breach and contain at least the information and measures referred to in points (b), (c) and (d) above. Art. 34 also has an area of exception, defined by three hypotheses: (a) in case of application by the controller of the technical and organizational measures appropriate to the data attacked by the violation, in particular measures to make the latter incomprehensible to persons not authorized to access it (such as encryption); (b) in the event of subsequent adoption, by the controller, of measures aimed at avoiding the occurrence of a high risk for the rights and freedoms of the data subjects; (c) in case the communication would require disproportionate efforts. In relation to this last hypothesis, the GDPR allows the controller to resort to a public communication or other measure to inform the interested parties with similar effectiveness.

The aforementioned communications are not merely a formal act but a tool for the protection of all data subjects. As a result, and according to normal legal canons, it is possible to reduce the burden of liability on the data controller for all those damages just mentioned that, as a result of the recommendations, are avoidable with the normal diligence of the data subject and without disproportionate effort.

10.6.4 Data protection impact assessment and prior consultation

The risk-based approach of the GDPR can be analyzed by looking at the Data Protection Impact Assessment (DPIA). According to art. 35, the data controller should conduct this assessment in three cases: (a) the systematic and global assessment of personal data relating to natural persons, based on automated processing (including profiling), whose decisions have legal effects or similarly can significantly affect natural persons; (b) the large-scale processing of particular categories of personal data or data relating to criminal convictions or offenses; (c) systematic large-scale surveillance of an area accessible to the public. Naturally, these cases tend to be "open," the boundaries of which have been more precisely defined thanks to the guidelines adopted by the WP29 and the lists drawn up by the supervisory authorities indicating the types of processing subject to this requirement.

Pursuant to art. 35(7), the DPIA shall contain at least: (a) a systematic description of the intended processing operations and the purposes of the processing, including, where applicable, the legitimate interest pursued by the controller; (b) an assessment of the necessity and proportionality of the processing operations in relation to the purposes; (c) an assessment of the risks to the rights and freedoms of data subjects and the related measures envisaged to address the risks, including safeguards, security measures and mechanisms to ensure the protection of personal data and to demonstrate compliance with the GDPR, taking into account the rights and legitimate interests of data subjects and other persons concerned.

Likewise, the supervisory authorities can also make public a list of types of processing for which the DPIA is not required. The evaluation consists of a systematic description of the envisaged processing and the purposes of the processing and includes an appreciation of both the necessity and the proportionality of the processing and the risks for the rights and freedoms of the data subjects, in addition to an indication of the measures envisaged to address the risks, such as guarantees, security measures and mechanisms to ensure data protection and compliance with the GDPR.

The need for prior consultation (art. 36) depends on the outcome of the DPIA, which must be carried out before the processing begins. It is required when the impact assessment indicates that the processing would present a high risk in the absence of measures taken by the controller to mitigate the risk. Here the controller will have to provide all the details necessary to identify the characteristics of the processing activity. The supervisory authority may provide a written opinion within eight weeks of the request for consultation, prescribing any corrective measures.

10.6.5 Appointment of a data protection officer

According to art. 37, another relevant obligation in the event of high risk is the designation of a data protection officer (DPO). This figure is separate from the data processor. The DPO acts as a supervisory body, accumulating functions that proceed from information and advice in favor of the controller to surveillance on the effective application of the GDPR, passing through cooperation with the supervisory authority, for which it acts as a contact point for relevant activities, including prior consultation. The DPO must be promptly and adequately involved in all matters concerning the protection of personal data and provided by the controller and processor with the resources necessary to carry out their duties, to access personal data and processing and to maintain their specialist training.

The DPO can be appointed based on competence and independence: they are in fact designated on the basis of their professional qualities (specialist knowledge of the legislation and practices of the sector) and cannot receive any instructions regarding the execution of their duties as controller. Furthermore, they cannot be removed or penalized by the controller or processor for the fulfillment of their duties, and they report directly to the top management. Despite the independence requirement established by the GDPR, the DPO can also be an internal subject, therefore an employee of the controller or processor, even though the role of guarantee would seem to suggest (without, however, imposing) the choice of an external subject. In any case, it is crucial that there are no conflicts between the duties that the subject has as an employee and their responsibilities as DPO. It is also possible to designate a legal person through a service contract (subject to the need for a natural person to be identified as a contact point, and that there is a clear definition of responsibilities within any team).

The designation of the DPO is mandatory in three cases outlined by the GDPR, outside of which it can instead be carried out on a voluntary basis: (a) if the processing is carried out by a public authority or by a public body (except judicial authorities when exercising their jurisdictional functions); (b) if the main activities of the data controller or data processor consist of types of processing that, by their nature, scope and/or purpose, require regular and systematic monitoring of data subjects on a large scale; (c) the main activities of the data controller or data processor consist in the large-scale processing of particular categories of personal data or data relating to criminal convictions and offenses.

10.7 Transfer of personal data

The transfer of personal data outside the territory of the Union is a central issue, especially given that in the information society, data is transferred through the network from one point on the planet to another, intersecting legal regimes that provide for different protections. While from an economic point of view the flow of personal data to and from countries outside the Union constitutes a necessary step for the purpose of expanding international trade, at the same time, the transfer of personal data to countries outside the territory of the Union poses several challenges regarding the protection of personal data, since third countries may have lower standards of protection than those established by the Union.

Before analyzing the rules provided for by the GDPR on the transfer of personal data outside the territory of the Union, it is necessary to proceed with some preliminary observations regarding the scope of the transfer regime. It should be noted that the GDPR limits the transfer of personal data to countries outside the European Economic Area or international organizations. The transfer restriction applies to all transfers, regardless of the size of the transfer or the frequency with which they are made. However, the types of data that are transferred must be considered. The transfer regime applies only to personal data according to the definition provided by the GDPR. If the transfer concerns data that do not fall within the notion of personal data (e.g., anonymous but not pseudonymous data), the transfer regime does not apply and therefore the data can be freely transferred outside the Union. Furthermore, the concept of transfer is different from that of transit. If personal data are simply routed electronically through a country outside the Union, but the transfer takes place between two countries of the Union, this activity does not fall within the scope of data transfer.

As will be further discussed in Chapter 14, arts. 44–50 should be taken into account. By focusing on the legal basis of the transfer, it is possible to identify three ways in which data can be transferred outside the Union: (a) transfer on the basis of an adequacy decision (art. 45); (b) transfer subject to adequate guarantees (art. 46); and (c) exceptions in specific situations (art. 49).

In the first case, the transfer of personal data to a third country or an international organization is allowed if the European Commission has decided that the third country, a territory or one or more specific sectors within the third country, or the international organization in question guarantees an adequate level of protection.

In the absence of this adequacy decision, pursuant to art. 46, the data controller or the data processor may transfer personal data to a third country or an international organization through a binding contract only if they have provided adequate guarantees and provided that the data subjects have enforceable rights and effective means of redress. The purpose of these guarantees is to ensure compliance with the data protection requirements, the EU general principles regarding the processing of personal data and with the principle of data protection by design and data protection by default. Adequate guarantees with the authorization of the supervisory authority consist in contractual clauses between the controller or processor and the controller, processor or recipient of the personal data in the third country or international organization, or provisions to be inserted into administrative arrangements between public authorities or bodies that include enforceable and effective data subject rights.

Moreover, the Regulation carefully takes into account the discipline of the binding corporate rules in art. 47. These clauses shall comply with specific criteria defined by the GDPR and are approved by the supervisory authority ensuring that they are legally binding and apply to all interested members of the business group or group of companies carrying out a joint economic activity, including their employees.

In the absence of an adequacy decision (art. 45) or adequate guarantees (art. 46), including binding corporate rules (art. 47), the transfer of personal data to a third country or organization is permitted internationally only under the conditions stated in art. 49.

10.8 Authorities and sanctions

Supervisory authorities, as defined in art. 4 as "an independent public authority which is established by a Member State pursuant to art. 51," play a unique role in enforcing data protection laws across the European Union and together with the EDPB provide guidance on the interpretation of the GDPR. Supervisory authorities are appointed by each Member State. In the context of the GDPR, all EU Member States have a data protection authority that serves as the main point of contact for stakeholders within that Member State. However, there are some exceptions, for example, in the scope of a group of enterprises with presences in different EU countries.

Each authority is responsible for monitoring the application of the GDPR in order to protect the fundamental rights and freedoms of natural persons in relation to processing and to facilitate the free flow of personal data within the European Union. The GDPR provides national supervisory authorities with significant powers to enforce its provisions, including:

a. a number of investigative, corrective and authorization and advisory powers (art. 58);
b. the power to advise individuals, private and public actors on the application of the GDPR;
c. the power to impose administrative fines on controllers and processors (art. 83).

As already discussed, controllers are required to report any personal data breach to their national supervisory authority without undue delay and in any event within seventy-two hours of becoming aware of such breach (art. 33(1)). Data subjects have a right to be informed, by the controller, of their right to lodge a complaint with the supervisory authority (arts. 13(2)(d) and 14(2)(e)). Data subjects have a right to lodge a complaint with the supervisory authority (art. 77). They also have a right to an effective judicial remedy against a supervisory authority and against infringing controllers and processors (arts. 78 and 79). Supervisory authorities are required to cooperate with each other and with the EDPB to ensure the consistent enforcement of the GDPR (arts. 60–76). Moreover, supervisory authorities are required to make annual reports summarizing their activities and decisions. They are also obligated to cooperate with other supervisory authorities in cases where multiple countries are affected, such as when dealing with multinational corporations.

Regarding the possible sanctions that can be imposed if an actor fails to comply with the GDPR, the new system of sanctions is based on a twofold need: the harmonization of the law, which requires the provision of equivalent administrative sanctions in all Member States; and its consistent application, which is expressed in the need to grant the supervisory authorities the same powers (including those of a sanctioning nature) and to guarantee the same methods of intervention. The lower levels of fines, up to 10 million euros or 2 percent of the company's global annual turnover, will be considered for infringements listed in art. 83(4) of the GDPR. This includes infringements relating to:

- integrating data protection "by design and by default";
- records of processing activities;
- cooperation with the supervising authority;
- security of processing data;

- notification of a personal data breach to the supervisory authority;
- communication of a personal data breach to the data subject;
- Data Protection Impact Assessment;
- prior consultation;
- designation, position or tasks of the Data Protection Officer;
- certification.

The higher levels of fines, up to 20 million euros or 4 percent of the company's global annual turnover, will be considered for infringements listed in art. 83(5) of the GDPR. This includes infringements relating to:

- the basic principle for processing, including conditions for consent, lawfulness of processing and processing of special categories of personal data;
- rights of the data subject;
- transfer of personal data to a recipient in a third country or an international organization.

If a controller or processor makes several infringements, the total amount of the administrative fine will not exceed the fine for the most serious infringement for the same or linked processing operations.

The GDPR also gives individuals the right to compensation of any material and/or non-material damages resulting from an infringement of the GDPR, in particular where the processing may give rise to discrimination, identity theft, financial loss, damage to reputation or any other significant economic or social disadvantage, where individuals might be deprived of their rights and freedoms. In certain cases, not-for-profit bodies can bring representative action on behalf of individuals. This opens the door for mass claims in cases of large-scale infringements.

10.9 Conclusions

As has been shown in this chapter, the GDPR is the most demanding and comprehensive data protection regulation to date. The GDPR aims to meet the current challenges related to personal data protection, strengthen online privacy rights and boost Europe's digital economy. It specifically aims to provide individuals with better capabilities for controlling and managing their personal data and thus to reinforce data subjects' trust in personal data collecting companies. Within the new data protection framework, individual service users may also benefit from the free movement of data if it results in the expansion of businesses with improved and personalized services.

In this context, taking into consideration all the above traits, the GDPR turns out to be a major step forward for enhancing the privacy of EU citizens, harmonizing data protection rules across Member States, and promoting privacy and security as core aspects of the European online personal data industry, with overall positive effects on the transparency of websites. It standardizes and strengthens the rights of all European citizens to data privacy. Moreover, it emphasizes transparency, security and accountability for organizations that collect, use, share and store personal data. At the center of the GDPR is the requirement for organizations to be fully transparent about how they are using and safeguarding personal data and to be able to demonstrate accountability for their data processing activities.

Still, the GDPR is just one piece of a broader European strategy in the field of data. The Data Strategy aims to establish the creation of a "single European data space." It consists of ten sectoral common European data spaces that are relevant for twin green and digital transitions. The Data Governance Act is the leading example of this approach. Likewise, the White Paper on artificial intelligence is another piece of the European strategy, which has been translated into the proposal for a regulation on artificial intelligence in Europe.

11 Privacy, Identity and the Right to Be Forgotten

11.1 Introduction

The previous chapters explained how the enjoyment and enforcement of the right to express one's opinions freely have changed within the digital environment. The Internet has created new ways in which one's personal identity is manifested and expressed. We experience this every day: from the voice assistant that programs our alarm clock every day to the apps we use to check traffic before going to the university or to the office, the thoughts and the photos we share with friends and acquaintances; these are all elements that make up a digital self through the act of sharing personal and non-personal data. And it is precisely the protection of personal data and digital identity that is one of the essential elements touched on by this handbook and to which the last chapters will be devoted.

To protect the digital exposure of individuals has become a priority because of the rise of technologies that, through the collection of vast amounts of data, can reduce the gap between the real and the digital. Data are revelatory of one's identity, which, in the digital space, is revealed beyond measure.

Therefore, as explained in Chapter 9, the fathers of privacy, Warren and Brandeis, created this concept precisely to protect the individual's private life from unwanted interferences. The boundary of one's personal identity radically changed in the digital environment, since the atomic identity is complemented by the digital one. This latter identity is composed of the information collected about the person and the information the person freely provides. Data are also obtained via tools that track their movements, their purchases, their reading habits and their hobbies. The identity, so framed, is increasingly fragmented and goes beyond the bodily dimension of the individual, projecting into the infinite memory of bits.

In this context, the right assigned by the General Data Protection Regulation (GDPR) – the right to erasure (or the right to be forgotten) – takes on a particular profile: balancing the needs for data circulation and sharing with the protection of personal identity and dignity. This right, before it was included in the Regulation, was at the center of a long judicial saga in the Court of Justice of the European Union (ECJ), which outlined its foundations through two important decisions that will be examined below, known as *Google Spain* and *Google v. CNIL.*

This chapter dissects how identity, privacy and data protection come into play with the right to be forgotten. Section 11.2 outlines the main contours of digital identity and how this element is reinforced by the right to privacy and to the protection of personal data. Section 11.3 frames the concept of the right to be forgotten, as distinguished from the right to erasure, and analyzes how it changed from its traditional definition (Section 11.3.1) to the Internet one (Section 11.3.2). Section 11.4 further delves into this shift by examining the facts (11.4.1) and the reasoning (11.4.2) behind the ECJ *Google Spain* case. Section 11.5 looks at the *Google Spain* aftermath, particularly the codification of the right to erasure into the GDPR (11.5.1), while eventually considering the problem of the territorial scope of application of the right to erasure (11.5.2).

11.2 Privacy and digital identity

Until the 20th century, a person's identity was only a physical one. That identity was encapsulated in the person's physical experience, that is, name, gender, height, special marks, residence, domicile and so on. From the mid-20th century onward, identity has been the subject of elaborate legal construction. Personal identity has, therefore, come to be composed of the right to be oneself, understood as respect for the public image, as well as for the private one. Therefore, personal identity, according to the definition established in the field of psychological and social sciences, is understood as the representation of an individual in relation to the social context in which they develop their personality.

This issue has much to do with that of privacy, but also more generally with the evolution of technology and, consequently, of each person's subjective position. Identity is a dynamic concept, changing with time, as indeed happens to physical identity. Therefore, in this digital context, the protection of personal identity is not only the individual's problem but, moreover, is a social issue. As Stefano Rodotà pointed out:

> in the face of the fragmentation that the person now undergoes in the informational dimension, the reference to identity (and its fullness) constitutes the instrument that allows for the reconstitution of the integrity of the person. … But just as the construction of the personality is the result of a selective process and not of a pure accumulation of events, so the projection into the legal dimension of personal identity requires the recognition of a possibility of selection, entrusted to objective criteria (time of preservation of the data collected) and to the decisions of the interested party. (Rodotà 2021, 65)

Hence, digital identity is considered to be the virtual identity that each individual creates for himself/herself on the Internet and indicates the set of information and resources provided by a computer system to a user of that system. The creation of an account on a social network, on an e-commerce site, or even on a government service, reflects the correlation between physical and digital identity.

Accordingly, digital identity is formed by two factors: the existence of a physical individual and the attribution to that physical individual of a set of electronic codes such that, once introduced in one or more computers, single or networked, the person can be identified, linking the codes to their identity. Therefore, the digital identity can be considered as a claim to regain ownership of one's personal history, and thus as a kind of right to self-determination in terms of information, that is, the individual's right to make their own decisions about the disposal and use of data about them.

As the concept of identity developed and broadened, the right to privacy and data protection were subject to extensive renovation, as Chapter 9 explains. The initial conception of the right to privacy also evolved thanks to the influence of the Council of Europe and the European Convention on Human Rights, which inspired the ECJ, in particular before the Charter of Nice entered into force. Therefore, the concept of privacy has been highly developed over the years and acquired a centrality that, according to some scholars, made it Europe's First Amendment.

Therefore, respect for one's private life is a concept that goes hand in hand with the notion of personhood and self-identity. Data protection can be understood as the exercise of control over the pieces of information that compose one's identity. Moreover, even ECJ case law indicates the extreme variety of aspects of the life of individuals that fall within the scope of private life and, consequently, the personal identity of individuals.

Therefore, the notions of private life and personal identity include, first and foremost, the principles of self-determination, the right to reputation and personal honor. These aspects come into consideration when it comes to balancing their protection with other rights, such as freedom of expression and information. Notably, the relationship between privacy and identity emerges in questions regarding the individual's control over their information expressed through their right to delete "personal data concerning him or her" (see art. 17 of the GDPR). This right captured the attention of policymakers and commentators since it is connected with the idea of informative auto-determination, meaning the data subjects' power to be anonymous or to remove their data (on the link between identity and auto-determination, see ECtHR *S.H. et al. v. Austria*, November 3, 2011; *Pretty v. United Kingdom*, April 29, 2002).

This means that the right to be forgotten (or the right to erasure) is the right that, being very much entrenched with personal identity, ensures that one can be forgotten and safeguards the confidentiality imposed by time on a piece of news and, therefore, personal data that is no longer up to date.

Hence, the right to be forgotten appears to be wedged between the right of society to access information and the individual's right to privacy. In this case, the right to privacy should be balanced with freedom of expression: it is clear that enforcing the right to be forgotten affects freedom of information and vice versa. There has been considerable debate over this right, in particular after the *Google Spain* decision (C-131/12) of the ECJ. In light of these premises, the following paragraphs analyze the essence of the right to be forgotten, under the lenses of the innovative interpretation of the ECJ rulings.

11.3 The right to be forgotten (or the right to erasure)

The essence of the right to be forgotten lies in the assumption that one's past should not clutter up one's present. This is the first understanding of the right to erasure – a right that is conditioned by the passing of time and concerns information (re)made publicly available. It also reflects the concept of privacy as imagined by Warren and Brandeis.

As noted in the previous chapter, the right to privacy, imagined as the right to be left alone, initially migrated from the United States to Europe. Since then, this right has evolved into protection of the individual's expectation of privacy and gone beyond a wholly negative and static dimension (the right to be left alone), extending its reach to the positive and dynamic dimension related to data protection.

The Charter of Fundamental Rights of the European Union (CFREU) protects the right to privacy under art. 7 and personal data pursuant to art. 8. The latter recognized the constitutional status of the right to data protection and also resulted in a shift from a merely economic dimension, inherent to Directive 95/46/EC, to a more comprehensive concept, where data subjects have more control over their data and data controllers are held accountable for their activities.

The dualism between the right to privacy and data protection is also reflected in the right to be forgotten. As Robert Post underlined, where the latter recalls a concept of fair processing of information and adequate measures of personal data protection, the former refers to the idea of dignity and protection of personal identity and private life. These two aspects emerged in the ECJ case law and were reflected in art. 17 of the GDPR, which protects the right to be forgotten. Hence, Post's conception of the right to be forgotten distinguishes between data privacy, as protected under art. 8 CFREU, and dignitary privacy, as protected by art. 7 CFREU. The first one is a bureaucratic concept that relates to data management and the exercise of control over personal data. In contrast, the second one, identified as "the right to be forgotten," refers to the protection of the dignity of human beings.

> As the author argues, "the RTBF applies to data management; the right to be forgotten applies to communication. The object of the RTBF is to give data subjects 'control' over their personal data; the object of the right to be forgotten is to protect the dignity of human beings. Although the RTBF makes sense in the context of large organizations that assemble big data to accomplish explicit purposes, its managerial logic is fundamentally incompatible with the communicative action required by the democratic public sphere. The right to be forgotten, by contrast, has been applied to the democratic public sphere in most legal systems for more than a century." (Post 2017, 993–994)

Before moving on to the analysis of the judgment that crystallized the right to be forgotten as conceived today, at least in the European context, it is necessary to focus on the conceptual semantics of this right. The right to be forgotten takes on different meanings. The first one recalls the concept of not republishing news already made known when a considerable amount of time has passed. The second meaning is based on updating and contextualizing news and personal information. The next subsection examines in depth the evolution of the right to erasure.

11.3.1 The traditional definition of the right to be forgotten

The first meaning of the right to be forgotten is the most time-honored one, elaborated by civil scholars and jurisprudence, in the era before the advent of the Internet. The right to be forgotten has traditionally referred to the right of a subject not to see published some news related to events, already legitimately published, for which a considerable amount of time has passed since their occurrence. The right to be forgotten, in this sense, relates to events that have constituted news facts or otherwise in relation to which publicization, that is, their removal from the sphere of confidentiality of those concerned, was to be considered lawful. The issue is whether the person or events legitimately publicized can always constitute the subject of new publicization or whether the passage of time and changing situations make it unlawful. Time also plays an important role in cases dealing not with news events but with events in relation to which a significant period has now passed and that lack elements of contextualization in time. In such cases, judgments have found a violation of the right to personal identity.

One example in this regard is judgment *no. 19681/2019* (Cass. Sez. Un., July 22, 2019, no. 19681). Here the court was called to ascertain whether an article in a newspaper recalling a murder that took place a long time ago (twenty-seven years earlier), within a column with a historical slant dedicated to certain facts of a crime, was still of public interest.

Hence, the court, while balancing the rights of the press and the right of the public to information with the right to privacy of the individual, clarified two aspects. First, even if the remembrance of a historical part recalls a public interest, this activity does not require identifying the individuals involved in the news unless it concerns individuals who have held a public position. Second, in the opinion of the court, this case was not about the right to report but about the right to the historical evocation of a news item.

On the subject of the relationship between the right to confidentiality (in its particular connotation of the so-called right to oblivion) and the right to the historical evocation of facts and events concerning past events, the judge – without prejudice to the freedom of editorial choice with regard to such evocation, which is an expression of freedom of the press and information protected and guaranteed by art. 21 of the Italian Constitution – has the task of assessing the public interest, concrete and current to the mention of the identification elements of the people who were protagonists of those facts and events. This mention must be considered lawful only in the hypothesis in which it refers to people whose destiny in the present moment is the interest of the community, both for reasons of fame and for the public role played. Otherwise, the right of the interested parties to confidentiality prevails with respect to past events that hurt their dignity and honor and of which the collective memory is now extinguished. (§11)

In another example, the Italian Supreme Court explained in decision *no. 5525/2012* (Cass. Civ., April 5, 2012, no. 5525) the right to contextualize information. The article that was the object of the decision reported the indictment of a politician for corruption. Although he had been acquitted, the news of his acquittal had been reported "quietly" by the newspapers. Therefore, if one did a web search, the article reporting the indictment still appeared. On this basis, the politician had requested the removal of the personal data contained in the newspaper article published in the historical archives of the online newspaper. The removal was refused both by the Italian Data Protection Authority and by the Court of Milan. However, the Court of Cassation considered that the news, although originally true, had not been correctly updated, thus resulting in a partial and untrue report.

In these two approaches, the connection between the right to protection of personal data and personality rights – including the right to rectification, the right to privacy, and the right to reputation, image and name – clearly emerges. Each fragment revolves around the concept of *protection of personal identity*. Therefore, the right to be forgotten, in this context, is not only recognized as a right to delete information the memory of which is no longer desired but as the right to give weight to information that protects the *social image* of the individual.

11.3.2 The right to be forgotten on the Internet

The right to be forgotten has changed with the use of the Internet and telematic networks due to the ways in which information is disseminated in these contexts. On the Internet, republication is no longer necessary since due to its very structure information is not deleted but remains available or at least abstractly available. In other words, it is not only or necessarily the republication of the information, but rather its permanence on the Internet, that is at issue. Thus, the role that time plays changes: it is necessary not just to not republish, but to place the publication, which may have been legitimate many years ago, in the current present.

The issue is to give weight to information, which on the Internet appears to be flattened, with the purpose of ensuring that a subject's identity is not misrepresented. Therefore, a third meaning of the right to be forgotten is that affirmed by the GDPR and the *Google Spain* decision, that is, the right to the erasure of personal data under certain circumstances. Therefore, due to its multifaceted nature, the right to be forgotten is well configured as a *personality right* that contains within itself the protection of the right to privacy, the right to personal identity and the right to the protection of personal data.

11.4 *Google Spain* (C-131/12) and the framing of the right to be forgotten in the digital age

The most famous and important decision regarding the right to be forgotten is the infamous *Google Spain* case. Here, the ECJ held that, under certain conditions, Internet search engine service providers are under an obligation, following a complaint by the data subject, to remove links to websites containing information that could harm the applicant's right to be forgotten, where personal data have been available for a significant period of time on the Internet. This decision, and in particular the approach taken by the ECJ, reveals the attempt to model a new right to privacy and data protection as a reaction to the challenges of the Internet.

11.4.1 Facts of the case and Advocate General opinion

The result of this ruling seems to be a right not to be found online rather than a true right to be forgotten, with the latter understood in the sense of a right to erasure of data. It seems appropriate at this point to retrace, albeit briefly, the court's reasoning.

In 2010, Mario Costeja González filed a complaint with the Agencia Española de Protección de Datos (AEPD), the Spanish Data Protection Agency, against a local newspaper, *La Vanguardia*, and Google Spain for claims relating to auction notices mentioning González that were published in 1998. The statements concerned real estate auctions held to secure repayment of González's social security debts. González contended that these pages were no longer necessary because "the attachment proceedings concerning him had been fully resolved for several years and that reference to them was now entirely irrelevant" (§15).

Mr. González made two requests: (a) he sought to have the local newspaper, *La Vanguardia*, remove or alter those pages so that the personal data relating to him no longer appeared or to use certain tools made available by search engines in order to protect the data; and (b) he also requested Google Inc. to remove the personal data relating to him. He stated in this context that the attachment proceedings concerning him had been fully resolved for a number of years and that reference to them was now entirely irrelevant.

By decision of July 30, 2010, the AEPD rejected the complaint as it related to *La Vanguardia*, taking the view that the publication of the information in question was legally justified as it took place upon order of the Ministry of Labour and Social Affairs and was intended to give maximum publicity to the auction in order to secure as many bidders as possible. At the same time, the AEPD found that search engines were subject to data protection legislation given that they carry out data processing for which they are responsible and act as intermediaries in the information society. Hence, the AEPD considered that the "obligation may be owed directly by operators of search engines, without it being necessary to erase the data or information from the website where they appear, including when retention of the information on that site is justified by a statutory provision" (§17). Therefore, the AEPD dismissed the plaintiff's claims against the newspaper but allowed those against Google.

Google appealed to Spain's High Court, which in turn referred three questions to the ECJ.

The judgment makes a preliminary ruling on the interpretation of Articles 12 and 14 of Directive 95/46/EC, dealing respectively with access to data and opposition to processing. In particular, the Court is asked to rule on the interpretation of Article 12(b) which states that "Member States shall guarantee any data subject to the right to obtain from the controller processing: (...) as appropriate, the rectification, erasure, or blocking of data the processing of which does not comply with the provisions of this Directive, in particular, because of the incomplete or inaccurate nature of the data," and Article 14, first paragraph, (a) where it is stated that "Member States shall grant the data subject the right: (...) at least in the cases referred to in Article 7 (e) and (f), to object at any time, for compelling legitimate grounds relating to his or her particular situation, to the processing of data concerning him/her, unless otherwise provided for by national legislation".

Hence, the content of the right to be forgotten to be investigated is related to the third meaning identified above: the right to erasure, data freezing and opposition to processing. These rights, as is well known, according to the conclusion reached by the court, can also be asserted against the search engine, which constitutes a data controller. Obviously, the search engine will not be able to delete personal data located with the data controller that publishes the information (i.e., on the website of the newspaper publisher, in many cases), only the link to that data, which may well remain with the data controller.

The Advocate General (AG) Niilo Jääskinen delivered his opinion in June 2012, providing a quite balanced view of the interests at stake. The ECJ, however, has departed from most of the arguments of the AG. First, it is worth exploring the opinion of the Advocate General in order to highlight the different approaches adopted by the ECJ. The reasoning of the AG Niilo Jääskinen is based on the interpretation of Directive 95/46/EC, even though the answers provide a more comprehensive overview of the legal issues implied by the balancing between the right to "oblivion" and freedom of information. The first question answered by the AG relates to whether an operator of a search engine meets the definition of "data controller" pursuant to the Data Protection Directive by reason of the activity carried out when indexing information retrieved from other websites. By interpreting art. 2 of the Directive, the AG found that the operations performed by the owner of a search engine (including copying, indexing, caching and displaying information collected from other websites) do fall within the scope of the processing of personal data.

Therefore, according to the AG, the provider (namely, Google) has no relationship with the content of third-party source web pages on the Internet where personal data may appear. Moreover, as the search engine works on the basis of copies of the source web pages that its crawler function has retrieved and copied, the service provider does not have any means of changing the information on the host servers.

The next step was to determine whether, in light of such processing of personal data, the owner of the search engine amounts to a "controller of personal data" pursuant to art. 2(d) of the Data Protection Directive. In this sense, the AG engaged in a teleological interpretation and ascertained that Directive 95/46/EC was no longer applicable and referred to a very different digital world. Therefore, the provisions of the Data Protection Directive simply do not take into account the fact that information can be hosted electronically and that its content can be copied and disseminated by parties having no relation whatsoever to the author. Thus, it would be misleading to rely upon a literal construction of art. 2(d). Hence, the AG rejected a "formal" qualification of the search engine as a data controller based solely on the circumstance that it is "materially" performing the processing of personal data.

Lastly, according to the AG, a national Data Protection Authority (DPA) cannot require an Internet service provider to withdraw information from its index except in cases where this service provider has not complied with the exclusion codes or where a request from a website regarding an update of cache memory has not been complied with. A possible "notice and takedown procedure" concerning links to source web pages with illegal or inappropriate content is a matter for national civil liability law based on grounds other than data protection.

The opinion has concluded that, except for the cases where a search engine provider fails to filter certain links or to apply exclusion codes, data protection authorities have no power to request them to remove links to third parties' websites. The approach followed by the AG engages in a balancing analysis where it is for the Member States, in his view, to implement such a remedy to ensure the enforcement of the right to be forgotten, but there is no such an obligation under the legal framework in force.

According to AG Jääskinen:

> The particularly complex and difficult constellation of fundamental rights that this case presents prevents justification for reinforcing the data subjects' legal position under the directive and imbuing it with a right to be forgotten. This would entail sacrificing pivotal rights such as freedom of expression and information. I would also discourage the Court from concluding that these conflicting interests could satisfactorily be balanced in individual cases on a case-by-case basis, with the judgment to be left to the internet search engine service provider. Such "notice and take down procedures", if required by the Court, are likely either to lead to the automatic withdrawal of links to any objected contents or to an unmanageable number of requests handled by the most popular and important internet search engine service providers. (§133).

This is the view expressed by the Advocate General Jääskinen in the concluding remarks of his opinion. The "balance" proposed by Jääskinen between the fundamental rights involved in the "particularly complex and difficult constellation" was nevertheless rejected by the ECJ.

11.4.2 To erase or not to erase? The ECJ reasoning

As mentioned, the decision of the ECJ has largely departed from the conclusions drawn by the AG. Even though the court has found, following the opinion of the AG, that the indexing of information retrieved from third parties' websites amounted to the processing of personal data, this has remained the only convergence. The relevance of arts. 7 and 8 CFREU was also crucial when the ECJ focused on the interpretation of the Data Protection Directive. However, the ECJ stretched the limits of EU legislation to make it fit with the interpretation that prioritized the right to data protection. This consideration is demonstrated by at least four respects in which the ECJ adopted a loose interpretation: the relevance of the case for EU law; the definition of the Internet search engine provider as a controller for data processing purposes; the application of art. 12(b) of the Data Protection Directive on the right to obtain the erasure, blocking and rectification of personal data; and the application of art. 9 of the Data Protection Directive on the exemption to the general rules laid down by the same Directive in the event that personal data are processed for the purposes of journalism.

The ECJ first ruled that the EU Data Protection Directive also applies to search engines. Articles 12 and 14 of the Directive were interpreted by the court as addressing the question whether the right to obtain the removal from the search results has legal grounds in EU law. The court found that both art. 12(b) and art. 14(1)(a) can be enforced by the data subject to request a search engine provider to remove certain contents from the search results (§21–26). With regard to art. 12(b), the ECJ ruled that the right to obtain the rectification, erasure or blocking of personal data extends to all circumstances where the processing of personal data does not comply with the principles laid down by the Data Protection Directive (§70). The ECJ held that search engines engage in the "processing of data" because they explore the internet "automatically, constantly and systematically in search of the information" (§28). The ECJ further held that search engines are "controllers" within the meaning of the Directive because they "determine … the purposes and means of" data processing (§23).

Second, the court concluded that because Google Inc. had a subsidiary (Google Spain) operating within the territory of a Member State (Spain), even though Google itself is based within a non-member state (the United States), the Directive properly applied to Google and Google operated as "an establishment" within the meaning of the Directive. Even if Google asserted that the data were not processed within Spain, the ECJ found that the company had an obligation to remove the links, as it aimed to "promote and sell, in the Member State in question, advertising space offered by the search engine in order to make the service offered by the engine" (§45).

The ECJ adopted a broad interpretation of the notion of "establishment" and of the words "in the context of the activities." The court justified this decision by saying that

> in the light of the objective of Directive 95/46 of ensuring effective and complete protection of the fundamental rights and freedoms of natural persons, and in particular their right to privacy, with respect to the processing of personal data, those words cannot be interpreted restrictively. (§53)

For these reasons, Google was found to have an obligation in certain cases to remove the links to pages displayed by third parties, even if the information published by those third parties is itself lawful.

The ECJ further held that search engines are "controllers" within the meaning of the Directive because they "determine … the purposes and means of" data processing (§23). The purpose of adopting such a broad definition of the controller was to grant as much protection as possible to the subjects. However, categorizing an entity as a data controller entails some other obligations under the Data Protection Directive which, if applied to an Internet service provider, are likely to conflict with the regime established by the E-Commerce Directive and, accordingly, the business model of search engine operators.

Following the above reasoning, the assumption of the court is that a search engine performs the processing of personal data pursuant to art. 7(f), which allows the data controller to use the data for fulfilling its legitimate interest (§74–75). According to the ECJ view, the processing is permitted "except where such interests are overridden by the interests or fundamental rights and freedoms of the data subject" (§74–75). Then, the court finds in this provision the basis for balancing the interests of the data controller and the right to personal data of the concerned individuals. Therefore, under the lenses of art. 14(1)(a), the court links the right to objection with the processing of personal data according to art. 7(f): in this matter, the ECJ finds that the data subject is entitled to object "on compelling legitimate grounds relating to his particular situation to the processing of data relating to him" (§76). On these grounds, the court has derived the right of the data subject to ask a search engine provider (and, where necessary, a court to order) the removal of the search results linked to certain contents.

The court also found that art. 6 requires that data is "adequate, relevant and not excessive in relation to the purposes for which they are collected," "accurate and, where necessary, kept up to date" and "kept in a form which permits identification of data subjects for no longer than necessary" (§7; §72). Moreover, in the view of the court, there must be a balance between the relevant rights at stake. Lastly, the ECJ focused on arts. 7 and 8 CFREU. In the view of the judges in Luxembourg, these provisions grant the data subject the right to determine that their personal data are no longer processed when the conditions set forth by the Data Protection Directive are met. However, in such a balance, the economic interest of the data controller may not prevail per se over the individual's right to data protection; rather, for the court, it is the general right to have access to certain information to be balanced with the "right to delete" of the concerned data subject. It should be pointed out that in the opinion of the court the exclusion of certain search results may occur regardless of the simultaneous removal of the contents from the relevant web pages (§82–83).

As was explained, this judgment contributed to framing the role of search engines as data controllers with respect to the pieces of personal information made available on third-party websites. This operation had the goal to make these huge operators accountable for the personal data they were processing. However, the court based its judgment almost exclusively on arts. 7 and 8 CFREU, scarcely considering the aspects related to freedom of expression.

Some specific parts of the judgment show how the ECJ has promoted protection of the right to digital privacy. More in detail, the ECJ stressed this aspect in finding that, when striking a balance between the right to information and the right to privacy, the latter is generally assumed to prevail, except where the removal of the information concerned might undermine the legitimate interest of Internet users in receiving it. In other words, the right to access information is limited to safeguarding other rights relating to the private sphere and the personal data of users. The former would only prevail over the latter as an exception, under certain circumstances and subject to certain specific conditions.

The reason why this bridge between data protection and other fundamental rights and freedoms, such as freedom of expression and freedom to conduct business, is still lacking is to be found in the aim of granting as much protection as possible to the right to digital privacy of data subjects. The ECJ acknowledged that, according to art. 12(b) of Directive 95/46, the data subject may ask for the erasure, rectification or blocking of data when they are not being processed in accordance with the principles laid down by the Data Protection Directive and, in particular, on the grounds that the data are inaccurate or incomplete. In this way, the ECJ established a basis for making any breach of the general principles set forth by the Data Protection Directive grounds for the data subject to take action to enforce their rights against the controller. Looking at the aftermath of the Google Spain decision, the consequence of the approach adopted by the ECJ resulted in a loose interpretation of EU law in light of arts. 7 and 8 of the CFREU. However, it also should be considered that burdening a search engine provider with an obligation to remove links, regardless of the activities carried out by the owner of the website concerned, is likely to result in reduced liability for those exercising editorial control and increased liability (perhaps excessively so) for the search engine.

The ECJ did not take this externality into account. Once again, the absence of any express reference to art. 11 CFREU at any point in the judgment in the *Google Spain* case is only one of many hints that confirm that the balance struck by the ECJ seems to be skewed toward the right to digital privacy. Another consequence of this overbalancing is the reduced level of protection for freedom of expression online. On the contrary, the ECJ seemed to delegate to search engines, as private actors, the task of carrying out activities in the public interest, including specifically the striking of a balance between the right to information and the right to privacy. The failure to clarify this point means that private actors are called on to assess such a proportionality test. In the *Google Spain* case, the ECJ has attempted to model a right to privacy, which Warren and Brandeis previously described with reference to the world of atoms, according to the characteristics of the digital world. Moreover, the conceptualization hereby realized has been further revised by the court in the aftermath of *Google Spain*, with the effect of depowering the original extent of the right to be forgotten. Such a trend is also apparent in relation to the European Courts of Human Rights, which, despite using different arguments, seems to have reached the same conclusions as the ECJ, downgrading protection for freedom of expression when it is exercised online.

11.5 The aftermath of *Google Spain*

After the ruling, Google had to take action to comply with the ECJ findings, consisting of making available a data removal application form, which must still be submitted for consideration by the company, in order to balance the privacy rights of the individual with the right of all to know and distribute information. Certainly, one cannot help but be puzzled, to say the least, by this para-constitutional function attributed to a private company, as recognized by the ECJ judge. But Google has also done something else: it has appointed an advisory committee on the right to be forgotten composed of international personalities, which opened an online platform (www.google.com/advisorycouncil/) asking for opinions on how a person's right to be forgotten should be balanced with the public's right to know.

11.5.1 Article 17 of the General Data Protection Regulation

In the aftermath, the new shape of the right to erasure was crystallized in the entry into force of Regulation EU 2016/679. Here, the right to be forgotten appears in Recitals 65 and 66 and, foremost, in art. 17 of the GDPR.

According to art. 17, the data subject shall have the right to obtain from the controller the erasure of personal data concerning them without undue delay, and the controller shall have the obligation to erase personal data without undue delay, where specific circumstances apply. Namely, when 1) the data subject withdraws consent on which the processing is based according to point (a) of Article 6(1), or point (a) of Article 9(2), and where there is no other legal ground for the processing; 2) the data subject objects to the processing pursuant to Article 21(1) and there are no overriding legitimate grounds for the processing, or the data subject objects to the processing pursuant to Article 21(2); 3) the personal data have been unlawfully processed; 4) the personal data have to be erased for compliance with a legal obligation in Union or Member State law to which the controller is subject; 5) the personal data have been collected in relation to the offer of information society services referred to in Article 8(1).

The right to be forgotten dovetails with the individual's right to access their personal information in art. 15. The right to control one's data is meaningless if people cannot take action when they no longer consent to the processing, when there are significant errors within the data or if they believe information is being stored unnecessarily. In these cases, an individual can request that the data be erased. However, as postulated by the article, this request is not an absolute one. Instead, the request must comply with letters a–f.

Hence, art. 17 GDPR outlines the specific circumstances under which the right to be forgotten applies. Therefore, a data subject has the right to have their personal data erased if: 1) Personal data is no longer necessary for the purpose an organization originally collected or processed it; 2) An organization is relying on an individual's consent as the lawful basis for processing the data and that individual withdraws their consent; 3) An organization is relying on legitimate interests as its justification for processing an individual's data, the individual objects to this processing, and there is no overriding legitimate interest for the organization to continue with the processing; 4) An organization is processing personal data for direct marketing purposes and the individual objects to this processing; 5) An organization processed an individual's personal data unlawfully; 6) An organization must erase personal data in order to comply with a legal ruling or obligation; 7) An organization has processed a child's personal data to offer their information society services.

However, an organization's right to process someone's data might override that person's right to be forgotten. According to the GDPR, the situations when this happens are the following:

> 1) The data is being used to exercise the right of freedom of expression and information; 2) The data is being used to comply with a legal ruling or obligation; 3) The data is being used to perform a task that is being carried out in the public interest or when exercising

an organization's official authority; 4) The data being processed is necessary for public health purposes and serves the public interest; 5) The data being processed is necessary to perform preventative or occupational medicine. This only applies when the data is being processed by a health professional who is subject to a legal obligation of professional secrecy; 6) The data represents important information that serves the public interest, scientific research, historical research, or statistical purposes, and where erasure of the data would likely impair or halt progress towards the achievement that was the goal of the processing; 7) The data is being used for the establishment of legal defense or in the exercise of other legal claims.

Even if art. 17 allows individuals to obtain from the controller the erasure of personal data and the abstention from further dissemination of the same under certain well-defined circumstances, the scope of application of the right to be forgotten may potentially be restricted by the safe harbor set forth under art. 17(3), which exempts data controllers from carrying out the erasure, among others, when the retention of personal data is necessary for exercising the right to freedom of expression. Moreover, under art. 85 of the Regulation, it is for the Member States to provide for exemptions or derogations from the general principles established by the Regulation "when reconciling the right to the protection of personal data ... with the right to freedom of expression and information, including processing for journalistic purposes and the purposes of academic, artistic or literary expression." The main issue with this provision is that it works as an empty clause that gives full discretion to Member States to regulate the exceptions to the right to be forgotten.

Second, the Regulation fails to foster harmonization of the relevant legal framework. Moreover, the right to erasure as framed does not seem to be a productive instrument that substantially empowers individuals to exercise control over their personal information. This particularly seems to happen, both because of legal and technical reasons, with artificial intelligence and blockchain technologies. In this framework, it is difficult to reconcile them with the GDPR's requirements that personal data must be amended (under art. 16 GDPR) and erased (under art. 17 GDPR) in specific circumstances.

Lastly, there are no specific requirements regarding the criteria that search engine operators and judicial or administrative authorities should adopt in order to assess whether there are compelling grounds for the right to information to prevail. While the decision in *Google Spain* could provide useful indications, then, as to the criteria for such a balance – and thus clarify the provision entrusted to arts. 17 and 85 of the Regulation – the ECJ actually seems to have missed a good chance to do so.

11.5.2 The territorial scope of the right to erasure

Meanwhile, the ECJ was called to decide on another dispute against Google, Inc. (now Google LLC). In 2015 the French Data Protection Authority (CNIL, acronym for Commission nationale de l'informatique et des libertés) ordered Google to deindex certain content from all versions of the search engine, including the so-called

.com version. Google resisted, stating that it would deindex the content only for users connecting to the version of the search engine accessible from that Member State. Google then referred the matter to the Conseil d'État, seeking the annulment of the CNIL sanction. Given the sensitivity of the issue, which involves the interpretation of European data protection law and, in particular, at the time, Directive (EC) 1995/46, the Conseil d'État decided to refer the matter to the ECJ. The latter was therefore called upon to define the boundary of its jurisdiction, or rather, the territorial boundary of the right to erasure.

On September 24, 2019, the Grand Chamber of the Court of Justice (hereafter: ECJ) released its judgment. In *Google v CNIL* the ECJ considered a preliminary reference concerning the territorial scope of the right to be forgotten online. The case arose out of a formal notice by which the President of the CNIL ordered Google to delist information concerning data subjects from all of its domain name extensions. Despite the proposal by Google to adopt geo-blocking measures, the CNIL nevertheless decided to sanction Google for a failure to comply with the order. Before the Conseil d'État, the point raised by Google concerning the vague boundaries within the *Google Spain* case led the administrative court to send a preliminary reference to the ECJ concerning the scope of search engine delisting obligations.

Starting from the opinion of AG Maciej Szpunar in *Google v CNIL*, it is possible to observe an approach characterized by self-restraint. According to AG Szpunar, neither the EU law nor the ECJ case law engaged with the territoriality of de-referencing within the context of protection for rights under arts. 7 and 8 CFREU.

First, the court considered whether EU law applies to the activities of search engines, and noting that the CNIL had rejected the proposed geo-blocking application as formulated by Google, the ECJ analyzed the questions proposed for a preliminary ruling: whether, according to arts. 12(b) and 14 of the Data Protection Directive and art. 17(1) GDPR, de-referencing is required on all versions of the search engine, or only on the versions of that search engine corresponding to all the Member States, or even only on the version corresponding to the Member State where the de-referencing was requested. The global nature of the Internet and the claims of the right to digital privacy and data protection seemed to open the door to a new phase in the extraterritoriality saga: "such considerations are such as to justify the existence of competence on the part of the EU legislature to lay down the obligation, for a search engine operator, to carry out, when granting a request for de-referencing made by such a person, a de-referencing on all the versions of its search engine" (§58).

Eventually, the ECJ highlighted the different approaches to the right to privacy and data protection in other legal systems as well as the relative nature of this fundamental right. Two of the pillars underlying the extraterritoriality effect seem to have fallen: on the one hand, the limited digital sovereignty of the EU has been recognized, or rather the presence of different sovereignties also within the digital world has been recognized. On the other hand, the trump card of the absolute right to data protection and privacy online appears, in part, to have become less powerful. As a result, even if, in light of the precedents, the coherent solution would have been to extend the right to be forgotten to a global scale, the ECJ opted for a self-restraint approach, motivated by the risk of a kind of European legal colonization in the name of cultural hegemony.

However, this decision seems to be more a tactical retreat than a surrender to criticism of the Europeanization of Internet regulation.

As the court held, there is little room for interpretation under the current legal framework of data protection to establish a global application of such a right. It highlighted the difficulties of global de-referencing, noting that the public interest in access to information varies substantially among third-party states, and therefore the balancing of fundamental rights would also differ. The court seemingly faced a difficult choice: either to consider a global application, which would ensure full protection of the right, at the risk of jeopardizing its legitimacy by encroaching on third-party states' sovereignty; or to avoid potential overreach by concluding a regional application that still provides its residents protection of their personal data, albeit limited, within the Union. Ultimately, the court went on to say that the EU framework does not provide for cooperation instruments and measures outside its territory and chose the EU-wide approach.

11.6 Conclusions

This chapter analyzed the long and complex evolution of the right to be forgotten. The latter does not constitute a right in itself since it appears to be instrumental, either to the right to personal identity or to the right to the protection of personal data. Nonetheless, it has entrenched a new accountability obligation on the data controller, shifting the focus from the topicality of the news to the updating of the data. This shift seems appropriate given the strong link between the right to erasure and the protection of individuals' personal identities. This very aspect is entrenched in the evolution of the concept that, at first, was related to human physicality and then, instead, to the digital *habeas corpus*, an evolution that culminated in the *Google Spain* judgment. This evolution also affected the right to erasure itself, the different stages of which were discussed in Section 3. Therefore, the result of this infamous ruling has been to affirm the right to delete data if they are inadequate, irrelevant or no longer relevant in relation to the purposes of the processing. This is not an *ad nutum* right but a right to erasure that must be weighed and exercised because of the characteristics of the data constituted by the adequacy, relevance or irrelevance of the processing in relation to the purposes. It is not about the right to delete data *tout court*.

Precisely because of the breadth but also the opacity of the court's reasoning, its consequences were wide-reaching, as demonstrated in the preceding section. In particular, Google, invested with this para-publicist power, has, from the very beginning, taken positive action to adjust itself to the role tailored by the court. Moreover, the entry into force of the GDPR marked a new stage in the evolution of the right to erasure, while the Court had to identify the territorial extension of this right, as in *Google v. CNIL*.

In conclusion, the right to be forgotten is dependent on the concepts of privacy, data protection and personal identity. The long evolution demonstrated that any solution will inevitably go through a complex process of balancing rights and, lastly, sovereign powers and jurisdictions. The critical issues raised in this chapter follow a trend developed by the ECJ, and also carry over to other open questions that will be addressed in the following chapters, in particular, that related to data retention and international transfer of personal data.

12 Transfer of Personal Data

12.1 Introduction

Cross-border data flows have been described as commerce-enabling hallmarks of 21st-century globalization and the connective tissue holding the global economy together. Moreover, Internet intermediaries, who have captured much of the value from the collection of personal data while the data subjects have received access to them, provide cross-border "free" digital services. These services have been estimated to have added between $240 billion and $3.2 trillion to trade in services in 2017. Such flows are ubiquitous, and with the Internet of Things there are huge volumes of international data transfers without human intervention. In addition, cross-border data flows allow enterprises to expand their businesses worldwide and access online digital services that can help them increase their productivity. International trade in data has grown rapidly in importance, in terms of both the amount of data flows and their financial value.

However, national and regional actors have not provided harmonious regulation for these increasing flows, or for data privacy more generally. Globalized trade in digital data and services has been accompanied neither by a general harmonization of internet law, nor by true data protection and data privacy law convergence, exemplified by the divergence between the two large Western blocs: certain obstacles to data privacy law harmonization exist between the United States and the European Union. This divergence exists despite the growing influence of the EU data protection model worldwide, with its GDPR.

Therefore, as previously shown in Chapter 11, transfers of personal data outside the territory of the EU are a central issue, especially if taking into account that in the information society data is transferred through the network from one point to another on the planet, intersecting legal regimes that provide for different protections. As previously explained, the transfer of personal data to countries outside the territory of the Union poses several challenges regarding the protection of this data since those countries may have lower standards of protection than those established within the Union. Therefore, it is necessary to understand how the GDPR deals with transfers of personal data outside the EU considering the massive flow of personal data outside EU borders.

This chapter analyzes the discipline set up by Chapter V of the GDPR, with which transfers of personal data must comply, specifically arts. 44–50 (12.2). Section 12.3 focuses on the legal challenges of international data transfers resulting from the recent ECJ decisions in Case C-362/14 and in Case C-311/18, *Schrems I* and *II*. These judgments invalidated EU–US cross-border transfers, making personal data transfers to the United States highly complicated. However, one caveat is that organizations have to perform a case-by-case assessment on the application of the standard contractual clauses (SCCs) and implement "supplementary measures" to compensate for the lack of data protection in the third country, where necessary. Regrettably, the ECJ missed the opportunity to specify what exactly these "supplementary measures" could be. As shown in Section 12.4, to fill this gap the European Data Protection Board (EDPB) adopted guidelines on the measures that supplement transfer tools to ensure compliance with the EU level of protection of personal data. In addition, on June 4, 2021, the European Commission issued new SCCs that replaced the previous SCCs that were adopted under the previous Data Protection Directive 95/46/EC. Moreover, the European Commission and the United States have recently agreed on a new Trans-Atlantic Data Privacy Framework that will foster transatlantic data flows and address the concerns raised by the ECJ in the *Schrems II* case.

12.2 Personal data transfers according to the GDPR

Regarding the transfer of personal data outside the European Union, the obligatory starting point is the regulation of the GDPR provided for by arts. 44–50. This observation seems, in particular, to be confirmed by the GDPR itself, which provides for a general principle in art. 44 according to which any transfer of personal data subject to processing or intended to be processed after the transfer to a third country or an international organization, including onward transfers of personal data from a third country or an international organization to another third country or another international organization, takes place only if the controller and the processor comply with the conditions set out by the GDPR, without prejudice to the other provisions of the Regulation. It follows that the transfer can only take place in accordance with the provisions of the GDPR.

However, it should be noted that Recital 102 specifies that these rules are without prejudice to the conclusion of international agreements concluded between the Union and third countries governing the transfer of personal data. Consequently, Member States may conclude international agreements for the transfer of personal data to third countries or international organizations, provided that such agreements do not affect the GDPR or any other provision of Union law and include an adequate level of protection for fundamental rights of the data subjects. And it is precisely the latter that is the cornerstone of the discipline, namely ensuring a level of protection equal to that established by the GDPR.

In this context, before analyzing the rules provided by the GDPR on the transfer of personal data outside the territory of the Union, it is necessary to make some preliminary observations regarding the scope of the transfer regime. It should be noted that the GDPR limits the transfer of personal data to countries outside the European

Economic Area or international organizations. The transfer restriction applies to all transfers, regardless of their size or the frequency with which they are made. However, what types of data are transferred must be considered. The transfer regime applies only to personal data according to the definition provided by the GDPR. If the transfer concerns data that do not fall within the notion of personal data (e.g., anonymous data, or data referred to companies), the transfer regime does not apply and, therefore, the data can be freely transferred outside the Union. Furthermore, the concept of transfer is different from transit. If personal data are simply routed electronically through a country outside the Union, but the transfer takes place between two countries of the Union, this activity does not fall within the scope of data transfer.

Focusing on the legal basis of the transfer, it is possible to identify three ways in which data can be transferred outside the Union:

a. transfer on the basis of an adequacy decision (art. 45);
b. transfer subject to adequate guarantees (arts. 46 and 47); or
c. exceptions in specific situations (art. 49).

12.2.1 Adequacy decisions

According to art. 45(1):

> the transfer of personal data to a third country or an international organization is allowed if the Commission has decided that the third country, a territory or one or more specific sectors within the third country, or the international organization in question guarantee an adequate level of protection.

In this case, the transfer does not require specific authorizations. It should be noted that, in assessing the level of adequacy, the Commission may decide, by means of implementing acts, that a third country, a territory or one or more specific sectors within a third country, or an international organization guarantees a level of adequate protection pursuant to art. 45(2). Consequently, the GDPR does not exclude that for some countries there may be an authorization for specific sectors or geographical areas. Furthermore, even once the authorization has been granted, the Commission can review its decision and revoke, amend or suspend it. To determine which countries of specific territories and sectors within a third country, and which international organizations, on which the Commission has expressed its assessment of adequacy, it is possible to consult the *Official Journal of the European Union* and the website of the Commission. Adjustment decisions made prior to the GDPR remain in effect unless the Commission expresses otherwise later.

To date, the Commission has expressed its assessment of the adequacy of the following countries and territories: Andorra, Argentina, Canada, Faroe Islands, Guernsey, Isle of Man, Israel, Jersey, New Zealand, Republic of Korea, Switzerland, United Kingdom and Uruguay. Meanwhile, the Commission has made partial assessments with regard to Canada, Japan and the United States. In particular, the suitability assessment for Japan covers only private sector organizations, while for Canada it only covers data subject to the Canadian Personal Information Protection and Electronic Documents Act (PIPEDA). With regard to the United States, before *Schrems II*, the suitability assessment for the United States only concerned transfers of personal data that fall within the framework of the so-called privacy shield between the European Union and the United States. This was a self-certification mechanism for companies established in the United States wishing to receive personal data from the European Union.

12.2.2 Appropriate safeguards

Where the Commission has not decided that a certain country ensures an adequate level of protection, the transfer of data to a third country or an international organization may be performed if the controller or processor has provided appropriate safeguards, and on condition that enforceable data subject rights and effective legal remedies for data subjects are available. The purpose of these guarantees is to ensure compliance with the data protection requirements with the EU general principles regarding the processing of personal data and with principles of data protection by design and data protection by default.

Art. 46 of the GDPR provides five types of appropriate safeguards that can be provided without requiring any specific authorization from a supervisory authority:

a. a legally binding and enforceable instrument between public authorities or bodies;
b. binding corporate rules in accordance with art. 47;
c. standard data protection clauses adopted by the Commission in accordance with the examination procedure referred to in art. 93(2);
d. standard data protection clauses adopted by a supervisory authority and approved by the Commission pursuant to the examination procedure referred to in art. 93(2);
e. an approved code of conduct pursuant to art. 40 together with binding and enforceable commitments of the controller or processor in the third country to apply the appropriate safeguards, including as regards data subjects' rights; and
f. an approved certification mechanism pursuant to art. 42 together with binding and enforceable commitments of the controller or processor in the third country to apply the appropriate safeguards, including as regards data subjects' rights.

Besides adequate guarantees, with the authorization of the supervisory authority personal data can be also transferred through:

a. Contractual clauses between the controller or processor and the controller, processor or recipient of the personal data in the third country or international organization.

b. Provisions to be inserted into administrative arrangements between public authorities or bodies that include enforceable and effective data subject rights.

Considering the latter, contractual clauses should be analyzed, specifically the standard contractual clauses issued by the European Commission. Models of such SCCs are set by the Commission in order to ensure adequate safeguards for the transfer of data to third countries. By the Decision of June 15, 2001, and the Decision of December 27, 2004, the Commission issued two sets of SCCs for data transfers from data controllers in the European Union to data controllers established outside the European Union or the European Economic Area (EEA). Moreover, the Decision of February 5, 2010, established one set of contractual clauses for data transfers from controllers in the European Union to processors established outside the European Union or the EEA. In addition, in 2021, the European Commission issued new SCCs to replace the previous ones. Furthermore, under the GDPR, standard data protection clauses may be adopted by a supervisory authority and approved by the Commission pursuant to an examination procedure.

Additionally, the GDPR provides for the possibility of stipulating binding corporate rules (BCRs). BCRs are an internal code of conduct operating within a multinational group that applies to restricted transfers of personal data from the group's EEA entities to non-EEA group entities. As stated in art. 47(1):

> The competent supervisory authority shall approve binding corporate rules in accordance with the consistency mechanism set out in art. 63, provided that they:
> (a) are legally binding and apply to and are enforced by every member concerned of the group of undertakings, or group of enterprises engaged in a joint economic activity, including their employees;
> (b) expressly confer enforceable rights on data subjects with regard to the processing of their personal data; and
> (c) fulfil the requirements laid down in paragraph 2.

These clauses shall comply with specific criteria defined by the GDPR and are approved by the supervisory authority, ensuring that they are legally binding and apply to all interested members of the business group or group of companies carrying out a joint economic activity, including their employees.

More specifically, under art. 47(2), BCRs shall specify at least:

a. the structure and contact details of the group of undertakings, or group of enterprises engaged in a joint economic activity and of each of its members;
b. the data transfers or set of transfers, including the categories of personal data, the type of processing and its purposes, the type of data subjects affected and the identification of the third country or countries in question;
c. their legally binding nature, both internally and externally;
d. the application of the general data protection principles;
e. the rights of data subjects in regard to processing and the means to exercise those rights;

f. the acceptance by the controller or processor established on the territory of a Member State of liability for any breaches of the binding corporate rules by any member concerned not established in the Union;
g. how the information on the binding corporate rules is provided to the data subjects;
h. the tasks of any data protection officer designated in accordance with art. 37 or any other person or entity in charge of monitoring compliance with the binding corporate rules within the group of undertakings;
i. the complaint procedures;
j. the mechanisms within the group of undertakings or group of enterprises engaged in a joint economic activity for ensuring the verification of compliance with the binding corporate rules;
k. the mechanisms for reporting and recording changes to the rules and reporting those changes to the supervisory authority;
l. the cooperation mechanism with the supervisory authority to ensure compliance by any member of the group of undertakings or group of enterprises engaged in a joint economic activity;
m. the mechanisms for reporting to the competent supervisory authority any legal requirements to which a member of the group of undertakings or group of enterprises engaged in a joint economic activity is subject in a third country that are likely to have a substantial adverse effect on the guarantees provided by the binding corporate rules; and
n. the appropriate data protection training to personnel having permanent or regular access to personal data.

Lastly, it should be noted that BCRs can be used both for arrangements among entities of the same corporate group, and by a group of enterprises engaged in a joint economic activity but not necessarily forming part of the same corporate group.

12.2.3 Derogations

In the absence of an adequacy decision (art. 45) or adequate guarantees (art. 46), including BCRs (art. 47), under art. 49, the transfer of personal data to a third country or organization is permitted internationally only under the following conditions:

a. the data subject has explicitly consented to the proposed transfer, after having been informed of the possible risks of such transfers for the data subject due to the absence of an adequacy decision and appropriate safeguards;
b. the transfer is necessary for the performance of a contract between the data subject and the controller or the implementation of pre-contractual measures taken at the data subject's request;
c. the transfer is necessary for the conclusion or performance of a contract concluded in the interest of the data subject between the controller and another natural or legal person;

d. the transfer is necessary for important reasons of public interest;
e. the transfer is necessary for the establishment, exercise or defense of legal claims;
f. the transfer is necessary in order to protect the vital interests of the data subject or of other persons, where the data subject is physically or legally incapable of giving consent; or
g. the transfer is made from a register that, according to Union or Member State law, is intended to provide information to the public and that is open to consultation either by the public in general or by any person who can demonstrate a legitimate interest, but only to the extent that the conditions laid down by Union or Member State law for consultation are fulfilled in the particular case.

The cases referred to in art. 49(1) (a-b-c) do not apply to activities carried out by public authorities in the exercise of public authority.

Even outside the aforementioned cases, the transfer is permitted only if it is not repetitive, it concerns a limited number of data subjects, it is necessary for the pursuit of the binding legitimate interests of the data controller, if the data controller has assessed all the circumstances relating to the transfer and, on the basis of this assessment, has provided adequate guarantees regarding the protection of personal data. The EDPB notes that the term "occasional" is used in Recital 111 and the term "not repetitive" is used in the "compelling legitimate interests" derogation under art. 49. These terms indicate that such transfers may happen more than once, but not regularly, and would occur outside the regular course of actions, for example, under random, unknown circumstances and within arbitrary time intervals. For instance, a data transfer that occurs regularly within a stable relationship between the data exporter and a certain data importer can basically be deemed systematic and repeated and therefore cannot be considered occasional or not repetitive. Besides, a transfer will, for example, generally be non-occasional or repetitive when the data importer is granted direct access to a database (for example, via an interface to an IT application) on a general basis.

In any case, it should be noted that the data controller has to inform the supervisory authority of the transfer. In addition to the provision of information referred to in arts. 13 and 14, the data controller informs the data subject of the transfer and of the binding legitimate interests being pursued. The latter case does not apply to activities carried out by public authorities in the exercise of public authority.

12.3 The *Schrems* saga

In order to understand the practical application of the discipline related to the transfer of personal data outside the European Union, it is necessary to analyze two of the most important rulings issued by the ECJ in recent years. These judgments invalidated EU–US cross-border transfers, making personal data transfers to the United States highly complicated. However, one caveat is that organizations would have to perform a case-by-case assessment on the application of the SCCs and implement "supplementary measures" to compensate for the lack of data protection in the third country, where necessary.

12.3.1 *Schrems I*

The *Schrems I* (C-362/14) case, which followed along the lines of *Digital Rights Ireland* and *Google Spain*, is one of the landmark decisions that demonstrated the role of the ECJ and its case law in building the practical application of the data protection right. This landmark judgment led to the invalidation of the adequacy decision known as safe harbor that, at the time, made it possible to transfer personal data from the European Union to the United States. This fundamental rights-based approach arose at several points in the judgment. It is not by coincidence that at the very outset, as a preliminary remark, the ECJ stressed that:

> the provisions of Directive 95/46, in as much as they govern the processing of personal data liable to infringe fundamental freedoms, in particular, the right to respect for private life, must necessarily be interpreted in the light of the fundamental rights guaranteed by the Charter.

This methodological premise paved the way for the ECJ to rely on a flexible and broad interpretation of the legal framework that was compatible with its purpose of a loose interpretation of the law. Another aspect that shows how the *Schrems I* decision reflects this goal is the enhancement of the powers vested in national data protection authorities. In particular, one of the questions raised by the national court was whether national regulators had *marge de manoeuvre* to challenge a decision adopted by the EU Commission when assessing the adequacy of the level of protection ensured by third countries' legal systems. According to the ECJ, although the decision adopted pursuant to art. 25 of the Data Protection Directive was binding on all Member States, the existence of such an act did not deprive individuals of the right to appeal to the competent authorities according to art. 28(4) of Directive 95/46/EC in order to protect their fundamental rights.

However, the ECJ stressed that the EU Commission's decision may not undermine the powers of the national regulatory authorities to protect individuals' rights. In this respect, therefore, the justification for manipulating the applicable legal framework took root when the ECJ provided a broad interpretation of the powers of these authorities to provide individuals with appropriate means to protect their personal data. According to the ECJ:

> it would be contrary to the system set up by Directive 95/46 and to the objective of arts. 25 and 28 thereof for a Commission decision adopted pursuant to art. 25(6) to have the effect of preventing a national supervisory authority from examining a person's claim concerning the protection of his rights and freedoms in regard to the processing of his personal data which has been or could be transferred from a Member State to the third country covered by that decision.

Thus, by interpreting the applicable legal framework also in light of art. 47 of the CFREU (protecting the right to an effective remedy and to a fair trial), the ECJ enhanced individuals' rights under arts. 7 and 8 CFREU, thus paving the way for enhancing the extent of the relevant protection.

However, the most important point that brings out the loose interpretative approach of the ECJ can be found in the part of the decision that considers whether Decision 2000/520 met with the conditions laid down by art. 25 of the Data Protection Directive, which requires an adequate level of protection for personal data transferred to third countries. This led the ECJ to consider whether the US legal system, and notably the safe harbor principles, afforded personal data of European residents "an adequate level of protection." Only if this requirement is fulfilled is the transfer of personal data to third countries lawful under the EU legislative framework (at the time, the Data Protection Directive, now the GDPR).

The ECJ pointed out that the Data Protection Directive assumed a relatively flexible notion of "adequate level of protection." A significant degree of ambiguity and vagueness thus surrounds this parameter. The Data Protection Directive did not set out in an exhaustive and systematic way the criteria to be applied by the competent European authorities when carrying out such an assessment, nor did it provide a specific definition of the concept of "adequacy." Art. 25(2) of Directive 95/46/EC only established that:

> the adequacy of the level of protection afforded by a third country shall be assessed in the light of all the circumstances surrounding a data transfer operation or set of data transfer operations.

In addition, it also suggested that:

> particular consideration shall be given to the nature of the data, the purpose and duration of the proposed processing operation or operations, the country of origin and country of final destination, the rules of law, both general and sectoral, in force in the third country in question and the professional rules and security measures which are complied with in that country.

In order to reduce this ambiguity and vagueness, the Data Protection Directive spelled out some factors that should be considered when assessing whether the level of protection offered by a third country is actually "adequate." Nonetheless, art. 25 of Directive 95/46/EC did not clarify whether these parameters were binding and exhaustive, thus preventing any evaluation from relying on different criteria.

On the one hand, the ECJ pointed out that art. 25(6) of the Data Protection Directive required (and the GDPR still requires) that a third country "ensures" an adequate level of protection by reason of its domestic law or its international commitments. On the other hand, according to the ECJ, the adequacy of protection must be assessed "for the protection of the private lives and basic freedoms and rights of individuals." The assessment is thus not purely normative but is more demanding, rooted as it is in fundamental rights.

In order to assess the compatibility of the Decision on the safe harbor agreement with the Data Protection Directive, in this case the ECJ acted as a fundamental rights adjudicator with a view to enforcing arts. 7 and 8 CFREU. In the following parts of the judgment, the ECJ provided arguments that confirm its focus on protecting fundamental rights through a strict interpretation of the reference to an "adequate level of protection." The ECJ converted this parameter into a standard requiring that there be some kind of equivalence between the legal orders being compared. In this respect, the ECJ referred back to the goal behind art. 25 of the Data Protection Directive, that is, "to ensure that the high level of that protection continues where personal data is transferred to a third country." This was clear when the ECJ stated that:

> the word "adequate" in art. 25(6) of Directive 95/46 admittedly signifies that a third country cannot be required to ensure a level of protection identical to that guaranteed in the EU legal order. However, as the Advocate General has observed in point 141 of his Opinion, the term "adequate level of protection" must be understood as requiring the third country in fact to ensure, by reason of its domestic law or its international commitments, a level of protection of fundamental rights and freedoms that is essentially equivalent to that guaranteed within the European Union by virtue of Directive 95/46 read in the light of the Charter. If there were no such requirement, the objective referred to in the previous paragraph of the present judgment would be disregarded. Furthermore, the high level of protection guaranteed by Directive 95/46 read in the light of the Charter could easily be circumvented by transfers of personal data from the European Union to third countries for the purpose of being processed in those countries.

Even though an adequate level of protection does not require third countries to adopt an identical standard, individuals may nevertheless enjoy a degree of protection that is "substantially equivalent" to that offered by EU law. The equivalence of the degree of protection is required, according to the court, "by virtue of an interpretation of the Data Protection Directive in light of the Charter."

The CFREU thus becomes the judicial device for the advancement of the level of protection required by EU law through a loose interpretation of the parameter of "adequacy." This approach is anything but rhetorical, since the ECJ was inspired by the entry into force of the CFREU to revisit the provisions enshrined in the Data Protection Directive and to renew its interpretation of it. Therefore, the meaning of the provisions of the Data Protection Directive changed and, accordingly, the level of protection granted to personal data was much broader even before the adoption of the GDPR.

Moreover, the judgment seems to pay attention to the dynamic nature of the level of protection, which may vary in line with a number of factors. This is essentially why the ECJ urged the EU Commission to carry out regular checks into whether the finding concerning the adequacy of the level of protection offered by third countries is still factually and legally justified. In addition, "such a check is required, in any event, when evidence gives rise to a doubt in that regard." To this end, the European institutions should take into account all factually and legally relevant circumstances once this assessment has been carried out. This approach mirrors a revisited interpretation of the standard of adequacy according to which a kind of "continuity" in the level of protection should be guaranteed not only from a geographical but also a temporal viewpoint. This dynamic view of the concept of adequacy arose even when the ECJ pointed out that:

> even though the means to which that third country has recourse, in this connection, for the purpose of ensuring such a level of protection may differ from those employed within the European Union in order to ensure that the requirements stemming from Directive 95/46 read in the light of the Charter are complied with, those means must nevertheless prove, in practice, effective in order to ensure protection essentially equivalent to that guaranteed within the European Union.

Therefore, the Data Protection Directive no longer constituted the sole basis on which the legitimacy of the Decision on safe harbor was based. The parameter that the ECJ used to the review the EU Commission's decision was the CFREU, the entry into force of which shifted the judicial perspective from a mainly market-oriented to a fundamental rights approach.

On the one hand, the ECJ stressed that such an adequate level of protection can be achieved through the implementation of measures that may not necessarily correspond to those practiced within the EU and provided for under Member States' domestic legislation. The ECJ seemed to step back by adopting an approach marked by self-restraint when recognizing that the goal of guaranteeing appropriate protection may be pursued by different means, tailored to the relevant specific legal context. On the other hand, the ECJ did not take this path. The ECJ examined the US legal instruments for determining whether these measures were compatible with the purpose of granting an adequate level of protection to personal data. The ECJ challenged the safe harbor system by adopting reasoning that is quite uncommon when it comes to protecting fundamental rights. In particular, the judgment is remarkable for its unambiguously pragmatic view, which is reflected in the efforts made by the ECJ to determine whether the objective of ensuring adequate protection is actually met.

These remarks constituted the premise for the analysis carried out by the ECJ into the compliance of the safe harbor principles with EU law. The ECJ reached the conclusion that the US measures did not provide personal data with adequate protection in comparison with EU standards. Although the review was formally conducted by comparing the Data Protection Directive with the content of the safe harbor principles, from a substantive standpoint, the decision found that the US legal system was not compatible with the protection of the fundamental rights enshrined in arts. 7 and 8 CFREU. In other words, in *Schrems I* the US framework operated as the parameter for assessing compliance with fundamental rights by an act from the EU legal order. The interpretation of "adequacy" was reviewed by focusing on the compatibility between the US approach and the CFREU since, as was recognized by the ECJ, the personal data of EU individuals were not properly protected by the US standard. Moreover, a factual element needs to be included in such an assessment. It is necessary to refer to the influence of the National Security Agency scandal, which at the time had captured the attention of the international community in the area of state surveillance.

Another important point concerns the protection of personal data in relation to national security, an interest that is generally evaluated at the discretion of the Member States. Protection of national security is not subject to harmonization at the EU level. Member States can adopt different solutions, which may also impinge upon the protection of personal data, despite the existence of a harmonized data protection legal framework. Here, the EU constitutional system can mitigate such asymmetry by harmonizing protection for such fundamental rights. In particular, art. 6(2) Treaty of European Union considers rights enshrined in the European Convention on Human Rights (ECHR) as general principles of EU law and, thus, art. 52(3) CFREU clarifies that protection for the rights enshrined in the CFREU shall be equal to the meaning and the scope of ECHR rights. As a result, the ECHR can be considered another (even implicit) parameter of the decision in question.

In addition to the above, it is worth recalling that in this case the ECJ also pointed out that it is for the EU Commission to regularly check whether the legal orders of the third countries concerned provide personal data with an adequate level of protection, in light of any legal and factual circumstances that may affect it. This statement reflects a dynamic, more practical and changing understanding of the standard of adequacy. It must, however, be considered whether the ECJ was affected by a decrease in the level of protection ensured by the US legal system, compared with the standard in force when the safe harbor agreement was concluded, or whether the judgement was instead a reaction to the risk of reduced protection for European residents in light of purely internal factors. In essence, the question is whether the ECJ's decision reflects an evolution of the relevant background or rather a regression that urged Europe to raise its defenses.

These considerations might contribute to defining a dynamic level of protection for privacy and personal data from at least two different perspectives. First, the range of factors that must be considered by the EU Commission when evaluating the adequacy of the protection offered by third countries becomes broader. The EU Commission would not limit its assessment to the status quo but rather would regularly check whether any assessment previously carried out still corresponds to the standard of adequate protection in light of the relevant factual and legal circumstances. Second, the ECJ recognized that the EU Commission's discretion in evaluating the protection offered by non-EU countries is narrow and that it is necessary to adopt strict scrutiny in relation to art. 25 of the Data Protection Directive (and now the corresponding provisions of the GDPR) in order to safeguard the right to privacy and data protection. The adoption of a kind of "strict scrutiny test" reflects the revisited understanding of Directive 95/46/EC. This act was intended, at the very beginning, to regulate purely economic matters, while it has been regarded more recently as the cornerstone for affording a high degree of protection to the fundamental rights to privacy and personal data. Finally, the ECJ basically rewrote the relevant criteria, from adequacy to essential equivalence. This constitutes further important evidence of the "manipulation through interpretation" in which the ECJ engaged through this decision.

12.3.2 *Schrems II*

In 2020, the ECJ added another piece of the puzzle in the *Schrems* saga. In *Schrems II* (C-311/18) the ECJ further strengthened its fundamental rights-based approach, and consolidated its power across the Atlantic, by invalidating the adequacy decision adopted in the aftermath of *Schrems I,* known as Privacy Shield.

Following the first judgment, the domestic court annulled the rejection of the applicant's complaint and referred the decision about the prohibition to transfer personal data back to the Data Protection Commissioner (Ireland). Facebook Ireland explained that a large part of personal data was transferred based on the SCCs and, therefore, the Commissioner asked the applicant to reformulate his complaint. The second claim concerned, inter alia, the possibility of surveillance and law enforcement authorities accessing data from Facebook and using this information in monitoring programs, thus interfering with arts. 7, 8 and 47 CFREU.

In 2016, the Data Protection Commissioner (Ireland) agreed with this position, observing that the standard data protection clauses in the annex to the SCCs Decision were not capable of remedying that defect, since they confer only contractual rights on data subjects against the data exporter and importer, without, however, binding the US authorities. The Commissioner decided to bring an action before the Irish High Court, which then made the reference for a preliminary ruling on the ECJ.

The shift was easier in this case than it was the first time around (*Schrems I*) because of Recital 104 of the GDPR, which states that "the third country should offer guarantees ensuring an adequate level of protection essentially equivalent to that ensured within the Union, in particular where personal data are processed in one or several specific sectors." However, art. 45 of the GDPR still clarifies that such cases only involve an evaluation as to the adequacy of the level of protection, and not a comparison. It should not therefore be surprising that the ECJ asserted that:

> the first sentence of art. 45(1) of the GDPR provides that a transfer of personal data to a third country may be authorised by a Commission decision to the effect that that third country, a territory or one or more specified sectors within that third country, ensures an adequate level of protection. In that regard, although not requiring a third country to ensure a level of protection identical to that guaranteed in the EU legal order, the term "adequate level of protection" must, as confirmed by recital 104 of that regulation, be understood as requiring the third country in fact to ensure, by reason of its domestic law or its international commitments, a level of protection of fundamental rights and freedoms that is essentially equivalent to that guaranteed within the European Union by virtue of the regulation, read in the light of the Charter.

Advocate General (AG) Saugmandsgaard Øe's Opinion had already paved the way for the ECJ's decision. When focusing on the extension of the assessment over national surveillance, the AG highlighted that, when adopting an adequacy decision, the EU Commission has to take into account, inter alia, the legislation of the third country concerned relating to national security. Despite such an extensive trend, he stressed that the resolution of the dispute in the case in question would not have required the ECJ to rule on the validity of the Privacy Shield Decision, since the same concerned only the validity of the SCCs Decision. Nonetheless, the AG raised doubts about whether the US legal framework met the standard of protection required to transfer personal data beyond EU territory. He expressly clarified:

> I doubt, as do Mr Schrems and the EPIC, that EO 12333, like PPD 28, which sets out guarantees applicable to all signals intelligence activities, are sufficiently foreseeable to have the "quality of law". Those instruments expressly state that they do not confer legally enforceable rights on the persons concerned. The latter cannot therefore rely on the guarantees set out in PPD 28 before the courts. The Commission considered, moreover, in the "privacy shield" decision, that although the guarantees set out in PPD 28 have binding force for the intelligence services, they are "not phrased in [...] legal terms". EO 12333 and PPD 28 bear more resemblance to internal administrative instruction that can be revoked or amended by the President of the United States. The ECtHR [European Court of Human Rights] has already held that internal administrative directives do not constitute "law".

At the same time, looking also at the case law of the ECtHR, the AG observed that the essence of arts. 7 and 8 ECHR was not compromised. Security is one of the possible justifications for restrictions to the right to privacy and data protection. According to him:

> I shall merely observe, on that subject, that the ECtHR has not had recourse, in its case-law relating to art. 8 of the ECHR, to the concept of violation of the essential content, or the very essence, of the right to respect for private life. It has not thus far considered that regimes that allow the interception of electronic communications, even on a mass scale, exceeded as such the margin of appreciation of the Member States. The ECtHR considers that such regimes are compatible with art. 8(2) of the ECHR provided that they are accompanied by a number of minimum guarantees. In those circumstances, it does not seem appropriate to me to conclude that a surveillance regime such as that provided for by EO 12333 would exceed the margin of appreciation of the Member States without undertaking any examination whatsoever of any guarantees that accompany it.

Concerning the safeguards, the AG expressed his concern about the lack of prior review. With specific regard to the first point, he observed:

> I have already pointed out that PPD 28 does not create rights for individuals. Next, I doubt that the requirement to guarantee surveillance "as tailored as feasible" is formulated in sufficiently clear and precise terms to forewarn the data subjects adequately against the risks of abuse. Last, the "privacy shield" decision does not establish that the surveillance based on EO 12333 would be subject to prior review by an independent body or might be the subject of post factum judicial review.

Similar concerns were expressed regarding the lack of effective remedies and the inadequacy of the ombudsperson mechanism. All these doubts led the AG to entertain certain doubts as to the conformity of the Privacy Shield Decision with art. 45(1) of the GDPR, read in light of arts. 7, 8 and 47 of the CFREU and of art. 8 of the ECHR.

The decision of the ECJ shed light on these concerns. The ECJ first underlined that the GDPR applies to the transfer of personal data for commercial purposes by an economic operator established in a Member State to another economic operator established in a third country, even if, at the time of that transfer or thereafter, those data may be processed by the authorities of the third country in question for the purposes of public security, defense or state security.

Like in *Schrems I*, the ECJ stressed that personal data can be transferred only pursuant to an essentially equivalent standard of protection. Moreover, the court underlined that the essentially equivalent level of protection applies not only to adequacy decisions by the EU Commission but also to the use of SCCs. By interpreting arts. 46(1) and 46(2)(c) with art. 45(2) of the GDPR, transfers of personal data based on SCCs have to take into consideration any access by the public authorities of that third country to the personal data transferred and the relevant aspects of the legal system of that third country, in particular those set out, in a non-exhaustive manner, in art. 45(2) of the GDPR.

The ECJ did not invalidate the SCCs Decision. Indeed, the ECJ underlined the role of economic operators in setting additional safeguards when contractual clauses cannot ensure the aforementioned level of protection. According to the ECJ:

> the standard data protection clauses adopted by the Commission on the basis of art. 46(2)(c) of the GDPR are solely intended to provide contractual guarantees that apply uniformly in all third countries to controllers and processors established in the European Union and, consequently, independently of the level of protection guaranteed in each third country. In so far as those standard data protection clauses cannot, having regard to their very nature, provide guarantees beyond a contractual obligation to ensure compliance with the level of protection required under EU law, they may require, depending on the prevailing position in a particular third country, the adoption of supplementary measures by the controller in order to ensure compliance with that level of protection.

Since SCCs are not capable of binding the authorities of that third country, the controller established in the European Union and the recipient of personal data have to verify, prior to any transfer, whether the level of protection required by EU law is respected in the third country concerned.

On the one hand, the ECJ seemed to underline the role of economic operators in assessing compliance with the SCCs. On the other hand, the ECJ underlined the primary role of the national competent authority in the context of third-country transfers of data. The ECJ clarified the primary role of supervisory authorities in case of the lack of a valid EU Commission adequacy decision. These authorities are required to suspend or prohibit the transfer of personal data to a third country on a case-by-case assessment, precisely if, in their view and in light of all the circumstances of that transfer, contractual clauses are not or cannot be complied with in that third country and the protection of the data transferred that is required by EU law cannot be ensured by other means, where the controller or a processor has not itself suspended or put an end to the transfer. The assessments focus on whether data protection clauses can be respected in that country and whether the protection of the data transferred that is required by EU law cannot be ensured by other means.

Once it had ruled on the application of EU law to the case in question and on the validity of the SCC system, the ECJ moved to the assessment of the validity of the privacy shield. The ECJ focused on appropriate safeguards, namely enforceable rights and effective legal remedies, in light of the fundamental rights, with a specific focus on privacy and data protection. The ECJ recognized that US law does not meet the standard of protection that should be essentially equivalent to the protection of EU law, precisely the principle of proportionality, since US surveillance programs are not limited to what is strictly necessary. Accordingly, the court said that:

> neither Section 702 of the FISA, nor E.O. 12333, read in conjunction with PPD-28, correlates to the minimum safeguards resulting, under EU law, from the principle of proportionality, with the consequence that the surveillance programmes based on those provisions cannot be regarded as limited to what is strictly necessary. In those circumstances, the limitations on the protection of personal data arising from the domestic law of the United States on the access and use by US public authorities of such data transferred from the European Union to the United States, which the Commission assessed in the Privacy Shield Decision, are not circumscribed in a way that satisfies requirements that are essentially equivalent to those required, under EU law, by the second sentence of art. 52(1) of the Charter.

According to the ECJ, these surveillance programs do not limit the power that US authorities can exercise in implementing them or in targeting non-US citizens. Even if formally US authorities have to comply with some safeguards, data subjects cannot rely on actionable rights before the courts against the US authorities. This is particularly relevant for ensuring the protection of art. 47 of the CFREU. It is not by chance that Recital 104 of the GDPR states, in that regard, that the third country "should ensure effective independent data protection supervision and should provide for cooperation mechanisms with the Member States' data protection authorities" and adds that "the data subjects should be provided with effective and enforceable rights and effective administrative and judicial redress." According to the ECJ:

> the very existence of effective judicial review designed to ensure compliance with provisions of EU law is inherent in the existence of the rule of law. Thus, legislation not providing for any possibility for an individual to pursue legal remedies in order to have access to personal data relating to him or her, or to obtain the rectification or erasure of such data, does not respect the essence of the fundamental right to effective judicial protection, as enshrined in art. 47 of the CFREU.

Even the ombudsperson mechanism does not provide enough guarantees from two perspectives. First, the ECJ recognized the lack of independence of the ombudsperson provided for by that mechanism. Second, the ECJ underlined that the ombudsperson could not adopt decisions that are binding on the US intelligence services. Regarding the first point, the ECJ observed that:

> in the letter referred to in para. 193 above, the Privacy Shield Ombudsperson, although described as "independent from the Intelligence Community", was presented as "[reporting] directly to the Secretary of State who will ensure that the Ombudsperson carries out its function objectively and free from improper influence that is liable to have an effect on the response to be provided". Furthermore, in addition to the fact that, as found by the Commission in recital 116 of that decision, the Ombudsperson is appointed by the Secretary of State and is an integral part of the US State Department, there is, as the Advocate General stated in point 337 of his Opinion, nothing in that decision to indicate that the dismissal or revocation of the appointment of the Ombudsperson is accompanied by any particular guarantees, which is such as to undermine the Ombudsman's independence from the executive.

Together with the lack of independence, data subjects do not have any cause of action before a body that offers guarantees substantially equivalent to those required by EU law:

> although recital 120 of the Privacy Shield Decision refers to a commitment from the US Government that the relevant component of the intelligence services is required to correct any violation of the applicable rules detected by the Privacy Shield Ombudsperson, there is nothing in that decision to indicate that that ombudsperson has the power to adopt decisions that are binding on those intelligence services and does not mention any legal safeguards that would accompany that political commitment on which data subjects could rely.

These were the primary reasons that led the ECJ to declare the Privacy Shield invalid.

The effects of this extension of European values is important as a limit on surveillance regulatory schemes that could undermine the principle of the rule of law and fundamental rights in the information society. The *Schrems II* case is a clear example of how the ECJ is trying to use the opening of the drawbridge of the European fortress to avoid disproportionate interference in a transnational digital environment. The judicial extension of EU values beyond national borders is also evident in the court's approach to the territorial scope of national orders to remove statements or data. As explored above, the ECJ has started to extend the geographical scope of EU law in the area of privacy and data protection. The EU system has created a *sui generis* system, an innovative and pervasive right to data protection and privacy that has transfigured the Internet and deeply influenced other legal systems, causing a new migration in relation to this right. However, this migration was preceded by an extensive ECJ case law that sought to apply the European vision of the right to digital privacy and thus to build a European "fortress." From *Digital Rights Ireland*, where the physical atomic infrastructure became a crucial criterion for assessing the validity of the Data Retention Directive, to *Google Spain* and *Schrems I* and *II*, where the ECJ expanded its scope to clashes between the US and European legal paradigms, the ECJ has provided a model for the codification of art. 3(2) GDPR, which now makes EU law on data protection applicable even to organizations based in third countries targeting EU residents. In this way, the court has ensured extraterritorial protection for the European right to privacy and data protection online *ante litteram*.

12.4 Recent developments

Given the uncertainty created in extra-EU transfers and especially in those to the United States, several acts and measures have been issued by European authorities. After the *Schrems* decisions, on November 10, 2020, the EDPB issued a six-step-approach Recommendations on measures that supplement transfer tools to ensure compliance with the EU level of protection of personal data. The EDPB Recommendations were intended to help organizations comply with the requirements established by the ECJ in *Schrems II*. Following the Recommendations, on June 4, 2021, the European Commission issued the long-awaited new SCCs for the transfer of personal data to third countries. Lastly, it should be noted that the European Commission and the United States in May 2022 agreed on a new Trans-Atlantic Data Privacy Framework that will foster transatlantic data flows and address the concerns raised by the ECJ in the *Schrems II*.

In its Recommendations the EDPB advised organizations to follow six steps to transfer personal data to third countries outside the European Union. To help exporters (be they controllers or processors, private entities or public bodies, processing personal data within the scope of application of the GDPR) with the complex task of assessing third countries and identifying appropriate supplementary measures where needed, the EDPB provides exporters with a series of steps to follow, potential sources of information and some examples of supplementary measures that could be put in place.

Moreover, the new SCCs are intended to provide "appropriate safeguards" under art. 46 GDPR by creating legal obligations for exporters and importers to ensure an appropriate level of data protection and GDPR compliance with respect to personal data transferred to countries that do not have adequacy decisions (art. 45). More specifically, the new SCCs are aligned with the GDPR and provide examples of technical and organizational measures in Annex III. They fill a long-existing gap in data protection law (since the former SCCs were adopted pre-GDPR), provide additional flexibility with regard to permitted cross-border data flows and help improve legal certainty for some international data transfers to third countries. It is expected that these modernized SCCs will enable businesses to account for a greater variety of complex data transfers and at the same time offer a safe exchange of personal data, adding uniformity and legal predictability to business transactions.

Lastly, the Trans-Atlantic Data Privacy Framework notably includes:

a. the free and safe flow of data between the EU and participating US companies;
b. the enactment of rules and binding safeguards to limit access to data by US intelligence authorities to only what is "necessary and proportionate" to advance defined national security objectives and without disproportionately impacting the protection of privacy and civil liberties;
c. the creation of a two-tier redress system to investigate and resolve EU data subjects' complaints regarding access of data by US intelligence authorities including the creation of a Data Protection Review Court that would consist of individuals chosen from outside the US government who would have full authority to adjudi-

cate claims and direct remedial measures as necessary. EU individuals will continue to have access to multiple avenues of recourse to resolve complaints regarding participating companies, including options for alternative dispute resolution and binding arbitration;

d. the obligation for companies processing data transferred from the European Union to meet high standards including requirements to adhere to, and self-certify their adherence to, the Privacy Shield Principles under the oversight of the US Department of Commerce;
e. the encouragement of US intelligence agencies to adopt procedures to ensure effective oversight of new privacy and civil liberties standards; and
f. the development of specific monitoring and review mechanisms.

12.5 Conclusions

In conclusion, as it has been shown, cross-border data flows are today an important component of international trade and the backbone of many digital service models. However, as explained in this chapter, in the context of "rival standards" and "rule overlap" of extra-territorial laws, restrictions on the transfer of personal data and data localizations, requirements have been made stronger. While these complexities have served to impede certain data flows, international agreements have been resorted to in order to allow for continued free flows of personal data, subject to providing certain protections of data subjects and their data. Accordingly, this chapter has analyzed the discipline set up by Chapter V of the GDPR with which transfers of personal data must comply, specifically arts. 44–50. Particularly, different legal basis exist, such as: (a) transfer on the basis of an adequacy decision (art. 45); (b) transfer subject to adequate guarantees (arts. 46 and 47); or (c) exceptions in specific situations (art. 49). As explained, according to art. 45, the transfer of personal data to a third country or an international organization is allowed if the Commission has decided that the third country, or the international organization in question guarantees an adequate level of protection. Where this decision does not exist, according to arts. 46 and 47, the transfer of personal data to a third country or an international organization may be done just in case the parties involved (controller or processor) have provided appropriate safeguards. In the absence of an adequacy decision (art. 45) or adequate guarantees (art. 46), including binding corporate rules (art. 47), under art. 49, the transfer of personal data to a third country or organization is permitted only under certain identified circumstances.

The chapter also discussed the legal challenges of international data transfers deriving from ECJ decisions in Case C-362/14 and in Case C-311/18 *Schrems I* and *II*. Both decisions showed the role of the ECJ and its case law in building the practical application of the data protection right. The first landmark judgment led to the invalidation of the adequacy decision known as safe harbor, whereas in the second decision the ECJ further strengthened its fundamental rights-based approach, and consolidated its power across the Atlantic, by invalidating the adequacy decision adopted in the aftermath of *Schrems I*, known as Privacy Shield. As shown in *Schrems I* and *II*, the ECJ provided a new model of application of the GDPR, which now makes it applicable even to organizations based in third countries targeting EU residents. In this way, the court has ensured extraterritorial protection for the European right to data protection online *ante litteram*.

Given the uncertainty created by extra-EU transfers and especially those to the United States, after the *Schrems* decisions, on November 10, 2020, the EDPB issued a six-step-approach Recommendations on measures that supplement transfer tools to ensure compliance with the EU level of protection of personal data. The EDPB Recommendations were intended to help organizations comply with the requirements established by the ECJ in *Schrems II*. Following the Recommendations, new SCCs for the transfer of personal data to third countries were issued. Lastly, it should be noted that recently the European Commission and the United States agreed on a new Trans-Atlantic Data Privacy Framework, which will foster transatlantic data flows and address the concerns raised by the ECJ in the *Schrems II*.

13 Data Retention and Law Enforcement

13.1 Introduction

The compatibility between the storage of personal data and its use by law enforcement agencies for investigation purposes has always been the subject of much debate, as well as of rulings by the European courts. On the one hand, limits must be placed on the storage of personal data in order to protect individual fundamental rights. On the other hand, this may collide with the need of law enforcement agencies to retain personal data for investigative purposes.

On this matter, in 2005 the European Commission proposed a Directive on data retention. The proposal was born of the idea that different retention requirements in the different Member States constituted obstacles to the internal market for electronic communication and that they therefore needed to be harmonized. Moreover, the European Commission argued that such differences also limited law enforcement's access to personal data and relevant information, thus impeding the fulfilment of their duties, including preventing and combating organized crime and terrorism.

To resolve all these issues, Directive 2006/24/EC was adopted, imposing a duty of retaining telecommunication data on service providers and obliging Member States to ensure access to data by "competent national authorities." The scope of the data covered by the Directive was broad and included information regarding the sources of communication; the date, time and duration of a communication; type of communication; and the location of mobile communication equipment. Specific elements of access to the retained data (e.g., procedure) were left to be regulated by Member States "in accordance with necessity and proportionality requirements."

Considering such an ample scope of application, the Data Retention Directive constituted a challenge in light of the case law of the ECtHR, since the ECtHR required proportionate and strictly tailored measures that would not only protect public security but also respect the essence of the right to confidential communication, private life and freedom of speech.

In 2011, the European Commission recommended the amendment of the Data Retention Directive and regulation of data retention as a security measure and not merely as a tool to harmonize the internal market. The Commission also emphasized the need to strengthen personal data protection within the scheme of telecommunication data protection by shortening the periods of mandatory data retention and ensuring independent supervision of requests for data access and retention, thereby reducing the data categories to be retained. The Commission directly referred to the standard established by the ECtHR in the *S and Marper v. UK* ruling, which balanced an individual's concerns about data collection against those of public safety and security.

At the same time, in 2012 the European Commission presented the first draft of a new Directive with the aim of harmonizing the processing of personal data in criminal law matters. Particularly, Directive 2016/680 (the Law Enforcement Directive, or LED) has a twofold aim: first, it ensures the protection of personal data processed for the prevention, investigation, detection and prosecution of crimes and the execution of criminal penalties. Second, it facilitates and simplifies police and judicial cooperation between Member States and, more in general, in addressing crimes in more effective ways. This two-pronged approach is similar to that of the GDPR. The LED covers activities by "competent authorities" for the "prevention, investigation and prosecution of criminal offenses or the execution of criminal penalties, including the safeguarding against and the prevention of threats to public security."

However, the problem of striking the right balance between the need to store personal data for investigative purposes and its access by law enforcement agencies has not yet been solved. This problem has been growing given the very rapid development of new technologies based on artificial intelligence and/or biometric data that allow the automated identification of suspects. In this regard, not even the most recent regulatory interventions (GDPR or the proposed Artificial Intelligence Regulation) have been able to efficiently resolve the balancing of opposing interests.

In light of all these considerations, Section 13.2 analyzes the first attempts to regulate the retention of personal data and the challenges raised by the adoption of Directive 2006/24/EC, which imposed a duty of retaining telecommunications data on service providers and obliged Member States to ensure access to data by "competent national authorities." Section 13.3 highlights how the Data Retention Directive also constituted a challenge in light of ECtHR case law, since the ECtHR required proportionate and strictly tailored measures that would not only protect public security but also respect the essence of the right to confidential communication, private life and freedom of speech. Lastly, Section 13.4 discusses Directive (EU) 2016/680 on protecting personal data processed for the purposes of law enforcement (LED), focusing on the main differences between it and the GDPR (Chapter 11).

13.2 First challenges to data retention

One of the most important cases challenging the Data Retention Directive is *Digital Rights Ireland*. In this decision invalidating the Data Retention Directive, the ECJ appeared to consider the fundamental rights established by arts. 7 and 8 of the CFREU as independent parameters to rule on the compatibility of such directive. In addition, this decision draws a clear distinction between the violation of the essence of fundamental rights and the assessment of proportionality in light of the objectives of protecting public order and combating terrorism. The hard core of the constitutional backbone to this case is captured in the words of Advocate General (AG) Cruz Villalòn:

> In the present cases, the Court has before it two references for a preliminary ruling on the validity of Directive 2006/24/EC, offering it the opportunity to rule on the circumstances in which it is constitutionally possible for the European Union to impose a limitation on the exercise of fundamental rights within the specific meaning of Article 52(1) of the Charter of Fundamental Rights of the European Union, by means of a directive and the national measures transposing it.

The ECJ did not pass up this opportunity. For the first time in the history of the European integration process, the ECJ decided to invalidate an act of EU secondary law on the grounds that it violated the CFREU.

The preliminary proceedings had been launched by the references of the High Court of Ireland and the Austrian Constitutional Court. The High Court of Ireland was considering a dispute involving Digital Rights Ireland and local authorities concerning national measures on the retention of data in relation to electronic communication. At the same time, the Austrian Constitutional Court had received a number of constitutional complaints by which the applicants sought to annul the domestic legislation implementing the Data Retention Directive.

The legal issues raised by this case originated from the fact that the Data Retention Directive allowed national authorities to collect intrusive information concerning multiple aspects of the private lives of subscribers of telecommunications services, such as the identities of the persons involved as well as the time and place where the communications took place. These pieces of information could provide precise details concerning the private lives of the individuals whose data had been subject to retention measures. Numerous claims had therefore been made in respect of both the Data Retention Directive and the domestic provisions transposing it, since the conditions under which such interference with the private lives of individuals could be justified were not established in a clear and precise manner.

Therefore, the ECJ enforced the CFREU as a constitutional principle, thus revealing its vocation as quasi-constitutional court and guardian of fundamental rights in Europe. It is no coincidence that a historic chapter in the case law of the ECJ was written in relation to substantive legislation such as the Data Retention Directive. Its provisions had already been brought before the ECJ in case C-301/16 (*Ireland v European Parliament and Council of the European Union*), although to no avail, as in that case the reference had been based on allegedly erroneous legal grounds for the act and not on insufficient protection for the fundamental rights at stake.

The Data Retention Directive resulted from the *security ethos*, as an immediate response to the attacks of September 11, 2001. This objective became apparent, in the first instance, as a functional requirement for the efficient implementation of the four fundamental freedoms established by the EU Treaties, and subsequently, following the entry into force of the Treaty of Maastricht, as an independent *telos* of the European Union. Imbued with a logic of preventive control and widespread suspicion, the Data Retention Directive carved out some exceptions to the protection of the right to respect for private life laid down by Directives 95/46 and 2002/58, as was noted by AG Cruz Villalòn. These instruments were intended to guarantee the confidential status of communications and traffic data and, in order to do so, established an obligation for telecommunication operators to delete or anonymize data where they were no longer required for the transmission of a communication, unless necessary for billing purposes.

Against this background, the Data Retention Directive stipulated that Member States must establish an obligation to retain data for a period no shorter than six months and no longer than two years for the purposes of investigation, detection and prosecution of serious crimes. The issue came as no surprise to the supreme and constitutional courts of the Member States, which were asked to review the legality of national legislation implementing the Data Retention Directive. Since 2008, national courts had been raising concerns regarding the insufficient protection afforded to the rights to privacy and data protection. AG Cruz Villalòn also contributed to clarifying the independent scope of arts. 7 and 8 of the CFREU:

> Article 8 of the Charter enshrines the right to the protection of personal data as a right which is distinct from the right to privacy. Although data protection seeks to ensure respect for privacy, it is, in particular, subject to an autonomous regime.

AG Cruz Villalòn sought to stress that there may be cases in which legislation restricting the right to protection of personal data according to art. 8 CFREU may nevertheless be regarded as a disproportionate restriction on art. 7 CFREU. In order to illustrate this point, AG Cruz Villalòn drew a distinction between "personal data" per se and data "more than personal." In the view of Cruz Villalòn, the former category concerns data that have exclusively the function of identifying a person and that have a neutral character, being as such "personal data and nothing more." These are the personal data for which the structure and the guarantees of art. 8 of the CFREU are the most appropriate. Data that are "more than personal" relate essentially to private life and its confidential status, including intimacy. According to Cruz Villalòn:

> in such cases, the issue raised by personal data commences, so to speak, further "upstream". The issue which arises in such cases is not yet that of the guarantees relating to data processing but, at an earlier stage, that of the data as such, that is to say, the fact that it has been possible to record the circumstances of a person's private life in the form of data, data which can consequently be subject to electronic processing.

A second distinction emerged in the reasoning of the ECJ and constituted an innovative departure from its previous case law. This distinction is based on the wording of art. 52(1) CFREU and concerns the assessment of possible violations of the essence of the rights under arts. 7 and 8 as well as the proportionality of the measures specified under the Data Retention Directive in order to achieve the objectives of safeguarding public order and preventing terrorism, which were considered to be legitimate by the ECJ.

Before this decision, the ECJ had focused on the first paragraph of art. 52 CFREU as a "single block" without considering the possibility that, even though a restriction of fundamental rights might not affect their essence, it could nevertheless be found to be disproportionate with respect to the goals pursued by the relevant legislation. By contrast, in the decision in question the ECJ not only held that "the interference caused by Directive 2006/24 with the fundamental rights laid down in Articles 7 and 8 of the Charter" was "wide-ranging," but also separately addressed aspects of art. 52(1) CFREU. Regarding the first aspect, the ECJ held that no violation had occurred of the essence of both the right to privacy and the right to data protection for two reasons. First, art. 5(2) of the Data Retention Directive prohibited operators from accessing electronic communications, thus granting a minimum level of protection at least to the content thereof, which is the most sensitive aspect of the data at issue. Second, according to the ECJ:

> Member States are to ensure that appropriate technical and organisational measures are adopted against accidental or unlawful destruction, accidental loss or alteration of the data.

In this way, the ECJ held that the measures for retaining data and communicating the relevant data to the national authorities were per se admissible. In the view of the ECJ, these mechanisms pursued objectives of general interest for the European Union such as the prevention of terrorism, the maintenance of international peace and security and, more generally, combating serious crime and, thus, protecting public safety.

However, the ECJ held that EU primary law had been breached when considering the proportionality of the collection and storage of data as provided for under the Data Retention Directive. Once the ECJ had established the wide-ranging interference with the rights protected under arts. 7 and 8 CFREU, the ECJ focused on the proportionality of such interference regarding the objectives pursued by the Data Retention Directive. The ECJ, thus, analyzed whether appropriate and necessary safeguards were in place in order to justify the proposed limitations on the relevant fundamental rights guaranteed by the CFREU.

The ECJ provided an in-depth analysis of the critical aspects of the Data Retention Directive. The ECJ first noted that the interference with the fundamental right to private life could affect the entire EU population, without any distinction. In this light, the ECJ pointed out that the collection of data affected individuals who were not necessarily suspected of having committed any crime. According to the ECJ, this processing was carried out regardless of any direct or indirect connection with the commission of a serious crime. In other words, the collection of data was neither limited to a certain group of individuals nor circumscribed to a geographical area or a specific period.

The ECJ held that the reference to "serious crimes" was not proper and generic and thus was incompatible with the principle of proportionality. According to the ECJ, while allowing each Member State to set its own definition of "serious crimes," the effect of the Data Retention Directive was that this notion was unlikely to be properly defined. The ECJ also stressed the lack of any substantive and procedural guarantee concerning access to data by domestic authorities. Moreover, it was not clear who within the respective authorities of each Member State had access to the retained data. Indeed, access to the data was not subject to prior scrutiny by any judicial or independent administrative authority. In terms of the retention period, the critical issues concerned the lack of any distinction between the various categories of data and the relevant duration of retention. This period should in any case be limited to the time necessary for the purposes of retention to be fulfilled.

On these grounds, the ECJ held that the Data Retention Directive did not establish clear and specific provisions and thus violated the fundamental rights enshrined in arts. 7 and 8 CFREU. Such wide-ranging interference could not be based on the principle of necessity, which could be seen as ancillary and supplementary to the principle of proportionality.

13.3 Data retention after *Digital Rights Ireland*

The cases of *Tele2 Sverige* and *Watson* are recognized as particularly important in developing the *Digital Rights Ireland* findings. In 2016, in the *Tele2 Sverige* and *Watson* joint cases (C-203/15 and C-698/15), the ECJ had the opportunity to return to the question of the balance between measures aimed to safeguard public interests and the protection of the right to privacy and personal data. In a way, the ECJ had to get rid of some measures that substantially reflected the content of the Data Retention Directive but that had been implemented without any connection to that EU law.

In particular, the ECJ had to review the compatibility of national measures implementing art. 15(1) of Directive 2002/58, which provides that Member States may derogate from the obligation to protect the confidentiality of electronic communications only by adopting necessary, appropriate and proportionate measures within a democratic society to safeguard national security, defense, public security, and the prevention, investigation, detection and prosecution of criminal offenses or of unauthorized use of the electronic communication system. To this end, Member States may, inter alia, adopt legislative measures providing for the retention of data for a limited period.

The measures adopted by some Member States on this legal ground were de facto reproducing the same consequences attached to the Data Retention Directive, for example, giving rise to the general and indiscriminate retention of all traffic and location data of all subscribers and registered users relating to all means of electronic communication, or giving access to national authorities to traffic and location data without prior review by a court or an independent administrative authority and in the absence of a requirement that the data are retained in the European Union. Therefore, the ECJ had to make new efforts to protect the fundamental rights under arts. 7 and 8 CFREU in this context. According to the court, such serious limitations of the right to privacy can be justified only in the case of "serious crime." However, this legitimate goal is not "strong" enough to justify "national legislation providing for the general and indiscriminate retention of all traffic and location data." The court stated that combating serious crimes cannot justify indiscriminate retention, otherwise it would become a general rule. Another shortcoming of national regulation was the lack of any relationship between data retention and threats to public security. Furthermore, there were no restrictions on time periods, geographical areas, groups of people likely to be involved or persons who could contribute to fighting crime. Consequently, the national legislation under review exceeded the limits of the "strict necessity" test and was not justified within democratic society. Nevertheless, the court noted that Directive 2002/58 and the Charter do not prevent "targeted retention" being limited "with respect to the categories of data to be retained, the means of communication affected, the persons concerned and the retention period adopted." This approach was considered following the decision in *Digital Rights Ireland* and suggested a possible method for limiting data retention. In *Tele2 Sverige* and *Watson*, the court specifically mentioned limitations based on geographical criteria. The approaches established in these cases would allow retention of telecommunications data where the level of crime is high and there is objective evidence to confirm the scope of the area. Moreover, the court made clear the notification requirement after authorities receive access to data to ensure an individual's right to a legal remedy. The court also noted the requirement of ensuring prior independent review of the processing of personal data based on art. 8 CFREU. A court or an independent administrative body must conduct a review into each request for data access, and each request must specify the reasons for data access for verification by the court or administrative body. The goal of data retention and access is limited only to fighting serious crimes, including organized crime, terror or those that pose serious public security threats. However, the Member State must decide which crimes are sufficiently serious to justify data retention and access.

The court's analysis led to a conclusion that EU law, specifically Directive 2002/58 and the EU Charter, prohibits the "general and indiscriminate retention of all traffic and location data of all subscribers." Moreover, access to such data collected based on "targeted retention" must meet the following set of requirements: the goal of data access is limited to "fighting serious crime"; data access is subject to prior review by a court and/or independent administrative authority; and the data are retained within the European Union.

In November 2021, three different Opinions of the AG published in relation to the joined cases C-793/19 and C-794/19, case C-140/20, and joined cases C-339/20 and C-397/20 reopened the debate on the issues linked, inter alia, to allowing the indiscriminate storage of telecommunications data for national defense and for internal security interests. According to the Opinion in case C-140/20, while in theory general access to telecommunications traffic and location data should be allowed for the protection of national security interests, the Irish legislation permits it for reasons other than those inherent in these interests, causing a preventive, broad and indiscriminate retention of traffic and location data of all users for two years. Specifically, permitting, for reasons going beyond those strictly connected to the protection of national security, the preventive, general and indiscriminate retention of traffic and location data of all subscribers makes the Irish legislation not compliant with the European legislation. Moreover, the Opinion assesses that, contrary to Irish law, the possibility for the competent national authorities to retain data should always be subject to previous review by a court or an independent authority.

The same idea and arguments have been expressed in the Opinion in joined cases C-339/20 and C-397/20, dealing with EU financial services law. The key issue here was whether an EU Member State could impose an obligation to retain electronic communications data in a general and indiscriminate way for insider dealing investigations. On this matter, like in the previous case, the AG opined that the retention of traffic data under EU Member State law for investigating insider dealing was flawed, as only national security purposes could justify such general and indiscriminate data retention.

Moreover, according to the Opinion in the joined cases C-793/19 and C-794/19, while the AG recognized the progress made in German legislation establishing a mandatory data retention period for telecommunications data, they determined that the general and indiscriminate storage obligation imposed by it covers a very broad range of traffic and location data for purposes beyond the protection of national security interests. Hence, the created legislative framework could potentially jeopardize the legitimate expectation of the individuals of their right to privacy and personal data protection, entailing a serious interference with individuals' fundamental rights.

In this context, even if national laws impose different retention periods, the AG considers that the range of data sets continues to be too wide and, therefore, detrimental to fundamental rights. As such, the main goal for national and EU legislators should be to strike a fair balance between two opposite needs: (a) the individual's rights to privacy and data protection, and (b) state authorities' need to access data for national defense interests.

13.4 Law Enforcement Directive

At the same time, in 2012 the European Commission presented the first draft of a new Directive with the aim of harmonizing the processing of personal data in criminal law matters. Directive 2016/680 (the LED) has a twofold aim: it ensures the protection of personal data processed for the prevention, investigation, detection and prosecution of crimes and the execution of criminal penalties as well as the harmonization of the processing of this personal data. This Directive was mostly based on the provisions in Convention 108 of the Council of Europe (also referred to as the Treaty of Strasbourg) from 1981. The Council of Europe published a recommendation that supplements Convention 108 for the use of personal data by the police in 1987. This recommendation specified who is permitted access to police data, under what conditions police data can be transferred to authorities in third countries, how data subjects can exercise their data protection rights and how independent supervision is organized. Those recommendations, however, were not legally binding and many Member States have not fully implemented them.

Since the processing of criminal law data is beyond the scope of Directive 95/46/EC, historically there was little harmonization within the European Union in this respect. After the September 11, 2001, terrorist attacks in the United States, the European Parliament repeatedly requested a legal instrument under the third pillar of the European Union, on Police and Judicial Cooperation in Criminal Matters. However, little progress was made. Only in 2008 did the European Union publish Framework Decision 2008/977/JHA on the protection of personal data processing within the framework of police and judicial cooperation in criminal matters. This Framework Decision was also based on Convention 108 and the Data Protection Directive principles. National security was beyond the scope of the Framework Decision. The aim of the Framework Decision is, on the one hand, the protection of personal data that are processed for the prevention, investigation, detection and prosecution of crimes and the execution of criminal penalties and, on the other hand, the facilitation and simplification of police and judicial cooperation between Member States.

In this context, a series of other legal instruments aim to advance the cooperation and sharing of information between Member States, such as the Schengen Information System (SIS) for international criminal investigation information); the Visa Information System (VIS) for visa data, including biometrical data; and the Customs Information System (CIS). Furthermore, the institutional regulations for Europol, Eurosur and Eurojust contain provisions for the exchange of criminal law information.

In 2012 the European Commission presented the first draft for a Directive that is much broader than the Framework Decision and that would harmonize the processing of personal data in criminal law matters. After that, a debate started between the European Parliament, the Commission and the Council, which took four years. In 2016, the legislative proposal was adopted, after amendments, in its current version as EU Directive 2016/680. In this Directive the deadline for implementation in national legislation is two years, with a final deadline in May 2018. Directive 2016/680 (the LED) repeals the current Framework Decision 2008/977/JHA as of that date.

Therefore, Directive (EU) 2016/680 on protecting personal data processed for the purposes of law enforcement (LED) entered into force on May 5, 2016, with the stated aim of ensuring the processing of personal data for police and judicial matters. With advances in technology and processing capabilities at the heart of its justification, the EU Parliament set about implementing a comprehensive approach to data protection regulation across almost all sectors of the EU community. Political consensus was found through negotiation, with the EU Parliament emphasizing a "package" approach to ensure that the GDPR – which was discussed in Chapter 10 – and the LED were dealt with in parallel. The LED covers activities by "competent authorities" for the "prevention, investigation and prosecution of criminal offences." The scope of the LED has been extended to cover the prevention of threats to the public, but not national security, while providing new rights for data subjects as well as new obligations for "competent authorities" processing data for "law enforcement purposes," that is, prevention, investigation, detection or prosecution of criminal offenses or the execution of criminal penalties, including the safeguarding against and the prevention of threats to public security.

13.4.1 Material scope

The scope and the objectives of the LED are presented in its first chapter, together with a set of definitions explaining the terminology used. The LED's foundations recognize the protection of personal data as a fundamental right and freedom of natural persons and lay the basis for ensuring the protection of the transfer of data among Member States.

The LED focuses on data processing by "competent authorities" as defined in art. 3(7). Competent authorities include:

a. any public authority competent for the prevention, investigation, detection or prosecution of criminal offenses or the execution of criminal penalties, including the safeguarding against and the prevention of threats to public security, and;
b. any other body or entity entrusted by Member State law to exercise public authority and public powers for the purposes of the prevention, investigation, detection or prosecution of criminal offenses or the execution of criminal penalties, including the safeguarding against and the prevention of threats to public security.

Perhaps the most obvious competent authorities are police forces and public prosecution services, but there may be a variety of competent authorities in national criminal law of EU Member States. For instance, in the domain of execution of criminal penalties, competent authorities may include the "regular" prison system, juvenile correction centers, forensic psychiatric centers, probation authorities and others.

The scope of the LED is limited to the processing of certain types of personal data. It should be noted that not all personal data processed by law enforcement agencies and the judiciary are included within the scope of the LED. Both data relevant to crimes that have already taken place (e.g., data regarding crime reconstructions and evidence for use in courts) and data relevant to crimes that still might take place (e.g., crime prediction models that police agencies use to prevent crime) fall within the scope of the LED. Data are not limited to criminal events but also apply to suspects, criminals, victims, witnesses, testifying law enforcement officers and police informants. In the case of crime prevention, there may be suspects involved (i.e., those preparing a crime) without a completed criminal act (as it was still in preparation).

Art. 4 of the LED provides a list of definitions. The definition of personal data is the most important. Similar to the GDPR text, personal data are defined as any information relating to an identified or identifiable natural person (the data subject). This means that data relating to legal persons (even when they are involved in criminal matters) are not within the scope of the LED. The processing of personal data includes the collection, recording, organization, structuring, storage, adaptation or alteration, retrieval, consultation, use, disclosure by transmission, dissemination or otherwise making available, alignment or combination, restriction, erasure or destruction of personal data. It should be noted that some types of data processing, such as anonymization, may transform personal data into anonymous (i.e., non-personal) data, putting it beyond the scope of the LED.

In addition, it should be noted that, like the GDPR, the LED pays special attention to sensitive categories of personal data and offers them additional protection. These include data the processing of which carries an additional risk for the rights of the data subject, such as potential discrimination. Sensitive data include data on racial or ethnic origin, political opinions and philosophical beliefs, trade union membership, genetic or biometric data, data concerning health, concerning a person's sex life or sexual orientation. These data are processed only when this is permitted by law to protect the vital interests of this or another person or where such data were manifestly made public by the data subject. Additionally, the automatic profiling of persons based on sensitive categories of data leading to discrimination is prohibited.

13.4.2 Principles of data processing

The main substance of the LED, like the GDPR, consists of the "fair principles" for the processing of personal data. These provide procedural rules and guidance for the processing of personal data in order to ensure fairness. The principles for the processing of personal data include fair and lawful processing, purpose limitation, accuracy of the data, adequate security safeguards and responsibility of data controllers. The principle of transparency is observed as much as possible, but there are differences in the phrasing of the GDPR and the LED, because full transparency may not always be realistic in criminal law, as it may interfere with or frustrate ongoing criminal investigations. Hence, the basic idea of informational self-determination and data subjects' control over their own data in the GDPR also underpins the LED.

The main principles for data processing reflect those in Convention 108 and the Data Protection Directive (see previous subsection) and include:

a. lawfulness and fairness;
b. purpose specification and limitation;
c. data minimization;
d. accuracy;
e. storage limitation;
f. appropriate security; and
g. accountability.

Personal data should be collected for specified, explicit and legitimate purposes within the LED's scope and should not be processed for purposes incompatible with the purposes of the prevention, investigation, detection or prosecution of criminal offenses or the execution of criminal penalties, including the safeguarding against and the prevention of threats to public security.

Moreover, the LED requires the clear establishment of time limits for storage and review. The LED states that Member States should provide for appropriate time limits to be established for the erasure of personal data or for a periodic review of the need for the storage of personal data. As such, storage time limits vary across Member States and for different situations, including different types of data subjects and different crimes. For instance, in Germany, data storage duration is limited depending on the type of person: ten years for adults, five years for adolescents and two years for children. Data on whistle-blowers and informants initially can only be stored for one year but this can be extended to three years. In addition, in the Netherlands the storage of personal data by the police is limited to one year, which can be extended to five years if the data are necessary for police tasks. In the United Kingdom, Section 39(2) of the Data Protection Act 2018 requires that appropriate time limits are established for the periodic review of the need for the continued storage of personal data for any law enforcement purpose.

Moreover, the LED explicitly distinguishes between different categories of data subjects, as art. 6 requires competent authorities to distinguish between suspects, persons convicted of a crime, victims and other parties to a criminal offense. Data controllers, therefore, should make clear distinctions between the personal data of different categories of data subjects. Lastly, the LED requires competent authorities to register facts and opinions separately. Art. 7 LED states that personal data based on facts are to be distinguished as far as possible from personal data based on personal assessments. Based on the concept of informational self-determination and data subject control over personal data, the LED contains a list of data subject rights and data controller obligations. These rights and obligations aim to provide further protection and control for data subjects via, inter alia, transparency and consent.

13.4.3 Logging

Under art. 25, Member States must provide for logs to be kept for at least the following processing operations in automated processing systems: collection, alteration, consultation, disclosure including transfers, combination and erasure. The logs of consultation and disclosure must make it possible to establish the justification, date and time of such operations and, as far as possible, the identity of the person who consulted or disclosed the personal data and the identity of the recipients of such personal data. The obligation to keep logs of six processing operations in automated processing systems is a distinct feature of the Directive that has no equivalent provision in the GDPR. This consolidation of the obligation to keep logs under the Directive as a comprehensive horizontal instrument is significant: from one processing operation (transmission) to six (collection, alteration, consultation, disclosure including transfers, combination and erasure); from a choice between logging or documenting to a standalone provision on logs, given that keeping documentation (records) is already stipulated in art. 24 of the Directive; and the applicability of the provision to all automated processing systems, which in practice means that all law enforcement databases must be in compliance with the obligation to keep logs. As law enforcement databases contain high volumes of information on a large number of individuals, a lot of which are sensitive data, the logs play a central role in ensuring that such databases are not being abused and are only accessed by persons with proper authorization and with valid reasons to access the retained data.

Out of six processing operations covered by this provision, the Directive gives particular importance to two processes: consultation and disclosure. These are the most common and the riskiest processing activities in databases, which is why the Directive provides much detail on the exact content of such logs. First, these logs should identify the person who consults the database or who discloses the information from the database to a third party. Second, in case of disclosure, the recipients of personal data should be identified as well. Third, the exact date and time of the consultation or disclosure must be recorded as a basic feature of the log. Fourth and most intriguing, a hitherto unprecedented requirement to be included in logs is the justification for performing a processing operation. When reading a log, it must be possible to conclude why a certain officer consulted a database or disclosed data to a third party. The justification may be demonstrated in different ways, depending on the nature of the database, its technical features and the user profile. Sometimes it will be sufficient to identify the user to understand why a certain database was consulted (as Recital 57 suggests).

Due to all these new logging requirements, under arts. 63(2) and (3) the Directive allows for a longer transposition period of art. 25(1) for databases set up before the entry into force of the Directive, that is, prior to May 6, 2016. Member States may take an additional five or even eight years to transpose this provision, by 2023 or 2026 respectively, if the transposition involves massive costs or jeopardizes the functioning of the database as such.

13.4.4 Transfers of personal data to third countries or international organizations

Under arts. 35–39, transfers of personal data to third countries must satisfy the conditions for international transfers laid down in Chapter V of the LED. Due to the different level of data protection standards within the European Union versus other parts of the world, arts. 35–38 stipulate additional restrictions to processing operations that are applicable when personal data are leaving the Union.

The articles in Chapter V are divided into general conditions for international transfers, transfers on the basis of adequacy decisions adopted by the Commission, transfers subject to appropriate safeguards and derogations from the general conditions for transfers in specific situations. Art. 39 lays down the conditions for so-called asymmetrical transfers that take place from Law Enforcement Agencies (LEAs)s in the EU Member States to private entities established in third countries. In particular, under the Directive, the logic applied to international transfers differs from that applied under the GDPR, although the architecture of Chapter V in both instruments is the same.

Apart from the requirement for international transfers to be based on an adequacy decision by the Commission, which is adopted according to the same procedure as an adequacy decision under the GDPR, the general principles for international transfers, set out in art. 35 of the Directive, are different from the ones stipulated under the GDPR. First, such transfers must be necessary for the purposes of the prevention, investigation, detection or prosecution of criminal offenses or the execution of criminal penalties, including the safeguarding against and the prevention of threats to public security. Second, and as a general rule, international data transfers may only take place via official channels, hence, from one law enforcement authority in the European Union to another one in the third country receiving the data.

Thus, where a Member State transfers data that were obtained from another Member State, the latter must, pursuant to art. 35(1)(c), authorize such an international transfer before it may be executed. This procedure can, in situations of an immediate threat to public security, be accelerated and may, pursuant to para. 2, take place without prior authorization. For example, if a French authority were to transfer personal data to a US authority, the latter would solely be allowed to further transfer such data to a Brazilian authority after the French authority authorized such an onward transfer.

As mentioned above, the conditions for adequacy decisions adopted by the Commission for international transfers are equivalent to those under the GDPR. Thus, it will be for the Commission to decide whether a third country ensures an adequate level of protection for personal data within the scope of the Directive. According to Recital 67 of the Directive, a third country should generally be able to provide a level of data protection that is "essentially equivalent to that ensured within the Union," as further required by the ECJ in its *Schrems* judgment (see Chapter 14). In the absence of the aforesaid decision, and in order to allow for more flexibility, the second step in the cascade is international transfers subject to appropriate safeguards. Article 37 foresees two situations in which such appropriate safeguards may exist, thereby departing from the similarities with, and being less specific than, art. 46 of the GDPR. In the first option, any appropriate safeguard must be guaranteed in a legally binding and enforceable instrument, to provide administrative or judicial redress to the data subject concerned. A typical example of an instrument created for this first option in accordance with art. 37 is the EU–US Umbrella Agreement. Another option provided for by art. 37 is a decision to transfer data based on a self-assessment evaluation carried out by the controller. In such a case, the controller must evaluate the circumstances of the transfer with regard to the existing data protection standards in the recipient state, inform the supervisory authority of the categories of data included in such a transfer and document the transfer for potential review by the supervisory authority.

The final step in the cascade is art. 38, under which the Directive allows Member States, in certain situations, to derogate from the conditions under arts. 36 and 37. Derogations are only permitted in individual cases and solely if they serve to protect the interests of the data subject, or if they are instrumental for the prevention of an immediate threat or the establishment, exercise or defense of legal claims. Where the fundamental rights and freedoms of the data subject prevail over the public interest, international transfers on the basis of art. 38 may not take place.

Moreover, as the most innovative provision of Chapter V, the Directive, under art. 39, provides the data protection framework for data requests from LEAs in EU Member States directly to private parties in third countries. Since the procedures for requests via official channels may be very lengthy, such asymmetrical transfers anticipate the prevention of obstacles and smoother, direct cooperation with third-country service providers. For that purpose, art. 39 imposes a number of conditions on the competent authorities in the Member States for data requests addressed to service providers in third countries, thereby derogating, in individual and specific cases, from the requirements in art. 35 to use the official channels only. However, in order for art. 39 to apply, all other conditions of the Directive need to be satisfied.

The legal basis for such transfers must be laid down in Union or Member State law (art. 8), and an adequacy decision under art. 36, appropriate safeguards pursuant to art. 37 or an individual derogation from art. 38 must exist, in line with the cascade described above. In addition, transfers under art. 39 must be strictly necessary for the investigation of a particular criminal offense. Thus, fishing expeditions or bulk transfers are not permitted. This requirement calls for a strong link between the main tasks of the transferring authority and the necessity to transfer personal data. The fundamental rights and freedoms of the data subject may not override the public interest for the purpose(s) for which the transfer is carried out and the service providers must be informed about the purpose(s) for which the transferred data may be processed. Furthermore, a direct transfer to service providers may only take place if the competent authority in the state of the establishment of the recipient is not trustworthy or is overwhelmed with requests, meaning that data exchanges cannot be carried out in a timely manner via the official channels. The third-country authority should nevertheless be informed of the transfer, but again, if the authority is corrupt or unavailable (for example, in a failed state) or simply prefers not to be notified, the competent authority in the transferring Member State does not have to comply with this requirement.

13.5 Conclusions

As has been analyzed in the first part of the chapter, the compatibility between the storage of personal data and its use by law enforcement agencies for investigation purposes has always been the subject of much debate, as well as of rulings by the European courts. The legislative and judicial life of data retention in the EU can be analyzed from different perspectives.

In balancing the compatibility of the Data Retention Directive with fundamental rights, ECJ case law has evolved and emphasized different aspects of the mass collection of telecommunications data. In *Digital Rights Ireland*, the court mainly analyzed the shortcomings of regulation on access to data retention by law enforcement, whereas in *Tele 2 Sverige* and *Watson* the court focused on the limits of data retention schemes. Ten years after the Data Retention Directive was adopted, the court concluded that the main idea of the Directive, the indiscriminate and untargeted collection of data traffic, is unacceptable under EU law. The decision in *Digital Rights Ireland* opened a real judicial discussion about data retention at the EU level, and *Tele 2 Sverige* and *Watson* certainly did not close it. The discussion may have intensified due to the requirements established in *Tele 2 Sverige* and *Watson*, which provide that there must be "objective evidence" proving that a given data retention system is "strictly necessary."

Finally, the Data Retention Directive saga shows how the ECJ evolved and proposed an innovative approach in balancing data protection and national security. However, the main concern is the implementation of *Tele 2 Sverige* and *Watson* by Member States facing their own shortcomings. The court certainly did not answer all the questions concerning data retention. Therefore, there are new reasons to discuss it in Member States with respect to other databases, including private ones gathering data on a voluntary basis. Because *Tele 2 Sverige* and *Watson* require the introduction of limitations to untargeted data retention based on objective evidence independently verified by courts or independent administrative bodies, it is likely that the real discussion about the effectiveness of data retention has just begun.

In addition, it has been shown that in 2012 the European Commission presented the first draft of a new Directive with the aim of harmonizing the processing of personal data in criminal law matters. The analysis of the LED can be considered equally important because it shows the discipline of the protection of personal data processed for the prevention, investigation, detection and prosecution of crimes and the execution of criminal penalties as well as the different regime provided by legislators for personal data processed by law enforcement agencies, compared with that required by the GDPR (Chapter 10). However, as has been shown, striking the right balance between the need to store personal data for investigative purposes for access by law enforcement agencies and the right to citizens' personal data protection is still an unresolved issue. In this regard, not even the most recent regulatory interventions (the GDPR or the proposal for an Artificial Intelligence Regulation) have been able to efficiently find the correct balance between the two aforementioned competing interests.

References

Chapter 1: The Law of the Internet

Barlow J.P., 'A Declaration of the Independence of Cyberspace' EFF (8 February 1996) https://www.eff.org/it/cyberspace-independence.

Easterbrook F., 'Cyberspace and the Law of the Horse' (1996) *University of Chicago Legal Forum* 207.

Goldsmith L., 'Against Cyberanarchy' (1998) 65(4) *University of Chicago Law Review* 1199.

Goldsmith L. and Wu T., *Who Controls the Internet? Illusions of a Borderless World* (Oxford University Press 2006).

Hardy T., 'The Proper Legal Regime for Cyberspace' (1994) 55 *University of Pittsburgh Law Review* 993.

Johnson D. and Post D., 'Law and Borders – the Rise of Law in Cyberspace' (1996) 48 *Stanford Law Review* 1367.

Lessig L., *Code and Other Laws of the Cyberspace* (Basic Books 1999).

Lessig L., 'The Law of the Horse: What Cyberlaw Might Teach' (1999) 113 *Harvard Law Review* 501.

Murray A., 'Internet Regulation' in David Levi-Faur (ed.), *Handbook on the Politics of Regulation* (Edward Elgar 2011).

Post D., 'Against "Against Cyberanarchy"' (2002) 17 *Berkeley Technology Law Journal* 1365.

Reidenberg J., 'Lex Informatica: The Formulation of Information Policy Rules through Technology' (1997–1998) 76 *Texas Law Review* 553.

Teubner G., *Constitutional Fragments. Societal Constitutionalism and Globalization* (Oxford University Press 2012).

Chapter 2: Internet and Jurisdiction

Balkin J.M., 'Free Speech Is a Triangle' (2018) 118 *Columbia Law Review* 2011–2056.

Goldsmith J.L., 'The Internet and the Abiding Significance of Territorial Sovereignty' (1998) 5(2) *Indiana Journal of Global Legal Studies* 475–491.

Hörnle J., *Internet Jurisdiction Law and Practice* (Oxford University Press 2021).

Kohl U., *Jurisdiction and the Internet* (Cambridge University Press 2007).

Pollicino O. and Bassini M., 'The Law of the Internet between Globalisation and Localisation', in M. Poiares Maduro, K. Tuori and S. Sankari (eds.), *Transnational Law: Rethinking European Law and Legal Thinking* (Cambridge University Press 2014) 346–380.

Reidenberg J., 'Technology and Internet Jurisdiction' (2005) 153 *University of Pennsylvania Law Review* 1951–1974.

Svantesson D.J., *Solving the Internet Jurisdiction Puzzle* (Oxford University Press 2017).

Chapter 3: Internet Access and Net Neutrality

Balkin Jack M., 'Free Speech Is a Triangle' (2018) 118 *Columbia Law Review* 2011–2056.

Cali B., 'The Case for the Right to Meaningful Access to the Internet as a Human Right in International Law', in A. von Arnauld, K. von der Decken and M. Susi (eds.), *The Cambridge Handbook of New Human Rights* (Cambridge University Press 2020) 276–284.

Cerf V., 'Internet Access Is Not a Human Right' *New York Times* (4 January 2012) https://www.nytimes.com/2012/01/05/opinion/internet-access-is-not-a-human-right.html.

Council of Europe, 'Freedom of Expression, the Internet and New Technologies', June 2018, 1.

De Hert P. and Kloza D., 'Internet (Access) as a New Fundamental Right: Inflating the Current Rights Framework?' (2012) 3 *European Journal of Law and Technology*.

DeLong-Bas N.J., 'The New Social Media and the Arab Spring' (Oxford Islamic Studies Online 2012).

'Dichiarazione dei Diritti di Internet', Internet Bill Of Rights, 14 July 2015.

Greek Constitution of 1975.

La Rue F., 'Report of the Special Rapporteur on the Promotion and Protection of the Right to Freedom of Opinion and Expression', 6 May 2011, A/HRC/17/27.

'Marco Civil da Internet' (Law 12.965/2014).

Mildebrandt H., European Parliament. Directorate-General for Parliamentary Research Services, *Internet Access as a Fundamental Right: Exploring Aspects of Connectivity* (Publications Office 2021) 1.

OECD (Organization for Economic Co-operation and Development), 'Strengthening Online Learning When Schools Are Closed: The Role of Families and Teachers in Supporting Students during the COVID-19 Crisis' https://www.oecd.org/coronavirus/policy-responses/strengthening-online-learning-when-schools-are-closed-the-role-of-families-and-teachers-in-supporting-students-during-the-covid-19-crisis-c4ecba6c/.

Pollicino O., 'The Right to Internet Access', in A. von Arnauld, K. von der Decken and M. Susi (eds.), *The Cambridge Handbook of New Human Rights* (Cambridge University Press 2020) 263–275.

Pollicino O. and Romeo G. (eds.), The Internet and Constitutional Law: The Protection of Fundamental Rights and Constitutional Adjudication in Europe (Routledge 2016) 1–272.

Portuguese Constitution of 1976, as amended in 2005.

Sassoli D., 'Video Debate with David Sassoli, on Internet Access as a New Human Right' 28 October 2020 (in part. min. 9:27) https://multimedia.europarl.europa.eu/en/video/-ideas-for-a-new-world-internet-a-new-human-right_I197966.

UNICEF (United Nations Children's Fund), 'How Many Children and Youth Have Internet Access at Home', https://data.unicef.org/resources/children-and-young-people-internet-access-at-home-during-covid19/.

Wired, 'Guide on Net Neutrality' (5 May 2020) https://www.wired.com/story/guide-net-neutrality/#:~:text=Net%20neutrality%20is%20the%20idea,otherwise%20discriminating%20against%20other%20material.

Chapter 4: Freedom of Expression and the Internet

Balkin J.M., 'Digital Speech and Democratic Culture: A Theory of Freedom of Expression for the Information Society' (2004) 79 *New York University Law Review* 1.

Barendt E.M., *Freedom of Speech* (Oxford University Press 2005).

Bollinger L.C., *The Tolerant Society: Freedom of Speech and Extremist Speech in America* (Oxford University Press 1988).

Bollinger L.C. and Stone G. (eds.), *The* Free *Speech Century* (Oxford University Press 2019).

Brunner L., 'The Liability of an Online Intermediary for Third Party Content. The Watchdog Becomes the Monitor: Intermediary Liability after Delfi v Estonia' (2016) 16 *Human Rights Law Review* 163.

Flauss J.F., 'The European Court of Human Rights and the Freedom of Expression' (2009) 84 *Indiana Law Journal* 809.

Katsirea I., 'Fake News: Reconsidering the Value of Untruthful Expression in the Face of Regulatory Uncertainty' (2019) 10(2) *The Journal of Media Law* 159.

Koltay A., New Media and Freedom of Expression: Rethinking the Constitutional Foundations of the Public Sphere (Bloomsbury 2019).

Pollicino O., 'Fake News, Internet and Metaphors (to Be Handled Carefully)' (2017) 9 *Italian Journal of Public Law* 1.

Pollicino O., Judicial Protection of Fundamental Rights on the Internet: A Road Toward Digital Constitutionalism? (Hart 2021).

Pollicino O. and Bassini M., 'Free Speech, Defamation and the Limits to Freedom of Expression in the EU: A Comparative Analysis', in A. Savin and J. Trzaskowski (eds.), *Research Handbook on EU Internet Law* (Edward Elgar 2014).

Post R.C., 'Participatory Democracy and Free Speech' (2011) 97 *Virginia Law Review* 477.

Rainey B., Wicks E and Ovey C., *The European Convention on Human Rights* (Oxford University Press 2017).

Rosenfeld M., 'Hate Speech in Constitutional Jurisprudence: A Comparative Analysis' (2003) 24 *Cardozo Law Review* 1523.

Schauer F., 'The Boundaries of the First Amendment: A Preliminary Exploration of Constitutional Salience' (2004) 117(6) *Harvard Law Review* 1765.

Sunstein C.R., *#Republic: Divided Democracy in the Age of Social Media* (Princeton University Press 2017).

Sunstein C.R., Liars: Falsehoods and Free Speech in an Age of Deception (Oxford University Press 2021).

Voorhoof D., 'Freedom of Expression and the Right to Information: Implications for Copyright' in Christophe Geiger, *Research Handbook on Human Rights and Intellectual Property* (Edward Elgar 2015).

Chapter 5: Internet Service Provider Liability

Balkin J., 'Free Speech in the Algorithmic Society: Big Data, Private Governance, and New School Speech Regulation' (2018) 51(3) *University of California Davis Law Review* 1149.

Bassini M., 'Fundamental Rights and Private Enforcement in the Digital Age' (2019) 25 *European Law Journal* 182.

Boyd D.M. and Ellison N.B., 'Social Network Sites: Definition, History and Scholarship' (2007) 13(1) *Journal of Computer-mediated Communication* 210.

Citron D.K. and Wittes B., 'The Internet Will Not Break: Denying Bad Samaritans Sec. 230 Immunity' (2017) 86(2) *Fordham Law Review* 401.

De Gregorio G., 'The Rise of Digital Constitutionalism in the European Union' (2021) 19(1) *International Journal of Constitutional Law* 41.

Frosio G. (ed.), *Oxford Handbook of Online Intermediary Liability* (Oxford University Press 2020).

Koltay A. and Wragg P. (eds.), *Comparative Privacy and Defamation* (Edward Elgar 2020).

Montagnani M.L. and Trapova A.Y., 'Safe Harbours in Deep Waters: A New Emerging Liability Regime for Internet Intermediaries in the Digital Single Market' (2018) 26 *International Journal of Law and Information Technology* 294.

Petkova B. and Ojanen T. (eds.), Fundamental Rights Protection Online: The Future Regulation of Intermediaries (Edward Elgar 2020).

Pitruzzella G. and Pollicino O., *Disinformation and Hate Speech: A European Constitutional Perspective* (Bocconi University Press 2020).

Riordan J., *The Liability of Internet Intermediaries* (Oxford University Press 2016).

Savin A., *EU Internet Law*, 3rd ed. (Edward Elgar 2020).

Taddeo M. and Floridi L. (eds.), *The Responsibilities of Online Service Providers* (Springer 2017).

Chapter 6: Hate Speech and Disinformation

Balkin J., 'Free Speech in the Algorithmic Society: Big Data, Private Governance, and New School Speech Regulation' (2018) 51(3) *University of California Davis Law Review* 1149.

Barendt E.M., *Freedom of Speech* (Oxford University Press 2005).

Bollinger L.C., *The Tolerant Society: Freedom of Speech and Extremist Speech in America* (Oxford University Press 1988).

Durante M., *Computational Power: The Impact of ICT on Law, Society and Knowledge* (Routledge 2021).

European Commission, *A Multi-Dimensional Approach to Disinformation. Report of the Independent High Level Group on Fake News and Online Disinformation* (Publications Office of the European Union 2018).

Lobba P., 'Holocaust Denial before the European Court of Human Rights: Evolution of an Exception Regime' (2005) 26(1) *The European Journal of International Law* 237.

Koltay A., *New Media and Freedom of Expression: Rethinking the Constitutional Foundations of the Public Sphere* (Bloomsbury 2019).

Pitruzzella G. and Pollicino O., *Disinformation and Hate Speech: A European Constitutional Perspective* (Egea 2020).

Pollicino O., 'Fake News, Internet and Metaphors (to Be Handled Carefully)' (2017) 9 *Italian Journal of Public Law* 1.

Pollicino O., *Judicial Protection of Fundamental Rights on the Internet: A Road Toward Digital Constitutionalism?* (Hart 2021).

Pollicino O. and Bassini M., 'Free Speech, Defamation and the Limits to Freedom of Expression in the EU: A Comparative Analysis', in A. Savin and J. Trzaskowski (eds.), *Research Handbook on EU Internet Law* (Edward Elgar 2014).

Pollicino O., Riccio G.M. and Bassini M. (eds.), *Copyright and Fundamental Rights in the Digital Age: A Comparative Analysis in Search of a Common Constitutional Ground* (Edward Elgar 2020).

Rosenfeld M., 'Hate Speech in Constitutional Jurisprudence: A Comparative Analysis' (2003) 24 *Cardozo Law Review* 1523.

Sunstein C.R., *#Republic: Divided Democracy in the Age of Social Media* (Princeton University Press 2017).

Sunstein C.R., *Liars: Falsehoods and Free Speech in an Age of Deception* (Oxford University Press 2021).

Wardle C., 'Understanding Information Disorder' (*FirstDraft*, September 22, 2020), https://firstdraftnews.org/long-form-article/understanding-information-disorder/.

Chapter 7: Copyright in the Digital Age

Bassini M., Internet e libertà di espressione. Prospettive costituzionali e sovranazionali (Aracne 2019).

Bassini M. and De Gregorio G., 'The Implementation of the Copyright Directive in Italy and the Proper Understanding of the "Best Efforts" Clause' (2021) 1–16, https://www.medialaws.eu/wp-content/uploads/2021/04/Policy-paper-ML-Article-17-and-best-efforts-5.pdf.

Bridy A., 'The Price of Closing the Value Gap: How the Music Industry Hacked EU Copyright Reform' (2019) 22(2) *Vanderbilt Journal of Entertainment & Technology* Law 323–358.

Koster A., 'Fighting Internet Piracy: The French Experience with the Hadopi Law' (2012) 16(4) *International Journal of Management & Information Systems* 327–330.

Mercanti L., 'La proposta di regolamento AGCOM sul "copyright enforcement": alcune note critiche alla luce dei modelli francese e statunitense' (2013) 2 *Informatica e diritto* 19–47.

Pollicino O., Riccio G.M. and Bassini M. (eds.), *Copyright and Fundamental Rights in the Digital Age* (Edward Elgar 2020).

Quintais J.P. and Angelopoulos C., 'YouTube and Cyando. Joined Cases C-682/18 and C-683/18 (22 June 2021) ECLI:EU:C:2021 (Case Comment)' (2022) 1(1) *Auteursrecht* 46–51.

Rosati E., '*GS Media* and Its Implications for the Construction of the Right of Communication to the Public within EU Copyright Architecture' (2017) 54(4) *Common Market Law Review* 1221–1242.

Shapiro T. and Hansson S., 'The DSM Copyright Directive: EU Copyright Will Indeed Never Be the Same' (2019) 41 *European Intellectual Property Review* 404–414.

Chapter 8: Audiovisual Media Services

Abbamonte G., Apa E. and Pollicino O. (eds.), *La riforma del mercato audiovisivo europeo* (Giappichelli 2019).

Bassini M., *Internet e libertà di espressione. Prospettive costituzionali e sovranazionali* (Aracne 2019).

Cabrera Blásquez F.J. and others, *Commercial Communications in the AVMSD revision*, IRIS Plus 2017-2 (European Audiovisual Observatory 2017).

Farchy J., Bideau G. and Tallec S., 'Content Quotas and Prominence on VOD Services: New Challenges for European Audiovisual Regulators' (2022) 28(4) *International Journal of Cultural Policy* 419–430.

Goanta C., 'Children on Social Media: A Comparison of COPPA [Children's Online Privacy Protection Rule] and the Revised AVMSD [Audiovisual Media Services Directive] (2020) 64 *TTLF Working Papers* 1–18. https://www-cdn.law.stanford.edu/wp-content/uploads/2020/10/goanta_wp64.pdf.

Psychogiopoulou E., 'The Audiovisual Media Services Directive and the promotion of European Works: Cultural Mainstreaming Revisited', in P.L. Parcu and E. Brogi (eds.), *Research Handbook on EU Media Law and Policy* (Edward Elgar 2021) 32–53.

Wagner M.A., 'Revisiting the Country-of-Origin Principle in the AVMS Directive' (2014) 6(2) *Journal of Media Law* 286–304.

Chapter 9: The Right to Privacy and Data Protection

Bygrave L.A., *Data Privacy Law: An International Perspective* (Oxford University Press 2014).

De Hert P. and Gutwirth S., 'Privacy, Data Protection and Law Enforcement: Opacity of the Individual and Transparency of the Power', in E. Claes, A. Duff and S. Gutwirth (eds.), *Privacy and the Criminal Law* (Intersentia 2006) 1–39.

De Hert P. and Gutwirth S., 'Data Protection in the Case Law of Strasbourg and Luxemburg', in S. Gutwirth, Y. Poullet, P. Hert, C. Terwangne, S. Nouwt (eds.), *Reinventing Data Protection* (Springer 2009) 3–44.

Gutwirth S, Leenes R. and De Hert P. (eds.), *Data Protection on the Move: Current Developments in ICT and Privacy/Data Protection* (Springer 2016).

Kuner C., *European Data Privacy Law and Online Business* (Oxford University Press 2003).

Lynskey O., *The Foundations of EU Data Protection Law* (Oxford University Press 2015).

Regulation (EU) 2016/679 of the European Parliament and of the Council of 27 April 2016 on the protection of natural persons with regard to the processing of personal data and on the free movement of such data, and repealing Directive 95/46/EC (General Data Protection Regulation).

Rodotà S., 'Data Protection as a Fundamental Right', in S. Gutwirth, Y. Poullet, P. Hert, C. Terwangne, S. Nouwt (eds.), *Reinventing Data Protection* (Springer 2009) 77–82.

Solove D.J., 'A Brief History of Information Privacy Law' (2006) 215 *Proskauer on Privacy* 12–51.

Warren S.D. and Brandeis L.D., 'The Right to Privacy' (1890) 4 *Harvard Law Review* 193.

Westin A.F., *Privacy and Freedom* (Bodley Head 1970) 1–558.

Chapter 10: The General Data Protection Regulation

Ausloos J., *The Right to Erasure in EU Data Protection Law* (Oxford University Press 2020).

Bygrave L.A., *Data Privacy Law: An International Perspective* (Oxford University Press 2014).

Gellert R., *The Risk-Based Approach to Data Protection* (Oxford University Press 2020).

Gutwirth S., Leenes R. and de Hert P. (eds.), *Reforming European Data Protection Law* (Springer 2014).

Kuner C., Bygrave L.A. and Docksey C., *The EU General Data Protection Regulation (GDPR): A Commentary* (Oxford University Press 2020).

Lynskey O., *The Foundations of EU Data Protection Law* (Oxford University Press 2015).

Von dem Bussche A. and Voigt P., *The EU General Data Protection Regulation (GDPR): A Practical Guide* (Springer 2017).

Chapter 11: Privacy, Identity and the Right to Be Forgotten

Ausloos J., *The Right to Erasure in EU Data Protection Law: From Individual Rights to Effective Protection* (Oxford University Press, 2020).

Bignami, F., 'Protecting Privacy Against the Police in the European Union: The Data Retention' (2007) 8 *Chicago Journal of International Law* 233.

Bignami F. and Resta G., 'Transatlantic Privacy Regulation: Conflict and Cooperation' (2015) 8 *Law and Contemporary Problems* 231.

Fabbrini, F., 'The European Court of Justice Ruling in the Data Retention Case and its Lessons for Privacy and Surveillance in the U.S.' (2015) 28 *Harvard Human Rights Journal* 65.

Fabbrini F. and Celeste E., 'The Right to Be Forgotten in the Digital Age: The Challenges of Data Protection Beyond Borders' (2020) 21(1) *German Law Journal* 55.

Kranenborg H., 'Article 8 Protection of Personal Data', in S. Peers, T. Hervey, J. Kenner and

A. Ward (eds.), *The EU Charter of Fundamental Rights: A Commentary* (Hart Publishing 2014) 231–289.
Petkova B., 'Privacy as Europe's First Amendment (2019) 27(2) *European Law Journal* 140.
Pollicino O. and Bassini M., 'Reconciling Right to Be Forgotten and Freedom of Information: Past and Future of Personal Data Protection in Europe' (2014) 2 *Diritto pubblico comparato ed europeo* 641.
Pollicino O. and Bassini M., 'The Luxembourg Sense of the Internet: Towards a Right to Digital Privacy?' (2015) *Global Community Yearbook of International Law & Jurisprudence 2014*, 223.
Pollicino O. and D'Antonio V., 'The Right to Be Forgotten in Italy', in F. Werro (ed.), *The Right to Be Forgotten: A Comparative Study of the Emergent Right's Evolution and Application in Europe, the Americas, and Asia* (Springer 2020) 163–177.
Post R.C., 'Data Privacy and Dignitary Privacy: Google Spain, the Right to Be Forgotten, and the Construction of the Public Sphere' (2018) 67 *Duke Law Journal* 981.
Rodotà S., 'Data Protection as a Fundamental Right', in S. Gutwirth, Y. Poullet, P. Hert, C. Terwangne and S. Nouwt (eds.), *Reinventing Data Protection* (Springer 2009) 77–82.
Rodotà S., *Riservatezza* (Treccani 2021) 1–108.

Chapter 12: Transfer of Personal Data

Bignami F. and Resta G., 'Transatlantic Privacy Regulation: Conflict and Cooperation (2015) 8 *Law and Contemporary Problems* 231–266.
Compagnucci M.C., Aboy M. and Minssen T., 'Cross-Border Transfers of Personal Data After Schrems II: Supplementary Measures and New Standard Contractual Clauses (SCCs)' (2021). Available at https://ssrn.com/abstract=3951085, 1–12.
Fabbrini F., 'The European Court of Justice Ruling in the Data Retention Case and its Lessons for Privacy and Surveillance in the U.S.' (2015) 28 *Harvard Human Rights Journal* 65–95.
Fabbrini F. and Celeste E., 'The Right to Be Forgotten in the Digital Age: The Challenges of Data Protection Beyond Borders' (2020) 21(1) *German Law Journal* 55–65.
Pollicino O. and Bassini M., 'Bridge Is Down, Data Truck Can't Get Through … : A Critical View of the Schrems Judgment in the Context of European Constitutionalism' (2017) *The Global Community Yearbook of International Law and Jurisprudence 2016* 245–265.

Chapter 13: Data Retention and Law Enforcement

Bignami F., 'Protecting Privacy Against the Police in the European Union: The Data Retention' (2007) 8 *Chicago Journal of International Law* 233–255.
Fabbrini F, 'The European Court of Justice Ruling in the Data Retention Case and Its Lessons for Privacy and Surveillance in the U.S.' (2015) 28 *Harvard Human Rights Journal* 65–95.
Grabowska-Moroz B., 'Data Retention in the European Union', European Constitutional Courts towards Data Retention Laws, (2021) *Law, Governance and Technology Series*, Springer, Cham, 3–17.
Leiser M. and Bart C,. 'The Law Enforcement Directive: Conceptual Challenges of EU Directive 2016/680' (2019) 5 *European Data Protection Law Review* 367–378.
Sajfert J. and Quintel T., 'Data Protection Directive (EU) 2016/680 for Police and Criminal Justice Authorities', (2017), available at https://ssrn.com/abstract=3285873, 1–22.

www.ingramcontent.com/pod-product-compliance
Ingram Content Group UK Ltd.
Pitfield, Milton Keynes, MK11 3LW, UK
UKHW051448290926
15471UKWH00008B/1084

9 788831 322706